The Complete Bilingual Lawn & Landscape Training Guide

By

Bryan P Monty

authorHOUSE

1663 LIBERTY DRIVE, SUITE 200
BLOOMINGTON, INDIANA 47403
(800) 839-8640
www.authorhouse.com

First Published by AuthorHouse 06/23/04

ISBN: 1-4184-0151-X (e-book)
ISBN: 1-4184-0152-8 (Paperback)

Library of Congress Control Number: 2004090560

This book is printed on acid-free paper.

Printed in the United States of America
Bloomington, IN

CONTENTS

INTRODUCTION

Welcome to the Complete Bilingual Lawn and Landscape Training Guide. This professional Training Guide uses the most effective, up-to-date work procedures. It will greatly improve the knowledge and work skills of everyone working in lawn care and landscaping. This Professional Guide is a must have resource for business owners, employees and even homeowners.

Each topic is broken down into easy-to-read, understandable step-by-step instructions. After reading this Guide, your work will become enjoyable, easier to complete, get done fast and correctly! You will reduce the risk of injury to yourself and to others. You will reduce damage to the property that you are working on and to the machinery that you are using.

Use this Guide to read about a select topic before starting that type of work or read the entire book to improve your knowledge and help you become a respected lawn and landscape professional.

Special thanks to Claudia Diaz and Banner Rosales for translating this Guide correctly into the Hispanic language. By using the most common Hispanic dialects, this bilingual Guide has proven to be a winner with the Hispanic reader.

LAWN AND LANDSCAPE MAINTENANCE SERVICES SPRING CLEAN-UP

(CHAPTER 1)

Spring clean up is the clean up of leaves, sticks, and debris that have blown onto a property over the winter months. Spring clean up should take place during early spring as soon as the ground is dry enough to work on. This service should be done before the lawn needs its first mowing. Leaves, sticks and debris will be easier to clean up while the lawn is short and still dormant from the winter.

You will need the following equipment to do a spring clean up.

- A ground blower.
- A backpack blower.
- Leave rakes.
- Tarp.
- Large landscape barrel.

You should wear:

- Gloves.
- Ear protection.
- Safety glasses, long pants and work boots while using any power equipment.

Ground Blowers

The ground blower is a blower that blows debris across the ground. It has more power than a backpack blower and it should be used on large areas of the lawn. There is a chute on the ground blower used to adjust the flow of air. If there are leaves stuck in the lawn, adjust the chute so more air blows down into the lawn. If there is only surface debris, adjust the chute to blow across the lawn surface. Always be careful when adjusting the blower chute. Turn off the machine first and **never** put your hands inside the chute. When working in heavy leaves, the vent in the front of the ground blower may clog up with leaves. When this happens, turn off the machine and remove the leaves by hand. **Never** clean this vent when the machine is running.

The ground blower should not be used in landscape beds; it is to powerful and will blow mulch or soil out of the bed. You can also damage plants very easily with a ground blower, so be careful where you use this machine.

Most ground blowers use regular gas. Fill the gas tank on the trailer or road while the engine is cool. Ground blowers use motor oil faster than any other machine. Check the engine oil level **two** or **three times per day**. Make sure you have extra engine oil with you before you go to the job site.

Backpack Blowers

The backpack blower is a 2-cycle machine. Use the backpack blower in landscape beds, sidewalks and smaller areas of the property.

Leave Rakes

Bring a few rakes so that if one breaks, you have an extra. Be careful while using rakes, do not push down to hard on the wooden handle or it will break. Check your rakes and make sure the part that does the raking is not worn out. When the end of the rake wears out, it will not work properly and it is time for a new rake.

Tarps and Landscape Barrels

During spring clean-up service, bring both a tarp and a landscape barrel. You should use the landscape barrel to pickup sticks and small piles of debris. If the debris is not too heavy, empty your barrel onto the tarp. Then when the tarp is full, make one trip to the dumping area. Do not to over fill a tarp or barrel or you may not be able to move it. Also be careful not to rip the tarp by pulling it across a sharp object. A few people will be needed to pull a full tarp. Teamwork always works best.

Spring Clean up (Work Procedures)

When you are doing a spring-clean up, it is very important to always work together with your co-workers as a team. The job will be easier and get done faster when you work together as a team!

Always wear gloves, safety glasses and ear protection while using any power equipment. We just spoke about the equipment needed for spring clean up, so now let's get to the work. Start by walking the property with the landscape barrel and picking up any sticks. Sticks

3

cannot be blown together so they should be picked up first. If there are a lot of small sticks, use a rake to make piles of sticks throughout the property, and then pick them up. After all the sticks have been picked up and dumped, you are ready to start blowing out the landscape beds. Gas up your blower and put on your safety equipment. Also, bring a rake and tarp with you. Start in the landscape beds against the house. Blow the debris out onto the lawn area. Be careful with the backpack around the house and plants. **You want to blow out the leaves and debris but not the mulch or topsoil.** Clean any debris stuck in or under the plants.

When debris is stuck and cannot be blown out easily with a backpack blower, you have to use a rake. Have a co-worker take a rake and lift up on the lower branches of the plant while you use the blower. Using a rake together with a blower will get the job done quicker and easier. First rake lightly throughout the bed to loosen up the debris, then the debris will blow out quicker and easier and the landscape bed will look professionally cleaned.

After the beds have been blown out onto the lawn, pick up the heavy debris with a rake and tarp and dump it either in your truck or at a dumping area on the property. Clean out any other landscape beds on the property the same way.

After all the beds are cleaned out, use the ground blower together with a backpack blower or a rake to clean the lawn areas. Work together as a team. Work back and forth across the lawn together. Use the backpack blower for any corners, edges, hills or small areas. Anywhere the ground blower has difficulty.

Use a backpack blower or rake to help loosen up debris stuck in the lawn. Work a few steps in front of the ground blower and loosen up the debris. Then the ground blower will be able to easily clean the debris once it has been loosened up.

While working back and forth, you will start to make a line of debris running across the lawn area. When this line of debris starts to build up, it will start to get difficult to move. Stop your machines and pick up the heavy debris with a rake and tarp. There is no need to blow the debris into a neat pile since you are not finished cleaning the lawn. Simply pull the tarp in front of the line of debris and rake it onto the tarp. Now you are ready to start the blowers again.

Once you are at the end of the lawn area, pick up the remaining debris and haul it away. Use a rake and backpack blower to make one final pile to be picked up. If you are working on a property where you can blow the debris into a wooded area, clean the lawn so that you finish up by the woods then you can blow the debris from the lawn into the woods. Clean off all the sidewalks, decks, patios, pools, and the driveway. **Close and lock any gates** and you are now finished with the spring-clean up.

Follow the spring clean up work procedures as we just discussed and each job will get done as quickly and easily as possible and when you are finished, the job will look great! Some companies also weed and edge the landscape beds during spring clean up. To learn about weeding and edging, turn to the next sections in this guide titled Weeding and Edging of Landscape Beds.

Spring Clean up Training and Safety Tips
- Always wear safety glasses, long pants, work boots, and ear protection when using any blower machine.
- Always work together. Teamwork gets the job done easiest and fastest.
- First pickup sticks with a rake and barrel. Don't be lazy and try to blow sticks together.
- Look against the house for any window wells, if they are dirty, clean up the debris by hand.
- Loosen up the debris in landscape beds with a rake, then blow the debris out with a backpack blower.
- First loosen up the debris in the lawn with a backpack blower or rake then finish up using the ground blower.
- A co-worker should push the ground blower behind the area that was just loosened up. Then **all** the debris will be removed and the lawn will look professionally cleaned.
- Look for wet areas on the property during spring clean up. Keep off of any wet areas with heavy machinery.
- Keep hands and feet away from all moving parts on all machines.
- Turn off the machine and be careful when adjusting the chute on a ground blower.

- Turn blowers off to unclog leaves from the fan area.
- Fill all machines on the trailer or road, not on the grass.
- Fill up the machines before you start working when the motor is cool.
- Make sure the gas caps are on straight before you tighten them.
- Do not over tighten the gas cap or you will break the seal and it will leak.
- Check the motor oil level in ground blowers at least twice a day.
- Keep all machines securely fastened on the trailer or truck during transportation.
- Always think safety first!!!

LAWN MOWING
(CHAPTER 2)

There are many different machines used in lawn mowing. We will talk about the most commonly used machines. They are the walk behind 21", 36" and 48" lawn mower. The reason we call them 21", 36" or 48" is because that is how wide the machine will cut. A 21" lawn mower is used to mow small pieces of lawn. A 36" lawn mower should be used on small to mid-sized areas of lawn and the 48" lawn mower works best on the largest areas of the lawn. To do a good job, be sure to use the correct size lawn mower for each different area of lawn.

Preparing Lawn Mower Machinery Before the Workday
Before you start the workday, you will need to check over a few things on all the lawn mowers that you will be using. **On a daily basis:**

- Check the oil level to make sure there is enough oil in the motor. If the motor is running without enough oil, the motor can get damaged or destroyed. Check the oil level when the machine is on level ground. Look for the mark on the oil dipstick and fill the oil up to this mark. **Do not overfill; too much oil can also damage or destroy the motor.**

- Check all the tires to make sure they have enough air pressure. If they seem low, fill them with air, then check them using an air pressure gage! All the tires must have the same air pressure or the machine will cut uneven and be harder to control. If you look on the tire, there will be writing on the tire that tells you how much air pressure the tire should have, such as 30psi. Follow this information for best results.

- Check any drive belts and pulley's to make sure they are clean and in good condition.
- Check to make sure nothing is loose on the machine.
- If the lawn mower is not working correctly, do not use the machine and tell someone in charge immediately.
- Make sure the mower deck is clean and the blade is sharp, otherwise the machine will not cut the grass easily. A dull blade will tear the grass, and will cause damage to the lawn. With a dirty deck, it will be difficult to collect the grass clippings and without a grass catcher, the grass will clump up instead of spreading out evenly on the lawn. Sharpen the blades and clean under the mower deck once a week for best results.
- Make sure that the grass catcher is also clean. If the vent holes on the grass catcher are clogged with dried up grass, the catcher will not work correctly and make your job more difficult. Clean the grass catchers with a wire brush whenever you sharpen the blades and clean the mower deck.
- Before you start the machine, be sure to check that there is enough gas in the gas tank. Never fill up the gas tank on the lawn and never fill the gas tank when the motor is hot. Most machines have a large gas tank so you can fill the machine in the morning and it will not have to be filled up again for a few hours.

- The last thing that should be checked is the mower height. In other words, how high the lawn will be cut. The lawn mower should cut the lawn at a height of approximately 2-1/2". In the summer, when it is hot, raise up the mower deck to cut on the highest setting. When the grass is cut higher, it will not burn out as easily from the hot summer weather. It is best to leave the mower height at the correct level and mow all the properties at this level. However, some customers may insist that they want their lawn mowed higher or lower. Then you will have to adjust the mower height before and after that job.

- **Make sure all lawn mowers are cutting at the same height.** Each machine has different settings. For example: Your 36" and 48" machine may be on notch number 3 to cut at 2-1/2" high, but your 21" machine may be on notch number 4 to get the same height of 2-1/2".

After you have checked all the machines as we just discussed, you are ready to work. First do a visual check of the lawn area you are going to mow. Pick-up anything that is in the lawn such as branches, toys, garbage, a garden hose, etc. If there are any people on the lawn area, make sure that they leave the area before you start working. Then choose the correct machine for the lawn area you need to mow.

Think about the easiest way to cut the lawn area. In most cases, you will run the machine across the longest area of lawn so that you do not have to turn the machine so often. Whatever size lawn mower you are using, the property should be visually checked to figure out the easiest way to cut the area. Obviously when you return to the same property the following week, you will know the best way to mow the lawn and you will not have to give it any thought. After a few months, you will need to change your mowing pattern, using the second easiest mowing pattern. Changing your mowing pattern every few months will be healthier for the lawn.

Operating A 21" Lawn Mower

Start up the lawn mower and turn the throttle up so the engine is running at full speed. By running the engine at full speed, the lawn mower will be able to cut the lawn easiest. Some 21" lawn mowers are self-propelled, while others you have to push. If you're using a self-propelled lawn mower, adjust the speed. If you're mowing an area that is flat, you can run the speed fast, but if you're mowing on a hill or slope, you should lower the speed.

First run the lawn mower around the outside edge of the area that you are mowing. Then run the machine across the lawn, back and forth in the pattern you planned out during the visual check. You should be mowing in a straight line. Turn the machine around and mow next to the area that you just cut. If you are using a self-propelled lawn mower, release the drive and turn the lawn mower around manually. While making the next pass, you should slightly overlap the machine onto the area that was just cut. By making a slight overlap, you will not miss cutting any areas of the lawn.

Once the grass catcher is full, park the lawn mower on level ground and turn off the motor. When you empty out the grass catcher, remove any grass that is clogging the chute of the machine. Again, **always** make sure the machine is turned **off** and wait at least a minute until the blade stops spinning before cleaning around the chute area. The chute will only clog up if the grass is very wet or if you over filled the grass catcher. If you are mowing an area that will fill up more than one grass catcher, be sure to bring a landscape grass barrel with you onto the area where you are working. Dump the full grass catchers into the barrel, then when you're finished mowing the area, you will need to make only one trip to dump out the grass.

Operating A 36" or 48" Lawn Mowers

Now that you're done using the 21", you can mow the larger areas of the property with the 36" or 48" machine. The 36" or 48" machine should have been gassed up and prepared as we previously discussed and the lawn area should be visually checked out as we previously discussed. When using a 36" or 48" **always** bring a landscape grass barrel with you to empty the grass catcher into. With most machines, you can put the barrel in front of the machine and push it to the area that you're mowing.

Note: Some lawn mowers may operate slightly different than described below.

Most machines operate in the following way.
- With the hand control levers out the lawn mower moves **forward**.

- Pull the hand control levers half way in, and lawn mower will be in **neutral**.
- Pull the hand control levers all the way in and the lawn mower will **stop**.
- Pull in the right lever to **turn right** and left the lever to **turn left**.

Before starting the machine, make sure that the control handles are closed and the parking brake is on so the machine does not start moving when you start it up.

Operating Procedures:
- Start-up the lawn mower.
- Put the machine in the correct gear, and then release the parking brake.
- Once the parking brake is released, raise the throttle so the engine is running at full speed.
- If you are on a lawn area, engage the blades.
- Put your hands on the hand control levers and slowly release the levers. The machine will start moving.
- **Never** let go of the hand control hand levers or you will loose control of the lawn mower.

An inexperienced person will take a day or two to become familiar with operating the lawn mower. Remember to never let go of the control hand levers while the machine is moving. To stop the machine, simply pull in both levers. Once you become familiar with the lawn mower and each property, the jobs will become much easier to complete.

At most jobs, you will be able to go around the driveway or street curbing to get onto the lawn area. However, if you cannot, you will have to get the lawn mower over the curb in the following way.

When going over a curb:
- Make sure that the blades are turned off and lower the throttle.
- Place the machine in neutral.
- Push down on the handlebars to lift up the front wheels over the curb then push the machine forward so the back wheels are next to the curb.
- Lift up the back of the machine while pushing forward, place the machine down once the back wheels have cleared the curb.

Once you are over the curb and on the lawn area to be mowed, adjust the throttle and drive gear as needed. Then start up the mower blades and you are ready to go to work.

Lawn Mowing Procedures:
First mow around the outside edge of the lawn area. If there are no people around, leave the grass catcher off while making the first pass around the lawn area. Position the lawn mower so that the grass clippings blow onto the lawn area and not into the beds, street or driveway. When you end up where you started, turn off the blades, put on the parking brake on, and then attach the grass catcher. Now

make the first pass across the lawn area, turn the machine around and continue with the next pass.

When turning a 36" or 48" mower, pull in the hand control levers to the neutral position then you will be able to manually turn the machine around. Use your body weight to help turn the machine, and never let go of the handles. Slightly engage the outside wheel to help make the turn. Do not lock up the inside wheel while making a turn. The locked wheel will turn in its place and damage the lawn. Always avoid locking up the tires or spinning the tires when making a turn.

Remember to slightly overlap onto the area that has just been mowed so you do not miss any areas. Try to keep the machine mowing in a straight line; this will give the lawn a professional appearance when you are finished. Slightly pull in on each hand control lever as needed to help keep the machine mowing in a straight line. When you come to a tree or landscape bed, go around it with the grass catcher to the **outside** of the tree or landscape bed. This way you will not damage anything with the grass catcher. Go around the entire bed, and then continue with the straight line-mowing pattern on both sides of the bed. Then you will have a professional look to the job when you are finished.

When you start to see small clumps of grass falling out near the grass catcher, it is time to empty the catcher.

- Park the lawn mower on level ground.

- Stop the machine and the blades.

- Engage the parking brake.

- Lower the throttle.

- Empty out the grass catcher.

- **Always keep your hands and feet away from the blade area even if the blades are turned off.**

If clumps of grass have spilled out onto the lawn from a full catcher, carefully pickup the grass by hand then run the lawn mower over that area again to pick-up the remaining clippings, or use a back pack blower to break up the clumps of grass.

Once you are finished mowing a lawn area, run the lawn mower around the outside edge of the lawn area again to give it a professional look. On a larger lawn area, or on a property that is not perfectly maintained, this last step may not be needed.

Belt Drive and Hydro Drive Lawn Mowers

Belt Drive Lawn Mowers

A standard walk behind lawn mower is driven by belts. The belts run from the transmission to the wheels. There are some problems with belt driven lawn mowers. Such as:

- When the belts and pulleys become clogged with dirt or grass clippings, the lawn mower will become difficult or impossible to operate.

Note: Inspect the belts and pulleys on a regular basis. If you see any dirt or grass clippings on the <u>inside</u> of the drive belts or on the pulleys, clean them off immediately. You will have to use a flat head screwdriver to clean the notch on the <u>inside</u> of the drive belts and pulley's. Always turn the machine off before cleaning the belts and pulleys.

- When the belts become wet, the lawn mower will become difficult or impossible to operate.

Note: Keep lawn mower and belts dry. Stay out of wet areas.

- When the belts get old, the lawn mower will become difficult or impossible to operate. The belts should be replaced as soon as they get worn. If the lawn mower is used on a regular basis, replace the belts once a year.

Hydro Drive Lawn Mowers

A hydro drive lawn mower has a hydro pump that drives the wheels instead of belts. Operating a hydro walk-behind lawn mower is slightly different than operating a belt drive.

Hydro Drive Operating Procedures:
- Let the hand control levers all the way out and the lawn mower will go **forward**.
- Pull the hand control levers half way in and the lawn mower will be in **neutral**.

- Slightly pull in the hand control levers and the lawn mower will **stop**.
- **Pull the hand control levers all the way in and the machine will not stop. Instead it will go backwards.**

After you learn how to operate the hydro lawn mower, it should be easier and less tiring for you to operate than the belt drive. *However, a hydro lawn mower can tear up the grass very easily when turning, so be careful.* When you have to mow under a tree or a hard to reach area, you will not have to manually pull the machine to get it out. Instead you will pull the control levers all the way in and the machine will drive out backwards.

The hydro pumps must also be kept well maintained or serious, costly damage can occur.
- Always keep hydro pumps filled correctly. Check the hydro pumps once a week.
- Hydro pumps have a separate oil tank which must be filled to the correct level and requires a special type of oil. **Do not** use regular motor oil and **do not** over fill the hydro pump oil tank.
- Change the oil and filters on a regular basis and **do not operate the machine if you spot an oil leak from any part of the machine.**

Ride-on Lawn Mowers

Ride-on lawn mowers operate basically the same as walk behind lawn mowers except you are sitting and riding on it while it is mowing. The control levers will be different, than a walk behind lawn mower. Each different brand of ride-on lawn mower will operate slightly different.

Note: Make sure that you clearly understand all of the control levers before you start to operate any ride-on lawn mower.

Most ride-on lawn mowers will cut 48" or larger Therefore you should only use the ride-on lawn mower on large open lawn areas. **Stay off of small areas or sloped areas.** Some ride-on lawn mowers may have a second motor used for the vacuum system. If the motor is mounded on the side of the ride-on, stay alert or you can destroy the motor or cause property damage by running it into something.

Mowing procedures are almost the same as the walk behind lawn mower that we just discussed. Follow these procedures and once you become familiar with the ride-on lawn mower that you are using, you will be able to quickly mow large areas of lawn without getting tired from constant walking.

Lawn Mowing Training and Safety Tips
Lawn mowing will be different at each property. Each property will have different terrain and problems that you will need to deal with. The information listed below will help you improve your lawn mowing skills. When you understand how to deal with different conditions, terrain, and problems, your job will become easier and always look professional. You will be safer towards yourself and

others. A lawn mower is a dangerous piece of equipment. **Always think safety first!**

- Always wear safety glasses, long pants and work boots when operating a lawn mower.
- When stopping a lawn mower for **any** reason, turn off the blades, lower the throttle, and use the parking brake.
- Do not park a lawn mower on a hill or slope because the machine might move or roll, even with the brake on.
- Do not use any machines when people or pets are in the area that you want to work in.
- Keep hands, feet, and all body parts away from any moving parts of any machine unless the machine is turned **off**.
- **Do not tear up lawn areas by locking up or spinning the tires!**
- If lawn mower tires are damaging the lawn from running over the same exact spot week after week. Move the lawn mower so the tires do not run over that damaged area again.
- Lift up on the machine to prevent a tire from dropping into a hole or low spot. If a tire drops into a hole, it will cause damage to the lawn and may damage the machine.
- Look ahead and stay alert when mowing.
- Do not let grass clippings blow into landscape beds, against a house, into pools, or near cars.
- Do not hit mail posts, trees, fences, rocks, or curbs with the lawn mower.

- Work slowly and carefully on wet lawns. Skip any lawn areas if they are too wet for the machine.

- If a lawn area is too wet for the lawn mower, use a string trimmer to cut the area. If extremely wet, skip the areas completely until the following week when conditions are drier.

- Do not gas up machines on the grass. Fill them up on the trailer or street when the engine is cool.

- Always bring a landscape grass barrel with you when bagging the lawn.

- Mow slower when there are bumps in the lawn, if the grass is wet or high, or when mowing on a slope.

- Run the engine throttle on full and always run the lawn mower in the correct gear.

- Avoid leaving any heavy clumps of grass throughout the lawn. Use a backpack blower to break up any heavy clumps of grass.

- Do not use 36" lawn mower where 21" should be used. Always choose the correct lawn mower for the area you are mowing.

- Visually check, inspect and plan out how you will mow before you start.

- Move all toys, hoses, etc. from lawn areas before mowing.

- After mowing, always shut and lock any gates!

- Take good care of all equipment.

- Do not leave grass catchers or landscape barrels full of grass overnight.

- Safety equipment on machines **must** be used. Do not disconnect or stop using safety equipment.

- Put safety cones out around your truck and trailer at every job site as soon as you park. Use at least two safety cones.

- When parking a truck on a hill, turn the wheels into the curb so it will not roll down the road if the parking brake fails.

- Check the trailer before driving to the next job to make sure everything is loaded up correctly.

- Do not spread tools and equipment around the parking area and property you are working at. Put tools and equipment back on to the truck or trailer as soon as you are finished using them. Be organized!

- Put all tools and equipment back where they belong. This way they will be in the same place all the time and will be easy to find the next time someone needs something.

- Drive trucks at or under the speed limit.

- On your truck, keep all rear view mirrors adjusted correctly. Always use these mirrors when driving.

- Stay alert! Do not run the trailer tires into curbs. Make wide turns to avoid running the tires into curbs.

- Do not use any machines that are broken or not working well.

- Always **think**…be smart and act **professional**!

- Organize each job. Think about how you can do the job the easiest and who will do what **before** you start, then work together. Teamwork is the best way to work and get a job done.

- Check each property before you leave. Check that the lawn areas are all mowed and trimmed correctly. Make sure that all gates are closed and all tools and equipment are put away. Make a note if there are any problems on the property.

- Tell your boss or foreman about any problems that you find on the property or with the machines.
- If you do not **completely** understand when your foreman or boss discusses a job, please tell them that you do not understand.
- Do not try to do something if you are not **100% sure** about what you are doing.
- Please be honest, work hard, smart, and safe.
- **Always think safety first!**

STRING TRIMMING AND CLEANING DEBRI (CHAPTER 3)

String Trimming

String trimming is done to cut the areas where the lawn mower could not reach. Such as: around trees, landscape beds, fences, sidewalks and driveways. All string trimmers are very similar. A few things to remember about these machines are:

- Be sure to use 2-cycle gas, not regular gas. 2-cycle gas is a gas and oil mixture.
- Before filling up the machine, shake the gas can so that the gas and oil are always mixed.
- Fill the machine before you start working when the motor is cool.
- Carefully screw the gas cap on. Make sure the gas cap is put on straight. Then turn it tight, but do not over tighten it or you will break the seal inside the cap. Then the gas cap will leak.
- When filling the trimmer head with string, make sure all the parts inside the trimmer head are kept clean. If there is dirt inside the trimmer head, it will not work properly.
- When using a string trimmer, the string should extend approximately 6 inches out from the head. If the string is shorter or longer, the trimmer will not work properly.
- There are two different types of trimmer heads. One type will release more string when you bump the bottom of the head on the ground. The other type will release more string when you lower

the engine speed then increase the engine speed and more string will come out.

- Some machines will have a string cut off on the safety guard which will cut the string to the correct length. But if you move the safety guard up, it will not work. If the trimmer doesn't have a string cut off, be careful not to let too much string out.
- Always leave the safety guard on the trimmer. Adjust it to where it seems best for you but never remove it. A trimmer without the safety guard can throw stones over 50 mph in all directions.
- Always wear safety glasses, long pants and work boots when operating a string trimmer.

Operating a String Trimmer

When you start string trimming, there are two different ways to use the trimmer. The first way is to hold the trimmer so that the string is horizontal with the ground. This is the same way that a lawn mower blade cuts. This should be done around trees, mailbox posts, fences, and small areas that where missed with the lawn mower. Cut the tall grass to the same height as the grass that has just been mowed. **Be very careful not to touch any trees, fences, etc. with the string.** The string trimmer will cause serious damage to trees, fences, etc. if you come to close and touch them.

The second way is to hold the trimmer so that the string cuts vertical (up and down). This is the same way that an edger blade cuts. This way should be used along walkways, driveways, and along landscape beds that have an edge. Many people make the mistake of trimming these areas with the string on a 45-degree angle, this is wrong. When you trim on a 45-degree angle, you're trimming the lawn to low. Then under any warm weather conditions, the grass will turn brown and die in these areas. Trimming on a 45-degree is not recommended in any situation.

When string trimming, start at one end of the property and work to the other end. Try to trim around the sidewalks and driveway first. Then a co-worker can blow off the sidewalk and driveway if you are still string trimming. Be careful not to over trim. When trimming sidewalks and driveways, do not make the space between the sidewalk and the lawn any larger than one inch. Trim these areas lightly or bi-weekly. Many areas on the property may be able to be trimmed bi-weekly, such as along landscape beds, sidewalks, and the driveway. During the summer months, you should also reduce string trimming. Do not trim any areas too low or the lawn areas will turn brown and die. While working through a property with the string trimmer, visually inspect the entire lawn. There may be areas where the lawn mowers have cut uneven. Use the trimmer to fix these areas. Trim down any obvious high spots to blend in with the lawn.

Remove any large weeds that are growing from curbing in the road or driveway. Try not to hit any loose stones when doing this.

Never operate string trimmers when there are people in the area where you are working. If you have to trim along a road with many cars, run the trimmer at a slower engine speed, and trim with the string in the horizontal position. This is the safest way to trim. Remember to always think about safety when using any power equipment.

Cleaning Debris

Cleaning debris from sidewalks, driveways and decks is the last step to a lawn mowing service. We recommend using a backpack blower. A backpack blower is a 2-cycle machine.

When you blow off the sidewalks, start at the front door. Run the engine **slowly** and blow off the front door area. Make sure that this area is left very clean since this is an area that many people will see. After the front door area has been blown off, clean the front walk. Once you are away from the front door, you can increase the engine speed to get the job done faster. Try to blow the debris off both sides of the walk. If there is a lot of debris, **do not** blow the debris onto the lawn that has just been mowed; and **do not** blow it into the landscape beds. Blow the heavy debris into a pile, then pick up the pile and take the debris away.

After the front walk is done, walk around to the back and do the same. While walking around the property, do a visual inspection of the property. Look for any heavy grass clippings left on the lawn or in the landscape beds. If so, blow these areas so there is no heavy grass left anywhere. If the property has a pool, clean this area slowly and carefully so you don't get debris into the pool. When cleaning off decks or patios, carefully blow off any outdoor furniture after the deck or patio area has been done. Be careful not to blow down any flowerpots or small things on the deck or patio. Blow off any outdoor mats and if they moved when you blew them off, straighten them out.

After the backyard is clean, **make sure that any gates are closed!** Make sure every gate is closed and latched or locked. Children or pets can be injured or killed if they get to places where they should not be. Remember all gates need to be closed and locked always.

The driveway is the last thing you need to clean. Try to blow the driveway to an area where you can get rid of the debris such as a sewer drain or wooded area. If the driveway is fairly clean, you can blow the debris off both sides of the driveway. If the driveway is a very dirty, you may need to make a pile, then pick up the pile and take it away. Be careful when working around any parked cars. After you are done blowing around the car, blow off the car itself to keep it clean. If you blow any grass into the road while mowing, be sure to blow off the road area as well as the driveway. Be careful and watch for oncoming traffic while you are in the road. When cleaning very large driveways or parking lots, a ground blower will get the job done better.

String Trimming and Cleaning Debris Training and Safety Tips
- Always wear safety glasses, long pants and work boots when using string trimmer or blowers.
- Keep the trimmer line at the correct length. If the string is too short or long, it will not work correctly.
- Do not work near other people.

- Be extremely careful when working near cars. Run the machine at a slow speed in the horizontal position.
- Keep the trimmer string away from stones or loose debris.
- Do not hit trees, mailboxes, etc. with the trimmer string.
- Keep the grass high along curbs and driveways or it will burn out during hot weather.
- Keep the space between walkways and grass no larger than one inch.
- Look for areas in the lawn where the lawn mower cut uneven. Then blend these areas in with the string trimmer.
- Keep hands and feet away from all moving parts on machines.
- Fill all machines on the trailer or street, not on the grass.
- Fill all machines before you start working when the motor is cool.
- Do not over tighten the gas cap or you will break the seal and it will leak.
- Make sure the gas cap is straight before you tighten it.
- Do not blow heavy debris into the landscape beds or onto the lawn that has just been mowed.
- Run the blower slowly when blowing near a house, pool, patio or cars.
- All gates need to be closed and locked always.
- Keep all machines securely fastened on the trailer or truck.
- Think safety first!!!

WEED REMOVAL (HAND WEEDING)
(CHAPTER 4)

Hand weed removal is the removal of unwanted weeds from landscape beds. You will remove these weeds by using your hands or a hand tool. Hand weeding of landscape beds must be done on a regular basis to keep a property looking its best. When removing weeds, you will need the following tools:

- A hand tool to help dig out the root system of the weed. There are many different types of hand tools used for weed removal. Some tools are simply a metal shaft with a few points on the end. Others tools look like a small pick or a small hoe. You should have a variety of different hand tools available.
- You will need a landscape barrel or wheelbarrow to collect the weeds.
- You will also need a pair of gloves to protect your hands.

Hand Weeding (Work Procedures)

Start removing weeds at one end of the property and work your way to the other end. Bring the landscape barrel and a hand tool and **be sure to wear gloves**. There are many different types of weeds. Some of them are poisonous and if you are not wearing gloves, you are asking for trouble. Poisonous weeds will leave you with a bad rash. Some people are more sensitive to these weeds and can even end up in the hospital if they make contact with them. When removing weeds, also be careful not to touch the weeds with your arms or face and be careful not to touch yourself with the gloves that you are wearing.

Before you start weeding an area, check to see that everything you are going to remove is a weed **and not a flower or perennial.**

Perennials are flowers that grow year after year. They are becoming very popular but the problem is that many of them look like a weed for part of the year. So be alert, and if you are not sure about what you are looking at, it is always better not to pull it out. Perennials are expensive and you can cause a lot of damage if you remove them. So, be careful!!

Weeds are removed much easier when the soil is moist. Try to take advantage of rainy days or the next few days after a rainfall to remove weeds. When you remove weeds from dry soil, it is almost impossible to remove the entire root system of the weed. **When you leave a piece of the root system in the soil, the weed will grow back in a few days and you will have to do the job again.**

When you grab a weed to pull it out, grab it as low to the ground as possible. Then slowly pull up on it. If the weed pulls out with the roots, you have done the job correctly. But if the weed is hard to pull out, take your hand tool and dig down to loosen the soil around the weed. Then slowly pull up and it should come out with the roots. Do not pull out weeds quickly or you will tear the roots and will not

31

remove the entire root system. Then the weed will grow back in a few days and you will have to do the job again.

All weeds are different. Some can be pulled out very easy because they have a shallow root system. Others are very hard to remove because they have a deep root system. With some experience, you will become familiar with which weeds are easy and which are hard to remove. While weeding, you will find that some weeds are very small and hard to grab. You can either leave these small weeds there and return in about seven days to remove them when they are larger. Or you can spray them with a chemical spray. A chemical spray should only be applied by a licensed applicator. We will discuss chemical weed control in the next section of this training guide.

Some types of weeds will always grow low to the ground and are almost impossible to remove by hand. In this case, if you are not qualified to spray, you need to use a hand tool. A tool that will scrap down into the soil and remove the weed and most of the roots. If the small weeds continue to return and you cannot spray them with a chemical, you will need to put down a layer of mulch. A heavy layer of mulch will stop any weed from growing. A few years ago, I came across a low growing weed that was almost impossible to stop. First we pulled it, then we sprayed it many times with chemicals. A month later, the weed would return. I sprayed it correctly with many different sprays and all of them did not work. The weed always returned one month later. We ended up putting down landscape fabric with a four-inch layer of mulch and the weed never returned. We will discuss mulching later in this training guide.

While you are weeding, be sure to look at the shrubs! Many people do not look at the shrubs. If you see anything growing out of a shrub, remove it. Follow the top of the weed down and pull it out with the roots so you don't have to do it again the following week.

Removing weeds from sidewalks, driveways, and patios is usually unsuccessful without a chemical spray. You can try to pull them out, but you usually will not get the roots. Also pulling weeds from a walkway by hand takes too much time. You can cut the tops of the weeds with a string trimmer, but they will grow back. Chemical spray may be the only way to permanently kill the weeds.

To remove poisonous weeds such as poison ivy or oak, first cut the vine part of the weed close to the ground. Then use a chemical spray and spray the leaves and the area that you cut open. Protect yourself when cutting a poisonous vine or plant. Throw away any gloves that made heavy contact with poisonous plants.

Once you are done hand weeding a property, you will need to dispose of the weeds that you just removed. Keep the weeds in a small compact pile and dump them as far away as possible because the weeds will dry out and any weed seeds can blow back onto the property, creating another problem. Cover the weeds with leaves or grass clippings if you are going to leave them on the job site.

Hand Weeding Training and Safety Tips

- Always wear gloves when weeding.
- If you are unsure if you are removing a weed or a flower. Do not remove it; stop and ask someone.
- Look out for poisonous weeds such as poison ivy or poison oak.
- Grab the weeds as low as possible and pull them slowly so the root system is removed with the weed.
- Use a hand tool to loosen the soil around the roots if the weed is hard to remove.
- Remember you must remove the roots or the weed will grow back.
- Take advantage of wet weather and get all your hand weeding done during this time.
- If weeds continue to grow back, a chemical spray should be used or apply landscape fabric and mulch over the problem area.
- Always think safety first.

WEED REMOVAL (CHEMICAL SPRAY)
(CHAPTER 5)

Chemical weed removal is done to control weeds in areas that are difficult to be removed by hand. Chemical spraying of weeds can also be done to control smaller weeds from growing larger and spreading. If done correctly, spraying can save time and do a professional job of stopping weed growth. Spraying weeds correctly will kill the entire root system of the weeds making it impossible for them to grow back. However, if spraying is not done correctly, serious problems can occur. Such as, damaging or killing landscape plants, damaging or killing lawn areas and creating a serious health problem to ourselves and everyone around us.

Most states require that you be licensed as a pesticide applicator or operator to apply weed control legally. Make sure you are properly trained and legally allowed to apply weed control before working at any job site. Always follow all rules required by your state.

Do not apply any chemical weed control in any way, shape or form if you are not licensed and trained. Reading this chapter of our training guide is your first step.

Chemical Spray Equipment

The equipment used to spray weeds is fairly simple. A backpack or hand held pump sprayer, rubber gloves, boots, a respirator and safety glasses.

Backpack Pump Sprayer

This type of sprayer works well and is most commonly used. The backpack pump sprayer will usually hold three gallons of mixture. Anything smaller is not recommended since you will have to stop to mix the chemical and water too often. The backpack sprayer has two straps and is carried on your shoulders and back. When opening and closing the cap, be careful to make sure the rubber seal/gasket on the screw on cap is correctly in place. Tighten the cap securely, but do not over tighten or you will break the seal and the cap will leak. When the cap starts to leak, the chemical will get onto your cloths, neck and back. Do not use the sprayer if the cap leaks.

There may be a filter under the cap to catch any debris before it gets into the tank. Use this filter and do not remove it. The filter sometimes makes it hard to get the cap on correctly so some people remove it. Do not remove the filter! You will only create more problems. At the bottom of the tank is the pump and a pump arm to give you the correct spray pressure. Then there is a hose connecting the pump to the sprayer handgun. There may be another filter in the handgun or before the spray nozzle. While using this sprayer, you will use one arm to control the pump arm to give you the correct spray pressure and you will use your other arm to hold the sprayer handgun.

Before going to a job site, make sure that all the filters are clean. Also, make sure that all the hose connections are tight and secure. Then check to make sure that the spray tip is clean and sprays correctly. The filters are in place to stop any debris from getting clogged in the spray tip. There is nothing worse than mixing the chemical and then getting to the job site and having the tip clog up every few minutes. Always clean and check the sprayer before using it.

Hand Held Pump Sprayer

The handheld sprayer is basically the same as the backpack except there is a pump and handle on top of the sprayer. You have to stop working and put the sprayer down on the ground every time you have to pump it. With the backpack you can pump and spray at the same time.

Safety Equipment

Wear the proper safety equipment, a respirator, glasses, rubber gloves, long pants and rubber boots.

Respirator

There are two types of respirators you can use. The first type is a rubber mask with two filter cartridges. When you breathe the airflows through the filter cartridges. There is a valve on the rubber part of the mask where you exhale. Make sure the cartridges are marked for pesticides and replace them as recommend by manufacture. Using the rubber respirator with the correct cartridges is the safest available way to protect yourself from breathing chemical spray mist.

The second type of respirator is a paper mask. The paper mask is smaller and easier to wear. The mask **must** be labeled for use with spray mists. The correct paper mask will reduce the amount of chemical mist you breathe, but will not stop 100% of it. The mask should be thrown out after it is used a few times. Both masks need to be kept as clean as possible. Keep them in the front of your truck; wrap them with a clean paper towel in between using them.

When using a backpack sprayer, you should be using a low pressure and you should be holding the spray tip about 6 to 12 inches off the ground. When used correctly, there is very little drift of chemical spray mist. Therefore the paper mask is most commonly used with a backpack or handheld sprayers.

In additional to wearing a respirator, you should be wearing safety glasses, rubber gloves (labeled for use with chemicals), long pants, and rubber boots. Leather work boots are not recommended because they will become saturated with chemical spray mist and chemicals will penetrate the boot if a spill occurs.

Mixing of Chemicals
Mixing of the chemical needs to be done very carefully.

- Always wear safety protection when mixing. The chemical is very strong before mixed with water; therefore safety protection is most important while mixing.
- Do your mixing on the ground where there are no other objects around that will create a problem.
- Do not get distracted from anything happening around you while mixing or you can make a serious mistake.
- Do not mix if there are any children, pets or activities in the area.
- Mix the first tank at the beginning of the day at the garage. Then if needed, mix the remaining tanks at the job site.
- Use only one measuring cup for the weed control chemical. Label the cup and do not use it for anything else.
- Make another mark on the measuring cup by the amount of product you use to make a full tank. This way you will not forget.

For example, if you are using a three-gallon tank and you need to mix (three ounces per gallon), you will need a total of (nine ounces to mix a full tank). Mark the measuring cup at nine ounces. You should also mark the gallons on the spray tank so they are easy to see.

- Try to use the same chemical throughout the year this way mixing will be easy to remember.
- Use a good quality product that will kill all different types of weeds, also grass, poison ivy, wild vines, and low growing brush. Most new products will not spread or seep in the soil. They should have a sticker in the chemical so the product stays on the weed

39

and will not wash off after it is dry for a few hours. Always read the label completely before using any chemical product. Instructions will vary based on each different application.

- Stay away from old products like Vegetation Killer. This product will kill all types of vegetation for up to one year. The soil will also be contaminated for up to one year. Under heavy rain conditions, the chemical may spread to other areas killing anything in its path and the chemical is very toxic.
- Stay with the best products. Completely read and understand the label and you should not have any problems.

Always make sure you completely understand everything about the product you are using. Ask questions if you are not 100% sure about the chemical, how to use it, what it does, and what the dangers of using it are.

Mixing a Three Gallon Spray Tank

- To mix your three-gallon tank, fill it with one gallon of water first. Then add the measured chemical.
- Fill up the measuring cup with water and dump it into the tank a few times until the measuring cup is clean, then add more water to get to the three-gallon mark on the spray tank.
- If there is a filter at the top of the tank, do not remove it. It will collect any debris before it enters the tank and causes a problem.
- Screw on the cap of the tank but do not over tighten it or you will break the rubber seal on the cap.
- Shake up the tank for 30 seconds to one minute.

- Rinse off the outside of the tank if needed.
- Put the chemical container and measuring cup in a safe place, locked and secured in a toolbox is best. Make sure the chemical container is secure and will not turn over or spill.
- Secure the spray tank in the back of the truck or trailer. The tank should be stored up high so children cannot reach the tank.

Spraying Weeds At the Job Site

- Once you are at the job site, put on your safety protection, shake the tank a little more and you are ready to spray.
- The areas you are going to spray should be hand weeded first. Remove any weeds larger than one inch; also remove weeds that are close to shrubs, trees, exposed roots, or hard-to-spray areas.
- Make sure there are no people or pets around when you are spraying.
- Start at one end of the landscape bed and work to the other end. While you are walking, cover an area of about six feet wide. Walk back and fourth reaching about three feet on each side of you. Walk through the bed similar to how you mow a lawn. Keep a straight line when walking back and fourth. By using this method, you will not miss any weeds or spray any weeds twice.
- Spray drift caused by over pumping is a very common mistake and can cause many problems.
- **Do not over pump the tank** or the spray will come out too fast. When the spray comes out too fast, it will make a lot of excess mist and drift onto undesirable areas. The spray mist will come up

into your face, and drift onto any plants in the area. If the chemical spray mist makes contact with any plants, it will cause serious damage or death to the plant.

- Only pump the tank enough so that the spray comes out slowly. It will take a little practice to get the spray pressure correct.
- Over-pumping happens mostly on backpack sprayers.
- Hold the spray tip about 6 to 12 inches off the ground. By doing this you will make good contact with the weeds. The spray will be very close to the ground and will not be able to drift too far.
- Also, hold the spray tip away from yourself so your clothes don't soak up the chemical spray.
- Spray the weed so that it is completely covered with spray. Once the weed is covered, stop spraying. There is no need to soak the weed or soil around the weeds.
- The weed will absorb the chemical through its leaves. Once the chemical is absorbed through the leaves, the weed will die including the root system.
- However, if the weed is not sprayed completely, it may not die; cover 100% of the weed.
- When you are spraying, stay away from all other plants. Stay away from ponds, streams, or running water. Stay away from any exposed surface roots from a tree or shrub.
- When you are finished with one area, wipe off your feet on dry soil. If there is a little bit of chemical under your boots and you walk onto a lawn area, you will kill the lawn from the chemical.

- If there are windy weather conditions, you are better off not to spray.

- If there is rain coming, do not spray. Most chemicals require about four hours of drying time before a rainfall or the chemical will not work.

- Most chemicals will take 7 to 10 days to kill the weed. A few hard to kill weeds may take a second application.

- Making a stronger chemical mix will not do a better job. If the chemical mix is too strong, you will burn the top of the weed off. Then the chemical will not get absorbed into the weed, the root system will not die and the weed will return in a few weeks. Never add extra chemical, only follow the recommended mixing instructions.

- Depending on the state you live in, you may have to put pesticide applied notification flags on the areas sprayed.

Be sure you understand and follow the procedures that we just discussed and follow chemical label instructions or you can create serious problems. Once you understand all the instructions and spray correctly, you will have excellent results in controlling unwanted weeds.

Chemical Spray Training and Safety Tips

- If you are not trained and 100% sure about what you are doing, do not use chemical spray. Most states also require you to be licensed to apply chemical spray.

- Wear safety glasses, gloves, respirator, rubber boots and a long sleeve clothing when mixing.
- Always read and understand each product label **before** using it.
- Do not mix near other people or pets. Avoid distractions when mixing.
- Make sure the tank is mixed thoroughly.
- Most sprayers have filters somewhere on the spray gun or hose and at the top of the tank. Keep these filters clean and check them often; do not remove them.
- Do not over tighten sprayer cap. Check to make sure that the rubber seal is always in good condition.
- Do not use any sprayers if they do not work properly. All equipment must be in 100% working order or it should not be used.
- Thoroughly wash off measuring cups, chemical containers and sprayers.
- Keep chemicals locked up.
- Keep the sprayer secure and four to five feet off the ground in your vehicle.
- Do not spray near people or pets. Avoid distractions when spraying.
- Wear proper safety equipment while spraying.
- Do not spray during windy weather conditions.
- Do not apply too much pump pressure while spraying. A low-pressure spray will come out coarse and not drift. A high-pressure spray will come out in a fine spray and drift.

- Be careful when spraying close to flowers, plants and root zone areas. These areas should be cleaned by hand weeding.
- Hold spray tip nozzle 6-12 inches off the ground.
- If the spray tip clogs, clean it with a knife or small wire brush. If this does not work, take the tip apart and flush it under water.
- Never blow out the spray tip with your mouth.
- If the tip continues to get clogged, flush out the entire sprayer and the filters.
- Always think safety first.

EDGING OF LANDSCAPE BEDS
(CHAPTER 6)

Edging of landscape beds is done to stop the grass from growing into the landscape bed area. It keeps the beds well defined and gives the landscape a professionally maintained look. You will need to have an edging machine, a spade shovel, a pick, and a wheelbarrow. When creating new landscape beds, you will need a paint gun to mark out where the new beds will go.

Edging Machine

The edging machine is a machine that has a metal blade on it. The blade spins very fast in a vertical direction. When the blade is lowered down, it will cut into the ground. Most edger machines have 2-cycle engines. The blade must be in good condition or it will do a poor job. Check the condition of the blade and get it changed when it is worn. Never use the machine if it does not have a safety guard and always wear safety glasses when operating this machine.

(Spade) Shovel

The spade is a type of shovel. The bottom part of the spade is not pointed, but flat. This shovel should only be used for edging beds. The flat part of the spade will fit down into the cut that you made with the edging machine. Or, if you don't have an edging machine, you can cut down into the ground with the spade.

Pick

The pick is a tool that has many purposes. If you have to remove grass or hard soil from the beds, it will be easiest to use a pick.

Wheelbarrow

The wheelbarrow will be used to pickup any grass or soil that needs to be disposed of after edging.

Paint Gun

A paint gun is a tool that is used to make marks on the grass or bed areas. It has a long handle and rolls on a wheel. By pulling the trigger at the top of the handle, paint will spray onto the ground. It is used when creating new landscape beds or can be used to re-shape an existing bed.

Edging of Landscape Beds (Work Procedures)

Re-edgings Existing Beds

First we will discuss re-edging of existing landscape beds. Landscape beds should be re-edged once a year. Before you start the edging machine, slowly walk along the area that you are about to edge. *Look up against the house or building for the box where all the utility wires are going. If there's a landscape bed in that area, be sure to be extra careful in that area. Use a spade and edge that area carefully by hand. Wires and pipes should be buried 6 inches deep but in many cases, they are only a few inches under the ground and can be cut while using an edging machine.* Look for anything that may get damaged from the edger blade or anything that may damage the blade on the edger machine. Such as:

- Wires for lights.
- Sprinkler system pipes.
- Sprinkler system heads.
- Cable TV and phone wires.
- Electrical wires.
- Large stones.

Another thing to be careful of is the invisible dog fence. This is a wire buried a few inches in the ground. It surrounds the entire property. The dog wears a special collar and gets a shock when he comes near the wire. If you see a dog on the property, ask the customer if they have an invisible fence. Make sure the customer clearly marks where the wire is or you cannot do the edging work.

Once you are aware of everything you need to avoid on the property, take another look at the area you are about to edge. Are there any landscape bed areas that need to be improved or expanded? The edge of landscape beds should run smoothly and have a good shape. If there are any bad looking areas, now is the time to improve them.

Before edging, ask yourself the following questions.

- Are there any areas where the bed needs to be cut larger?
- Are there any areas that you can reshape to look better?

Think about it and make the change if needed. Do not re-edge exactly on the old existing edge if it doesn't look its best. If needed, use a paint gun to re-shape the bed this way you will have a mark to follow.

There will be some jobs where the beds **do not** need improvement or reshaping. So you can simply run the edger blade along the existing contour. When the beds do not need improvements, cut **as little as possible** from the edge of the bed. Then there will be very little grass and soil to remove and pickup.

Start up the edger machine and run the motor at full speed and then make the cut. Cut down approximately 2 to 3 inches into the ground. If you are cutting through grass, cut approximately 2 inches down below the layer of grass. Push the machine while running the motor at full speed. Skip any areas where there are stones, sprinkler heads, etc or where there may be wires buried. Reshape any bed areas that need to be improved.

Now that the edge has been cut, you are ready to use your spade or pick. Push the spade into the groove that you just cut. Then lift up and remove the soil or grass on the **inside** of the landscape bed. Remove all the grass and weeds inside the landscape bed area, close to the edge that was just cut. Keep a straight, sharp edge where the edger blade cut down into the ground.

The spade is the most commonly used tool for edging. The spade works well if you are removing small amounts of soil or grass.

If you have to remove a lot of grass, and weeds, or if the soil is very hard, a pick will work better. Use the wide part of the pick, dig down and lift up the grass. Use the pick in the same direction as the edge was cut. You should be able to remove the soil and grass and leave the cut edge undisturbed.

After the edge has been cut and dug out, you need to pick up the grass or soil that was removed. **Try to leave most of the soil in the bed**. If there are any large pieces of grass with soil on them, shake the grass so most of the soil falls off and back into the bed. Pickup grass, weeds, rocks, etc and put them into your wheelbarrow. In most cases, it is easiest to pickup the grass, etc with your hands. After the grass, etc has been cleaned up, the job is done. At some jobs, you may also remove weeds from the entire landscape bed while edging. Then you might mulch the beds. We'll discuss mulching in the next chapter of this training guide.

Edging New Landscape Beds
Edging of new landscape beds is done almost the same except the new bed is first marked out with marker paint. Then you cut along the marked line and remove everything inside the new bed.

Edging of Tree Rings
Tree rings are small circular beds around ornamental trees. They protect the trees from lawn mowers and string trimmers. They also help protect the root system during hot and cold weather conditions.

To edge an existing tree ring, first check to see if the existing shape looks good and adjust it if needed. Then use the same procedures as we just discussed. As the tree grows larger, the tree ring should also be made larger. Increase the size of tree rings as needed, usually every two or three years the ring should be made slightly larger.

To edge a **new** tree ring:

- Make a mark where you want the edge to be.
- Use a piece of rope; wrap it loosely around the tree trunk.
- On the other end or the rope, tie a can of marker paint.
- You should be able to swing the rope around the tree.
- Adjust the paint can so it will make a mark where you want.
- While you swing the rope around the tree, spray the paint onto the ground. This will give you a nice even circle around the tree and the job will look professional.

Edging Sidewalks and Patios

If a property has not been maintained, it may have grass growing onto the sidewalks or patio. Using the edger machine, run the blade against the outside edge of the walkway or patio. Then, remove any grass or soil that is on the walk or patio. There should be a small space between the grass and a walkway or patio. Remember to look for any wires, pipes, etc. before edging.

Edging of landscape beds should be done once a year. The springtime is the best time of year to do the job since the ground is usually soft and easy to work in. Edging in hard, dry soil is very difficult and

51

should not be done if possible. The edges should be maintained with a string trimmer during the lawn mowing service. Hold the string trimmer so the string cuts vertical down into the existing edge. This should be done about every two weeks and will keep the property looking great.

Edging of Landscape Beds Training and Safety Tips

- Always wear safety glasses with edger machine.
- Always check the area you are going to edge before you make to the cut. Look for cable and phone lines, lighting, sprinkler pipes, stones and other problems. Cut theses areas carefully by hand.
- If the shape of the bed or tree ring is not perfect, fix it when you make the new edge. Don't follow the same shape if it does not look good.
- Make your cut as close as possible to the old edge. Then there will be less soil and grass to remove and the job will be much easier.
- Keep hands and feet away from all moving parts on machines.
- Fill machines on trailers, not on grass.
- Do not over tighten the gas cap or you will break the seal and it will leak.
- Keep all machines securely fastened on the trailer or truck.
- Do not remove any safety guards.
- Always think safety first!!!!!

MULCHING OF LANDSCAPE BEDS
(CHAPTER 7)

Mulching is done for many different reasons. First it will help to protect landscape plants. Throughout the year, a layer of mulch will help hold water and moisture around the root zone area of plantings. Landscape plants will be able to hold water longer, stay healthier, and be able to withstand dry weather conditions better. During the winter, mulch will help protect the plants root system from bad weather conditions. Plants will be healthier and have a better chance of survival during stressful conditions with mulch around them. Mulch will reduce the amount of weed growth in landscape beds. Weeds will grow very quickly and be hard to control in a bed without mulch. Mulch will also help prevent soil erosion. Without mulch, the soil in the landscape beds will start to wash away with a heavy rainfall. Mulch will decompose after a few years and slowly turn into soil. The soil will be rich in organics and some nutrients will be added to the landscape beds. Another reason to mulch is because it looks great and it gives the beds a clean, professional look.

There are many different types of mulch available. Mulches will be different in color, material and cost. Stay away from using the very cheap mulches. Most of the very cheap mulches have garbage ground up into it, such as old construction debris, pallets or wood that is rotten or contaminated with chemicals. These cheap, low quality mulches can do more harm than good. I have seen landscape plants die from a poor quality contaminated mulch being used. If there is any chemical in the mulch, and it washes into the soil during a rainfall, there will be some serious damage done to the existing soil and plants. Make sure you are getting your mulch from a reliable, reputable company. Check the mulch throughout the year and make sure it is a good quality all year long.

Sometimes a supplier will have a very large pile of mulch and by the time they get down to the bottom of the pile, the mulch may have already started to decompose. Then you will have mulch that is already starting to turn to soil. If the mulch has some soil in it, it should not be used. Mulch should be made up of various pieces of ground up wood, without any soil in the mixture. How will the mulch control weeds if there is already soil in the mulch? Some suppliers will sell you anything, so be careful. Inspect the mulch you are buying throughout the year.

Mulch is usually bought by the cubic yard. A yard is a measurement that is 3 feet by 3 feet by 3 feet, in the shape of a cube or square. When it is sold, it will be dumped into your truck with a tractor bucket. You can measure the truck bed that you are using to determine how much mulch will fit into it.

If your truck bed is:
- 9 feet long by 6 feet wide by 3 feet high (multiply $9 \times 6 \times 3 = 162$ square feet).

- One cubic yard is $3 \times 3 \times 3$ (a total of 27 square feet).

- Divide 162 by 27, which totals 6 yards.

- If filled level, the truck will hold a total of 6 yards.

Types of Mulch

Lets now talk about the different types of mulch that are available. We will talk about the most popular and commonly used mulches. Depending on what part of the country you are working in, you may use a mulch that we have not discussed. Such as in the Southern states there are many pine trees. People in this area of the country use the pine needles as a mulch since it is easy to get together and sell. But remember all mulches basically do the same thing. Protect the plants, protect the ground from erosion, help prevent weed growth, and look great. We'll start discussing the cheapest mulch in cost and quality and work up to the best.

Wood Chips

Wood chips are the cheapest and lowest quality mulch. They usually are available from a local tree service company. The tree service runs branches through their chipper/shredder to make the mulch and dispose of their branches. Wood chips are very rough-cut and they may have insects in the chips if an infested tree was chipped up. They may also have small sticks and other debris in them. Wood chips should not be used around the foundation of a house. They should be used for large beds away from the house or can be spread out along a woods line after the woods have been cleaned out. A heavy layer of four to five inches of chips will help hold down weeds and brush and give the woods a clean maintained look. Wood chips are large in size and will not decompose as quickly as regular mulch. Wood chips can be bought directly from a local tree service for the best price.

Playground Wood Chips

Playground wood chips are wood chips that are very clean. There are no small sticks, leaves, or debris in playground wood chips. They are used mostly around children's play areas. A layer of 3 to 4" will keep children from getting dirty and will be safer than falling onto the hard ground. Playground wood chips are available at most garden centers.

Hardwood Mulch

Hardwood mulch is made up of different types of hard wood. It is ground up twice so it is finer than wood chips and is usually brown in color. Hardwood mulch is very popular because it is not too costly and looks fairly attractive. Be careful when purchasing hardwood mulch. Sometimes the manufacturer will grind up construction debris and other garbage into this type of mulch. Inspect the mulch and if you find any garbage in it, do not use it. Some types of hardwood mulch will have a bad odor to them. The odor may last for a few weeks. Hardwood mulch will last about one year. After one year it will look old and start to decompose. When using hardwood mulch, you should give the landscape beds a layer of approximately 1 to 2-1/2" per year. Hardwood mulch can be purchased at most garden centers or directly from the manufacturer for the best price.

Root Mulch

Root mulch is a mulch that is dark brown/black in color. Root mulch is made from tree stumps and aged to turn into a dark color. Root mulch will last about one to two years before it will need to be replenished. Root mulch is sold at most garden centers and will cost a little more than hardwood mulch.

Colored Hardwood Mulch

Colored Hardwood mulch has become popular over the last few years. This product is colored to look reddish-brown. The color stays onto the mulch for a year or more. There is almost no fading of the color. Most other mulches fade on color after a few months. Make sure the customer has a sample of any colored mulch before you do any work. Some people like the color while other people find it very unattractive. Also colored mulches will slightly vary in color. Be sure to purchase all the mulch for a job from the same stockpile because the next pile may not be an exact color match. The product is available at most garden centers but is fairly expensive.

Hammermill Mulch

Hammermill mulch is a high quality mulch that is available in different shades of brown. When Hammermill mulch is made, only the best quality woods are used. The mulch is ground into pieces that are slightly different in size. Hammermill mulch will last longer than Hardwood mulch. Another good thing about Hammermill mulch is that it does not smell bad. Many of the hardwood mulches have a bad odor to them for a week or two. A bad smell may give you an unhappy customer. Hammermill mulch will still need to be replenished in one to two years. Hammermill mulch is not being used as often as Hardwood mulch because of its cost. Hammermill usually costs about twice as much as Hardwood mulch. Hammermill mulch is available from all garden centers. If purchased in a large quantity, it can be bought directly from the manufacturer.

Cedar Mulch

Cedar mulch is the best mulch you can buy. It is reddish-brown in color and is made from cedar trees. Cedar wood will outlast all other woods. It will not decompose as fast as other mulches. However the color will fade about the same as most other mulches. Cedar mulch is great to use around the foundation beds of a house. For about one month the cedar will have a good smell to it. Cedar mulch is the only mulch that insects will avoid. Insects will not make a home in cedar and don't even like to walk across it. If you have a customer with an ant or termite problem, cedar mulch is the mulch to use. The cost of cedar mulch is its only bad point, it cost about three times more than Hardwood mulch.

Tools Needed For Mulching

You will need the following tools when mulching:
- A jumbo and regular sized wheelbarrow.
- A large and regular sized pitchfork.
- A metal bow rake.
- A leave rake.
- A flat shovel.

- A backpack blower.
- A dump truck or someone to deliver the mulch to the job site.

Be sure to bring the correct amount of tools to the job site. If you are working as a two-person crew, you will need two wheelbarrows, two pitchforks, and two rakes. If you are working as a three-person crew, bring three of each of the tools. It is unprofessional and unproductive to have a three-person crew working with only one or two wheelbarrows and sharing one metal rake and one pitchfork. Even if you are working together as a team and not using all the tools at once, it is always best to have spare tools on the job site.

Wheelbarrows

The jumbo-sized wheelbarrow should have dual wheels and be able to hold about double the amount of a regular size wheelbarrow. The regular sized wheelbarrow should be used when you need to fit into small areas between plants, trees or fences. It will also work better when you are working on a hill. Whatever size wheelbarrow you are using, make sure that the tires have enough air pressure. The job will be twice as hard if you are pushing a full wheelbarrow with a tire that is half flat. Always keep an air pump in your truck; then when you are on the job site and you notice a low tire, you can fix the problem and don't have to suffer all day.

Pitchforks

Pitchforks are used to pick up the mulch. A large sized pitchfork works best when filling up the wheelbarrows from the mulch pile. A smaller sized pitch fork with a long handle works best when you are taking mulch out of the wheelbarrow and putting it in hard to reach areas. It can also be used to start to spread out the piles of mulch that are dumped throughout a landscape bed.

Rakes, Shovel and Back pack Blower

A metal bow rake should be used to spread out the piles of mulch. Some people finish spreading out the mulch with the metal rake, while other people use a plastic leave rake to finish. When using a plastic leave rake you can lightly rake out any areas that are not perfectly smooth. This will give the bed a professional look. The leave rake, flat shovel, and backpack blower are all used to clean up an area where a mulch pile was dumped, such as a driveway or road area. You should also rake up or blow any mulch that was spilled onto any lawn areas.

Dump Truck

You will need a dump truck to get the mulch to the jobsite. The dump truck you are using must have the correct air pressure in the tires and will need a tarp to cover the load of mulch. You need the correct tire pressure on your truck because if one tire has less air then the others, the truck will tilt when loaded up. This will put even more stress on the low tire and the truck can roll over if it tilts too far while driving. Yes, it can happen to you. Check the air pressure before the truck gets loaded up. You will need a tarp to cover the mulch loaded in the truck. The dump truck needs to have a tarp and roller put on the front top of the dump body. You should not pick up mulch or other supplies without a tarp. You will get a ticket by the police if you are caught driving a loaded truck without a tarp over the material.

Getting Mulch to the Job Site

You will need to have the mulch delivered to the jobsite with your dump truck or by the local supplier or garden center. Most landscapers pick up mulch with their company dump truck. When you pick up the mulch in your own truck, you can dump the piles in the best location on the job site. You can also work directly out of the truck if the job calls for only one truckload or less. If you have a very large mulch job of 50 or more yards, you should consider having it delivered in one large truck directly from the manufacturer. Mulch always cost less when it is bought in bulk directly from the company who makes the mulch. Sometimes it may be easier to get the job done if you are working from many small piles while other times it may be better to work from one large pile. Think and plan out each job before you have mulch delivered.

Usually when you have a large amount of mulch delivered, it has to be dumped on the side of the road. When dumping mulch on the side of the road, you must follow some rules.

- *You must always put out safety cones on both sides of the pile to clearly alert all oncoming traffic.*
- *You will need to have the pile removed from the road by the end of the day or you may get a ticket from the police.*

- *Some busy roads will require a permit when dumping mulch on them.*

- *Every worker must always be very careful of oncoming traffic while working on the side of any road.*

The boss or foreman is usually making the discussion about mulch pick up or delivery. However, everyone should give each job some thought and then talk to each other about the best way to complete each job so that the job is being done as easily and effectively as possible. **Always look for ways to get each job done faster, easier and better.**

A Typical Mulch Job

Each mulch job will be different and will require a different amount of mulch. The job that we will be discussing will need a total of 50 yards. An agreement has been made with the customer to spread 50 yards of mulch on their property. It is a large property with beds in many different areas of the property. One large truck can deliver the mulch but it will be hard to work from that pile since it can only be dumped in the road. So you will pick up and deliver the mulch to the job site yourself. Five truckloads of 10 yards each will give you the total of 50 yards.

Each Job Needs To be Explained and Organized

Before starting any job, **everyone** should know how much mulch is going to be used, where it needs to be spread and any other details about the job. Before you start working, everyone must walk the job site together and discuss what exactly needs to be done. The job will go much easier and faster when everyone knows exactly what needs to be done. If you are unsure about what needs to be done at a job site, ask questions until you are 100% sure. After you walk and discuss the job site, you need to get organized.

Every type of landscape job needs to be explained and organized before you start working. Be aware that you will have to re-organize each job a few times throughout the workday.

At the job we are discussing, you will need to do some work in the landscape beds before you can spread the mulch. You have decided that two workers will weed and edge the beds while another worker picks up and delivers the mulch to the job site.

Picking up and Delivering Mulch

When you get to the mulch supplier, back the dump truck up to the mulch pile. This way if any mulch comes off the back of the truck while it is being loaded up, it will fall back close to the pile. Once the truck is loaded, climb up onto the truck with a metal rake or shovel and level out the pile. Push the high spots of mulch into the low areas and clear off any mulch on the tailgate of the truck. Pull the tarp over the mulch and tie the tarp down. The tarp should come over the back of the tailgate of the truck.

While driving back to the job site, drive carefully since the truck is loaded up. While driving with weight in the truck, you should go slower around curves and slow down earlier when coming to a stop. Before you get to the job site, think about the best spot to dump out the mulch or where it would be best to park if you are going to work out of the truck. Talk with your co-workers to decide where the best place or places will be. There is one obvious basic rule to keep. Bring the mulch as close as possible to the beds that you are mulching.

At the job we are discussing, you will need a total of 50 yards which is a total of five truckloads. After planning out and organizing this job, you have decided to dump three truckloads in the corner of the driveway close to the garage. This mulch will cover all the beds around the house and the back yard. Then you will dump one truckload in the street. The last truckload will not be dumped. You will work out of the truck and you will use the last truckload to mulch a few beds on the far end of the property.

You will need to back into the driveway with the truck. Before backing up into the driveway:
- Call a co-worker to help.
- Your co-worker needs to direct you and may need to direct traffic if you are working on a busy road.
- If you are working on a busy road, you should have two co-workers directing you. One person should be in the driveway and the other person needs to be in the road to stop any oncoming traffic if needed.
- Wait until there is no oncoming traffic in site, then start backing up toward the driveway.

- Look in the rear view mirrors for the **curbs** of the driveway.

- Get onto the driveway and off the road as soon as possible.

- If a car comes while you are backing up, your co-worker needs to put his hand up high to make a stop sign. He should put his hand up early so the driver of the car can clearly see and understands what to do before getting close to you. You also might consider purchasing red flags to hold up because they are a lot more visible.

- **Watch the curbs while backing up**. If you rub against any curbing with a loaded truck, you will damage or destroy the tire. Driving with a damaged tire is very dangerous because the tire can blow out and may cause the truck to rollover.

- Even if the driveway is easy to back up on, you should still have someone directing you. Children, dogs, cats, tools, toys, landscape lighting and curbing will create a serious problem if they are hit.

- Never back into a driveway without someone directing you.

Dumping out the Mulch

- Always park the truck on hard level ground and use the parking brake.

- Do not lift up the dump body if the truck is not parked level.

- Always take a look at what's above you. Stay away from tree branches and wires.

- Give yourself room to move the truck forward. Leave about 15 feet for room so you can pull up the truck while dumping it.

- Once the mulch is out, put the dump body down immediately.

- Never drive with the dump body up.

- One last thing to remember is to never block up the driveway or garage area unless you first spoke to the property owner to make sure it is okay. Try your best to leave the driveway and garage open, so if someone needs to get in or out, they can do so. If you must block the driveway, always ask first.

Mulching Work Procedures

Now that the first load of mulch is dumped, one worker will go to the pick up the next load while the other two workers start mulching. Since the job is fairly large, you should have three wheelbarrows on the job site. Put the three wheelbarrows next to the mulch pile.

Start taking mulch from the area that came out of the truck last. This way you will make the pile smaller and when the next load of mulch comes, it can be dumped almost in the same spot, by dumping as close as possible to one spot it will be easier to clean up the area when you are finished.

Organize the job, one person should be filling the wheelbarrows while the other should be pushing the wheelbarrows and dumping them it out into the beds. By using three wheelbarrows, there will always be a full wheelbarrow to push and a wheelbarrow to fill up. There will be no time wasted waiting for a wheelbarrow.

Before you start dumping mulch into the beds, make sure you know how deep the mulch should be at each job. Some jobs will require only a light covering of mulch, while other jobs will require a depth of two or three inches. Landscape beds should have about two-to-three inches of mulch in them. If the beds still have mulch in them from the previous year, you will only need to put down another inch. If there is no mulch at all, you will need to put down at least two inches; however, this depends on what the customer will pay for. **Everyone must know how deep the layer of mulch should be spread and how much mulch can be used at each job**. If a job needs to be completed with 10 yards and you do not finish with 10 yards it will create a serious problem. **Always understand the amount of mulch that can be used and the approximate depth the mulch should be spread before you start each job!**

The job you are currently working at will require about 1-1/2 to 2 inches of mulch. Start dumping piles of mulch throughout the landscape bed. Try to space the piles out so that when they are spread, the mulch will be about 1-1/2 to 2 inches deep. This will take a little practice. It will always be better to put down a little **less** mulch at first. Once you spread out the mulch and if you need a little more, you can always bring another wheelbarrow to finish. But if you dump the piles to close, the mulch will be spread to deep and you will not finish the job with the amount of mulch that is required.

When using the large sized wheelbarrow, you can dump small piles out in a few different places. It is better to make a few small piles instead of one large pile. Then the piles will be easier to spread out. If there are any tight areas where you cannot fit the large wheelbarrow, use the smaller one. Be very careful not to run into any shrubs with the wheelbarrow. You will break the branches and the branches will turn brown and die. If the smaller wheelbarrow is still too big to fit into a tight area, use a pitchfork.

A regular sized pitchfork with a long handle works best. Take the mulch out of the wheelbarrow and spread it into the hard to reach tight areas. You should also use the pitchfork to toss mulch under plants that are hard to reach. **Make sure to get mulch under each plant**. When you are mulching around ground cover plants, a pitchfork also works best. Call a co-worker to help you; one of you should lift up the branches so the other can toss mulch under the plant.

Continue to work as a team with one-worker filling the wheelbarrows while the other dumps piles into the beds. When the landscape bed is covered with piles about half way, one worker needs to start spreading out the piles. The other worker will then fill, push, and dump more piles in the bed alone.

To spread out the mulch piles, use a metal bow rake. If the piles are large and hard to spread with the metal rake, use a pitchfork first to break up the piles. If while spreading the pile, you find areas where you need a little more mulch, call over your co-worker to dump a little more mulch where needed.

When you are spreading mulch up against a house, make sure that the mulch does not touch the siding. Siding is made of wood, vinyl, or aluminum and the mulch should never be put up against it. The mulch should only be put against the foundation which is concrete. Leave at least a one-inch space between the mulch and the siding. If the bed is higher than the siding, use a shovel and dig out an area so you can start one inch below the siding. Then the rest of the landscape bed should slope away from the house and foundation so that rainfall runs away from the house.

While you are spreading the mulch throughout the bed, try to rake it out so the beds are smooth and even when you are finished. If there are any low spots in the beds, add a little more mulch to fill in the low spots. If there are high spots, put less mulch on them. Once all the mulch is spread evenly throughout the bed, give the bed one final inspection to make sure all areas are evenly covered. Then you may want to use a plastic leave rake to lightly rake the mulch one last time. A plastic leave rake works well for the final light grading of the mulch.

At the job we are discussing, you now have the three truckloads of mulch dumped in the corner of the driveway near the garage, which is being used to mulch around the house and the backyard. You also have one full truck of mulch to use at the end of the driveway near the road. You will need to dump this truck load on the side of the road so the truck can pickup the fifth and final load of mulch. But you will not dump that fourth truckload until you are finished working around the house.

Never dump a pile of mulch on the side of the road until you are ready to work from that pile. If you are dumping a large pile, make sure that you have enough time during the day to completely remove the pile from the road before the end of the day. Always use safety cones when dumping or parking on the side of any road.

Now that you have three workers on the property, you should make sure everyone is still organized. Even if you are not in charge, if you think of an easier way to get the work done, make a suggestion to your boss, foreman or co-workers on what may work better. **Always** stay alert and think about the best way to complete each job. Watch and learn from experienced co-workers and make suggestions if you see a better way to complete the work.

After re-organizing the job, you now have three wheelbarrows next to the mulch pile. One worker is filling the wheelbarrows, the second worker is pushing and dumping small piles throughout the beds, and the third person is spreading out the piles. If a lot of piles build up in the beds, switch positions. Two people should spread and one person fill and push the wheelbarrows to the beds. If the mulch gets spread out and more piles are needed. Switch back to having only one-person spread. Talk with each other about the job throughout the day so everyone knows what to do and no mistakes are made. Then the job will go as quickly and easily as possible.

Now that you have finished the mulching around the house and backyard, you need to clean up the driveway area where the mulch pile was. First use a metal bow rake, flip the rake over and use the backside of the rake to push the mulch into a pile. Then use a plastic leave rake. Pick up the mulch with a flat shovel. After you have picked everything up with a shovel, blow off the area with a backpack blower.

Then walk around the landscape beds that have just been mulched. Pick up any mulch that was spilled on the grass, walks, etc., then blow off these areas. Check to make sure all your tools are off the area of the property that was just finished. Keep all your tools together so nothing gets lost. Then as always, make sure any gates are securely shut before you leave the area.

Now that you are ready to mulch the beds at the end of the driveway and need to park the truck on the side of the road, check for oncoming traffic and have someone direct you if needed. Once the truck is parked where you want to dump out the mulch, put out the safety cones. You need to use two or three safety cones so on-coming traffic has plenty of notice that there is something on the side of the road. Put one cone approximately ten feet away from the pile. Then put another about twenty feet away. Use safety cones even if you are working on a street with very little traffic. There are many bad drivers on the road and if an accident happens near your mulch pile, you and your company will be to blame. If safety cones are used correctly, there will be little or no problem if an accident occurs. If safety cones are not used and an accident occurs, you and your company will be held responsible.

Before dumping, check for any dangerous wires or tree limbs. Also make sure the truck is parked on hard level ground. When working near any road, you always need to be careful of oncoming traffic. Organize the job and get to work done.

Your last truckload of mulch will not be dumped out. Work the mulch directly out of the truck whenever possible. If you are working on a job that needs only one truckload of mulch or less, or when you are working on your last truckload, leave the mulch in the truck. This way if you have any extra mulch, it will not be dumped on the ground. You will not have to clean up as much and you can drive around to different areas of the property when the mulch is in the truck.

At the job we are discussing, you have some beds at different areas around the outside of the property. It will be easiest to park the truck at different areas of the road so you are as close as possible to these beds, always use safety cones.

When you are working out of the truck, stand on the tailgate and remove the first half of the mulch pile. After half of the mulch is out of the truck, close the tailgate and raise up the dump body. Raise it up until the mulch from the front of the truck falls to the back of the truck, then lower the dump body down. Now you can easily reach the rest of the mulch and you don't have to walk back and forth in the truck to put the mulch into the wheelbarrows.

Remember to organize and plan out each part of each job. Then your job will turn out looking great and you will have gotten the job done as quickly and easily as possible.

Mulching Training and Safety Tips

- Think about each job and organize it before you start and re-organize as needed throughout the workday. Work together as a team.
- Everyone must understand what needs to be done and how much mulch can be used at each job before you start working.
- Keep enough air pressure in truck tires when driving with a full load of mulch.
- Level out the mulch in the truck, clean off the tailgate and use the tarp.
- Keep enough air pressure in the wheelbarrow tires and the wheelbarrow will be easier to push.
- When you put pitchforks on the ground or in the truck, keep the points facing down.
- Keep wheelbarrow tires away from the pitchforks.
- Keep the truck tires away from curbing or anything that can damage the tires. Especially when the truck is loaded up.
- Always park on level ground when dumping out mulch. Look above you for any wires, tree branches, etc.

- Always use safety cones.
- Always organize and think safety first.

PRUNING OF SHRUBS AND ORNAMENTAL TREES (CHAPTER 8)

Why is Pruning Needed?

- *Pruning of shrubs and ornamental trees is needed to keep plants healthy and looking their best.*

- *If you do not prune plants on a regular basis, they will grow out of control, grow into each other, become unhealthy, unattractive and die prematurely.*

- *Correct pruning will increase the plants overall health and life. The plants will produce more flowers or fruit and have more colorful leaves and branches.*

- *Pruning will reduce the risk of damage during stressful conditions, such as extreme weather conditions, or during attack from insects or disease.*

- *Pruning is done to control the overall size of the plant and to direct the plant to grow a certain way.*

- *Pruning is also done to remove sick or damaged branches from the plants.*

Knowing What to Prune and When

As a landscape professional, you should know how to correctly prune many different types of shrubs and ornamental trees. Shrubs will vary greatly in size and shape, from a low growing ground cover to a large 15 foot diameter plant, from a weeping to an upright plant, from an evergreen to a deciduous plant. Ornamental trees are small trees that grow to about 25 to 30 feet in height and usually have flowers. Any trees that are larger than 25 to 30 feet would be considered a full sized tree and should be pruned by a tree company, not a landscape company.

The best time for pruning most plants is during the summer months or soon after the plants have flowered. By July and August, most plants have already flowered and have a lot of new growth on them from the spring. About 70% of a plants new growth happens during the spring and early summer months. So by pruning in the late summer, you will not have a lot of additional new growth coming onto the plant after you have pruned it. The plant will keep its pruned shape until the next spring.

If you prune too late in the year, such as the late fall, the plants that flower may not have enough time to grow new buds for the next spring season. The buds are where the flowers come from. So if you prune too late and remove the buds, the plants may not flower the following spring. If you prune in the early spring, you will remove the buds just before they are ready to flower and the plant will look like it needs pruning again later on in the season. Stay with a schedule of pruning during the summer unless it is a special situation.

Most shrubs and ornamental trees need to be pruned on a yearly basis. If you skip a year or two, there will be two or three years of new growth on the plant and it may not be possible to prune the plant down to its original size. If unmaintained for a few years, the center of the plant may start to die. Lack of airflow and sunlight to the center of the plant will cause insects and disease to damage to the center part of the plant. Then, it will not be possible to prune it down to its original size since there will be nothing alive in the center of the plant, only brown dead branches. Note: Never prune a plant down to the brown dead branches in the center of the plant. By removing all of the green growth from the branches, you will damage or destroy most plants.

By pruning every year, you will avoid this problem, the plant will look better and live a lot longer.

Tools and Equipment Needed

You will need the following tools to prune shrubs and ornamental trees.

- Power trimmers, (one small size and one larger size).
- Extended reach power trimmers.
- Hedge shears.
- A small power chain saw.
- A hand saw.
- Hand shears.
- Loppers.
- A combination pole saw/loppers.
- A step latter.
- Rakes.
- A landscape barrel.

- A tarp.

- A backpack blower.

- You will also need bee and wasp spray in case you run into a bee's nest.

- Alcohol for cleaning the tools.

Power Trimmers

Power trimmers are most commonly used when pruning shrubs. There are two blades on power trimmers. The blades have nuts and bolts going through them to hold them together. The nuts and bolts should be tightened so there is little or no space between the blades. If there is a space, you will get a bad cut. However, if the bolts are too tight, the blades will not be able to move. Make sure the blades are adjusted correctly. The blades also need to be sharp, if the blades are not sharp, you will get a bad cut and have problems pruning. Check the space and sharpness of the blades after each job and have them repaired if needed.

After each job, you should clean the blades by using a rag with alcohol to wipe them down. During the summer months, there are many active diseases in the shrubs that you are pruning. By wiping down the blades, you will remove any disease and you will not spread the disease to the next property. When you are on the job site and see a shrub that looks heavily diseased, wipe down the blades after you prune it and **before** pruning the other shrubs. Wipe down all other tools such as hand shears, saws, loppers or pole saws if they have made contact with any diseased plants and after each job.

Power trimmers use 2-cycle gas. Fill up the gas tank before each job at your truck, not on the lawn or beds. When tightening the gas cap, make sure it is straight before you screw it on. Also be careful not to over tighten it or you will break the seal inside the cap. When you break the seal, gas will leak out. If gas leaks on the plants you are pruning, there will be dead spots all over the plants. If gas leaks from the cap or anywhere else, stop immediately and do not use the machine.

Power trimmers are very dangerous, if you touch the blades with your arms or legs you will cause serious injury to yourself. Be careful and stay alert! It is best to have two different sized power trimmers; one with a regular sized blade about two feet long for pruning small to medium sized plants, the other with the longest blade length possible, three or four feet long. Use it for large or hard to reach shrubs, hedges, and evergreen trees.

Extended Reach Power Trimmers

Extended reach power trimmers are now available. These machines have the blades mounted on one end of a shaft and the motor mounted at the bottom of the shaft. The shaft is about five to six feet long and the blades can be adjusted to different cutting angles. Many power equipment manufacturers have a string trimmer where the head can be easily removed and power trimmers can be mounted in its place. The machine is also lightweight and easy to work with. Extended reach power trimmers will make many jobs much safer since you will not have to hang off a latter to trim hard to reach areas. The jobs will also get done faster since you will not have to go up and down a latter as much. I highly recommend using extended reach power trimmers.

Starting the power trimmers can sometimes be a problem. All machines will start slightly different. However, most machines start easiest by using these procedures.

First use the choke on the machine with the throttle on only about half way. When the machine sounds like it has almost started, turn off the choke and apply the throttle about half to three quarters of the way open and the machine should start. The mistake that many people make is that they hold the throttle on full and apply too much gas or they leave the choke on too long. This will flood out the motor and then the machine will not start. Always be careful not to apply too much gas or you will have a problem.

All machines will start differently. Once you find the easiest way to start a machine, **repeat that process every time you need to start it up**. Once the machine is warm, it will start easier and you probably will not have to use the choke. Safety glasses, ear protection and gloves should be worn while using this machine.

Hedge Shears
Manual hedge shears will cut similar to power trimmers. They have a long cutting blade approximately two feet in length.

Small Chain Saw

- Before using the chain saw, make sure that the chain is not loose. The chain should never be loose; it should fit snug around the bar. As soon as the chain gets a little loose, stop using it and have it tightened. Do not over tighten the chain or you will burn out the chain, bar and motor. **Always** keep the tools needed to tighten the chain wherever you go with the chain saw.

- You will also need to check the chain to make sure it is always sharp. If the chain gets dull after a job, **make sure** you tell someone in charge to have it sharpened **before** going to the next job.

- A chain saw uses 2-cycle gas and has another tank used for bar and chain oil. Always fill both tanks together; when you fill up the gas, fill the oil up also. If you run out of bar and chain oil, motor oil can also be used. Bring bar and chain oil or motor oil wherever you go with the chain saw. Using the chain saw without oil will destroy the bar and chain.

- Safety glasses, ear protection and gloves should be worn while using this machine.

Be careful when starting up the chain saw. Chain saws have the same problem as power trimmers, they flood out very easily. Once the motor is flooded with gas, the machine will not start. Apply the choke and throttle carefully and use the same starting procedure as we discussed with power trimmers.

When using a chain saw, make sure you are always standing in a well-balanced position. Keep the chain away from your body and only cut small branches. Large branches are under pressure and can snap suddenly. Large branches should be removed by a tree professional, not a landscaper.

When cutting small branches, you want to make a flush, even cut. First make a small cut at the bottom side of the branch, then cut from the top. The reason you first make the small cut on the bottom is to cut through the bark, so when the branch falls, the bark will not peal. Without the cut on the bottom side, the branch can fall and peal the bark. If the bark peals off from areas that you do not want to remove, it will look very bad and unprofessional. Insects and disease can infect these areas of the tree where there is no bark. If you left a stub, cut it flush to the larger branch.

The best way to cut off a branch and avoid pealing is to make a double cut. First cut the branch off as we just discussed but leave a stub about one foot long. Then make a flush, even cut when removing the smaller piece.

When you are making a cut, do not push the saw to hard, only put light pressure on the saw. If you push to hard, you will have two problems.

- First you will be cutting to fast, when you cut too fast the woodchips get caught up in the saw. This will cause the saw to work poorly or stop working from the woodchips jammed up into the machine.

- Second, you might hit another branch, cut into the dirt, hit a stone, or slip and loose your balance when you get through the branch and the saw is free.

You need to put a little pressure on the saw when you are cutting, then ease up when you are almost through the branch.

The most common problem landscapers have when using chain saws is that they touch dirt or stones with the chain. The chain can only cut wood. Once it touches dirt or a stone, it will become dull and will not cut. A tree professional will use the same chain all week because they are careful to only cut wood. You can do the same if you try.

Hand Saw

A handsaw can be used instead of a chain saw. It is much safer and it won't break down like a chain saw. But you will have to work harder and each job will take longer to get done. If you are cutting only a few branches, use the hand saw. Keep a handsaw in your truck, then if your chain saw breaks down, you can always finish the job using the handsaw.

Hand Shears

Hand shears are used to cut small branches. Hand shears should not be used to cut anything larger than ¾ of an inch. If you try to cut something larger, your hand shears may break. Hand shears should only be used to cut wood. Once the blade on the hand shears gets dull, they will work very poorly and should not be used. Use a sharpening stone to sharpen the blade of the hand shears a few times a year. Do not sharpen the blade on a grinding wheel.

When you are pruning shrubs and trees, the hand shears should always be kept with you; in your back pocket or in a case that hooks onto your belt. **Never** put a pair of hand shears down on the ground. They will get lost very easily. Put them back into your pocket or case when you are not using them. Hand shears are expensive and the easiest tool to loose. Make a place in your truck where the hand shears always belong. Then they will not get lost and can always be found without wasting any time.

Loppers

Loppers are like very large hand shears. They will cut branches from ½ to about 2 inches thick. Use loppers to remove branches that are too big for power trimmers or hand shears. Loppers also work well on branches that are not stable. Some branches move around too much to use a saw; loppers will work better on unstable branches.

Combination Pole Saw and Loppers

A pole saw with loppers is the next tool you will need. A pole saw is used to prune hard to reach branches from a large shrub or a small tree. Most pole saws are about eight feet long and can extend to about 16 feet. With a pole saw, you can saw off branches or use the loppers to cut off the branches.

- If the branch you have to remove is stable and not moving around, use the saw to remove it.

- If the branch is unstable and moves around, put the branch into the loppers, then pull on the rope that is attached to the pole saw. By pulling the rope you will open and close the loppers.

- Make sure you are well balanced when using a pole saw. Do not try to reach a branch that is too far away or you may fall. Be especially careful when working on a latter.

- When the saw blade of the pole saw does not cut easily, replace it. Never try to work with a dull saw blade on a pole saw, it is very dangerous, tiring, and the job will take twice as long as it should.

Step Latter

You will need a step latter when pruning shrubs and ornamental trees. A step latter opens up and does not have to rest on anything like a regular latter. You can open it up, place it on level ground and walk up the latter. It is best to have two different latter sizes; a small one that is easy to pick-up and move around between shrubs and a larger one that should be used for tall shrubs and ornamental trees. Latter's will be made of either wood or aluminum. Wood latter's are very dangerous because they can fall apart when they get older. If you are using a wood latter, inspect it before each job. If it is not stable, or if any part looks weak or worn out, do not use it. Most people use aluminum latter's because they are stronger and last much longer. But aluminum latter's can also break; so it is a good idea to open it up and inspect it before each use.

Always make sure the latter is stable before working on it. If you are working on any type of slope or uneven terrain, have a co-worker hold the latter while you are working on it. While working on a step latter, do not use the last few steps. There will be a notification near the top of the latter which will tell you not to go any higher. Do not disregard this notice, standing on the top of a step latter is very dangerous and falling off can cause serious injury.

Other Equipment Needed

You will need a backpack blower, a few rakes, a landscape barrel and a tarp for cleaning up the debris from pruning. Bring at least two rakes. Bring a barrel so you can put debris in the barrel when cleaning hard to reach areas. Spread out the tarp and dump the full barrels onto the tarp. Then using a few workers, dump the full tarp of debris in your truck or at the dumpsite on the property. After you clean up, use a backpack blower to blow together the smaller debris and to blow out any debris that is stuck in the shrubs that you have just pruned.

When pruning, bring along safety glasses, ear protection, and gloves. You will also need bee and wasp spray. Keep the can of spray close to the area where you are working at, then if you run into a bee's nest you will not be helpless. Bee's nests are very common during the summer months. Bring along a container of alcohol and a rag. If you prune a shrub at the job site that is heavily diseased, wipe down your tools before pruning the other healthy shrubs. Also after each job, wipe down the blades of any tools used so that you kill any disease that have made contact with the blade. This way you will not bring the disease onto another property. Take a minute and wipe down the tools after each job.

Before driving to the job site, make sure that you have all the tools and safety equipment loaded into your truck and secured. Make sure that your power trimmers or chain saw will not roll or slide around in the truck. Tie down the latter's and anything else that might move around.

Organizing and Inspecting the Job

Once you get to the job site, get organized.

- With a two-person crew, you can both prune until you are about half way through the job. Then one person should continue pruning while the second person rakes up the debris. With a three-person crew, two people should prune while the third rakes up the debris.

- Gas up all your power equipment at the truck. If you run out of gas during the job, return to the truck to gas up. Remember to only lightly tighten the gas caps on the machines, if you over tighten the cap, you will break the seal inside and the gas cap and it will leak gas. Bring all your machines and tools onto the property, close to where you will be working. When everything is close to you, you do not have to walk back and forth to the truck every time you need a different machine or tool.

Before you start pruning, it is important to take a walk around the property to inspect the shrubs and trees and discuss exactly what needs to be done. Each job will be different and have different things that need to be done. Before pruning, look at each individual shrub and ornamental tree and imagine how you will prune it to make it look better.

Plant identification is important when pruning. Each plant grows differently; some grow slow; some grow fast; some have flowers and others do not. Some plants that loose their leaves they are called deciduous. Other plants stay green all year long and they are called evergreens. If you are not familiar with the plants you are about to prune, make sure someone knowledgeable walks the job site with you. Discuss all the plants and how to prune each plant the correct way. **Never prune shrubs or trees unless you are 100% sure about what needs to be done**. Incorrect pruning can do more harm than good. Each plant may require a different pruning method. Now lets talk about these different methods of pruning.

Shearing of Landscape Shrubs

Shearing is when you cut back the outside surface of a plant using power trimmers or hedge shears. You will create a smooth, uniform outer surface on the plant. Shearing shortens all the outer branches of the plant. By doing this, you will encourage the outside of the plant to grow thicker. New growth will increase on the outside of the plant, creating a dense outer shell. When shearing a plant year after year, the inside of the plant will slowly die because it cannot get enough sunlight or airflow.

Shearing will quickly bring a plant down in size but will leave you with an unhealthy plant that will easily get infected with insect and disease problems. Insects and diseases like the inside of a sheared shrub since there is very little sunlight or airflow. Overall shearing will create poor plant health and shorten the life of the plant. Shearing plants should rarely be done. Shearing does work well on some hedges or on sculptured ornamental plants.

Unfortunately, many landscape companies across the country are shearing almost all the plants that they have to prune because it is the fastest and easiest way. Company owners need to explain to their customers the correct way to prune. They should charge correctly so the job can get done the correct way.

Thinning of Landscape Shrubs

Thinning is the best way to prune shrubs but it will take the most time. Try to picture how you want the plant to look before you start pruning. Using your hand shears, find the branches that are sticking out from the plant. Reach down on the branch into the center of the plant, then cut it off with your hand shears. Continue to prune off the longest branches. You will be reducing the size of the plant while opening it up to allow sun and air to reach inside. Try not to cut off any branches that will leave large open spaces in the plant. At times you may have to cut off only half of the branch.

Carefully remove a few of the older branches from the plant. This will encourage the newer branches to grow healthy and strong. Be very careful when removing old branches; when you remove older branches, there should always be a younger branch that will grow into its place.

Look for any branches that are damaged from disease or insects and remove them.

Do not remove more than 25 to 30% of the plant. If you remove 30% of a plant and it is still too large, you should wait until the next year to remove the rest.

You may have to use loppers for the larger branches. Do not use a chainsaw because you may hit and damage the branches that you want to keep. After removing select branches and thinning out the plant, you may need to lightly prune the outside surface of the plant. Prune the outside of the plant if you want to further reduce the overall size or to repair a poorly shaped shrub. Thinning can be done to all evergreen and deciduous plants. So that brings us to the next pruning method, shearing and thinning.

Shearing and Thinning of Landscape Shrubs
First look at each plant and picture in your mind how that plant should look when you are done pruning it. Look to see if there are any areas of the plant that need to have more or less removed. If a plant should be round, but has a flat spot in it, do not cut the flat spot. Let that area grow back and the plant will have the correct shape the following year. Using your power trimmers or hedge shears very **lightly**, shear

and shape the outside of the plant. After **lightly** shearing and shaping the outside of the plant, use your hand shears to **thin out** the plant. When thinning a plant:

- **Remove select branches all around the plant.**
- **Grab the branches and remove them from the inside of the plant.**
- **Try to remove the older branches. Be careful when removing branches that are large or you will leave the plant with a large open hole in it.**
- **Do not leave any stubs when you cut off parts of a branch.**
- **Always cut the branch so that there is younger, smaller branch left to grow in its place.**
- **Never remove more than 25 – 30% of a plants branches in one pruning.**
- When you are finished thinning a plant, **the outside of the plant should look shaped but loose and fluffy so the sun and air can reach the center of the plant**. When thinning out a plant you remove part of the inside and outside of the plant. Then new growth will take place on both the inside and outside of the plant. This is how a healthy plant should grow. Light shearing and then thinning is a good way to get the pruning job done quickly and correctly. However, this method should not be used on all plants.

Renewal Pruning of Landscape Shrubs

Renewal pruning is done to improve the overall health and looks of an old plant. By renewal pruning, you can transform a big, ugly, overgrown plant into a smaller healthier and better-looking plant.

Renewal pruning should only be done to some plants, mostly deciduous plants. What you need to do is remove all of the oldest branches of the plant and let the new younger branches grow. Never remove more than 30% of the plant in one pruning. Cut the branches off by the base of the plant.

Use hand shears, loppers or a hand saw. Be careful not to cut or damage any of the younger branches when removing the older ones. If you have removed 30% of the plants largest and oldest branches, and there are still more to prune, you will have to wait until the following year. This process may take up to three years to completely remove all of the older branches while letting the younger branches grow. The end result will be worth the wait and will leave you with a plant that will look good and stay healthy for many more years.

Ornamental Tree Pruning

Ornamental trees are trees that grow approximately 25 to 30 feet in height. They can be Evergreen or Deciduous. First we will explain pruning of deciduous trees such as Flowering Dogwood, Cherry, or Plum trees.

Before pruning, give the tree a visual inspection to find out the problems with the tree. Then visualize in your mind what you will do to correct these problems and improve the tree. Look at the main tree trunk, then look at the main branches that form the tree. These are the branches that you want to keep and let grow. Then look to **remove** the following:

- Remove sucker branches. Sucker branches are very young, new branches that rapidly grow straight up from around the tree trunk and main branches.
- Remove branches that are crossing each other or rubbing together.
- Remove branches that are growing in the wrong direction. All the branches should be growing out from the center of the tree. Remove any branches that are growing into the center of the tree, or that are growing straight up.
- Remove main branches that are growing too close to each other. Remove branches that are on top of each other.
- Remove branches that have a **narrow** crotch angle since they will grow weaker than branches with a wide crotch angle. A narrow crotch angle is when branches grow in the shape of a V. A wide crotch angle is when branches grow in the shape of an L. A wide crotch angle is best.
- Remove branches that are damaged from insects or disease.
- Remove branches that are cracked or damaged.
- Remove dead or dying branches.

When pruning, start from the bottom of the tree and work your way up to the top of the tree. Most of the pruning can be done with a pole saw with loppers. First use it at the eight-foot length, then extend it when you work higher up the tree. However, you may need other tools to get the job done, such as hand shears, hand loppers, a handsaw or chain saw.

When removing smaller branches, make one even flush cut. Do not leave any stubs after removing the branch. Make a quick cut through the branch using the loppers. By making a quick cut, the loppers will not get pinched or stuck when the branch starts to fall.

When using a hand saw, hold the branch in one hand while cutting it with the other to avoid it from falling down and pealing the bark by the cut. When cutting larger branches, make a small cut through the bark on the bottom of the branch then cut it from the top. For larger branches, make the cuts leaving a stub. Let the large branch fall and then remove the stub leaving a flush cut.

When pruning the middle to top part of the tree, you should use a pole saw/loppers. First work from the ground, then when you start working higher up in the tree, you will have to use a step latter. If the tree is fairly large, you may also be able to climb inside the tree to reach more branches for pruning. **Only** climb inside the tree if the tree is large enough to support your weight. When using the latter, make sure the latter is secure or have someone hold it while you are working. While pruning, use the loppers on the pole first since they will make a quick cut and the bark will not peel. If the branches are too thick use the saw. Make a small cut on the bottom side of the branch, then cut from the top. While you are working on the latter or inside the tree, it will become difficult to see all the branches that need to be pruned. Have someone on the ground help point out what needs to be done.

After you have pruned off all the branches inside the tree, you may need to reduce the overall size of the tree.

The best way to reduce the overall size of the tree is to locate the large branches that are extending out from the trees shape. Remove these branches from inside the tree. You will be thinning out the outer branches to reduce the size and allow sun and airflow to reach inside. Then after thinning, you should shear off any smaller outer branches if needed. The outer shape of the tree should have a natural, loose looking appearance.

Only remove 25 to 30% of a tree's branches, if more pruning is needed after 30% of the branches have been removed, wait until the following year. Evergreen trees should be pruned using the shearing and thinning method that we discussed earlier.

Clean-up

To clean up you will need a rake, a landscape barrel, a tarp, a backpack blower and a pair of hand shears. Start by lightly raking the clippings off the shrubs. If there are any large branches stuck in the shrub, remove them by hand. After you rake and remove the clippings off the shrub, you may notice a branch that was missed during pruning. Keep a pair of hand shears with you so if you notice any branches that have been missed during pruning, you can snip them off. After you have cleaned the clippings from the shrubs, rake the debris into a few small piles around the landscape bed area. Rake lightly so you do not remove the mulch while cleaning up. Some of the very small clippings will not be able to be raked up. Leave them in the bed and you will blow them out with a backpack blower later. After making many piles, put the piles onto a tarp or into a landscape barrel and dump them in your truck or dumping area on the property.

After you have picked up the piles of debris, use the backpack blower to blow off the shrubs and then lightly blow the bed area.

It is important to remove all of the clippings from the shrubs. After a few days, the clippings will turn brown and if they are not removed properly, there will be brown clippings in and around the shrubs. This will look unprofessional.

The bed area should be blown very lightly so you do not remove any mulch or topsoil. It is important to leave each job as clean as possible. Before you leave, walk the job site and inspect the work that you have just done. Make sure all your tools and equipment are cleaned and put back into your truck.

Pruning Training and Safety Tips

- Wear safety gear as needed, such as safety glasses, ear protection and gloves.
- Always **clearly** understand what needs to be done **before** you start pruning.
- **It is always better to remove a little less than too much. Once you remove too much from a plant, it will take years to grow back. In some cases, you may cause permanent damage**.

- Always be careful when using power trimmers. Keep them far away from your body while using them.

- Be careful when working on any type of latter. Make sure the latter is on solid ground. Have someone hold the latter if you are working near the top. Do not use the last few steps on a step latter.

- During the summer and early fall, be on the look out for bees. Their nests can be in the ground in shrubs and trees or in the siding of a house.

- Do not over tighten the gas caps or you will break the seal and cause the cap to leak.

- Do not prune with a gas cap that leaks.

- Always fill machines at the truck or trailer, not on the grass.

- Keep all tools sharp, clean and maintained.

- Keep all machines and gas cans securely fastened on the trailer or truck.

- Always think safety first!!!

FALL CLEAN-UP
(CHAPTER 9)

Fall clean-up service is done to remove leaves, sticks and debris from lawn and bed areas. Fall leave clean up will take place from September to December depending on the area of the country you live in. The leaves will clean up easier if you make a few visits to each property during the fall season. If leaves are left on a lawn area for a long period of time, they will damage or kill the lawn. Also, leaves will get stuck in the lawn which makes cleaning-up even harder. Try to make fall clean-up visits every 7 to 14 days. During the early fall, start to mow the lawns you are maintaining slightly lower than normal. By doing this, it will be easier to remove the leaves during clean up.

The equipment needed during fall clean up is basically the same equipment you use during spring clean up. You will need the following equipment to do a fall clean up:

- A ground blower.
- A backpack blower.
- Rakes.
- A tarp.
- A large landscape barrel.

You should wear:

- Gloves.
- **Ear protection**.
- Safety glasses.

Ground Blower

The ground blower is a blower that blows debris across the ground. It has more power than a backpack blower and it should be used on large areas of the lawn. There is a chute on the ground blower to adjust the flow of air. If there are leaves stuck in the lawn, adjust the chute so more air blows **down** into the lawn. If there is only surface debris, adjust the chute to blow across the lawn surface. Always be careful while adjusting the blower chute. Turn off the machine and never put your hands inside the chute. The ground blower should not be used in landscape beds. It is too powerful and will blow mulch or soil out of the bed.

Most ground blowers use regular gas. Fill the gas tank on the trailer or road while the engine is cool. Ground blowers use motor oil faster than any other machines. **Check the engine oil two or three times per day**. Make sure you have extra engine oil with you before you go to the job site.

Backpack Blower

The backpack blower is a 2-cycle machine that uses a gas and oil mixture to run. Use the backpack blower for landscape beds, sidewalks and smaller areas of the property. Be careful not to damage anything with the blower on your back. While you are working in landscape beds, against a house, it is easy to back up into the house or into a tree or shrub and cause damage. Be careful when you are working close to a house, cars, trees and shrubs.

Rakes

Bring a few rakes to the job site so that if one breaks, you have an extra. Do not push down to hard on the wooden handle or it will break. Check your rakes and make sure the part that does the raking is not worn out. When the end of the rake wears out, it will not work properly and it is time for a new rake.

Tarps and Barrels

Bring both a tarp and a landscape barrel. Each property will require something different. Use the landscape barrel to pickup sticks and small piles of debris. Empty your barrel either in your truck or onto the tarp. Then when the tarp is full, bring it to your dump truck or to the dumping area on the property. Do not over fill a tarp or barrel or you may not be able to move it. Be careful not to rip the tarp by pulling it across a sharp object.

Leave Vacuum

A leave vacuum is an optional machine used during fall leave clean up. A leave vacuum is a machine that sucks up leaves and debris through a large hose that is about 12 inches wide and 20 feet long. Once the leaves go through the hose, they go through a fan that is spinning very fast. When the leaves go through this fan, they break apart. Then the leaves will come out of a chute. The chute will go into the back of your truck. Your truck needs to be sealed off with a mesh tarp so the leaves that blow into the truck cannot escape. The tarp needs to be securely connected to the truck. You must use a mesh tarp so that air can escape through the tarp but the leaves cannot. The broken up leaves will come into the truck with pressure, this will allow you to fit almost double the normal amount of leaves into your truck. Most leave vacuums are mounted on the truck tailgate and some are mounted on a trailer. The tailgate mounted leave vacuum is better because you can easily back up the truck into driveways or hard to reach areas.

You need to have the exhaust chute of the leave vacuum machine mounted near the top of the truck. By having the chute mounted at the top of the truck, you can fill the truck to the top. Once the truck is filled to the top, loosen the tarp and crawl inside the truck. Try to push the leaves down with your body. By doing this, you can push the leaves down a few feet and then fit even more into your truck.

Most leave vacuums will also pick up grass clippings and small sticks. However, stay away from large sticks since they will get caught up in the hose and then cause a clog up. Also stay away from loose stones; picking up stones will damage or destroy the machine in a short period of time.

When picking up wet leaves, the machine can also get clogged up very easily. Do not force too many wet leaves into the hose at once.

Listen to the motor and leaves going into the truck. If the motor sounds strange and there are no leaves going into the truck, you have a clog. Also if you loose vacuum power at the end of the hose, you may have a clog. **Stop** the machine and remove the hose, then clean out the fan, hose and exhaust chute. Cleaning the machine from a clog takes a lot of time and is not easy. So try to use the leave vacuum correctly to avoid this problem.

There are two ways to use the leave vacuum hose. The first way is to use the handles on the end of the hose, move the hose back and forth across a pile of leaves. The second way is to put the hose on the ground and rake the leaves into the hose; both ways work well. One or two workers should operate the machine; there is no need to have any more than two workers using the leave vacuum. However, once the truck is full and ready to be dumped out, you will need at least two strong workers to lift the machine off the truck tailgate.

Always wear ear and eye protection when using this machine. Check the gas tank before starting the machine and only fill the gas tank when the motor is cool. **Remember to check the motor oil level at least twice per day**.

Now that we have discussed all the equipment used for fall clean up, lets discuss how to do the job correctly and efficiently.

Completing a Fall Clean-up Job

As with every landscape job, you need to plan out and organize before you start to work. When you get to the job site, everyone should take a look at what needs to be done. Then discuss how the job will be done and who will use what machine. Work together as a team to get the job done. After you have determined the best way to do the job, gas up your machines, check the motor oil (at least twice per day), put on your safety equipment and you are ready to start. Make sure that there are no people in the area where you are going to work. If there are people in the area that you want to work, ask them to leave while you are working. If this is not possible, it is better to leave and return to the job site at another time when the area is clear of people. Never operate any power machinery near other people.

In the beginning of the fall season, start by cleaning-up the lawn areas only. When you clean the landscape bed areas, you will remove some of the mulch. Therefore it is better to clean out the landscape beds only two or three times during the fall.

When you are cleaning up the lawn areas only, it will be easiest to simply mow and bag the lawn to collect a **light** covering of leaves. Remember to cut the lawn slightly lower than normal during the fall. Then it will be easier to blow off the leaves at the next clean-up visit.

When the leaves start to become heavier, it will be too difficult or impossible to bag them. Now you will need to use the blowers to clean off the lawn.

- First use a backpack blower and clear an area about five feet wide around the edges of the lawn area.

- Then another person should put the ground blower into this cleared area. Start walking and blowing back and forth across the lawn using a ground blower and a backpack blower. Move a few feet forward with each pass across the lawn.

- If there are any landscape beds in the lawn area, go around them using the backpack blower. Never use a ground blower in a landscape bed since it will blow the mulch or topsoil out of the bed and onto the lawn.

- Continue to work back and forth across the property. Once the leaves become difficult to blow, make a pile, then rake the pile of leaves onto a tarp and haul them away. Continue to blow and clean the lawn area.

- Skip cleaning all the landscape bed areas. But **do not** blow leaves into the beds when you are cleaning off the lawn. This will make cleaning the beds very difficult in the future. It will look messy and is an unprofessional way to clean off the lawn.

- After the lawn area is clean, you may need to mow the lawn or it may be possible to skip the mowing until the next visit. If you are not going to return to that job for 10 to 14 days and the weather is still warm, you will be better off to mow the lawn or the job will be very difficult at the next visit.

Cleaning the Entire Property

At your next visit, it should be time to clean the entire property including the beds. Do not wait too long to clean out the landscape beds. If the leaves get too heavy and it rains, the beds will be very hard to clean.

Using a backpack blower, clean off all the shrubs and the landscape bed. While one worker is blowing the shrubs and bed area, a second worker should help move the leaves with a rake.

Wherever the leaves build up and get heavy, rake them out. Leaves get caught in-between branches and under shrubs. Use the rake to lift up the branches of shrubs or ground cover plants while a co-worker blows out the debris.

When you are working in a landscape bed, be careful not to damage any of the shrubs or trees by walking on them while you are cleaning. Be careful when walking backwards with a backpack blower, you may back into a shrub or tree and break off the branches or damage the house. A backpack blower extends almost two feet off your back, so be careful.

While backpack blowing, do not let any leaves accumulate near the fan of the backpack blower. There is a small space between the padded area that mounts to your back and the fan. During leave clean up, this area can become clogged with leaves. When the area gets clogged, the blower will loose power and damage the to the motor will occur. It is hard to notice if there is a problem since you cannot see the area when you are using the blower. So look out for each other during clean up, and if you spot this problem, notify your co-worker immediately.

Turn the machine off and remove the leaves by hand, or turn the clogged machine on idle and using another backpack blower, blow out the leaves clogged in the machine. Never stick your hand in the area to remove leaves while the machine is running. Some newer blowers come with a cover over this area to prevent this problem.

Continue to work together as a team blowing and raking the leaves from the beds. **Be careful** not to blow too hard on the mulch. Try to keep the mulch in the beds and not blown out onto the lawn. After you have cleaned the bed area, you may need to lightly blow off the house or building, especially when working in dusty conditions. Look at the house and windows and if you see a layer of dirt, blow it off. If any windows are open, notify the homeowner to shut them before you start working. If this is not possible, blow very slowly and use a rake to clean the area so you do not blow dirt and dust into the house. Once the beds are cleaned out, clean the lawn area a few feet so that the ground blower can start in this area. Then start to clean the lawn area the same way as we discussed earlier.

You will have to use a tarp to pick up and haul away the leaves more often when the leaves are heavier. You will either haul the leaves to a dumping area on the property or have to put them in your truck.

If you are dumping the leaves into a wooded area on the property, pull the tarp as far back as possible into the woods so the leaves are not easily seen and will not blow back onto the area that you cleaned. Be careful not to rip the tarp when pulling it through the woods. Remember after you dump, spread out the piles so they are not noticeable. If you are blowing leaves into a woods line, get them back as far as possible or they will blow back. Use a backpack blower or rake to spread out the leaves and reduce the height of the leaves when blowing in any wooded area. Whenever dumping into a wooded area, be careful that you do not fill in any streams or areas where water flows through during a rainfall.

If you are removing the leaves from the property and hauling them away in your truck, there are two ways to get the leaves into your truck either by hand or by using a leave vacuum. When you are putting leaves into your truck by hand.

- First remove the landscape trailer from the truck.
- Put safety cones out around the trailer, then park the truck as close as possible to the area of the property that you are working at.
- If there are a lot of leaves, you will have to put them on a tarp. Putting the leaves in a landscape barrel will take too much time.
- Once you have the leaves blown into a pile and then raked onto a tarp, tie the two back corners of the tarp together. Then grab the other two front corners and pull the tarp up into the back of your truck.
- If you are working by yourself, you will have to use a small tarp. In most cases there will be two or three people working together.

107

Use a larger tarp when you are working with a larger crew; the larger tarp will get the job done quicker and easier. Tie the two back corners of the tarp together, have one person grab each front corner, then get up into the truck and pull the tarp of leaves while the third person lifts and pushes from the back. With teamwork, you can get a lot of leaves into your truck quickly.

- After dumping the leaves into your truck, walk up and down or the leaves. Try to compress them so you can fit as much as possible into your truck.
- Always cover the leaves with a tarp before driving. There should be a tarp and roller mounted on your truck. Cover the leaves even if the truck is only half full. If any leaves are blowing out while driving, you can get a ticket from the police.

The other way to get leaves into your truck is by using a leave vacuum. The leave vacuum will be mounted to the back of your truck or may be mounted to a small trailer. When using a leave vacuum, you will probably have to pull the landscape trailer with a second vehicle. The leave vacuum and mesh tarp must be properly mounted on your truck or you will have ongoing problems while using the machine. The tarp must completely cover the back of your truck. There can not be any small openings or leaves will escape through the opening when you are using the machine. A mesh tarp must be used so airflow can escape through the tarp but not the leaves.

Check the gas and motor oil level before each time you use the leave vacuum. Use the light flashers on the truck while operating the leave vacuum. If you are working near the road, make sure you have safety cones out all around the area you are working in. Use flashers and safety cones at all times even if you are working in a low traffic area. Before you start using the machine, put all the leaves together into a pile. Create a pile in an area that is easiest to reach with your truck. Do not put the leave piles on gravel driveways or any area where there is a lot of stone. Also, do not block the use of someone's driveway with leave piles.

A two-person crew works best when using the leave vacuum. One person to hold the hose while the other person rakes the leaves close to the vacuum hose, or to back the truck up further into the pile as needed. Work slower while vacuuming up wet leaves and do not force too many leaves into the vacuum at once to avoid clogging up the vacuum. As discussed earlier, remember to avoid vacuuming up stones and any branches over one foot in length. When the truck is full, climb into the truck under the tarp. Push the leaves down with your body and you will then be able to fit more into the truck.

Drive carefully with a fully loaded truck and make sure you have the correct amount of air in the truck tires. Never load up the truck when the tires are low on air.

Final Fall Clean-up Visit
After most of the leaves have been cleaned from each job site and you are making your final visit of the year, it may be easier to collect the leaves with a lawn mower again. First blow out the beds for the last

time. Pick up the debris from the beds if it is too much for the lawn mower to pickup. If there are any sticks on the lawn or beds, pick them up and put them in a barrel. Look against the house for any window wells, if they are dirty, clean out the debris by hand. Then mow the grass with the bag to collect a light covering of leaves. If there are heavy leaves on the lawn, you will need to clean them up as we just discussed before the final mowing. This will give the property a professional look for the winter.

Working in Windy Conditions

During the fall, there may be days where the wind makes the leave clean up difficult or almost impossible. Obviously if you are in the early fall season or late fall season, and you are only picking up the leaves with the lawn mower, you will not have a problem. During windy days, you must realize that you cannot do a perfect job. Your goal should be to remove the heavy leaves and then return a week or two later to do a better job. Before you start working, try to find which way the wind is blowing, then blow the leaves in the direction that the wind is blowing. Some days this will work out, other days it will not. Sometimes the winds blow in many different directions making clean up even harder or impossible. While cleaning up during windy conditions, pick up the leaves more often then usual.

If you get the leaves onto a tarp or barrel quickly, they will not be able to blow back on the area that was just cleaned. Try to watch and learn about each property. Some houses will always be winder than others. On a windy day, choose the properties that usually have less wind.

Don't waste time. If you have tried your best on a windy day and it is almost impossible to get anything done, think about some other jobs that can be done, such as: equipment maintenance or a small landscape job or take the day off.

Fall Clean-up Training and Safety Tips

- Always wear **ear protection** because you can cause permanent damage to your ears from the loud noise of the blowers. Also wear other safety equipment such as safety glasses and gloves.
- Think about each job and organize before you start.
- Work together as a team.
- Fill up machines with gas on the trailer when the motor is cool.
- Do not over-tighten gas caps.
- Check the motor oil level at least twice per day.
- Keep hands and feet away from all moving parts on all machines.
- Be careful when adjusting the chute on the ground blower.
- Turn off the motor to unclog leaves from the blowers.
- Keep machines securely fastened on your trailer or truck.
- Always think safety first.

LANDSCAPE SERVICES CHOOSING AND HANDLING PLANT MATERIAL (CHAPTER 10)

Choosing and handling of plant material must be done carefully and correctly or the plant that you are about to install **may not survive**. Plant material is very expensive and replacing it after you have installed it is a serious loss to everyone. By following a few simple work procedures, you will be successfully choosing, handling and installing plant material that will grow healthy and look beautiful for many, many years.

Preparing to Choose and Pick-up Plant Material From the Nursery

Preparing a Plant List and Selecting a Nursery

Before you make a visit to your local nursery, you need to create a list of all the plants that you need. Try to group a few small jobs together so when you visit the nursery you can get the needed plant material for a few different jobs all in one visit. Your list should have the names of the plants, the quantity you need and the sizes you need. Once the list is ready, someone will need to call the nursery to see if the plants that you need are available. Do not waist your time driving to the nursery if you are not sure about what they have in stock.

You should do business with a few different nurseries. Pick the best three nurseries in your area. Then learn about each nursery; for example: One nursery may always have a large selection of trees while another nursery may always have a large selection of smaller plants. Then you will know who to call for the plant material that you need.

Preparing Your Truck and Trailer

Once you are ready to pickup the plant material, choose the correct truck and/or trailer for the material that you are going to get. The truck and trailer needs to be perfectly clean of any gas or oil. If you had a gas or oil spill on your truck or trailer, put down a solid tarp before loading up any plant material.

You will also need a mesh tarp to cover the plants during transportation. By covering the plants, you will protect them from getting damaged or stressed from the wind or warm weather. The tarp that you use to cover plant material must be mesh so air can still flow through it and so the plants can breathe.

Never use a solid tarp to cover plant material. The nursery should supply you with rope to tie down any plants; however, it is a good idea to have rope on your truck for emergency situations. Check the tire pressure on your truck and trailer before loading up with plant or landscape material. When you get to the nursery look for someone to help you right away. Always pick out and load up the largest trees and shrubs first, then you can fit the smaller plants in between the larger ones. The larger plants will help support the smaller ones and help keep them from moving around while you are driving.

Delivery Options

At times, it may be better not to take the plants on the same day that you inspect and purchase them. Depending on your job situation, it may be better to tag the plants and then pick them up on the day that you will be installing them.

Plant material should be moved around as little as possible and must be watered on a regular basis. Do not bring plants to your garage or job site if you are not going to install them right away.

If you need a large number of plants, you should consider having the plants delivered. Most of the time it will be easier and cheaper to pay for a delivery instead of driving back and forth to the nursery all day long. The boss of foreman at your company should make this decision.

Tagging Plant Material

When tagging plant material **double** tag each plant. Then there will be less of a chance of someone else removing the tag from your plant and putting your tag on a different plant. Double tagging works best by using a regular tag with your company name on it and then wrapping the plant with a piece of colored plastic marker tape. You will need to bring the plastic marker tape yourself. Keep it in your truck throughout the year.

Inspecting Plant Material

Obviously you want to pick out the healthiest and best look plants. So you need to take a few minutes to inspect each plant before you buy it. **Never buy plant material without inspecting it first.** As a landscape professional, you should only buy plants that are of good quality and in good condition. Do not settle for anything less.

Inspecting and Choosing Trees

The first thing you should do is look at the overall shape of the tree. Pick a full tree with a lot of healthy branches. The branches should be growing in the correct shape. Avoid choosing trees with only a few branches or branches that are growing irregular. It will be very hard to find trees or shrubs that have all four sides perfect in shape. If three sides of the tree look good and the fourth side as a **slight** problem, you should still be able to use it. **You should always install trees or shrubs so that the worst side is facing away from the area that is most visible.**

After you choose a tree with a good shape, you should also inspect the following:

- Inspect the condition of the leaves, branches and needles. The leaves, branches and needles should have a good color and should be firm and upright. Avoid trees that have a weak color or sagging leaves, branches or needles. Avoid trees with brown leaves or branches. Run your hand over the needles and if a lot of needles fall off, the tree is weak and stressed. Look around the root ball,

115

and if a lot of leaves or needles have fallen off, avoid choosing that tree.

- Inspect the leaves, needles and branches for any signs of insects or disease. If there are any insects or disease on the tree, avoid choosing that tree.

- Inspect the trunk of the tree. The trunk should be straight and healthy and have undamaged bark. Avoid trees with a crooked trunk. Avoid trees that have splitting or damaged bark.

- Inspect the size of the root ball. If the tree is fairly large and has a small root ball, it may not survive. Sometimes you will find trees where the root ball seems small compared to the size of the tree. If the root ball was cut too small, many of the roots have been removed. This puts the tree in a stressful condition. Only choose trees where the root ball seems to match the size of the tree. Avoid trees where the root ball seems too small.

- Inspect the root ball to make sure it has not been damaged. After looking at the size of the root ball, look for any damage. Most root balls come balled and burlaped in a metal cage. Some smaller trees may come in a plastic container. Check the condition of the burlap and avoid burlap that is old and starting to rot. **However, if the tree looks strong and healthy and has roots growing through the old burlap it can be wrapped with new burlap and used if the root ball is solid and not damaged.**

- Choose a tree with a **solid** root ball. The dirt of the root ball should **not** be broken up and loose. Avoid trees with rotten burlap, or with a root ball that is not solid. Also avoid trees with large punctures into the root ball.

- Choose a tree that has the trunk **centered** in the root ball. Do not choose the tree if the trunk is not in the center of the root ball.

- Using your hands, grab onto the tree trunk about four feet up from the root ball. Then move the trunk back and forth. If the trunk seems very loose and is not solidly connected to the root ball, it may be damaged. Avoid choosing that tree.

- Try to choose balled and burlapped grown trees over trees that are grown in a plastic container. Trees that are balled and burlapped are usually stronger and easier to install.

- Be extra careful when there are only a few trees left to select from. Usually the last trees of a bunch are the ones with the problems.

Inspecting and Choosing Shrubs

- Again, first look at the overall shape of the shrub. Make sure that at least three sides of the shrub look good and that the forth side has only a slight problem.

- Inspect the color of the plant and check the condition of the leaves, branches or needles.

- Inspect the leaves, needles and branches for any signs of insects or disease. If there are any insects or disease on the shrub, avoid choosing that shrub.

- Inspect the base of the shrub where the trunk or branches grow from and carefully move the trunk or branches. If the trunk or branches feel loose and not secure to the root ball, avoid choosing that shrub.

- Check the size of the shrub compared to the root ball. If the plant is very large compared to the root ball, the shrub may be stressed. Only choose plants where the root ball size matches the size of the shrub.

- Make sure the shrub is centered in the root ball or container. A plant that is not centered has not been removed from the ground correctly. The root ball was cut uneven; this will cause additional stress to the plant.

- Check the burlapped root ball or plastic container. Make sure it has not been damaged in any way. If it was damaged, avoid choosing that shrub.

- Again, be extra careful when there are only a few shrubs left to choose from. Usually the last few plants of a bunch are the ones with the problems.

Inspecting and Choosing Ground Covers and Perennials

- Perennials are plants that return year after year. They go dormant and are usually not visible during there dormant time. Then they return during the growing season. You should choose perennials during the growing season. Avoid choosing perennials when they are dormant since you will not be able to know if the plant is strong and healthy or small and weak.

- Look at the color of the plant. Choose plants with a strong color, this indicates that the plant is healthy.

- Make sure the leaves, branches and needles are growing upright. Avoid plants with sagging branches, leaves or needles.
- Inspect the plant for any signs of insects or disease and avoid the plant if you find any problem
- Make sure the plant container and the soil in the container has not been damaged in any way.
- Again be extra careful when there are only a few plants left to select from, since the last few plants of a bunch are usually the ones that have problems.

Inspecting and Choosing Flowers and Bulbs
Annual Flowers

Annual flowers grow only during warm weather and will die when they are exposed to freezing temperatures. Therefore, they are planted every year (annually). They should be planted in the spring after the last chance of a frost or freezing temperatures. Then they will grow until the cold weather returns in the fall.

When choosing annual flowers:
- Make sure the color of the leaves are strong, not weak and faded.
- Make sure the leaves are growing upright; not sagging.
- Choose plants that have only a few flowers or no flowers at all. Then they will have a longer flowering time where they are installed.
- Choose flowers that are a good size. **Not too large, but not too small**. Small flowers are hard to install and can die very easily.

- Choose flowers that do not have any type of damage to them or to the container that they are growing in.
- Look for insect or disease problems.
- If there is a small selection of flowers to choose from, and they are not in good condition, do not buy them.

Bulbs

A bulb is a dormant flower. It is small in size and usually similar to the shape of an onion. Bulbs are perennials; they are planted in the ground and produce a flower for a few weeks every year. Then they go dormant until the next year.

- When choosing individual bulbs, hold each bulb in your hand. Then look for any soft spots on the bulb. Soft spots are damaged areas on the bulb. The bulb should be firm and should not have any soft spots.
- If you are buying a box of bulbs, open the box and check the bulbs. If most of the bulbs are in good condition, you can buy the box. If you find a lot of damaged bulbs, do not buy them.
- Do not buy the bulbs unless you are going to plant them shortly after. If you have to store the bulbs, keep them in a cool, dry place.

Handling of Plant Material

Whenever a plant is removed from the ground, transported to a nursery, unloaded and placed on the ground, it will be stressed out and has a chance of dying. As a landscape professional, you must be aware of this. To reduce the risk of having the plants die, you must handle all plant material correctly and handle the plants as little as possible. Your goal is to get the plant material from the nursery to the job site and installed correctly in the ground, without adding any additional stress to the plant.

Picking up and Moving Plant Material

- As we just discussed, handle and move all plant material as little as possible.
- **Never** pickup or move the plant by grabbing onto the branches or trunk.
- Only grab onto the root ball to pick-up or move the plant. If the plant is in a plastic container, grab onto the container to pickup or move the plant. If the plant root ball is wrapped in burlap, there should also be a metal cage wrapped around the burlap. Grab onto the metal cage to pickup or move the plant.
- Avoid dropping the plants or handling the plants roughly. By dropping the plants, you can break the roots and root ball and cause the plant to die.
- Do not try to move a plant that is too heavy for you. Use a tree cart or a machine to move large plants.

Loading up the Plant Material

Inspect and choose the large plant material first. After the large plants are loaded up, inspect and choose the smaller plants. Then the smaller plants can be placed in between the larger ones and will not get damaged.

Loading up Large Plant Materials (Trees and Large Shrubs)

- As we just discussed, load up large plant material first.

- Before loading up trees it is usually better to tie up the branches. By tying up the branches, you will reduce the risk of damage to the tree and you will have more space on your truck or trailer. The nursery employee should supply you with rope and help you tie up the trees.

- Plan out the best way to load up the trees and large plants. By planning it out, you will be able to fit more onto your truck and trailer.

- Avoid bending the plants branches.

- If the branches are rubbing on anything like the back of your truck, use some burlap to protect the branches.

- Try to keep all plant material laid down so it will not move from the wind when you are driving. The wind is also stressful for the plant and can damage or kill the plant.

- After the trees and large shrubs are loaded up, make sure that they will not move during transportation. If there is any chance that they might move, tie them down. If large plant material moves during transportation, it can create a serious problem. Make sure everything is secured.

- All plant material must be covered with a breathable mesh tarp. The tarp will protect the plants from heat and wind damage during transportation.

Loading up Smaller Plants

If you have large plants loaded up on your truck and trailer, you can usually place the smaller plants in between the larger ones. Then the larger plants will help support the smaller ones. If this is not possible or if you are only buying small plants, you will have to group them together. By grouping the small plants together, they will help support each other and be less likely to move around. Once all the plants are loaded up, cover them with a mesh tarp. Make sure that the tarp is tied down and you will be ready to drive to the job site.

During transportation, drive slowly. Avoid sudden stops or rapid acceleration. Drive slowly and steady and your plants will be in good condition when you get to the job site.

INSTALLING TREES AND SHRUBS
(CHAPTER 11)

Before installing any plant material, research must be done to insure that the plant is best suited for the chosen location. Sun, shade, wet or dry soil, deer problems and designing of the landscape must all be well planned out before purchasing and installing any plant material. After the correct plant has been chosen for the location, it must be spaced out properly. There must be enough space to allow the plant to grow into its mature size. After you inspect and choose healthy plant material, they must be installed correctly to grow strong and healthy and live a long life. As a landscape professional, you are responsible to install all plant material correctly so it does not die prematurely.

New research has shown that many of the standard planting methods used for many years are becoming outdated. There are now tested and proven, better ways to install plant material which will give the plant the best chance of growing strong and healthy and living a long life.

You will need the following tools and equipment when installing trees, shrubs, ground covers, perennials, flowers and bulbs. A tree cart, .a wheelbarrow, shovels, a pick, a metal bow rake, a leave rake, a pitchfork, hand shears, a hand shovel, a hand sized pick, a utility knife, and a backpack blower.

Wear work boot and gloves. If you are bending over a lot or lifting a lot, you should wear kneepads and a back support.

Installing Trees (Balled and Burlaped)

- Bring the trees over to the location where they are going to be installed. **Note:** Handle the trees very carefully. Use a tree cart or machine to move the trees. Never use the tree trunk or branches as a handle. Only grab onto the root ball to move a tree.

- Before you start digging, the trees should be spaced out correctly and then clearly marked **exactly** where they are to be installed. **Note:** The owner or foreman should be responsible to space out and mark exactly where the trees are to be installed. **Never** install any plant material if you are not 100% sure of the correct location.

- The tree's root ball should be placed very close to where it is going to be installed. Then when you have finished digging the hole, the root ball can be carefully placed into the hole.

- Dig the hole using a shovel and a pick to loosen up the soil before you dig it out.

- Dig the hole twice as wide as the root ball but no deeper than the depth of the root ball. If you don't have a tape measure, measure the root ball with the handle on a shovel. Grab onto the handle with your hand and use it as a measuring stick.

- Check the width and depth of the root ball and compare it to the hole you are digging. Remember **twice** as wide but no deeper than the depth of the root ball. Dig the hole wider at the top so the hole has a saucer shape.

Using the old planting method, you would also dig the depth twice as deep and then backfill the hole with soil. The problem with that method is that the backfilled soil will settle causing the tree to sink deeper into the hole. Then new roots can get torn off when the tree settles.

- When the root ball is put into the hole, the top of it should be slightly higher than the existing ground. If you dig the hole too deep, backfill with soil and **firmly pack** it down.
- **Loosen** up the sides and bottom of the hole with a pick or shovel.
- **Double-check the size of the hole one last time. It is very important to have the exact depth.** If you put a heavy tree into the hole and the hole is too deep or not deep enough, you will create additional work for yourself and you may not be able to lift the root ball back out of the hole.
- Once you are 100% sure that the hole is correct, a few people should grab onto the root ball. Grab onto the metal cage or onto the ropes wrapped around the tree. Never use the tree trunk to lift or move the tree. When you grab on, make sure you can also let go quickly and easily or you may hurt yourself when you put the root ball into the hole.
- Carefully lift the root ball into the hole. **Do not** drop the root ball into the hole. Let it slowly slide into the hole, then stand it up and move it to the center of the hole. If you cannot slide the root ball into the hole, try to **turn** it while pushing and pulling on it to

move it a few inches at a time, then let it slowly slide into the hole.

- After positioning it to the center of the hole, turn the tree so that the best side of the tree is facing the most visible area. Then make sure that the tree is straight. If needed, add some soil under the root ball until the tree is standing perfectly straight.

- After the tree is positioned correctly and you do not have to move it anymore, untie all the rope and peal back the rope, burlap and metal cage as best as possible.

- Backfill the hole with soil. Make a mixture using about 50% of the soil that you removed from the hole and 50% topsoil. **Be sure to mix it up thoroughly as you are back fill the hole.** Avoid putting stones back into the hole.

New research has proven that a plant will be able to grow better in the new location if the new roots can establish in the existing soil. The old planting method is to dig a hole and fill it with 100% topsoil. The problem is that once the new roots grow past the area of topsoil they may not grow into the existing soil Instead they circle around in the topsoil. This causes the tree to do poorly and die prematurely.

- **After the hole is halfway backfilled, check to make sure the tree is still straight**, then **lightly** press the soil down around the root ball. Then backfill the remaining part of the hole and **lightly** press down the soil when you are done.

- After the tree has been installed, prune off any broken branches, also prune any branches that are hanging low or out of place. **Only** prune a few branches off the tree; do not over prune.
- Edge out a tree ring around the tree if it has been planted in a lawn area.

Most plants do not need to be fertilized when they are installed. Plants are feed at the nursery. Applying too much fertilizer can damage or kill the plant. Most plants do not need fertilizer until their second year installed. If you choose to fertilize when planting, only use an organic slow release product.

- Build a ring of soil a few inches high around the outer part of the root ball. This will help bring water to the root ball and prevent water from running off the surface.
- Apply a two to three inch layer of mulch around the root ball. **Keep the mulch away from the tree trunk.**
- If the tree is very top heavy or is located in a windy exposed area or commercial area, it should be staked. When you stake a tree, make sure that the ties are left loose so the tree can grow. Then remove the stakes and ties after one year.

To stake a tree:

Use 2×2 pressure treated wood or fence posts 4 to 6 feet tall depending on the size of the tree. Use two or three stakes to support each tree, space them out evenly around the tree. Hammer the stake into the ground next to the root ball. Hammer the stakes into the hard existing soil and not into the area that has been dug up during planting. Hammer the stake down approximately 1-1/2 feet deep. Tie the tree to the stakes. Using the new plastic ties made for tree staking work best. Or support the tree the old way by using wire and running the wire through a piece of garden hose to protect the tree bark. Always leave the ties loose around the tree trunk, then pull each tie tight and wrap it around each stake to support the tree.

- Thoroughly water the tree and make sure that the owner of the new tree clearly understands watering responsibilities. Give your customer an information sheet explaining how to take care of their new plants. See the example below.

Important Instructions for Your Installed Landscape Plants
The plants installed are free of diseases and insects, are sound in structure, healthy and viable at time of installation.

It shall be solely the responsibility of the purchaser to provide adequate care and protection for the plants after installation. **Please follow the instructions below:**

- Make sure plants get adequate water. Water them twice a week for the first month. If temperatures are over 80 degrees, water three times per week. (A light rainfall is not considered a proper watering. If there is a good amount of rainfall, it can be considered as a watering.)
- Water plants in the morning or early evening (morning is preferred). Water the root zone area, not the branches. With a

garden hose, water each plant for approximately one minute, then repeat the process. For larger plants or trees, put a garden hose on the root ball. Then let the water slowly run for approximately 5-10 minutes per plant. If using an irrigation system, make sure all the plants are being covered and the root zone area is getting enough water. **Water must penetrate the surface and soak the plants root system**. If you're using a soaker hose, check the area after running the hose for about one hour.

- In the fall, reduce watering to once a week until late October.
- For the following years, start to water at least once a week as soon as temperatures reach 80 degrees.
- If plants are not 100% deer resistant, protect them over the winter months with netting or spray.
- After the plants have been installed for one year, it is a good time to feed them. (Do not feed them any earlier.)
- Always keep a layer of mulch around plants approximately 2" thick.
- Contact us if you see any problems such as discolored or drooping leaves or leaves or needles falling off the plant.

With proper care your landscape plants will increase in size, beauty and value. Please call if you need any further information. Thank you for your business and enjoy your landscape.

Installing Shrubs (Balled and Burlaped)

Balled and burlaped shrubs are installed basically the same way as a balled and burlaped tree. Lets briefly review the correct procedures to install a shrub:

- Handle the shrubs carefully; use a tree cart or wheelbarrow to move them. Never pickup the shrubs by the branches, only pickup or move them up by grabbing onto the root ball.
- Bring the shrubs over to where they are going to be installed.
- Before you start digging **make sure** the shrubs have been spaced out and marked correctly.
- Dig a saucer shaped hole twice as wide as the root ball. Dig the depth no deeper.
- Measure the depth of the root ball and the depth of the hole. Be 100% sure that the hole is the correct size.
- The top of the root ball should be level or slightly higher than the existing ground.
- Lightly loosen the soil at the bottom and sides of the hole and then carefully put the shrub into the hole.
- Position the shrub so the best side is facing the most visible area. Then make sure the shrub is sitting straight. If needed, add some soil under the root ball until the shrub is straight.
- Remove the rope and burlap from the shrub as much as possible. Use a utility knife to cut it off. Do not disturb the root ball while removing the rope and burlap.
- Back fill the hole with soil. Use approximately 50% existing soil and 50% topsoil and **be sure it is thoroughly mixed when backfilling the hole.**
- After the hole is halfway backfilled, check to make sure the shrub is still straight then lightly press the soil down around the root ball. Fill the rest of the hole and lightly press down the soil again.

Do not break any branches off when pressing down the soil around the shrub.

- Prune off any broken branches, also prune off any branches that are hanging low or out of place. **Only** prune a few branches off the shrub, do not over prune.

- Build a ring of soil around the outer part of the root ball.

- Apply a 2-3 inch layer of mulch around the shrub and give the shrub a good watering.

Installing Trees and Shrubs (in Plastic Containers)

If your trees or shrubs come in a plastic container, there are some different procedures to follow when installing them.

- To avoid damaging the plant, pickup or move it by the container only.

- Bring the plants to the location where they are going to be planted. Make sure the plants have been spaced out correctly and marked exactly where they are to be installed.

- Remove any roots that are growing out of the holes at the bottom of the container, if these root are not removed, you will not be able to remove the plant from the container. Always check the bottom of the container first.

- Water down the soil and root system inside the container. By watering it down, it will be easier to slide out of the container and the soil will stay together better than if the soil is dry.

- The hole should be dug out, measured and prepared the same way as we discussed using a balled and burlaped plant.

- Slowly and carefully remove the plant from the plastic container. If the plant is very small, you will be able to turn the plant upside down then a co-worker can remove the plastic container. If the plant is too large to handle, lay it on its side and carefully pull off the container.

- If the plant is difficult to remove from the container, make two or three cuts down the sides of the container with a sharp utility knife.

Some container grown plants will break apart very easily. To help prevent the soil from breaking apart, wet down the soil, then handle it very carefully and as infrequently as possible. Container plants may have roots growing and circling around the outside surface of the root ball. Using a utility knife, cut through the mass of roots all around the plant. By doing this, the roots will be re-directed so they can grow outward instead of circling around as if they were still in the container.

- Position the plant correctly in the hole and then backfill with soil. Prune, mulch and water as we discussed earlier.

Installing Trees and Shrubs (Bare Root)

Bare root plants are not used frequently; however, they are inexpensive and still used at times. Bare root plants are exactly that, bare rooted with no soil around them. Some tips on installing bare rooted plants are:

- Keep the root system moist or wet at all times. If the root system dries out, the plant may not survive. Plant them immediately after purchasing them.

- After the hole has been dug out, measured and prepared, put the same soil into the hole. Then carefully put the plants root system on top of the soil. Adjust the plant to the correct position and correct height.

- Position the plant so it is planted at the same level as it grew in the nursery.

- Move the soil in between the root system by hand. Be careful not to damage the roots, and avoid having any large air pockets. The roots must have good contact with the soil.

- Carefully backfill the hold and then lightly press the soil down around the plant.

- If there are any damaged branches, prune them off. Mulch and water thoroughly.

INSTALLING GROUNDCOVERS, PERENNIALS, FLOWERS AND BULBS
(CHAPTER 12)

Installing Groundcovers

A groundcover is a plant that will grow into a low, dense mass that covers the ground. After a groundcover has established, it will require very little maintenance and will look beautiful. For a professional job, install groundcover plants using the following procedures.

- For best results and for a rapid establishment of the groundcover, it is best to prepare the bed area before you install the plants. To prepare a landscape bed area for planting, turn over the soil with a shovel or roto-tiller. Remove any weeds, stones and unwanted debris. If the existing soil quality is poor, improve it by turning in a good quality topsoil and or peat moss.

- If you do not prepare the landscape bed as we just discussed, you will have to dig a separate hole for each plant. This method will work but the groundcover plants will take much longer to establish since the soil may be hard and compact in between each plant.

- Groundcover plants usually come in a tray, the tray is called a flat. Each flat will have soil in it and will have 50 to 100 small plants. When you remove each plant from the flat, it will come out without any soil around it so it will be a bare-root plant. Larger groundcovers will come in small containers. With container grown plants, there will be soil around the roots and they should be installed the same way as a container grown shrub.

- Spacing of the ground cover plants is very important. Most plants are installed approximately 8 to 10 inches apart. They can be installed closer for a quicker establishment or spaced out further to cut down on the cost of the job. Avoid spacing the plants any further than 12 inches apart. Container grown ground cover plants are larger and may be able to be spaced further apart. Check the label and spacing recommendation before installing them.

- If the landscape bed has been turned over and prepared for the plants, they will be easy to install. Use a hand shovel or small pick to make a small hole. Make sure the holes are spaced out properly. Then install a plant into each hole and lightly press down the soil around each plant with your hands. *To install the groundcover plants quickly, space out and dig all the holes first then install the plants.*

- If the landscape bed was not prepared, the holes will be harder to dig. If the soil is a very poor, mix in a little topsoil or peat moss when planting. Spread the topsoil or peat moss over the bed area first. Then when you are installing the plants, mix some of the topsoil and existing soil together.

- Container grown groundcover plants should be handled and installed the same as container grown shrubs. Please refer the earlier in chapter where this was discussed.

- Once the plants are installed, apply a layer of mulch to help keep the plants from drying out and to help prevent weed growth. Apply a layer of mulch every year until the groundcover is fully established.
- Water the new plantings the day they were installed and then on a regular basis.
- A **light** balanced fertilizer can be mixed into the bed area when planting, then do not apply fertilizer until one year later.

Installing Perennials

Perennials are plants that return year after year. They die down to the ground after each growing season. Then they lay dormant in the ground until the following year. Perennials come in two different ways; bare rooted or in a small container. Container grown perennials are most common. If you are installing a lot of different perennials into a landscape bed, it would be best to prepare the soil in the bed before you install the plants. If you are only installing a few perennials throughout different areas of the landscape, it would be best to dig a separate hole for each plant.

Installing (Container) Grown Perennials

Container grown perennials should be handled and installed the same as container grown shrubs. Lets review the planting procedures:
- Handle the plant by the container not by the leaves or branches.
- Bring the plants to the location where they are going to be installed. Make sure the plants have been spaced out correctly and marked exactly where they are to be installed.

- Remove any roots that are growing out from the bottom of the container.

- Water down the soil and roots system inside the container.

- Dig out and prepare the holes for the plants. Dig twice as wide but no deeper than the plants root ball. Lightly loosen the soil on the bottom and sides of the hole. Check to make sure the depth is correct. The top of the plants root ball should be level or slightly higher with the ground when installed.

- Turn the plant upside down, hold your hand over the top of the root ball and catch the plant as it slides out.

- Using a utility knife, make a few cuts around the root ball. This will encourage the roots to grow out instead of circling around the root ball.

- Position the plant in the hole and then backfill with soil. Lightly press down on the soil around the plant.

- Apply a layer of mulch around the plant and water it.

Installing (Bare Root) Perennials

- Keep the root system moist at all times. Store the plants in a cool, dark area. Avoid storing them any longer than a day or two. Install them as soon as possible.

- Lay out and prepare the holes for the plants.

- Put some soil into the hole. Then carefully put the plants root system on top of the soil. Adjust the height of the plant so that it is not too deep or not too high.

- Put more soil around the root system with your hands. Lightly press down on the soil and roots. Avoid having any pockets of air. The roots must have good contact with the soil.
- Apply a layer of mulch and water.

Installing Flowers (Annuals)

Annual flowers give color to the landscape; they usually flower for a long period of time. However, they cannot survive any cold temperatures. Therefore, they are planted in the spring after the last frost and will live until the first frost in the fall. A few types of annuals can survive a frost, but most of them will not. As discussed earlier, select annual flowers that are not too small but also not too large in size. Most annual flowers come in flats. A flat is a tray that holds small plants such as annual flowers or ground cover plants. When purchasing a flat of annual flowers, there usually is another small tray inside the flat. This smaller tray has individual compartments. Each compartment will hold one flower. Flats vary in size; an average flat will hold about 48 flowers.

Try to install flowers immediately after you purchase them. If you have to store them for a few days, keep them watered on a daily basis. Only water them in the early a.m. or late p.m. Watering during the hot, sunny daytime hours can cause damage to the tender flowers. Try to keep the flowers in a shady area until they are planted.

To install the Annual flowers:

- Mark and plan out the areas where you are going to plant. Check the label for spacing requirements. Most Annual flowers are spaced about 12 inches apart.

- Prepare the soil in the planting area. Turn over the soil so that the soil is loose and the roots will be able to grow easily. If the soil is very poor, turn in some good quality topsoil and/or peat moss.

- For best results, turn some plant food (fertilizer) into the soil. **Make sure** the plant food you use is labeled for Annual flowers and **do not** over apply the fertilizer or you will cause more damage than good.

- Using a hand shovel, make a hole wherever you are going to install a flower. Space the holes out as recommended on the label. Do not space any further apart then recommended.

- Water the cell packs, then turn the cell pack upside down and the flower should come out. If the flower does not come out, push the bottom of the cell pack to help it come out. Be careful not to drop the flowers as they come out. Work close to the ground when removing the flowers. **Never** pull on the flower to try to remove it from the cell pack.

- Once the flower is out, look at the root system, if there is a massive root system, you will need to gently break the roots to help the roots grow into the soil when planted. Use your hands and gently tear the bottom of the roots system or use a pair of hand shears to cut into the mass of roots.

- Put the flower into the hole; be careful not to plant it too high or too deep. Then push soil around the flowers root ball and lightly press down on the soil.
- Apply a layer of mulch and water the entire area.

Installing Bulbs

Most bulbs are sold and planted during the fall. Then they will flower the following spring and return year after year. To install bulbs, follow these procedures.

- Choose only the best bulbs; avoid bulbs that have soft spots on them. Keep bulbs in a cool dry area until they are planted.
- Plan out and mark the areas where you are going to plant.
- Make sure you know how deep the bulb should be planted. Some bulbs need to be 8 inches deep, while others should be only 3 inches deep. Read the label and understand exactly how deep the bulb needs to be. Also check the label to see how far apart the bulbs are to be spaced.
- Prepare the planting area. If you are planting a lot of bulbs close together in a small area, you should turn over the soil in that area.
- If you are planting the bulbs in different areas throughout the landscape, it will be better to dig an individual hole for each bulb. Remove any stones and improve the soil if needed.
- After the holes are all prepared, you are ready to plant. Inspect the bulb to make sure you clearly understanding what is the top and what is the bottom of the bulb. On the bottom side, you can usually see the root system.

- Do not put fertilizer or bone meal in the hole with the bulb.

Do not use bone meal when installing bulbs. Bone meal attracts animals and some animals will eat the bulbs if they find them in the ground. Bulbs can be lightly fertilized in the early spring before or after they have flowered. This will help them grow larger and flower more the next year.

- After you have determined the bottom side of the bulbs, place one into each individual hole, push down lightly on the bulb so it make good contact with the soil at the bottom of the hole. Then backfill the hole with soil, mulch the area for a professional job.
- Since the bulbs are dormant when they are installed, they will not need to be watered.

Remember that as a landscape professional, you are in control of how a plant will grow and how healthy it will be. By installing all plant material carefully and correctly, you will help make a beautiful, long-lasting landscape. You will help give yourself and your company a good reputation and gain respect from other people that notice your good work.

INSTALLING LANDSCAPE BEDS AND SOIL TESTING
(CHAPTER 13)

Many landscape beds are simply edged out in an existing, poor quality soil. Then plants are installed into the bed but are unable to grow healthy and strong. Hard soils or sandy soils can be improved by mixing and turning in good quality topsoil with organic matter. By professionally installing a new landscape bed or by improving an existing bed you will create an environment for all plant material to grow healthy and strong.

You will need the following tools and equipment to install or improve a landscape bed. An edger machine, a few wheelbarrows, shovels, picks, metal bow rake, a spade shovel, a paint gun, measuring tape, a backpack blower, and a roto-tiller (optional).

You should wear boots and gloves and consider wearing kneepads and a back support belt while working.

Installing Landscape Beds
The first step needed would be to plan out the shape of the new bed. Generally when beds are installed around a house they will vary in size from 5 feet to 25 feet. The boss or foreman will need to design the landscape beds based on that property and based on what is going

to be planted in the beds. Once the shape is determined, a paint gun is used to mark the shape of the new bed on the ground. If you are working off of a blue print use a tape measure and make measurement marks. After the measured marks are made, connect the marks with the paint gun to give you the shape of the new bed. The shape should have free flowing lines and curves and should not have any irregularities.

After the lines are established on the ground, make sure there is nothing that can get damaged in the bed area such as electrical wires, sprinkler heads, etc. Mark anything that you find so that you do not dig in that area.

Now start up the edger machine and cut along the marked line as discussed in the previous chapter. Then remove everything on the inside of the bed such as grass, weeds, etc, and then dispose of the debris.

After the new beds has been edged and cleaned out, you will need to add soil and nutrients to the beds. Landscape beds should be raised up at least 5 inches high. Add a good quality topsoil to raise the beds. As a landscape professional, you should also add peat moss, manure or some type of organic matter such as compost. You can also add a balanced granular fertilizer at this time. This will increase the nutrients available in the soil. *Note:* A soil test is recommended before improving any landscape bed areas. Then the correct soil amendments can be added. Soil testing will be discussed later in this chapter.

After the beds are raised up with topsoil and soil amendments, you will need to turn this mixture down into the existing soil. This can be done manually using a pick and shovel or by machine using a roto-tiller. Whatever you use, it is important to dig down at least one foot deep into the existing soil and thoroughly mix it with the new topsoil and soil amendments.

Many landscapers simply add a few inches of topsoil on top of the existing poor soil. This is unprofessional and a poor quality job. The landscape plants will do poorly when they try to grow larger in these poor soil conditions.

The next step after improving and turning over the landscape bed is to shape and grade the bed. If the bed you are installing is around a house or building, make sure that the beds slope away from the house. Then during a rainfall most of the water will run away from the house. Keep the soil line about four to five inches away from any siding on the house. Leave two to three inches for mulch. Then there should still be a space in between the landscape bed and the siding. The soil and mulch should only make contact with the concrete part of the house and **never** touch the siding. Use a metal bow rake to shape and grade the bed. Break up any large pieces soil while grading the bed. Even if you are working in a landscape bed that is away from the house it should still slope slightly down.

Now the newly installed landscape bed is complete. It is ready for plants to be installed and mulch should be applied as soon as possible. Mulch will help hold the soil in place and prevent it from washing away in a heavy rainfall. It will also help prevent weed growth and protect the landscape plants.

Soil Testing

A soil test should be done when:

- Established plants are weak and unhealthy even after you have applied a balanced fertilizer.
- To improve the soil condition before installing new plant material, seed or sod.

Soil Test

To take a soil test, first remove the top layer of mulch or leaves from the landscape bed. Then using a hand shovel or special tool for removing soil samples, dig down at least six inches deep and put the soil into a bag. Repeat this process at least six times and take the samples throughout different areas of the landscape bed. Then thoroughly mix the pieces of soil together in the bag and bring it to a soil-testing laboratory.

A soil test can be done by your Local Cooperative Extension Service (usually this is part of an agricultural college) or by a private soil-testing laboratory. The results will include: Nitrogen, Phosphorus, Potassium, Soil pH, Organic content, and Micronutrients.

- Nitrogen, Phosphorus and Potassium are the three major nutrients that all plants need. If one of these elements is low, there will be a problem. The soil test results will indicate any problems.

- Soil pH. Even if all the other nutrients are available in the soil, they may not be able to be absorbed by the plant if the soil pH level is incorrect. Soil pH levels range from 1 to 14 and a level between 6.0 and 7.5 works best. The level between 6.0 and 7.5 is called Neutral. **Anything below 6.0 is called Acidic soil; anything above 7.5 is called Alkaline.** By having the correct pH level, the plant will be able to absorb all the nutrients in the soil and become healthier and stronger. To adjust the soil pH level to neutral:

- When the soil is Acidic, apply limestone to **raise** the pH.

- When the soil is Alkaline, apply sulfur to **lower** the pH.

Organic Content—The soil test should also let you know how much organic matter is in the soil. Than you can add organics such as, peat moss, manure or compost to improve the soil.

Micro Nutrients—Micronutrients are secondary nutrients that the plant needs. They include Calcium, Magnesium, Iron and other nutrients. Micronutrients are very important and you must add micronutrients to the soil if needed.

INSTALLING LANDSCAPE FABRIC
(CHAPTER 14)

Landscape fabric is used to stop weeds from growing in the landscape beds. It can be used to stop an existing weed problem or to prevent weeds from growing in the future. Installing landscape fabric will reduce the amount of maintenance needed to keep landscape beds weed free. The fabric can also be used underneath decorative stone. When installed under decorative stone, it will help prevent the stones from sinking into the ground and it will help prevent weed growth. Landscape fabric is made so that water and air can penetrate the fabric but weeds cannot. It is very important that the root system of the existing plants in the landscape bed can easily get water and air. If the plants have trouble getting water or air, they will become stressed, unhealthy, and may die. Always use a good quality fabric that is specifically made for landscape beds. Never use any other type of product.

You will need a tape measure and a sharp utility knife when installing landscape fabric.

Installing Landscape Fabric (Work Procedures)

- Before installing any landscape fabric, make sure that the bed is graded correctly. Make sure the bed is sloping away from the house. Rake out any high or low spots in the bed and add additional topsoil if needed.

- If perennials are planted in the landscape bed, make sure they are all clearly marked so you do not install fabric over them. Also if there are any large planting areas that are used for annual flower plantings, mark these areas and leave them open. But if the annual flower planting areas are small, it will be easier to cut the shapes out after the fabric is installed.

- After the beds have been graded and marked, you need to take a rough measurement of the beds to determine how much fabric you will need. Then plan out the best way to install the fabric. Fabric comes in rolls 50 to 100 feet long. The width of the fabric can be anywhere from 3 to 10 feet wide. Choose a size that is best suited for your job when installing the fabric. You want to keep the pieces as large as possible.

- The fabric will be installed easiest and fastest when two people are working together. One person should hold one end of the fabric in place while the second person rolls out the fabric across the landscape bed. Then using a sharp utility knife cut the fabric to the correct length.

- When laying down each piece of fabric, make sure you overlap it onto the piece that is on the ground. After a few pieces have been put down, you will need to secure them to prevent them from moving. You can use large stones or bricks. Put the stones on the fabric to hold it down. Walk carefully so you do not move the fabric. After you put mulch or decorative stone on top of the fabric, you can remove the stones. Landscape staples can also be used. On a flat surface, staples are not needed, but if you are installing fabric on a slope or where there is heavy water running, install the staples and leave them in place. Staples need to be hammered into the ground with a hammer.

- Cut around all the plants that are in the landscape bed. You can install the fabric under the plants branches right up to the trunk. When making any difficult cuts, use your measuring tape to mark the fabric correctly and avoid making mistakes.

- After the fabric is installed, apply mulch or decorative stone on top. **Be very careful not to move the fabric when you dump and spread out the mulch or stone. You will have to work slowly and carefully to avoid a problem.** Now you can remove any of the stones or bricks that you put on the fabric to help hold it in place.

Note: We will discuss mulching and decorative stone in the next chapter in this manual.

Landscape fabric works very well, especially when used with decorative stone. The problem with mulch is that it will start to decompose and then create a small layer of soil over the fabric. After a few years, weeds will start to grow in that small layer of soil.

INSTALLING DECORATIVE STONE
(CHAPTER 15)

Decorative stone is used in landscape beds instead of mulch. Decorative stone can be used in small areas of a bed along with mulch or it can be used on its own. Careful thought must be given to the color and size of stone that will be used and where in the landscape it will be installed. When decorative stone is chosen, designed and installed correctly, it will add variety and beauty to the landscape.

The tools that you will need to install decorative stone will include the following:

- Wheelbarrows.
- Shovels.
- Metal bow rakes.
- Backpack blower.
- A dump truck (a chute on the tailgate is optional).

You will also need the tools needed to install landscape fabric. Landscape fabric should always be installed before covering the bed with decorative stone. The fabric will help prevent the stones from settling into the ground and will help prevent weeds from growing.

Calculating Job Supplies

Before purchasing the stone, the landscape beds should be measured so that you can determine exactly how much stone will be needed. Measuring and determining the amount of supplies needed is usually done by the boss or foreman; however, it is good for everyone to know. This method can also be used to determine how much mulch or topsoil is needed to cover an area.

Follow these steps to determine how much material is needed for an area:

Example 1

- Measure the length and width of the landscape bed. This measurement will give you the square feet of the bed. For example: (40 feet × 8 feet = 320 square feet.)
- Determine how deep you want the stone, mulch or top soil to be. In this example we will stay two inches deep.
- Stone, mulch and topsoil are sold by the cubic yard. One cubic yard is a measurement of 3 feet by 3 feet by 3 feet. This measurement is in the shape of a square or cube. Multiply this together and you will get (3 × 3 × 3 = 27 square feet) for 1 cubic yard.
- Now you must change the **height** of the cube from feet to inches. 3 feet = 36 inches.
- You want the stone to be 2 inches deep so divide the 36 inches (the height of the cubic yard) by 2 (or 2 inches). Therefore 36 ÷ 2 = 18. (You will get 18 layers, 2 inches thick.)

- Now multiply the **width** and **depth** of the cube ($3 \times 3 = 9$ square feet).

- Multiply 18 by 9 square feet = 162 square foot per yard. At a depth of 2 inches you will cover 162 square foot **per yard**.

- The landscape bed that you want to cover is 320 square feet. At a depth of 2 inches you will cover 162 square foot per yard.

- Now divide $320 \div 162 = 1.975$ yards.

- A total of 1.975 will be needed to cover the area of 320 square feet with 2 inches of stone.

Lets review another example. However, this time we will not explain everything in detail.

Example 2:

- The bed area is 50 feet $\times$ 4 feet = 200 square feet.

- You need the material 3 inches deep.

- Divide the height of a cubic yard by 3 (or 3 inches). 36 inches $\div$ 3 inches = 12.

- The width $\times$ depth of a cubic yard is ($3 \times 3 = 9$ square feet).

- Multiply $12 \times 9 =$ (108 square feet per yard at 3 inches deep)

- Now divide $200 \div 108 = 1.851$ yards.

- You will need 1.851 yards to cover the area 3 inches deep.

Stone, mulch and topsoil is sold by the yard so round off all calculated numbers.

Example # 1: 1.975 yards (purchase 2 yards).

Example # 2: 1.851 yards (purchase 2 yards).

Installing Decorative Stone (Work Procedures)

After you have determined how much stone is needed for your job, you will be ready to pickup the stone. Obviously a dump truck will be best to pickup and deliver the stone. However, if you only need a small amount, a pickup truck can also be used. Whatever vehicle you are using following these instructions to avoid problems.

- Check the trucks tire pressure before loading up the truck. Never load up if the tires are low on air.
- Make sure that the truck is clean of any other debris so that the stone stays clean.
- Do not overload the truck, stones are very heavy. You will have to make a few trips if you need a lot of stone.
- Keep stones away from the tailgate and clean all stones off of the trucks tailgate. If the stones fall off your truck while you are driving, they can cause damage to another car.
- Do not to hit any curbs or other objects with the tires.
- Drive slowly and carefully and always think safety first.

Once you get to the job site, park the truck as close as possible to the area where you are working. Park on level hard ground and use the parking brake. If you are using a dump truck, make sure there are no wires or branches above the truck. You will need to raise up the dump body so it will be easier to remove the stones from the truck. Avoid dumping the stones out, some stones can damage a driveway and it will be much harder to pickup the stones from the ground.

Organize the job, walk the property and discuss what needs to be done. Everyone should know exactly what is going to be done **before** you start working. If you are unsure about what is going to be done, ask questions.

Before installing the decorative stone in the landscape beds, you will need to install the landscape fabric. Landscape fabric should be used under all decorative stone, even if the areas are very small. (Installing landscape fabric was explained in the previous chapter).

After the landscape fabric is installed, you will be ready to cover the bed with the stone. If you are using a dump truck, raise up the body about half way, then the stones will be easier to shovel out. Some dump trucks have a chute on the tailgate, put a wheelbarrow under the chute and you will be able to fill it up quickly and easily. Be careful not to over fill the wheelbarrows or they will be very difficult to push. Also make sure the tires on the wheelbarrow have plenty of air.

Usually one worker will fill up the wheelbarrows while the second worker pushes them and dumps the stones out in the bed. You will need at least two wheelbarrows so that one is being filled while the other is being pushed to the bed. When dumping the stones in the bed on top of the fabric, dump the stones **slowly** so you do not move the fabric.

Make small piles throughout the bed. Be careful not to dump the stones to close together. After the bed is about half way filled up with piles of stone, one worker should start to spread them out. Use a metal bow rake to spread the piles. **Be careful when spreading stones over the seams of the fabric. If you are not careful, you will move the fabric and push the stones under the fabric**. Once you have a layer of stone over the fabric, it will be easier to spread the remaining stones.

Decorative stones are usually spread about 2-1/2 inches deep. This depth works well for small stones. When installing large stones, you will have to go deeper. As a general rule, you should not be able to see any of the fabric through the stone. Large stones will be more difficult to install. They are harder to pickup with a shovel and harder to spread out with a metal bow rake. Sometimes it may be easier to spread them out by hand.

If you used stones or bricks to hold down the landscape fabric, while covering it with the decorative stone remove them and fill in the areas as needed. Inspect the job, clean up your tools and you are finished.

INSTALLING BASIC DRAINAGE SYSTEMS
(CHAPTER 16)

Basic drainage systems are installed to carry water from one place to another. Drainage systems will help keep important areas of the landscape dry and usable. We will discuss a gutter drainage system first. Drainage pipes are installed around the foundation of a house to collect all the water from the gutters and downspouts and then bring it out to the street. By installing a gutter drainage system around a house, you will keep the area drier and help prevent water from soaking the house foundation and seeping into the basement. The second type of drainage system we will discuss will help dry out wet areas on a property and will help lower a high water table. The third type of drainage system we will discuss will dry out wet areas, help lower a high water table and collect surface water that is flowing over the ground.

You will need the following tools and equipment when installing a basic drainage system.

- Wheelbarrows.
- Shovels, picks, metal bow rakes.
- Tape measurer, hand saw for PVC plastic.
- A standard level and a line level, string and stakes.
- Utility knife.
- Paint gun.

- Black marker pen.

- Backpack blower.

- Dump truck.

- Back-hoe machine (optional).

Safety equipment to consider:

- Gloves.

- Knee pads.

- Back support belt.

Installing a Gutter Drainage System

Before starting any manual work, you will need to plan out the job.
First look at all the downspouts coming off of the house. Plan out the
best way to connect all of these downspouts. The pipes connecting the
downspouts will be installed right up **against** the foundation of the
house. Then a few pipes will run out away from the house and bring
the water either to the street, a wooded or unused area of the property,
or to a dry well.

- *Make sure that the drainage pipes you are installing do not
  direct water onto the neighbor's property.*
- *If you are directing water out into the street, you will need a
  permit from the township where are you are working.*
- *Call the local utility company to mark all buried utility wires and
  pipes and check with the homeowner to discuss the location of*

other wires, sprinkler lines, etc. before you plan out a drainage system design.

Plan out the front, back and sides of the house. The best situation would be to have only two pipes running out away from the house; one in the front and one in the back. However, this will not be possible on every house. Some jobs will require four pipes running out from the house, one in the front, one in the back, and one pipe on each side. Try to avoid using sharp bends and plan on installing clean out connections every 50 feet throughout the system so it can be cleaned out if needed.

After you have planned out the best way to install the pipe, you will be ready to start the job:

- Using a paint gun, mark out the areas where all the pipes will be installed. Measure all the marked areas, then you will know exactly how much pipe to purchase. There are two different types of plastic pipe you can use. The first kind is called ADS. It is four inches wide, comes in a roll of 100 feet and it is flexible. The problem with this pipe is that it will settle into any uneven areas in the bottom of the trench you are digging. If the pipe settles into a low spot, water will have trouble flowing through it and the low spot may cause a clog.

- The second type of pipe is called PVC. It is a hard plastic pipe that is not flexible. It usually comes in lengths of 10 feet and is also 4 inches wide. It can be put into a trench that is not perfectly smooth and it will not sink into any low spots. Both pipes can be cut to any length and various fittings are available for them. The hard plastic PVC pipe will give you a better quality job.

- Dig out a trench against the foundation of the house. Start at the downspout that will be the **first** to be connected to the pipe. Dig the trench about 6 inches wide and about 6 inches deep.

Keep the bottom of the trench smooth and as even as possible. Do not remove too much soil from the bottom of the trench. If you remove too much soil, you will have to back fill the trench to raise it up, then the backfilled soil can settle which may cause the pipe to move. If the pipe moves, the water may not be able to flow out.

- Slope the entire length of the trench so that it lowers at the rate of at least 1-1/4 inch for a ten-foot length of pipe or 1 foot for every 100 feet. To measure the slope, you need to use a level. Place the level on top of the pipe to take a measurement. After the first piece of pipe is installed at the correct slope mark the location of the bubble on the level. Then use the marked level to correctly install the rest of the pipes.
- You will have to install elbows or tee-fittings to connect to the downspouts. There is another connection that will be installed on top of the elbow or tee fitting that will connect to the gutter.
- When connecting the pipes, elbows, tee-fitting or gutter adapters together, clean the pipe using PVC plastic cleaning solution. Then apply PVC plastic glue to both sides of the pipe and press the two

pieces together. Avoid breathing the fumes from the cleaner or glue and avoid making contact with them.

- Some pieces of pipe will have to be cut to a certain length. Before cutting the pipe, make an accurate measurement and mark the exact spot the pipe will need to be cut. Use a black marker pen to make a mark. Use a hand saw with a ridged metal blade, or use a saw that is made to cut PVC plastic. Make the cut as straight as possible through the pipe.

- After the pipe has been installed around the foundation of the house, you will need to dig out and install the pipes that will carry the water away from the house. These lines should be kept as straight as possible. If many long sections of pipe need to be installed, it may be easier to dig out the trench with a small backhoe machine. Since the pipe is sloping 1-1/4 inch deep for every 10 feet length the trench will have to be deeper the further you get from the starting point.

- To measure the slope on a long straight length of the trench use a string and a line level. Rough out the trench and be careful not to dig too deep. Then put the string on the bottom of the trench where it is the correct depth **(this point will be where the last piece of pipe was installed)**. Hammer a spike into the ground and tie the string onto the spike. Run the string down the length of the trench and hammer a second spike into the ground and tie the string to it. Attach the line level to the center of the string. Adjust the string at the far end until it reads level. Then move the string down at the far end to get the correct slope.

For example:

If the trench is 100 feet long, the far end of the line needs to be 1 foot lower than the starting point. If the trench is 50 feet long, the line should be lowered 6 inches. If the line cannot be lowered because the trench is not deep enough, remove soil as needed.

Note: If you do a lot of drainage work, you may want to rent or purchase a surveyors transit or laser level. These tools will make the job much easier.

- Your pipe may discharge in the street, if so, be sure to get a permit and follow the township requirements. If the pipe does not discharge in the street, it may run into a wooded or unused area of the property or into a drywell.

A drywell is an area where water runs into and then seeps into the ground. A typical dry well is about 4 feet wide by 4 feet deep and filled with stone or a plastic insert. Dry wells will not work, if you have a high ground water table. Check township requirements and permits before installing drywells.

- After the pipe is installed, backfill the trench and finish grade all surface areas.

Underground Drainage System

The second type of drainage system we will be discussing will help dry out wet areas on a property and will help lower a high water table.

The water table is the level at which ground water lays under the surface of the ground.

To install this type of system, you will have to use perforated plastic PVC pipe that is 4 inch by 10 feet long. It is the same pipe that we used to install the gutter drainage system except this pipe will have holes in it. The pipe will be installed throughout wet areas of the property.

Installing an Underground Drainage System

- Plan out the drainage system, where it will start and where the water will be discharged. Remember to have all utilities etc. marked before you layout the system. Also remember that the pipe will need to slope at least 1-1/4 inch per ten feet or 1 foot per 100 feet of length. Try to avoid using sharp bends in the system and plan on installing a clean out connections every 50 feet throughout the system so it can be cleaned out if needed.
- After the system has been planned and marked, you can start to dig out the trench. Dig the trench approximately eight inches wide and start with a depth of approximately 12 inches deep.

Try to install the drainpipe as deep as possible but remember that the end of the drain will have to be deeper than the starting point. On some jobs, it may be better to start at the lowest point (which should be the end of the drain) and work backwards up to the highest point (or beginning of drain). By installing the pipe as deep as possible, you will lower the ground water table and dry out the area the most. The holes in the pipes are placed on the bottom of the trench. Then as the ground water rises up, it will flow into the holes and flow out to the end of the drainage system.

- Dig the trench about two inches deeper than where you want the pipe to be installed. The bottom two inches will be filled up with stone. The pipe will be installed with (¾ inch) clean stone all around it. This will help draw more water into the pipe.

- Before installing the stone, you will need to lay landscape fabric into the trench. Cut the fabric so that it will be able to wrap around the pipe with two to three inches of stone around the pipe. The fabric is installed to keep dirt out of the stones and pipe. Fabric that will just cover the pipe is also available. It is faster and easier to use, but cost more money. Installing the fabric around the stone and pipe is best.

- Make sure that the trench has the correct slope. Then install the landscape fabric throughout the length of the trench.

- After the fabric is installed, fill the bottom of the trench with approximately two inches of stone. Try to keep the stone the same depth throughout the trench, then grade the stone with a metal bow rake.

- After the layer of stone is graded at the bottom of the trench, start to install the pipe. Install the pipe so that the holes are facing down. You will have to check each piece of pipe with a level to make sure it is slopped correctly. If the slope is not correct, you will need to add or remove stone until the pipe lies on the correct slope.

- Cut and glue all the pipes as we discussed earlier. When the pipes are all installed, add more stone on the sides and top of the pipe. There should be about two inches of stone around the top, bottoms and sides of the pipe.

Note: Be careful not to dig the trench to wide. Keep the trench no larger than eight inches wide. If the trench is too wide, you will waste time and materials filling it up with stone.

- Wrap the fabric over the top of the stone and pipe. Then back fill the trench with soil. Be careful not to let any soil in-between the fabric or it will get into the drainage system. You will need about 6 inches of soil on top of the stone so grass can grow.
- The system should end up (or discharge) into an unused area of the property, into the street or drainage system located in the street, or into a drywell.
- By planning out and then installing an underground drainage system as we just discussed, you can convert a wet ground area into a usable piece of property.

There is one other way to install an underground drainage system, which will require less labor, but it will not work as well as the type that we just discussed. You would install the system the same way but you would not put stone around the pipe. This will reduce the labor and cost of the job but also reduce the quality of the job.

Installing an (Open) Underground Drainage System

The third type of drainage system we will discuss will help dry out wet areas and help lower a high water table and collect surface water that is flowing over the ground. This drainage system is designed and installed the same way as the underground drainage system that we just discussed **except** the trench is not backfilled with soil. Instead it will be backfilled with stone until the stone is level with the ground. By filling the trench up with stone instead of soil, any surface water will easily fall into the drain. Install this type of drain wherever there is a problem with surface water flowing over the ground. Decorative stones can be installed on top of the drain so that it will look better in the landscape.

Combining Different Types of Drainage Systems

Each property you are working at will have different drainage problems. There will be many jobs that require a few different types of drainage systems to resolve the problems on the property. The three types of drainage systems that we discussed can all be combined with each other if needed.

By planning out and installing a drainage system correctly, you will be able to improve a property by changing a wet unusable area into a dry usable piece of property, you will also help prevent water from damaging a home or building and increase the value of the property.

INSTALLING PAVING STONE WALKS, PATIOS AND DRIVEWAYS

(CHAPTER 17)

Paving stones are man made stones used for walks, patios and driveways. They are similar to old fashion bricks except they will last much longer and are available in many different colors and shapes. Paving stones have become very popular and as a landscape professional, you should know how to install them correctly. When installed correctly, a paving stone job should last forever. However if they are installed incorrectly, they will sink into the ground and leave you with a poor quality job and an unhappy customer. If you follow the instructions in this chapter, your paving stone job should last a lifetime.

Tools and Equipment Needed

You will need the following tools and equipment to install a basic walkway, patio or driveway.

Wheelbarrows, shovels, picks, a metal bow rake, a grading rake, a broom, a tape measure, a paint gun, a regular level and a line level, strings and stakes, a rubber hammer, a straight piece of wood, (2) 1 inch diameter pipes that are about 10 feet long, a vibrating plate tamper, a hand tamper, a masonry saw to cut the paving stones, and a backhoe (optional).

Safety Equipment Needed:

Gloves, safety glasses, a dust mask, kneepads, and a back support belt.

Installing a Paving Stone Walk

Choosing the Stones, Pattern and Layout

The first step to installing paving stones is to choose the correct stone, pattern and layout of the job; this is usually be done by the boss or foreman of your company.

- There are many different types of paving stones which will vary in color and shape. When choosing a color and shape, bring a brochure to the customer, most brochures will show all the different colors and shapes available. Brochures should be available from your local paving stone dealer. After a color and shape have been chosen from the brochure, bring a few stone samples to the customer so that the customer clearly understands how the paving stones will look.

- The pattern is the next thing to choose and confirm with the customer. Patterns are also shown in the brochure. The pattern is the way the paving stones are installed. They can be installed straight or on an angle. Some larger jobs can have two or three different patterns. Let the customer know that the job cost will vary base on the pattern that is chosen.

- The layout of the job will also need to be planned out. The width, length and shape need to be determined. A job with a lot of curves will require a lot of cuts, making the job more difficult and costly.

While a job layout that is straight will be easier to install and less costly.

During the layout process, you will also have to determine if the area has the correct slope. If the slope is not correct, you may have to change the slope by excavating the area. During the layout process, look for any buried wires or pipes in the area. If you are not 100% sure where the utilities are buried, call up the utility company so that they can mark them. Also, make sure the property owner advises you of any other hazards such as, sprinkler pipes or landscape lighting wires. If lighting might be installed in the future, plan on installing a plastic PVC pipe through the base of the job so that wires can then be installed through the pipe and on both sides of the job.

After the stones, pattern and layout have been confirmed, you will be ready to start the installation process.

Installation Process
Note: Always check the manufacturers exact recommendations before installing paving stones.

Layout
Measure and mark the area where the walkway will be installed. You will need the base material to be approximately one foot larger on both sides of the walk. Installing the base material larger than the walk will prevent the edges of the walk from moving and settling. Use

a tape measure and paint gun to measure and mark the area. Do not do any digging until everything is clearly marked.

Excavation

A properly installed base is a very important procedure when installing paving stones. The base material for walkways should be four to six inches deep. Then add three inches onto the base depth to determine the total depth required. The additional three inches are excavated to allow for the stone dust and paving stones which will be installed on top of the base material. Base material should consist of (0 to ¾ inch) stone. You will need to excavate a total of nine inches for the walkway that we are discussing.

To remove the soil, use a shovel and pick. Put the soil into a wheelbarrow and dispose of it. On some jobs, you may need to use this soil to re-grade an area near the walk or somewhere else on the property. If you need to excavate a large amount of soil, it will be easier and faster to rough out the area using a backhoe. Check the depth of the excavated area with your tape measure. Try to keep the bottom of the excavated area smooth and keep the sides of the area straight. Hand rake the bottom of the excavated area so it is as smooth as possible. Then compact the ground with your vibrating plate tamper. This will compact any soft areas in the ground before you add the base material.

Base Material

If you are working in a wet area, a special landscape fabric should be installed at the bottom of the excavated area. The fabric will make the base stronger and will prevent the base material from seeping into the existing soil. Your local paving stone supplier will be able to recommend and supply you with the correct fabric.

After the fabric is installed, you can start to fill the area with the base material. Again, base material should consist of (0 to ¾ inch) stone. Install a four-inch layer, then rake the stone level and compact the material with your vibrating plate tamper. (Never install more than 4 inches of base material without grading and compacting it first.) Wet the base material with water and make several passes over the area with the tamper. Then add two more inches of base material, rake it level and repeat the compacting process. Check the area with a level in various places to make sure the base material is level and the same throughout the entire walk.

Edging

The manufacturer of the paving stones will supply you with a special edging that is to be used with their paving stones. Most edging pieces are made of plastic. They are flexible so they can be easily installed around any curved areas and usually come in 12-foot lengths. Spikes are hammered through the edging and into the ground to hold it in place. Most paving stone manufacturers recommend installing the plastic edging on top of the base material.

Install the plastic edging on **one side** of the base material. Using 10-inch spikes, install one spike every two feet. Starting from the plastic edging that you just installed, layout a small section of paving stones across the walk in the pattern that you will be using. Then take a measurement from one side of the walk to the other. Use that same measurement to measure and mark areas along the opposite side of the walk. Then install the edging on these marks.

Setting Material

The setting material is the material that the paving stones will be set on top of. Stone dust or concrete sand should be used for setting material. Spread a 1 to 1-1/2 inch layer of setting material on top of the base material. Rough grade the setting material with a metal rake. For drainage purposes, there should be a two percent incline on the setting material. The two percent incline will allow rainfall to easily flow off the walk. The two percent will equal ¼ inch per foot. Therefore, if your walkway is three feet wide, the incline from one side of the walk to the other side should be ¾ inch. The incline should always slope **away** from a house or building. Some jobs may already have an incline that allows water to easily flow off the paving stones.

If the plastic edging has been installed, you can use the edging as a guide to finish grade the setting material. You will need to use a straight piece of wood. Cut a notch at both ends of the wood so that it will rest on the edging but also fit inside the edging. Adjust the notch so that you also get the correct incline on the setting material. Then pull the board across the walkway to finish grade the setting material.

Add or remove setting material as needed. This will take a little practice but is easy after you do it once or twice. After the setting material has been graded properly, be careful to stay off the area. The setting material does not get compacted until after the paving stones have been installed.

Installation of Paving Stones

Place the paving stones down in the pattern that you have chosen. Start the pattern at the widest area of the walkway. Usually this would be the area by the front or back door. Start by installing a small section of pavers. Check the pattern and angle of stones to be sure it is correct before you continue working. Carefully walk onto the pavers that you installed, work forward, always working on top of the pavers that you just installed. To get an even distribution of color and texture, it is recommended that you choose paving stones from more than one pallet at a time.

As always, you should have the job organized at all times. When installing the pavers, one person should install them while the second person selects the pavers from the pallets and places them where they will be easiest to reach for the person installing them.

Paving stones are manufactured with side spacers. The side spacers will keep a space of 1/8 inch between each paver. When you are finished installing the pavers, sand will be swept into these spaces to help hold the pavers together. When you place each paver down, gently place it up against the last paver. Look for the 1/8 inch space in between the pavers. If the space in between the pavers is larger than 1/8 inch, they have not been installed correctly. Some people lightly tap each paver with a rubber hammer after it is set correctly. While installing the pavers, check the pattern to make sure it is not changing or moving in the wrong direction. On larger jobs, you may be able to install a string, then you can use the string as a guide to keep your pattern straight and correct. Install all the solid paving stones first. Leave an open space where the pavers will need to be cut.

Cutting the Paving Stones

Measure and mark all the pavers that need to be cut. There are two types of saws that can be used to cut the stones. A table saw or a hand held saw. Both saws should have a special blade that should be used only to cut stone. Cut the stones so there will be a space of 1/8 inch on all sides of the stone, then the stones will fit easily into their space. Never force a paver into its space; if it does not fit easily, you must cut off a little more. When cutting the pavers, you will make a lot of dust. Water can be used to help control the dust problem. Always wear safety glasses and a dust mask when cutting the pavers.

Stabilizing the Paving Stones

After you have finished installing all the pavers, you will need to stabilize the pavers by using a vibrating plate tamper. This procedure will press the pavers down into the setting material and will level the surface of the walkway. For best results, run the plate tamper over the pavers two or three times in both directions. The paving stones will settle into the setting material by about 3/8 inch. After using the plate tamper, you will need to spread sand over the pavers. The sand will fill in the 1/8 inch spaces in between the paving stones. Use a broom to brush the sand over the walkway. Add more sand until all of the spaces are filled up. Once all the spaces have been filled up with sand, run the plate tamper over the area again. The plate tamper will help the sand settle into the spaces. Add more sand to any spaces that are not completely filled. Repeat this process until all the spaces are filled until the sand will not settle any further. Remove the excess sand from the surface of the walkway, and then moisten the area with water to stabilize the sand even further.

Installing a Paving Stone Patio or Driveway

Note: Always check the manufactures exact recommendations before installing paving stones.

A patio or driveway is installed almost the same as a walkway except for a few changes. These changes will include:

- The area must be excavated deeper since the base material will need to be deeper. Follow the recommendations on the chart.

Walkway:	Base material depth approximately 6 inches
Patio:	Base material depth approximately 8 inches
Driveway:	Base material depth approximately 12 inches

- Grade and compact every four-inch of base material.
- Set the correct incline on the base material, not on the setting material.
- When grading the setting material, large areas will have to be graded in sections. Lay down two pipes that are one inch in

diameter and approximately 10 feet long. Space them approximately six feet apart. The pipes should lay on the base material. Then fill in between the pipes with the setting material. Then using a board that is perfectly straight, put the board on top of the pipes. Drag the board towards you to grade the setting material. Add or remove setting material as needed. After the area has been graded, carefully remove the pipes and move them to the next section. The spaces left from the pipes will be filled in by hand when installing the pavers.

- A string should be set up and used as a guide when installing the pavers. By working with a string, you will help prevent the pattern from moving while installing the pavers in a large area.

Note: Before attempting to complete a large complicated job, you should get experience from completing smaller, less complicated jobs. Each job will give you more experience and confidence. Then each job will get done easier and faster and look professional.

INSTALLING DECORATIVE STONE WALLS
(CHAPTER 18)

Decorative stonewalls are used to hold small amounts of soil and they add beauty to the landscape. A decorative stonewall will range in height from 6 inches to a maximum height of 2-1/2 feet. If the wall is any higher than 2-1/2 feet, it is considered a structural retaining wall. A decorative stonewall and a structural retaining wall are installed almost the same except the structural retaining wall will require some additional reinforcements (we will be discussing decorative stone walls only).

Types of Walls

There are many different types of stonewalls, we will discuss the most popular ones.

Pre-fabricated Retaining Wall System

Pre-fabricated wall systems have become very popular over the past few years. They are man made blocks that are available in various colors and shapes. They are made of material similar to paving stones. They will not crack or fall apart when they get older. The blocks are simple to install and do not require any maintenance once they are installed. Pre-fabricated wall blocks are taking the place of wooden tie walls. Wooden tie walls will last 40 years then the wall will need to be replaced. Pre-fabricated wall blocks will last a lifetime.

Wall Stone

There are many different types of wall stone. The stones will vary in color, texture and shape. Wall stones are basically flat in shape and are installed without using any cement. Wall stones come from the earth and will give the landscape a natural look. When installed correctly, a job with wall stone should last a lifetime.

Landscape Boulders

Natural or man-made boulders are also used to make decorative walls or placed separately throughout the landscape. There are many different types of boulders to choose from. Boulders always add beauty when chosen and placed in the landscape correctly.

Tools and Equipment

You will need the following tools when installing any type of decorative stonewall.

- Wheelbarrows, a tree cart, shovels, picks, a metal bow rake, a broom, a tape measurer, a paint gun, a level, string, a rubber hammer, a hand tamper, a masonry saw, a hand sledgehammer, and a masonry chisel.

Safety equipment:

- Gloves, safety glasses, a dust mask, kneepads, and a back support belt.

Installing Pre-fabricated Wall Blocks

- The first step to installing a decorative wall is to choose the correct type, color and size block then plan the layout of the wall. This is usually done by the boss or foreman.

- Measure and mark the area where the wall will be installed. Mark any utilities that are buried near the wall. **Never** start excavating until you are 100% sure nothing is buried under the area where you will be working.

- Excavate a trench approximately 12 inches wide by 6 inches deep. Start excavating where the **lowest** part of the wall will be installed. This will be the area where the ground is the lowest. The bottom of the trench should be level, smooth and compact. Make sure that the bottom of the trench is well compacted. Use a hand tamper to compact the soil if necessary.

- Install approximately 2-1/2 inches of (0 to ¾ inch) stone into the trench. Rake the stone as level as possible, then compact the stone with a hand tamper. This will be the base of the wall. Install another ½ inch of stone and rake it until it is level. Check the base material with a level every few feet. The entire length of the base material must be level before installing any of the wall blocks. Do not compact the last ½ inch of the base material.

- Install the first row of wall blocks. Level each block from side to side, front to back and make it even with the block next to it. Use a rubber hammer to help level the blocks.

Note: If you are installing a wall on an uneven slope, you will may have to excavate, grade and install the first row of blocks (starting at the lowest point). Then re-excavate and grade to install the following rows until the blocks are installed around the entire shape of the wall.

- Installing the first row of wall blocks must be done correctly since all the other blocks will be placed on top of the first row.

- When installing the second row of blocks, place the block down so that the center of the second block covers the joint of the blocks below. Most wall blocks will have a small extra piece on the back, bottom side of the block. Slide the blocks forward until the piece on back bottom side makes contact with the blocks below.

- The procedure is fairly easy after you get a little practice. Only the first row needs to be leveled. After the first row is leveled correctly, all the other rows on top do not need to be leveled.

- Backfill behind each row of blocks with ¾ inch stone. The stone is installed behind the wall for drainage purposes to keep water away from the wall. Install the ¾ inch stone approximately one foot wide and the same height as the wall. Then backfill the remaining area with soil.

- (Optional.) When you set to the top row of blocks, a special (cap) block can be installed. The (cap) block will give the job a better look. Cap blocks will need to be secured with a concrete adhesive.

Installing Wall Stone

Wall stone is a natural type of stone. The stones are installed without any cement. The stones are placed on top of each other. Smaller pieces of stone are put into the spaces in between the larger stones and behind the wall. This will help make the wall stable. Installing wall stone will take longer than installing pre-fabricated wall blocks, and it will require more skill. By reading the instructions below and working on the job site, you will gain knowledge and experience and become a professional after a few jobs.

- **Choosing the Stones**—The wall stones will usually come on a pallet. The pallet is covered with wire to hold the stones together. Look for a pallet that has the best-sized pieces. Choose a pallet that has mostly flat average sized stones. Stay away from stones that are very small, very large or round in size. These stones will be very difficult to work with and will make your job harder. Whenever loading a pallet of stones in your truck, make sure the tires have enough air pressure. Make sure that the parking brake is on before the pallet is loaded up. Place the pallet in the center of the truck and **secure the pallet** so it will not slide when you are driving. Drive carefully and do not accelerate or brake too quickly.
- **Layout**—Measure and mark the area where the wall will be installed.
- **Excavation**—Excavate a trench approximately 12 inches wide by four inches deep. Start excavating where the lowest part of the wall will be installed. The trench will need to be level. After

excavating, make sure the bottom of the trench is well compacted. Use a hand tamper to compact the soil if necessary.

- **Base material**—Fill the trench with (0 – ¾ inch) stone. Install approximately two inches of stone into the trench. Rake the stone as level as possible, then compact the stone with a hand tamper. Install another ½ inch of stone and rake it level. Check the base material with a level every few feet. The entire length of the base material must be level before installing the wall stones. Do not compact the last ½ inch of the base material.

If you are installing a wall on an uneven slope, you will have to excavate, grade and install the first row of stones (starting at the lowest point). Then re-excavate and grade to install the following rows until the stones are installed around the entire shape of the wall.

- **Installing the stones**—Install the first row of stones on the base material. When installing the stones, put the best side of the stone facing the outside of the wall. Each row of stones must be centered on top of the joint of the stones below. Use smaller pieces of stone to fit into the spaces in between the stones until it is secure and will not move. Use a level to keep the stones and wall straight. Since the stones are irregular, it will be difficult to get an exact reading from the level. Use the level to get an approximate reading. Some of the larger pieces of stone can be split and reduced in size by using a hammer and mason chisel.

- **Back filling**—After a few rows of stone have been installed, backfill behind the wall with (¾ inch) stone. Using your hands or a shovel, fill in the spaces in between the stones behind the wall. Then add stone to a width of 6 to 12 inches behind the wall. The stone will help support the wall and keep water away from the wall. **Back filling is very important**. Many unprofessional landscapers skip this step and only back fill with soil. Then the soil settles and the wall starts to fall backwards. To do a professional job, always back fill with (¾ inch) stone.

- **Final Step**—Try to find some good looking pieces of stone to cap off the wall. Set these pieces aside while you are constructing the wall. There will be many small pieces of stone left over. Use some of them to fill the larger spaces in front and back of the wall. Use any small unusable pieces to back fill behind the wall. Save any good sized pieces for your next job.

Installing Landscape Boulders

Boulders are large stones, usually natural. However, some are man made. There are many different types of boulders. They will vary in color, shape and texture. Boulders will add beauty to the landscape when chosen and installed in the correct areas. Boulders can be placed close together to create a natural looking wall. Boulders can also be placed in the landscape separately, and then plantings can be installed around them. As always, the boss or foreman must talk with the customer and confirm the type of boulders to be used and where the boulders will be installed. After the job has been confirmed with the customer, you will be ready to go to work.

- Boulders are usually sold separately. Choose boulders that are large, but not too large or you will not be able to move them unless you are using some type of machinery. Do not overload your truck and drive carefully to the job site.
- Once you are at the job site, mark the areas where the boulders will be installed.
- If you are not using machinery to move the boulders, there are two ways to move them manually.

The first way is to use a large sized wheelbarrow. Put the wheelbarrow against the back of the truck. While one person is holding the wheelbarrow, slide a boulder off the truck and into the wheelbarrow.

The second way is to dump out the boulders. **Make sure you dump the boulders on an area that will not get damaged.** After the boulders are dumped on the ground, use a tree cart to move each boulder to its spot in the landscape. Before moving the boulders into the landscape, prepare an area for each stone. Dig out an area so that the boulder will not move when in place. Boulders are usually installed so that they are partially buried in the ground. Be very careful when moving the boulders. Keep your hands and feet away from the underside of the boulder. Work together when moving and positioning each stone.

- After the areas have been prepared, select the best side of the boulder and set the best side forward. Then back fill with soil and mulch. This will give the landscape a natural look. The boulders should look like they are part of the landscape and have always been there. Think about the best way to position each boulder before you install it and your job will look great when you are finished.

(LAWN CARE SERVICES)
OPERATING DIFFERENT TYPES OF
APPLICATION EQUIPMENT
(CHAPTER 19)

(Note: Please be aware that your application equipment may work slightly different than described in this training guide.)

Spreaders

There are two different types of lawn spreaders that are used to apply fertilizer, grass seed and other dry materials. The most commonly used lawn spreader is called a rotary spreader. The second type of lawn spreader is called a drop spreader.

Rotary Spreader

The rotary spreader spreads material in a wide arc. Material can be spread 6 to 10 feet wide in one pass. This type of spreader should be used on large areas of lawn. The operator of the spreader needs to be very careful. If the rotary spreader is not used properly, material will be spread into landscape beds, driveways, walkways, etc. As a professional, you must operate the rotary spreader so material is spread **evenly** onto the lawn areas only.

Before using the spreader, you will need to inspect it. If the spreader does not work properly, you can cause poor results or serious damage to a lawn area. On a **daily** basis you should inspect the following.

- Make sure the entire spreader is always clean. The rotor that spins and spreads the material should be checked most often. It will get clogged up with material quickly. If this material is not cleaned off, the spreader will not work correctly.
- Check the tires to make sure they are both filled with air. If the tires are low on air, the spreader will be difficult to operate.
- Grease all the moving parts on the spreader.
- Look for any loose or damaged parts on the spreader. If you find a problem, get it repaired before using the spreader.

As a lawn care professional your spreader should have a cover. The cover goes over the top of the spreader and will prevent the material from dumping out if the spreader tipped over. The cover will also protect the material from wet weather conditions.

A deflector should be installed onto your spreader. The deflector is mounted on the side of the spreader. When the deflector is used, material will not be distributed on one side of the spreader. The deflector should be used around sidewalks, driveways, landscape beds and small areas of lawn. It will prevent material from getting into unwanted places.

There will be a hand control lever at the top of the spreader near the handles. This lever is used to open or close the flow of material. It will start or stop the material from spreading onto the lawn. There is also a rate gage lever that is used to adjust the rate that the material is used. The rate gage lever has letters or numbers. Adjust the rate gage lever onto a selected letter or number then the material will be released at the correct rate. If the material is released incorrectly, poor results or serious damage can occur to the lawn area.

Always read and understand the label on the product that you are using. All lawn care products will have a label. The label will give you instructions, warnings and the recommended rate that the material should be applied. The label will give application rates for a few different types of spreaders. Therefore, you must know the name brand of spreader that you are using.

Next to the name brand of the spreader will be a recommended application rate. This rate will be a letter or number. **After you know the application rate, adjust your spreader to the recommended letter or number.** Make sure you tighten the knob on the rate gage or the lever may move and change the rate setting while you are working.

Professional spreaders come with a hand held calibration gage. By using this type of gage, you will get the most accurate spreader setting. The calibration gage measures the holes in the bottom of the spreader that release the material. To adjust the spreader to the letter or number recommended on the product label.

Look on the hand held calibration gage for that letter or number, then insert the gage into each hole on the spreader. Adjust the holes until the calibration gage fits snug, then tighten the knob on the gage to lock the lever on your selected setting.

You should be wearing boots; long pants covering the top part of your boots, a long sleeve shirt, gloves, safety glasses and a respirator or a dust mask (if recommended on the product label). If you will be using the spreader throughout the day, you should consider wearing some type of dust mask even if the material you are using is not hazardous.

Always read and understand the product label before applying the product to the lawn area. Each product will have different instructions to follow. Poor results or serious damage can occur if you do not follow the instruction on each product label.

Operating a Rotary Spreader

- Before operating your rotary spreader, inspect the spreader and adjust it to the recommended rate setting as we just discussed. Put on all your safety equipment and you are ready to start work.
- Before filling the spreader with material, make sure the hand control lever is closed. If it is not closed, material will pour through the spreader and onto the ground.

- The spreader should always be filled on a hard level surface. Then if you spill material, it can be easily cleaned up. Never fill the spreader on the lawn areas.

- *There should be a screen inside the spreader. The screen is used to catch any large or irregular pieces of material before they clog up in the bottom of the spreader. Clean out the screen when it starts to fill up with debris. Always use the screen and do not operate the spreader without it.*

- *If you are using the spreader on level ground or a slight slope, you can fill the spreader all the way up. But if you are using the spreader on a steep slope, you should only fill the spreader ¾ of the way full. A full spreader can tip over very easily on a steep slope. Also, a full spreader will be very difficult to push on a steep slope. Filling it ½ or ¾ full is recommended.*

- After you have filled the material into the spreader, put the cover on the top of the spreader. Check to make sure the deflector is all the way up and locked in place. If the deflector is not locked in place, it may start to move. If it moves, it will create a problem while you are operating the spreader.

- Visually inspect the lawn area that you are going to apply the application to. There should be no people, children, pets or toys on the lawn area. Pick up anything that is on the lawn area.

- The lawn area should also be clean. If the lawn has a lot of leaves, sticks and debris on top of it, the application will not work correctly. If the lawn has lots of debris on it, it may be better to return after the lawn area has been cleaned.

- Once the lawn area is clean, plan out the best way to push the spreader over the lawn area. The spreader needs to be pushed in a straight line as often as possible. Also, plan out a pattern where you will not have to turn the spreader around very often.

- Always try to start against a straight edge such as the curbing on a road, driveway or walkway. If there is no straight edge to start from, push the spreader in a straight line across the lawn area. Use that first pass across the lawn as a guide, then make all other passes in the same direction.

- After you have chosen the pattern that you will use, you will need to choose a walking speed. Your walking speed should be approximately 3 mph. This is an average walking speed; not too fast, but not too slow.

When you push a spreader at the correct speed (approximately 3 mph), the material will be spread out at the correct width and rate. Usually the material will be spread approximately 4 feet on both sides of the spreader. This will give you a total of 8 feet of treated lawn area for each pass walking at 3 mph. If you walk slower, the width of the material will be less than 8 feet and the material will be applied to heavy. If you walk faster, the width of the material will be more than 8 feet and the material will be applied too light. Always push the spreader at the same walking speed throughout the entire lawn area or poor results or serious damage can occur.

- It is very important that you push the spreader at the same walking speed throughout the entire lawn area. By pushing the spreader at the same exact speed throughout the lawn area, you will apply the material evenly and professionally. If you walk at different speeds, the material will be applied differently. This will cause poor results or serious damage to the lawn area. Pushing the spreader at the same speed on a steep slope or small lawn area can be difficult. Stay alert and only push the spreader at one speed.

- Position yourself and the spreader so that you are ready to make the first pass across the lawn. Position yourself so that you are a few feet behind or to the side of the area that you are going to treat.

- Start to walk forward. Within a few steps, you should be pushing the spreader at the correct speed. Then quickly open the lever to let the material out.

- While you are pushing the spreader along the first pass across the lawn, look on both sides of the spreader to see exactly how far the material is being spread. Remember how far the material is being spread.

- When you get towards the end of the first pass, do not slow down. Continue to walk at the correct speed. If the material is spreading four feet in front of the spreader, you will need to close the lever to stop the material approximately four feet before the end of the pass.

- After the first pass is done, position the spreader for the next pass. You will have to **slightly overlap** the material with each pass that you make. This is why you must **always** watch how far the material is being spread.

- Before each pass, remember that you will need to start a few feet behind or to the side of the area you want to treat.

- *If you start the spreader at the top of the pass you are going to make, you will not cover your starting point area. Therefore, you must start the spreader a few feet behind or to the side of your starting point. Remember that all the lawn areas you are treating must receive the same amount of material.*

- When you open and close the lever to let the material start or stop, the spreader must always be moving at the correct speed. Once the spreader is moving at the right speed and positioned correctly, you must use this lever quickly. Also at the end of each pass, the lever must be closed quickly.

- *The lever that lets the material out should also be used as an emergency lever. If you hit a hole in the lawn and the spreader stops, quickly close the lever. Whenever you have a problem or difficulty, close the lever immediately. By closing the lever immediately, you will prevent material from dumping onto the lawn.*

- Continue to make each pass across the lawn as we just discussed. If there is a tree or landscape bed in the lawn area, stop the spreader. Then start the spreader on the other side of the tree or landscape bed. *Never push the spreader over a lawn area that has already been treated. If you push the spreader over a lawn area that has already been treated, you will be applying the material at double the recommended rate. Most materials will cause damage to the lawn if they area applied heavier than the recommended rate.*

- When treating small areas, you may need to use the deflector. The deflector will stop material from coming out of one side of the spreader. Use the deflector on all small or narrow areas of lawn. Never spread material into landscape beds, sidewalk or driveways. Use the deflector for a professional job.

- Whenever using the spreader, remember to always watch the material. Watch how far it is spreading and if it is spreading evenly. At times, the material may clog in the spreader or the spreader may not work correctly. If you see a problem, stop the spreader. Then remove the material from the spreader. Clean and inspect the spreader then re-fill it with material and try it again.

- Some professionals like to first make a pass around the outer edge of the area being treated. And then make straight passes back and fourth across the area. Whatever way you choose, make sure all the lawn areas are being treated evenly.

Clean up

After you have finished applying the lawn application, you will need to clean up any material that is on the driveway, sidewalks or road. If you applied the lawn application correctly, there should be very littler material on these areas. You will need a backpack blower or hand held blower to clean the material.

When you clean the material off these areas, you must blow off the material evenly. **Do not** blow the material into a pile or into one area. By blowing the material into a pile or into one area, the lawn area it makes contact with will die. The area can also get contaminated from the heavy material. **Always blow off the material evenly**. If there is **heavy** material on an unwanted area, do not blow it off. Use a broom to sweep it into a pile, then pick it up with a shovel and remove the heavy material from the area and job site.

Drop Spreader

The drop spreader is the second type of spreader used to apply dry materials. It is used for very small lawn areas. It can also be used to apply grass seed or other material along the edges of a lawn area since the spreader applies material accurately.

Drop spreaders come in different widths. Most drop spreaders are about four feet wide. The material will drop straight down. Therefore if the spreader is four feet wide, the material will be spread at a width of four feet.

Before using the drop spreader, you will need to inspect it the same way you inspect a rotary spreader.

- Make sure the entire spreader is always clean.
- If the tires have air in them, make sure they are both filled with air and not low.
- Keep all moving parts on the spreader greased.
- Look for any loose or damaged parts on the spreader. If you find a problem, get it repaired before using it again.

The drop spreader will have a hand control lever at the top of the spreader, near the handles. This lever is used to open and close the flow of material. The drop spreader will also have a rate gage used to adjust the rate that the material is being released. The hand control lever and rate gage will work basically the same as on the rotary spreader.

Always read the product label to determine the correct application rate. Adjust the rate gage as needed before applying any material.

Safety Equipment

A drop spreader is safer than a rotary spreader because the material is released very close to the ground and will not drift. However, you should still wear long pants, boots, a long sleeve shirt and gloves. Also wear safety glasses and a respirator or dust mask if recommended on the product label.

Operating A Drop Spreader

- Before operating your drop spreader, inspect it and adjust it to the recommended rate setting as we just discussed. Put on your safety equipment and you are ready to work.
- Make sure the hand control lever is closed, then fill up the spreader with material.
- Visually inspect the lawn area that you are going to apply the application to. The area must be clean and there should be no people, children or pets on the area.
- Plan out the best way to push the spreader over the lawn areas. Then operate the drop spreader the same way as the rotary spreader. The only difference is that the material will only be spread out four feet wide for each pass.

Hand Held Spreader

A hand held spreader is used to spot treat areas in a lawn. The hand held spreader is used most often when spot seeding. It will spread seed quickly and evenly. These spreaders are held at waist height in front of your body. The spreaders will only hold a small amount of material. Some hand held spreaders may have a strap that will go around your body. The strap will help support the weight of the spreader when it is full. On the bottom side of the spreader there is a rotor. There is a handle that will make the rotor spin. The handle is located on the side of the spreader. There is also a lever that will start and stop the material from coming out of the spreader and a rate gage to adjust the amount of material that will come out.

Before using your and held spreader:
- Make sure it is clean and maintained.
- Make sure it is working correctly.
- Wear protective clothing and safety equipment as needed.
- Adjust the rate gage as needed.
- Inspect the areas that you are about to treat. The area should be clean and prepared for your application.
- Place one hand on the on/off lever so that you can quickly and easily start or stop the material from coming out of the spreader.

When using the spreader, always turn the handle at one constant speed. Start turning the handle, then open up the on/off lever. Watch the material as it comes out of the spreader and falls to the ground. Walk slowly around the area that you want to cover. Close the on/off lever as soon as you are finished.

Using a hand held spreader will take a little practice. Once you know how to operate it, you can quickly and professionally spot treat select lawn areas.

Tank Sprayer

A tank sprayer is a large sprayer that is used to apply a liquid application to either lawn areas or to shrubs and ornamental trees.

As a professional, you should use one tank sprayer for lawn applications only and a second tank sprayer for shrubs and ornamental trees only. Lawn tank sprayers are usually used to apply liquid weed killer applications. Even if you flush out the tank sprayer, there will still be some chemical residue left inside. If you treat shrubs and ornamental trees with the same tank sprayer that you applied weed killer with, some of the weed killer chemical residue may come out onto the shrubs you are treating. If any weed killer chemical residue makes contact with shrubs or ornamental trees, serious damage can occur. Therefore, it is better to keep a separate tank sprayer for only lawn applications and a separate tank sprayer for shrubs and ornamental trees.

Tank sprayers are mounted in the back of a truck or on a trailer. The tank that holds the liquid material will vary in size. Most tanks will hold between 100 and 300 gallons of liquid material. There will be marks on the tank that will indicate how many gallons are in the tank. Usually there is a mark for every 20 gallons. It is important that you can easily read how many gallons are in the tank so that you can mix the material and water correctly.

All tank sprayers have a lid on the top of the tank. This is where you pour the chemical material and water into the tank. There should be a screen filter mounted below the lid. The screen filter will stop any debris from getting into the tank and clogging it. There should also be a filling attachment mounted on the top of the tank.

You will connect a hose to this attachment to fill up the tank with water. This attachment will keep a space between the fill hose and the tank. The space will prevent liquid material from flowing back into the hose. This attachment is required by law in most states.

Never put the fill hose inside the tank. There must always be a space in between the hose and the tank.

There is a metal frame that will hold the tank, motor, pump and hose. Most tank sprayers have the motor and pump mounted on the lower part of the frame. Then the sprayer hose and hose reel are mounted above the motor and pump. There is a button to push, which will turn the hose reel. The hose must be pulled out manually, but will wind up by an electrical motor. When winding up the hose, guide the hose so that it wines up as close together and as even as possible.

The motor is usually a 4-cycle motor that will take regular gas. Check the motor oil level on a daily basis. The pump will pressurize the liquid material so that it can spray out of the hose. Whenever using the tank sprayer, start the pump at a low pressure. Then slowly increase the pressure to the correct level. There is a pressure gage on the pump that is used to adjust the pump pressure. Tank sprayers have two filters. One mounted below the lid and a second filter mounted between the tank and the pump. Make sure these filters are kept clean.

Inspecting and Preparing the Tank Sprayer

Before using your tank sprayer, it should be inspected.

It is very important to inspect your tank sprayer on a daily basis. Serious damage can occur if the tank sprayer breaks and liquid material leaks out at the job site.

On a daily basis, inspect the following:

- Fill the gas tank while the motor is cool. Check the motor oil level.
- Check the filter mounted between the tank and the pump. Clean it if it is a little dirty. To clean the filter, put on a pair of rubber gloves and safety glasses. The sprayer tank must be empty or you must close the valves to stop the liquid from flowing from the tank. Unscrew the filter, then bring the filter to a hose and flush out the debris from the filter. Before installing the filter, put a light layer of grease on the screw threads. The grease will prevent the filter from getting jammed up and will make it easy to remove the next time you clean it. Carefully screw the filter back on and tighten it lightly by hand.
- Remove the lid and inspect the filter mounted below the lid and clean it if needed.
- Attach the hose onto the hose attachment mounted on the top of the tank.

- Fill the tank with 5 to 10 gallons of water. Then start up the motor. Never run the motor at full speed. Adjust the throttle so the motor is always running between ½ and ¾ of the way open.
- There is a lever on the pump that will engage or disengage the pump. There is another lever to adjust the pump pressure. Engage the pump and slowly increase the pump pressure.

For lawn applications, the pump pressure should be between 50 and 100 psi. For shrub and ornamental tree applications, pump pressure should be between 100 and 250 psi.

- When the motor is running and the pump is engaged, do a visual inspection of the entire tank sprayer. First look on the outside of the tank. Look for any leaks from the hoses or pump. If there are any leaks, do not use the sprayer. The leak must be repaired before the tank sprayer can be used.
- Check the handgun mounted on the end of the sprayer hose, make sure it operates and is not leaking or dripping any liquid material. After the outside of the tank sprayer has been inspected, look inside the tank. When looking inside the tank, make sure that the agitation devise is working.
- All tank sprayers will have either a jet or mechanical agitation devise inside the tank. This agitation devise deeps the liquid material mixed at all times. If the liquid material is not mixed, the chemical and the water may start to separate. If the chemical and water separate and are then applied to lawn or shrubs, serious

damage can occur. Make sure the agitation devise is mixing up the liquid material. If the agitation devise is not mixing the liquid in the tank, do not use the tank sprayer until it is repaired and works properly.

- After your tank sprayer is inspected and prepared, you will be ready to mix the material and water. Always read and understand the product label before mixing.

Calibrating Your Spreader

As a professional you will need to calibrate your tank sprayer. By calibrating your tank sprayer, you will know how much liquid material will be applied to a certain area. Calibrate your spreader at the beginning of the year before you start using the tank sprayer on the job sites and again every few months.

Follow these steps to calibrate your tank sprayer.

- Measure and mark an area on the lawn that is 1,000 square feet. The area will need to be 20 feet wide by 50 feet long (20 × 50 feet = 1,000 square feet).
- Fill the tank sprayer with exactly 20 gallons of water.
- Attach the sprayer handgun to the hose. The sprayer handgun must be the one that you are going to use on a daily basis.

If you change the sprayer hand gun or nozzle the calibration will change. You will have to re-calibrate the sprayer if you change the sprayer hand gun or nozzle.

- Start up the motor and adjust the throttle to the motor speed that you will be using on a daily basis. This motor speed should be between ½ and ¾ of the way on. Make a mark on the throttle or motor so you can set the throttle speed the same each time you use the tank sprayer. Or, you can leave the throttle set at the correct speed and only use the on/off switch and choke when starting or stopping the motor.

- After the motor speed is correctly set, engage the pump. Then adjust the pump to the pressure that you will be using on a daily basis. For lawn applications between 50 and 100 psi. You will need to use the same pump pressure on a daily basis or the calibration will change.

- Bring the hose over to the 1,000 square foot area that you marked off. Then apply the water to the lawn area the **same way** you would apply an application. Try to walk at one standard walking speed. Apply the water until it has made good contact with the lawn. Cover the entire 1,000 square foot area.

- After the area has been treated, turn off the motor and pump. Then determine how much water is left in the tank. If there is 17 gallons left in the tank and you started with 20 gallons, you used 3 gallons of water. Now you know that you will be applying approximately 3 gallons of liquid material for every 1,000 square feet.

- Repeat the entire process that we just discussed and you should end up with approximately the same number (3 gallons per 1,000 square feet).

This number will change if the motor speed is changed, if the pump pressure is changed, if the handgun or nozzle is changed or if the applicator changes the walking speed.

As a professional applicator, you should be maintaining the same motor speed, pump pressure and application techniques on each job. By being consistent, each application will be applied correctly and you will avoid poor results or damage.

Safety Equipment

When operating a tank sprayer, you should always be wearing long pants, rubber boots, a long sleeve shirt, chemical resistant rubber gloves and safety glasses. You may also have to wear a respirator. Read the product label to see if wearing a respirator is recommended.

There are two types of respirators you can use. The first type is a rubber mask with two filter cartridges. When you breathe the airflows through the filter cartridges. There is a valve on the rubber part of the mask where you exhale. Make sure the cartridges are marked for pesticides and replace them as recommend by manufacture. Using the rubber respirator with the correct cartridges is the safest available way to protect yourself from breathing chemical spray mist.

The second type of mask is a paper mask. A paper mask is much easier to wear, but will not give you as much protection. **Make sure** the mask is labeled for use with pesticide spray mists.

Mixing

After you have inspected your tank sprayer, you can mix the liquid material. Read the product label to determine how much material will be mixed with how much water. Make sure that the mixing rate is 100% correct. After you know the mixing rate, write it down in your notebook, then it will be easy to locate in the future. Different materials will come in different forms. Materials come in liquid, granular or powder.

(Mixing) Liquid Material

- Start to fill the tank with water.
- Put on your safety clothes and equipment. Always wear glasses and a respirator when mixing.
- Carefully pour the correct amount of liquid material into your measuring cup.

You should have a separate cup for weed killer and a separate cut for insecticide and disease control. Label each measuring cup before using them.

- There should be no people or distractions around you when you are mixing. Concentrate on what you are doing so you do not make a mistake.
- Carefully bring the cup over to the tank and pour it inside the tank. Rinse out the cup with the water that is flowing into the tank. Rinse the cup several times.

- Put away the liquid material and measuring cup.

- Start up the motor and pump so that the tank mixture is being agitated. Then continue to fill the tank until the water reaches the correct amount of gallons needed.

- Remove the hose, screw on the lid and turn off the pump and motor.

(Mixing) Granular or Powder Material

A granular or wet able power is a dry material that is mixed with water. You will need to follow all the mixing instructions as above. However, there will be one additional step. Before pouring the material into the tank, it should be **pre-mixed**. Granular and power materials do not mix easily with the water in your tank. If the material does not mix correctly, poor results or serious damage can occur. By pre-mixing the material, it will mix easier with the water in your tank.

To pre-mix material use a clean 5-gallon bucket and fill it ½ way with water. Then carefully pour your measured material into the bucket. Thoroughly mix the dry material with the water. To mix the material and water, use a small stick. The best way to mix is to use a power drill and a paint mixing attachment. This will quickly, easily and thoroughly mix the dry material with the water.

After material is thoroughly mixed, carefully pour it into the tank and follow the instructions that we just discussed.

Driving With a Full Tank Sprayer

You will have to drive very carefully when you have a full tank of liquid material. Before driving, make sure the truck tires have enough air pressure. If a tire looks low on air, do not drive the truck until it is fixed. Your tank sprayer must be bolted to your truck or trailer so it cannot move during transportation. While you are drive, do not speed. Start to brake early when coming to a stop. Since the truck will be harder to stop. Never drive close behind another car. Always stay alert.

When you get to the job site, park on a hard level surface. If parking on a hill, turn the front tires towards the curb, but never rub the tires against the curb. Always use the parking brake and make sure the truck is in the parking gear. Put safety cones out around your truck as soon as you park.

Applying an Application With A Tank Sprayer

When you get to the job site, your tank sprayer should have been inspected and prepared as we just discussed.
To make an application with a tank sprayer, you must be properly trained and you should be licensed as a lawn applicator or operator.

Follow these steps when making an application with your tank sprayer.

- Visually inspect the area you are about to treat. If you are spraying close to a house or building, make sure all the windows are closed.

208

- Put a notification flag in the ground at the entrance of the property. Check your state regulations to make sure you are installing notification flags correctly.

Depending on your state regulations, you may have to let the property owner know that you are going to make an application on their property. This may have to be done with a letter a few days before you get to he job site. You may also have to notify people when you get to the job site, before you spray. In some states, neighbors of the property you are going to treat will have to get notified. Make sure you are aware of all notification rules and follow them correctly.

- After the area has been visually inspected and proper notification has been given, you should put on all your safety gear.
- Start up and set the motor and pump.
- Check your tank to see how many gallons are in the tank.
- Pull the sprayer hose out to the farthest area on the property. When you pull the hose, never pull it by the sprayer handgun. **Only grab and pull the hose.**
- Visually check the area you are about to treat. Plan out the best spray pattern to use.
- For lawn areas, you should walk back and forth the same way you walk with a spreader. Hold the handgun in one hand and hold the hose in the other hand. Remember to never pull the hose by the handgun. When you are walking across the lawn area, you should

be able to treat an area about six feet wide. By reaching your arm and the handgun from your right side to your left side. You should treat about three feet on each side of you for a total of six feet. Hold the handgun at waist height.

- Most materials will require that you spray the lawn or weeds until the plant is completely covered. Be very careful not to treat one area twice or you will cause damage to the lawn. Maintain an accurate walking pattern and look at what you are spraying to avoid this mistake.

- When spot treating weeds, use the same application method, except look for the weeds in the lawn and only treat them. If there are a lot of small weeds in an area of the lawn, treat that entire area.

- Be very careful when spraying weed killer around flowers or plants. You can slightly lower the height of the handgun so it is closer to the ground. When lowering the handgun closer to the ground, be careful not to over apply material to that area.

- If there is any wind blowing, do not treat the lawn areas that are close to any flowers or plants. On a windy day, the spray can drift very easily and cause serious damage to whatever it makes contact with. On a very windy day, it is best not to spray at all.

- After you have finished the lawn application, turn off the pump and motor. Roll up the hose as even as possible. Remove your safety gear and look at how many gallons are left in the tank. Then figure out how many gallons were used on the property and record this information in your application record book.

Check your state requirements for recording application information.

Backpack Sprayer

This type of sprayer works well and is most commonly used. The backpack pump sprayer will usually hold three gallons of mixture. Anything smaller is not recommended since you will have to stop to mix the chemical and water too often. The backpack sprayer has two straps and is carried on your shoulders and back. When opening and closing the cap, be careful to make sure the rubber seal/gasket on the screw on cap is correctly in place. Tighten the cap securely, but do not over tighten or you will break the seal and the cap will leak. When the cap starts to leak, the chemical will get onto your cloths, neck and back.

There may be a filter under the cap to catch any debris before it gets into the tank. Use this filter and do not remove it. The filter sometimes makes it hard to get the cap on correctly so some people remove it. Do not remove the filter! You will only create more problems. At the bottom of the tank is the pump and a pump arm to give you the correct spray pressure. Then there is a hose connecting the pump to the sprayer handgun. There may be another filter in the handgun or before the spray nozzle. While using this sprayer, you will use one arm to control the pump arm to give you the correct spray pressure and you will use your other arm to hold the sprayer handgun.

Before going to a job site, make sure that all the filters are clean. Also, make sure that all the hose connections are tight and secure. Then check to make sure that the spray tip is clean and sprays correctly. The filters are in place to stop any debris from getting clogged in the spray tip. There is nothing worse than mixing the chemical and then getting to the job site and having the tip clog up every few minutes. Always clean and check the sprayer before using it.

Hand Held Pump Sprayer

The handheld sprayer is basically the same as the backpack except there is a pump and handle on top of the sprayer. You have to stop working and put the sprayer down on the ground every time you have to pump it. With the backpack you can pump and spray at the same time. The hand held sprayer is more compact and will take up less room on your truck or trailer.

TYPES OF LAWN CARE APPLICATIONS
(CHAPTER 20)

Always read and understand each product label before making an application. You should be properly trained and licensed before applying most products listed in this chapter. Understand all your state requirements before making any applications. Always wear the correct safety clothes and equipment. Determine the total square feet of each lawn area before you make any applications. Keep notes and records on each lawn area that you maintain. To determine the total square feet of a property, measure the length and width of the front, back and sides. Then separately calculate each area and add up the total. See example:

Front property	*100 feet × 50 feet =*	*5000 square feet*
Back property	*100 feet × 25 feet =*	*2500 square feet*
Right side	*55 feet × 25 feet =*	*1375 square feet*
Left side	*70 feet × 10 feet =*	*700 square feet*
Total:	*9575 square feet*	

Fertilizer

Fertilizer is the most commonly used lawn application. Fertilizer provides nutrients to the lawn. A lawn cannot grow healthy without the correct nutrients. There are three main nutrients in all fertilizers; nitrogen, phosphorus and potassium.

- Nitrogen—Nitrogen helps the lawn grow and turns the lawn green in color. Nitrogen will promote top growth on the lawn but will not help the root system grow. If you apply too much nitrogen, the lawn will grow too fast. This is unhealthy for the lawn. Also, if nitrogen is applied too heavy, the lawn area can get damaged or die.

- Phosphorus—Phosphorus helps the lawn grow a strong root system. A fertilizer with a lot of phosphorus is applied when seeding or sodding since it will encourage root growth. Phosphorus also helps reduce some lawn diseases.

- Potassium—Potassium is needed to keep a lawn healthy. Without the correct amount of potassium, a lawn will become unhealthy and more likely get a disease.

A symbol is used to describe these three main nutrients. Nitrogen is simply called (N), Phosphorus (P), and Potassium (K). Plants use these three nutrients in large amounts. Many fertilizers have other nutrients besides NPK. These secondary nutrients are called micronutrients. Micronutrients are also needed to keep a lawn healthy and strong but are not used as often as NPK. Some commonly used micronutrients are iron and magnesium.

Fertilizer can come in a variety of different nutrient ratios. The nutrient ratios are listed on the product label, for example: 24-5-11. These numbers indicate the amount of NPK nutrients. The first number indicates the amount of (N) Nitrogen, the second number indicates the amount of (P) Phosphorus and the third number indicates the amount of (K) Potassium.

The product label will also indicate if there are any micronutrients in the product and if any of the nutrients are slow release. Many fertilizer products have some nutrients that are **slow release**. This means that the nutrients will gradually be released in to the soil. When NPK nutrients are released into the soil all at once, there is a chance of damaging the grass if the fertilizer was applied too heavy. A slow release product will last longer and should not damage the lawn when applied correctly.

There are two different types of fertilizers; synthetic and organic.

- Synthetic fertilizers are most commonly used. A synthetic fertilizer is a man made chemical fertilizer. A lawn will respond quickly from this type of fertilizer because it is a concentrated product. However, no mistakes can be made when applying a synthetic fertilizer or damage can occur to the lawn. Use a slow release synthetic fertilizer for best results.

- Organic fertilizers are all natural, they are made from animals and plants. They release nutrients into the soil slowly. You will not notice a quick response to the lawn after applying an organic fertilizer. Organic fertilizer will gradually improve the soil and health of the lawn. Organic fertilizers are safer to apply but are usually more difficult to apply and more costly than man made synthetic fertilizers.

215

Fertilizers are applied in granular or liquid form. Dry granular fertilizer products usually come in bags and are applied with a spreader. Always read the label to find out the recommended application rate. Then adjust the setting on your spreader as needed. Many granular fertilizer products are in slow release form. Most lawns will require approximately four fertilizer applications during the year.

When applying a granular material with a spreader, you should wear work boots, long pants, a long sleeve shirt, gloves and safety glasses. Fertilizer is not a hazardous chemical so a respirator is not needed. However, a dust mask can be worn if needed.

Liquid fertilizers usually come in a dry powder form and must be mixed into water. Liquid fertilizers are usually not in slow release form and will have to be applied more often than a granular product. Liquid fertilizers need to be mixed correctly and are applied with a tank sprayer.

When applying a liquid material with a tank sprayer, you should wear rubber boots, long pants, a long sleeve shirt, rubber gloves and safety glasses. A respirator can be worn to prevent breathing the mist from the spray.

Pre-emergent Crabgrass Control
Pre-emergent crabgrass control prevents crabgrass seeds from growing. Once crabgrass is established, it is very hard to kill.

Therefore it is easier to stop the crabgrass seeds from growing. An application of pre-emergent crabgrass control will create a chemical layer on the surface of the soil. The lawn area must be clean before the application is applied. The lawn should not be disturbed after the application is applied. The lawn area can be mowed with a lawn mower, but should not be raked, cleaned, de-thatched, aerated or seeded after the application. Grass seed will not grow on a lawn that has been treated with pre-emergent crabgrass control until the chemical is no longer in the soil. If an application has been applied in the spring, seeding must be done in the fall.

Pre-emergent crabgrass control must be applied in the early spring. The application will last into the summer. However, if the lawn and soil surface was disturbed after application, poor results will occur. Also, if there is a lot of rainfall during the spring, the chemical control will not last as long. If the lawn you are treating has a bad crabgrass problem, two applications can be applied. Check the product label for information on application rates and double treatments.

Most pre-emergent crabgrass control applications are granular and are applied with a spreader. Usually a combination product is used such as fertilizer with pre-emergent crabgrass control. When applying a granular application, it is very important to make sure the edges of the lawn receive the correct amount of the product. Crabgrass likes to grow near the edges of a lawn area and in areas where the lawn is not very thick.

Crabgrass will grow best in a sunny location. The lawn area must be cleaned of any debris before the application is applied. When applying a liquid application, the lawn should be prepared and treated the same way.

Most pre-emergent crabgrass products have a yellow color to them. This color will stain wood or stone surfaces. Blow off any granular material when you are finished with your application. Liquid applications must be applied very carefully, you should not make contact with any wood or stone surfaces.

Weed Control (Post-emergent)

A post-emergent weed control application will kill any weeds that are visibly growing in a lawn. Post-emergent means that the weeds have already germinated and grown. This type of weed control application will not kill any weed seeds. A post-emergent liquid weed control application is the most popular way to kill weeds in a lawn area. Usually the weeds are spot treated.

A post-emergent weed control application is applied onto the leaves of the existing weeds. The weed control material must make good contact with the leaves of the weed. However, do not apply too much material or you will also kill the lawn area around the weeds. When the weed control material is applied correctly, the weed will start to absorb the weed control material through its leaves. Then the material will flow through the entire weed and the weed will die. The weed must be **actively growing** or it will not absorb the material and it will not die. Therefore, the best time to apply this application is when the weeds are growing rapidly. Mid spring is the best time to make a weed control application and the second best time would be in the early fall. **Weed control should not be applied when the temperature gets very warm (over 85 degrees) or when the soil is very dry.**

When temperatures are very warm, the weed control product may kill the lawn area around the weeds you are treating. The second problem is when it gets very warm, most weeds will not grow rapidly. If the weeds are not growing rapidly, the material will not be absorbed through the weed and it will not die. Dry soil conditions are another problem. If the soil is very dry, most weeds are not growing rapidly and the weed control results will be poor. Also the lawn around the weeds will be under stressful conditions if the soil is dry. Therefore the lawn may die very easily if you apply weed control to the area. For best results, the lawn and weeds should be allowed to grow before your application. Avoid making an application when the lawn has just been mowed. If the weeds have been cut from a lawn mower, there will be less leave surface on the weed. When there is less leave surface on the weed, the application will not work it best.

Apply the liquid weed control until the entire weed has been covered, then stop immediately. If you apply too much liquid weed control, you can damage or kill the lawn area around the weeds. However, if you do not apply enough, the weed will not die.

Stay away from flowers, plants or the roots of plants. Do not apply liquid weed control on windy days. After your application, all people and pets must stay off the area. Most products will require that the application dries and stays on the weeds for a few hours before it will work. Therefore, do not apply weed control if rain is expected. Always read the product label for instructions, recommendations and safety precautions before using it.

Before making an application, plan out a walking pattern on the lawn. Then be very careful not to treat an area twice or serious damage can occur. On warm days, sidewalks and driveways will heat up. You must be careful when treating weeds around these areas since the soil may be very warm and dry. If you apply weed control to areas that are very warm and dry, the lawn may die.

Granular products are also used to kill weeds. However, they are very difficult to use. For a granular product to make contact with the weeds, the weeds must be wet. If the weeds are not wet, the product will not stick to the weed and poor results will occur. The lawn and weeds should not be cut short before the application and you will have to stay off the area for a longer period of time. Avoid making contact with flowers, plants, or the roots of plants.

Most products, liquid or granular will take about 7 to 14 days to completely kill the weed. Some hard to kill weeds may need a second application to completely stop the problem.

Weed Control (Pre-emergent)

A pre-emergent weed control application will kill weed seeds before they can germinate and grow. This type of weed control application is not used very often to control weeds in a lawn area. The application is expensive and you must treat the entire lawn for it to be effective. This type of application is used more often in landscape beds.

The best time to apply a pre-emergent weed control application is in the early spring. The application will last a few months and can also be applied during other times of the entire year. The lawn area must be clean before the material is applied and the lawn should not be disturbed after the treatment.

The application works the same as pre-emergent crabgrass control except the chemical material will control weeds instead. A dry granular product is used most often, however a liquid product is also available.

Surface Insect Control

Surface insect control is used to kill insects that are feeding on a lawn. Whenever an insect feeds on a lawn, damage will occur. If the problem is not stopped quickly there will be permanent damage to the lawn. Surface insects are insects that feed on the top part of the grass plant, they do not feed on the root system. These insects can travel from one lawn to another. When they find a lawn area that they like, they will make a home there. Then they will feed on the lawn and increase their family members.

These insects usually start creating lawn damage when the temperature gets warm in the spring and early summer. When there is a week or two of temperatures over 75 degrees, these insects will become active. Then they can do damage throughout the year until temperatures stay well below 75 degrees.

Most surface insects prefer a sunny lawn area. Lawns that have a thick layer of thatch will get insects more often. The thatch layer is the layer of old dead grass between the top of the lawn and the soil. Insects like to make a home in a thick layer of thatch. Surface insects also prefer a lawn that is well-fertilized or over fertilizer. Over-fertilizing creates lots of tender new growth, insects prefer a lawn with lots of tender new growth.

Surface insects will discolor areas of the lawn when they are feeding. After the lawn discolors, it may turn brown and die. If you see any discolored areas of the lawn, inspect it more closely to determine if there is an insect problem.

Many times, surface insects will be too small to see with the human eye. Use a magnifying glass, an insect identification book and think about the site conditions to determine the problem. If you are still unsure, take a sample of the discolored lawn and bring it to a local garden center or college. When taking samples, remove a partially discolored area and not the lawn areas that are already completely brown and dead. Remove the entire grass plant including the roots. Put the sample in container or wrap it in paper. Then get it looked at as soon as possible.

There are many different types of insect control products. You should identify the type of insect before choosing a control product. Then read the product label to make sure it will kill the insects causing the problem. Both liquid and granular products work well. When applying a liquid material, you will kill the insects immediately. When applying a granular material, the application will not work until it is watered in correctly.

Once the material is released onto the lawn, it will kill any insects on the area. Then it will stay effective and protect the lawn for a period of time. Different products will be effective for different periods of time. Some products last only a few days while other products will stay effective for weeks.

Soil Insect Control

Soil insects live in the soil and feed on the root system of a lawn. The most common soil insect is called a grub. Grubs feed on the lawns root system, and if left untreated, they will cause serious damage. Most of the damage is done in the late summer and early fall. However, if there is a large population of grubs in the soil, damage can also be done in the spring.

Grubs also prefer sunny lawn areas. However, grubs will live on almost any lawn. You can get a grub problem if the lawn is highly maintained or not maintained at all. To locate a grub problem, look for discolored areas of lawn during the **late summer and early fall**. If there are a lot of birds digging in the lawn, there will most likely be a grub problem. Birds like to eat the grubs. Grab onto the discolored lawn and if the lawn lifts up easily, you have grubs. Grubs will eat all the roots, then the top of the lawn will lift off the ground very easily. If you lift up the lawn and look at the soil, you should be able to find some grubs. They look like small white worms that are about one inch long. They are usually curled up in the soil.

There are two different ways to control grubs and other soil insects; pre-emergent or post-emergent.

Pre-emergent Grub Control

Pre-emergent control is usually applied when you know there was a grub problem during the previous year or to a highly maintained lawn area. This application is applied in the spring or early summer. The material will be released into the soil and kill the grubs before they can damage the lawn. This application is usually a granular treatment. By applying the pre-emergent control, you know that the lawn area is safe and no damage will occur.

Post-emergent Grub Control

Post-emergent control is applied directly to the active problem. Some lawn damage is usually done before making an application. Most products will only be effective for a few days; therefore, the application cannot be applied until you visibly see a problem.

There are liquid or granular products available; however, granular products are used most often. Any granular material must be watered immediately after the application or it will not be effective. If there is a large grub problem or if there is a heavy layer of thatch, a second application may need to be applied.

Crabgrass Control (Post-emergent)

Post-emergent crabgrass control is used to kill any crabgrass that has started to establish in a lawn area. This application will be a spot treatment to select areas. The application must be applied when the crabgrass is still young. Once the crabgrass is fully matured, it will be almost impossible to kill and the application should not be made.

A pre-emergent crabgrass application is easier to apply and will control crabgrass better than a post-emergent application. To control a crabgrass problem, always apply a pre-emergent application in the early spring.

If a lawn has a serious crabgrass problem or if the pre-emergent application was applied incorrectly, some crabgrass will start to grow during the early summer. Also, if there was a lot of rainfall during the spring, the pre-emergent application may have gotten washed out of the soil too early, then crabgrass will be able to grow.

If you see any crabgrass starting to grow in a lawn in the early summer, a post-emergent application should be applied immediately. If the crabgrass was found in the summer when it has already matured, it will be best to wait until the next year to control the problem.

When the crabgrass is young and actively growing, apply a post-emergent spray. Post-emergent crabgrass control is a liquid application. It is usually mixed in a small amount and sprayed from a backpack sprayer. The crabgrass you are spraying must be **actively growing** and the crabgrass plant should not be cut before your application. The crabgrass must be left as long as possible so that the spray can make good contact with it.

Most products will need to stay on the crabgrass for at least 24 hours to be effective. A second application is usually needed to completely kill the crabgrass. Return in about 7 to 14 days to make a second application. Always read the product label and instructions before making any application.

When you make the application, you will be spot spraying each crabgrass plant. Apply the spray until the crabgrass is completely covered, then stop immediately. Crabgrass control will kill the lawn area if it is applied too heavy. Avoid spraying if the soil is very dry and if the lawn around the crabgrass is under any stress. The lawn should be healthy and actively growing or the application should not be made. Spraying onto a stressed lawn area will kill the lawn.

Post-emergent crabgrass control will not work or cause more damage than good if it is not applied correctly. If the conditions are not right, do not make the application. This product is also very expensive, therefore, if you have a large area infested with crabgrass, it would be best to wait until the next spring when you can apply a pre-emergent application.

If all the conditions are right and if the application is made correctly, crabgrass can be stopped with a post-emergent spray before it grows into a large ugly weed. If you are unable to make the application, keep the lawn mowed as high as possible. This will make it harder for the crabgrass to grow. Crabgrass will turn brown and die with the first frost. Then be sure to make a pre-emergent application next spring.

Wild Grass Control

Wild grasses are unwanted wild types of grass that infest and spread throughout a lawn area. Wild grasses are aggressive and will spread quickly throughout a lawn area if left untreated. Pre-emergent crabgrass control or weed control will not kill most types of wild grass.

A special product can be used to treat most wild grasses. The wild grass control product is a post-emergent spray. It is similar to post-emergent crabgrass control. The conditions must be just right and the product must be applied correctly or it will not work. Wild grass control is applied from a backpack sprayer.

Follow these instructions when applying a wild grass control application.

- Spot treat wild grass **before** it spreads into large areas. trying to control large areas of wild grass in a lawn will be very expensive and difficult.

- Read the product label to find out general instructions and if the product will kill the wild grass you are spraying. Identify all the wild grasses you are trying to kill and make sure you are using the correct product.

- Treat the wild grass when it is young and actively growing. If the wild grass is already mature, two treatments may be needed. Do not make application during hot or dry weather.

- Do not cut the wild grass with a lawn mower. The wild grass must be as large as possible so that the spray can make good contact with it. When the spray makes good contact with the wild grass, it will be most effective. If the wild grass has been cut with a lawn mower, the application will not work.

- Make the application with a backpack sprayer or hand held sprayer. Most products need to be thoroughly mixed before each job and the mixture should be finished during the day.

- Apply the spray until the wild grass is completely covered, then stop immediately. If you over apply, the product will kill the lawn around the wild grass.

- After the application has been made, do not cut or water the treated wild grass for at least 24 hours.

Some wild grasses cannot be killed from wild grass control products. If you have identified the wild grass and if there is no wild grass control product available, you will have to use a non-selective control product.

Non-selective means it will kill everything **including** the lawn. A non-selective control product is also much less expensive than wild grass control. When using a non-selective control product, you will have to re-seed the areas that you treated. Therefore, it is best to make an application in the late summer and return in the early fall to re-seed the areas that you treated.

When spot spraying wild grasses in a lawn area with a non-selective control product, you must be very careful. Hold the spray tip close to the ground, use low pump pressure, and never make the application during windy weather.

Sometimes manually removing the wild grass will work best. If the wild grass does not have a deep root system, remove it with a pick. Then you can reseed the same day. By manually removing the wild grass, there will not be any ugly, brown spots in the lawn from the chemical spray.

Disease Control
There are many different types of disease. Disease can occur and cause damage to a lawn area during any time of the year. However,

most lawn diseases will be active during the spring and summer. Weather conditions will cause lawn diseases and damage to increase or decrease. When weather conditions are very rainy and wet, or when it is humid, disease will increase. Also if a sprinkler system is watering the lawn too often or at the wrong time of the day, a lawn disease will get worse. If the lawn area is healthy, it may be able to withstand the disease. A healthy lawn may also repair itself after the disease has stopped. An unhealthy lawn will get a disease much easier, and will not be able to repair itself after the disease has stopped.

Disease control applications are **very** expensive and must be applied many times to prevent or stop a lawn disease. It is always best to try to prevent a lawn disease **before** it happens. As a lawn care professional, you should know how to help reduce and prevent disease before it happens. Then if a lawn disease still occurs, it will require less chemical control application.

To help prevent lawn disease problems, follow these instructions.

Keep the lawn healthy by fertilizing it on a regular basis throughout the year.
- Give the lawn a soil test to determine if there are any soil deficiencies. Then correct any soil deficiencies as needed.
- Check the soil pH level and then make lawn application as needed to correct and maintain the soil pH level.

- Remove any heavy thatch from the lawn. Disease will live in the thatch layer and it will be very difficult to control unless the heavy thatch is removed.

- Mow the lawn on a regular basis. Keep the lawn cut high; do not cut the lawn too low. When the lawn is cut too low, it will get disease much easier.

- Make sure your mower blades are always sharp. Dull blades will tear the grass instead of cutting it. When the lawn was cut with a dull blade, disease can infect the lawn very easily.

- If the lawn has any disease, collect the grass clippings when you mow the lawn.

- When you are finished mowing a lawn with disease, clean under the mower deck before you use the lawn mower again. Scrap under the mower deck, then spray it with a 50/50 bleach and water mix.

- If the lawn has a sprinkler system, make sure it is used correctly. Water in the morning only; between 4:00 a.m. and 9:00 a.m. Never water at night. If the lawn is wet overnight, a disease problem will occur much easier than if it was dry.

- Give the lawn a **heavy** watering a few times per week. This will help the lawn develop a deep root system and will allow the lawn to dry out in between waterings.

- **Do not** water the lawn lightly and on a daily basis. When you give the lawn many light waterings, the lawn will be constantly wet. The root system will not get the water and will become unhealthy. Instead of growing deep into the soil, the roots will grow near the surface. With a shallow root system, the lawn will become unhealthy and get diseases easier.

- Improve drainage conditions if the lawn is constantly wet. Core aeration will help improve drainage. It will also help reduce thatch and promote a deep root system.

If there is an active disease in a lawn that is causing damage, you will need to apply a chemical control to stop the problem. It is best to control any disease as soon as it starts. Then you can control the disease before it spreads and the areas may only need to be spot treated.

Before treating any lawn disease, you must identify the type of disease. As a lawn care professional, you should become familiar with the most common diseases in your area. Take a class at your local college and get a good book on lawn disease identification. Then keep the book in your truck to help you identify a disease when you find one. If you cannot correctly identify the disease, take a sample and bring it to your state agricultural college. They will be able to identify the disease and may also recommend the correct control product.

Never apply a chemical control application to a lawn disease if the disease was not identified. There are many different types of diseases and chemical control products. Always read the product label to make sure it will stop the disease that you identified. Disease control products are very expensive and will not work if they are not chosen and applied correctly.

Disease control products will be granular or liquid. Some granular products must be applied when the lawn is wet so the product sticks to the lawn. Then the lawn must remain dry and undisturbed; avoid using this type of product. The second type of granular product is used more often. It is applied to the lawn when it is dry. Then the product must be watered in. Liquid products will work best. Liquid products can be mixed in a backpack sprayer or tank sprayer. Liquid products will start to work as soon as they make contact with the lawn and do not have to be watered in.

If the disease is bad, it may require a second or third application. Always read the product label for instruction and recommendation on the product. Always wear the correct clothes and safety equipment when making an application.

Limestone
Limestone is used to adjust or maintain the soil pH level. By having the correct soil pH level, the lawn will be helped in the following ways.

- The lawn will be able to absorb all the nutrients from the soil. With an **incorrect** pH level, the lawn will **not be** able to absorb the nutrients that are available in the soil.
- Better results from fertilizer application.
- Increased green color of the lawn.
- With the correct pH level, the lawn will not get disease as easy.

- Thatch problems will take longer to develop.
- The correct pH level will give the lawn better overall health. A healthy lawn will be more resistant to disease, insects, weeds and stress from bad weather.

To find out how much limestone a lawn needs, the area should be measured to determine the total square feet. Then a soil pH test should be taken. By knowing the total square feet of the lawn area and the soil pH results, you will be able to determine how much limestone is needed for the lawn area. Instructions and application rates will be found on the product label.

Do not apply limestone if you do not know the soil pH level. Some lawns may not need any limestone. Applying the incorrect amount of limestone to a lawn area can cause poor results or even add stress to the lawn. Always take a soil pH test before making any application. After the test has been done, you can correct and maintain the soil pH level. If you maintain the correct soil pH level, a test will not be needed the following year.

Limestone is a granular product that usually comes in 50 lbs. bags. It comes pulverized or pelletized. The pelletized is best because it will not blow away when used in windy weather conditions. Avoid getting the limestone into the landscape beds. The product is very safe; however, the dust can irritate your nose. Wear a dust mask when applying limestone. Limestone will take a few months to break down into the soil. You will not get quick, noticeable results from limestone. Limestone can be applied any time of the year; however, it is usually applied during the late fall or early winter. Then the application will be effective for the following season.

CORE-AERATION AND DE-THATCHING
(CHAPTER 21)

To maintain a healthy lawn, you will have to do more than basic lawn care applications. Over the years, a lawn can decline because of compacted soil or excessive thatch build-up. Core-aeration or de-thatching will be needed to stop these problems and to maintain a healthy lawn. Both of these services should be done in the late summer to fall season. During the spring, there are many active weeds. When a lawn is aerated or de-thatched, soil will be exposed. Then weeds may grow in the exposed soil areas before the lawn can. Spot seeding or over-seeding is usually done with aeration or de-thatching. Late summer and fall are the best time for seeding.

Core-Aeration
Benefits of Core-Aeration
A lawn can never grow healthy and strong with compacted soil Water and nutrients cannot penetrate the surface of compacted soil. Soil also needs air, if the soil is compact with little or no air, the lawn will do poorly. If this problem is not corrected, the lawn will not be able to develop a deep root system, instead the lawn will develop a shallow root system. A lawn with a shallow root system cannot take any stressful conditions and will die very easily or may die out on it's own.

Lawns gradually compact over the years from simply walking on them. When heavy lawn mowers are used or if the lawn is used for sports or parties, the soil can become compacted in a year or two.

To keep a lawn healthy and avoid compact soil, core-aeration should be done every two years. After the lawn and soil are aerated, the lawn will benefit in many ways.

- Lawn applications will be more effective since they can reach the root zone area. The lawn absorbs applications from the roots. If the application cannot reach the root zone poor results will occur.

- Water will also be more effective since it will reach the root zone much easier. This will allow the grass to grow a deep root system. With a deep root system, the lawn will be able to withstand stressful conditions. When the soil is hard and compact, a lot of water will run off the lawn and will not penetrate the soil.

- If a sprinkler system is used, you will be able to reduce the amount of water being put on the lawn since each watering will be more effective.

Note: When watering each section of lawn, you will need 30 to 45 minutes of water. A heavy watering will encourage a deep root system and a healthy lawn. If you reduce watering, it is better to eliminate one day instead of reducing the time.

- Air will be able to penetrate the soil. As we discussed earlier, air is needed in the soil to grow a healthy lawn.

- Aeration will help improve drainage. If water is laying on the surface of the lawn, aeration will help it penetrate the soil and keep the area drier.

- Aeration stimulates new growth. An unhealthy lawn will have all the benefits we just discussed; therefore, it will be able to grow stronger and healthier after aeration.

Core-aeration (Work Procedures)

Most aerating is done with a power aerator machine. A power aerator has many hollow metal tubes (tines) that slowly spin around as the machine moves. The tines press into the ground and pull out a plug of grass and soil. Then the plugs fall back into the lawn. The plugs do not have to be raked up, they will dry up and fall apart in a few weeks. A manual aeration tool should be used for small pieces of lawn or on areas that are hard to reach with the power aerator machine.

Core aeration should be done shortly after the lawn has been cut. Before aerating any lawn area, you **must** inspect the entire lawn area. Using 12 inch marker flags, mark anything in the lawn that needs to be avoided. Such as: sprinkler system heads or exposed pipes; any exposed drain, sewer, gas, or water pipes; any electrical wires that are not buried correctly; invisible electrical dog fence; large stones or objects that can damage the aeration machine.

Always talk with the property owner before aerating to determine what needs to be marked. After everything has been clearly marked, you will be able to work.

Operate the aerator across the lawn the same way you would operate a lawn mower. First go around the outside perimeter. Then make passes back and forth across the lawn. Most aerators have a bar that will lower or raise the tines. The tines will have to be raised up out of the ground whenever you make a sharp turn. Then lowered back down for the next pass. When making a gradual turn, you should be able to leave the tines down and manually turn the machine while it is moving.

A control lever will engage or disengage the tines from turning. **Do not** engage the tines until they are lowered into the ground. Disengage the tines before raising them up. When the tines are turning in the ground, the machine will move forward. When using the machine on a straight, flat surface, you can run the machine at full speed. When working on a slope or hill, be very careful. Work across the hill, not up and down since the machine has no brakes. Also, run the machine at a slower speed. Keep the tines away from stones, sidewalks or driveways. Damage can occur to both the tines and the sidewalk or driveway.

When you are finished with the entire lawn, remove all the marker flags and you are finished. After the job is done, water and fertilize the lawn area. Spot seeding or over-seeding can also be done after aeration. We will discuss spot seeding and over-seeding in the next chapter.

De-thatching

Thatch develops from the build up of old grass parts. As the grass grows, it sheds off these old dead parts. These old dead parts of the grass plant decompose very slowly and develop into a spongy layer between the grass and the root system. Thatch happens naturally and is not caused by grass clippings left on the lawn. Grass clippings decay quickly and do more good than harm to a lawn.

If a lawn is fertilized incorrectly, by constantly using a high nitrogen fertilizer thatch buildup will occur much quicker than normal. Compacted soil and the constant use of pesticides will help a thatch build up quicker than normal. Mowing too much of the grass off in one mowing, or mowing infrequently will also increase the thatch layer. Some grass types such as Blue grass, Bermuda grass and Zoysia grass produce thatch quicker than other grass types.

To determine if a lawn has a thatch problem, use a spade to remove a small section of the lawn. The layer between the root system and blades of grass is the thatch layer. Look at your sample piece. If the thatch layer is ½ inch or thicker, the lawn has a thatch problem. Also, when you walk on a lawn with a thatch problem, it will feel very spongy.

A thin layer of thatch is normal and needed. The thin layer of thatch protects the grass plant, but a layer of ½ inch or more will prevent lawn applications, water and air from penetrating into the soil and root system of the lawn. A shallow root system will develop since all the water is trapped in the thatch layer; a lawn with shallow roots is unhealthy. The moist thatch layer will become a home for insects and diseases. Problems will increase and the lawn beauty will decrease. The heavy thatch layer must be reduced to solve all of these problems.

De-thatching (Work Procedures)

Most de-thatching is done with a power de-thatching machine or (power rake). The de-thatching machine will quickly rake out and reduce a heavy layer of thatch. It can be adjusted higher or lower, to take the thatch to the level you want.

De-thatching should be done shortly after the lawn has been cut. Inspect and mark any objects to avoid in the lawn. Such as sprinkler heads, pipes or stones. Operate the de-thatching machine the same way you mow a lawn. First go around the perimeter, then make passes back and forth across the lawn. Most de-thatching machines have two levers; one to engage the power rake and another to raise or lower it into the ground. Start with the machine on the highest setting, engage the power rake and push the machine across a small section of the lawn. Lower the setting until the machine removes almost all of the thatch layer. Do not go too deep or you can damage the lawn. If you see a lot of soil, you are going too deep. After you find the correct setting, push the machine across the entire lawn. When the power rake

241

is engaged and lowered in the ground, the machine will be easier to push. Avoid hitting any sidewalks, driveways or stones. Small areas of lawn can be de-thatched manually with a de-thatching rake.

When you are finished using the machine, you will need to rake up and dispose of all of the thatch that was removed from the lawn. This should be done with a leave rake. Using a leave rake together with a ground blower will get the work done faster. Bring some large wheelbarrows to put the piles of thatch into, then dispose of the thatch.

After the job is done, water and fertilize the lawn area. Spot seeding or over-seeding can also be done after de-thatching. We will discuss spot seeding and over-seeding in the next chapter.

SPOT SEEDING, OVER-SEEDING, AND SLICE SEEDING
(CHAPTER 22)

Seeding of an existing lawn area is done for various different reasons. Spot seeding is done to repair poor areas of an existing lawn. When spot seeding, it is very important to use the **same** type of grass seed as the existing lawn. If you use a different type of seed, the spot seeded areas may look different from the rest of the lawn.

Over seeding is done to blend a newer, better quality seed into an older lawn. Over seeding will help convert a thin, weak lawn into a thick healthy lawn. Many of the new types of grass seed are more resistant to insects and diseases. They are also more resistant to drought, have an improved appearance and are greener in color. Over seeding is also done when property conditions have changed. Over the years, trees grow larger and create more shade. If the lawn consists of a grass seed that requires sun, it will start to decline as the shade increases. To have a thick, healthy lawn, a shade seed will need to be over seeded into the lawn.

Slice seeding is used in the lawn renovation process or to incorporate a newer seed into an older, poor quality lawn. The slice seeding machine will cut through the thatch layer and into the surface of the soil. Then the grass seed will fall into these slices and make contact with the soil. Seed to soil contact is needed for grass seed to germinate. A lawn that has been slice seeded will establish quicker and thicker than the over seeding method.

Grass seed comes in a variety of different mixtures such as: Full Sun, Sun, Sun & Shade, Shade and Dense Shade. Make sure that you choose the correct seed mixture to meet the specific conditions of each job. Always choose a top quality seed mixture.

Before you purchase grass seed, read the grass seed label and look for the following:

- Conditions where the seed will grow.
- Names and percentage of grass types.
- Germination percentage of at least 85%.
- Weed seed content no more than 0.5%.
- Inert matter no more than 1%.
- Unwanted seed types no more than 1%.
- A date for freshness that is less than a year old.

In most regions of the country, the best time to grow grass seed is in the **early** fall. In the fall, the ground is still warm which helps speed up the germination process. The air is cool during the night. The cool air helps the soil stay moist for a longer period of time. The seed must remain moist or it will not germinate, when grass seed is established in the fall, it has more time to develop a strong root system before stressful summer conditions arrive. Early spring is the next best time to grow grass seed. Never try to establish grass seed during the summer.

Tools and Equipment

You will need the following tools and equipment to spot seed, over seed or slice seed. A slice seeding machine, a de-thatching machine, rotary spreader, drop spreader, hand held spreader, a clean five gallon bucket for seed, a lawn roller, a utility knife, wheelbarrows, plastic leave rake, metal bow rake, grading rake, de-thatching rake, shovels, and a back pack blower.

You should wear gloves and consider wearing a dust mask.

Spot Seeding (Work Procedures)

- Inspect the job site and determine the correct type of seed to be used. If the wrong type of grass seed is used, the spot seed areas will look different than the rest of the lawn. Determine how much seed will be needed.
- Determine if any additional topsoil will be needed on the areas to be spot seeded. If the soil conditions are poor or eroded, additional topsoil should be used.
- Before starting the work, the lawn should be mowed. Mow the lawn slightly lower than normal.
- Prepare the areas for the grass seed. If the areas to be seeded are mostly soil, use a metal bow rake to thoroughly loosen up the surface of the soil. If there is thatch in the lawn areas to be seeded,

remove the thatch with a de-thatching rake. If the soil conditions are poor or eroded, spread a layer of topsoil over the areas.

Note: All the areas to be spot seeded must be prepared correctly or the seed will not grow.

- The seed can be spread out over the areas by hand or by using a spreader. If you are spreading the seed by hand, put the seed into a five-gallon bucket. Then toss the seed over each area. **Make sure the seed is spread evenly**. Do not get any seed into landscape beds or unwanted areas. If you are using a spreader, set the spreader to the correct setting. Then carefully spread the seed over each area. Be careful when using a rotary spreader. The rotary spreader will spread seed six to eight feet wide. A drop spreader will only spread seed 3 to 4 feet wide; therefore it works best when seeding near landscape beds or sidewalks. When spot seeding, it is always best to apply a generous amount of seed for the best results.
- Apply starter fertilizer at the correct rate over each area with a rotary or drop spreader or by hand. Do not apply the starter fertilizer any heavier than the recommended rate or you may damage the seed.
- Apply hay over each area. Spread the hay as evenly as possible. Apply more to sloped areas or to open topsoil areas. Starter mulch is a new product that will protect the grass seed and works better than hay. This product comes in bags and can be spread by hand or from a drop spreader. The product material comes in pellets.

These pellets dissolve after a heavy watering and form a protective layer over the grass seed. The product stays on the ground and will not blow away like hay does. Starter mulch works great for spot seeding but is too expensive to cover larger areas.

- After the areas have been seeded and covered with starter mulch or hay, you will need to roll each area. Rolling will press the seeds into the soil. The seeds **must** make good contact with the soil or they will not grow. Fill the lawn roller with water and roll all the areas you seeded.

- Make sure that the property owner waters each area on a daily basis until the seed is a few inches tall. Then continue to water every few days for eight weeks. Poor results will occur if watering is not done properly. Detailed watering instructions will be explained later in this chapter.

Over seeding (Work Procedures)

- Inspect and measure the lawn area to determine the correct type of seed to use and the amount of seed needed.
- Only use high quality seed.
- Read the label on the seed and find out the recommended amount of seed required for your job. You will need to measure the area to determine the square feet. Then you will be able to purchase the correct amount of seed for your job.
- To determine the square feet of a property, measure the length and width of the front, back and sides or property. Then separately calculate each area.

For example:

Front property:	100 feet × 50 feet =	5000 square feet
Back property:	100 feet × 25 feet =	2500 square feet
Right side:	55 feet × 25 feet =	1375 square feet
Left side:	70 feet × 10 feet =	700 square feet
total of property:		9575 square feet

Round off the number. 9,575 square feet would be rounded off to 10,000 square feet. Now you can purchase enough seed to over-seed a lawn that is 10,000 square feet in size. Always purchase a little extra seed. You will need extra seed so that you can apply it generously and so that you have some extra to spot seed any areas that did not grow.

- De-thatch the entire lawn area (as discussed in the previous chapter).

Note: Over seeding will not work unless the thatch layer is removed and the grass seed can make contact with the soil.

- Mow the lawn area slightly lower than normal. After the lawn has been over seeded, you will need to stay off the areas for as long as possible. By mowing the lawn low, you should be able to stay off the lawn for about two weeks.
- Add topsoil to any poor areas of the lawn.

- For best results, a soil test should have been taken a few weeks before starting the job (as discussed in Chapter 5 of this book). Apply the correct type of application as recommended by the soil test. **If fertilizer is needed to correct a soil deficiency, the nutrients may be available in the starter fertilizer that will be applied. Be careful not to apply too much fertilizer or the seed can get damaged and may not grow.**

- Apply an application of starter fertilizer. Starter fertilizer is used to help establish the root system of seed and sod. **Always check the recommendation on the bag of starter fertilizer. Never apply any more than recommended. If you apply more than recommended, you may burn out the new seed because the fertilizer application is too strong.**

- Apply seed to all the edges of the new lawn area. Use a hand spreader or put seed into a clean bucket and spread it by hand. Be careful not to get any grass seed into the landscape beds or other areas where grass is not wanted. The seed must be applied evenly and at the correct rate. **Avoid applying the seed too heavy or too light. Avoid clumps of seeds on the ground.** Apply the seed at least two feet wide from all the edges. The edges can also be seeded by using a drop spreader. A drop spreader will spread the seeds close to the edges without getting the seeds into the landscape beds.

- After the edges have been completed, use a rotary spreader to spread seed on the larger areas of the property. A rotary spreader will spread seed approximately six to eight feet wide in one pass. A drop spreader will spread seed approximately three feet wide in a pass. Adjust the spreader to the correct rate. When applying the seed, walk at the same speed throughout the entire area. By walking at the same speed, the seed will be applied evenly. Slightly overlap the seed when making each pass with the spreader.

- Cover the entire area with hay. They hay will help hold moisture around the seed and it will help prevent damage to the new seed from a heavy rainfall. It will also help discourage birds from eating the new seeds. Put the bails of hay into wheelbarrows to move them around the property. **Spread the hay by hand as evenly as possible.** If there is a slope or area that will get a lot of run off from a rainfall, apply more hay to protect the area.

- Then, you will need to roll the entire area. By rolling the area, you will push the seeds into the soil. The seeds must make good contact with the soil or they will not grow. Fill the lawn roller with water and roll the entire area.

Slice Seeding (Work Procedures)

Note: If the lawn has a heavy thatch layer, de-thatching should be done first.

- Inspect and measure the lawn area to determine the correct type of seed to use and the amount of seed needed.
- The lawn should be mowed slightly lower than normal.
- Mark any sprinkler heads, pipes, etc. in the lawn area.
- Fill the slice-seeding machine with seed and adjust it to the correct rate. Most machines have a rate chart that will tell you the correct

setting for each type of seed. There is a control lever used to turn the seed on or off.

- A lever is used to drive the machine forward or in reverse. The machine can also be raised or lowered similar to the de-thatching machine. Always start the machine on the highest setting.

- Underneath the machine there are blades that spin and will cut into the ground. A control lever will turn the blades on or off.

- Place the machine on the lawn. With the machine on the highest setting, engage the blades and drive forward a few feet. Inspect the lawn, the blades should cut through the lawn and thatch and scratch the surface of the soil. **The blades must scratch the surface of the soil but not cut too deep into the soil.** When the correct height is set, you will be able to start seeding. Open the seed control lever.

- Operate the slice seeder around the perimeter of the lawn area first. Then make passes back and forth across the lawn similar to the way the lawn is mowed.

- Turn off the seed when turning the machine. Stay away from any flagged off areas. Refill the machine with seed as needed.

- After the lawn has been slice seeded, apply starter fertilizer and any applications needed to correct soil deficiencies (as per soil test)

The correct instructions must be followed after the seed has been installed or poor results will occur. Read the following information, then make sure the customer is fully aware of these instructions and what they need to do to get the seed established.

1. Watering of entire area must be done as needed in order to keep seed, sod, and soil moist at all times.
2. Lawn areas must remain moist for 4 to 8 weeks to insure proper germination and root development. Seeds germinate at different time periods; continue to water up to 8 weeks for best results. After an 8-week period, water generously at least twice per week throughout the remaining year.
3. **Do not** discontinue watering when some green up is noticed.
4. Make sure to allow the lawn and ground to completely dry before mowing. To accomplish this you should not water the day before mowing. The first 4 to 8 mowings should be done very carefully since the grass has not matured, and root system is not fully developed. Keep the mower height on highest setting possible.
5. Try and keep people and pets off new lawn area for 4 to 8 weeks, or damage and poor results will occur.
6. Regular scheduled fertilizer applications should be applied starting approximately 30 days after seeding.
7. Do not apply pesticides to your new lawn area until approximately 12 weeks after germination, carefully read the label on any lawn products you may apply.
8. Additional spot seeding of new lawn areas may be needed to insure a beautiful thick lawn. Spot seed as soon as possible after first seeding is approximately 75% established; this will also help avoid a weed problem.

RENOVATING, SOIL TESTING AND MAINTAINING AN EXISTING LAWN (CHAPTER 23)

In this chapter, we will explain how to change (renovate) a poor quality unhealthy lawn into a healthy and beautiful lawn.

We will also discuss how to professionally maintain an existing lawn. Before you start to maintain a lawn, you should make an inspection of the area. Some lawns will have many different problems. Applications alone may not improve the lawn. You should consider renovating when:

- The existing lawn is not thick, green and healthy. It has deteriorated throughout the years.
- The existing lawn has not improved much from the lawn applications.
- The existing lawn has constant insect and disease problems.
- The existing lawn is made from a low-quality grass seed mixture.
- The existing lawn needs to be improved by blending a new high quality grass seed mixture into the lawn.
- An existing lawn area has been changed from a sunny area to a shady area because trees have grown larger. The lawn needs to be upgraded by blending a (shady) grass seed mixture into the lawn.

- If you are trying to reduce pesticide use, upgrade a lawn by blending an (endofyte) enhanced grass seed into the lawn. Endofyte enhanced grass is resistant to some insects and diseases.

After you have determined that a lawn needs a renovation, you will need to plan out the job. If there are weeds and other problems with the lawn, the renovation process can take a full year to complete. Plan on removing any weeds, insects, wild grasses, etc. in the spring and early summer. Then the lawn area will be ready for a late summer/early fall seeding. All renovations will be slightly different. Some will take a full year to complete while others can be done in one visit.

We will now discuss the steps needed to complete a lawn renovation. The lawn we are discussing is in very bad condition and the renovation will take a full year to complete.

Lawn Renovation (Work Procedures)
- Measure the lawn area to determine the total square feet (as explained in the last chapter).
- Take a soil test. By taking a soil test, you will find out if there are any soil deficiencies. Then you can correct the deficiencies before seeding the lawn. A lawn will never grow healthy and strong if there are soil deficiencies. You must take a soil test.

Soil Test

To take a soil test, you will need a small hand shovel or a special tool used for removing soil samples. Try to remove a piece of soil that is approximately six inches deep and one or two inches wide. Remove a small piece of soil from this sample and put it into a bag. Repeat this process at least six times and take the samples from different areas of the lawn. Then thoroughly mix the pieces of soil together in the bag and bring it to a soil testing laboratory.

A soil test can be done by your Local Cooperative Extension Service (usually this part of an agricultural college) or by a private soil-testing laboratory. The results will include: Nitrogen, Phosphorus, Potassium, Soil pH, Organic content, and Micronutrients.

Nitrogen, Phosphorus and Potassium are the three major nutrients that all plants need. If one of these elements is low there will be a problem.

Soil pH. Even if all the other nutrients are available in the soil, they may not be able to be absorbed by the plant if the soil pH level is incorrect. Soil pH levels range from 1 to 14 and a level between 6.0 and 7.5 works best. The level between 6.0 and 7.5 is called Neutral. Anything below 6.0 is called Acidic soil; anything about 7.5 is called Alkaline. By have the correct pH level, the lawn will be able to absorb all the nutrients in the soil and become healthier and stronger.

To adjust the soil pH level to neutral:

- When the soil is Acidic, apply limestone to **raise** the pH.

- When the soil is Alkaline, apply sulfur to **lower** the pH.

Organic Content—the soil test should also let you know how much organic matter is in the soil. Organic matter is needed for a lawn to grow healthy.

Micro Nutrients—Micronutrients are secondary nutrients that the plant needs. They include Calcium, Magnesium, Iron and other nutrients. Micronutrients are very important and you must add micronutrients to the soil if needed.

A good soil test can also help you adjust the pH level, organics or micronutrients of the soil. After the lawn has been measured and a soil test has been taken, continue with these lawn renovation work procedures.

- Make any applications needed to correct soil deficiencies and apply a balanced fertilizer application (spring).
- Apply a pre-emergent crabgrass control application (early spring).
- Make a weed control application (spring).
- If there is any chance that the lawn area has a grub problem, make a pre-emergent grub control application (late spring/early summer).
- Treat any surface insects if a problem emerges (late spring/early summer).

- Treat any wild grass or crabgrass that emerges during the summer. You will need to use a post-emergent control (summer).
- Apply a balanced fertilizer application (summer).
- Set an approximate date for seeding. The best time will be during the late summer or early fall. Also choose a grass seed mixture that will work best at the job site. Such as Sunny, Sun and Shade, or Dense Shade mixture. By using the total square feet measurement you will be able to determine how much seed to purchase. Remember it is always best to purchase a little extra.
- Depending on the condition of the existing lawn, you will have to do one or more of the following before seeding.

De-thatching—If there is a heavy layer of thatch, it must be removed before seeding. De-thatch all lawn areas that have a heavy thatch layer. (De-thatching was discussed in detail earlier in this training guide.)

Core aeration—If the existing soil is very hard and compact, it should be aerated. Grass seed will not be able to establish a strong root system if the ground is hard and compact. Core aeration will create a good environment for grass seed to establish. (Core-aeration was discussed in detail earlier in this training guide.)

Repairs—Fill in and repair any holes or bad areas in the lawn. Fill these areas in, and then compact the soil with a lawn roller. After the soil was compacted lightly, regrade the area with a metal grading rake. When seeding, apply extra seed and hay to these areas. Then carefully push the lawn roller over these areas to help press the seed into the soil.

Slice Seeding or Over Seeding—Slice seeding is the best way to get the seed down into the existing lawn. If you are over seeding, dethatch the lawn first then apply the seed. Use a lawn roller and roll the lawn area after over seeding. (Slice seeding and over seeding were discussed in detail earlier in this training guide.)

- After the lawn has been seeded, apply additional seed to select areas as needed. Any areas that are all soil with little or no existing grass will need additional seed. Also apply hay and roll the areas.
- Apply a starter fertilizer application. *Note:* Do not over apply the starter fertilizer or it will be too strong for the seed.

The correct instructions must be followed after the seed or sod has been installed or poor results will occur. Read the following information, then make sure the customer is fully aware of these instructions and what they need to do to get the seed established.

1. Watering of entire area must be done as needed in order to keep seed, sod, and soil moist.
2. Lawn areas must remain moist from four to eight weeks to insure proper germination and root development. Seeds germinate at different time periods; continue to water up to eight weeks for best

results. After an eight week period, water generously at least twice per week throughout the remaining year.

3. **Do not** discontinue watering when some green up is noticed.

4. Make sure to allow the lawn and ground to completely dry before mowing. To accomplish this, you should not water the day before mowing. The first four to eight mowings should be done very carefully since the grass had not matured and the root system is not fully developed. Keep the mower height on the highest setting possible.

5. Try to keep people and pets off new lawn for four to eight weeks or damage and poor results will occur.

6. Regular scheduled fertilizer applications should be applied starting approximately 30 days after seeding.

7. Do not apply pesticides to your new lawn area until approximately 12 weeks after germination, carefully read the label on any lawn products you may apply.

8. Addition spot seeding of lawn areas may be needed to insure a beautiful thick lawn. Spot seed as soon as possible after first seeding is approximately 75% established.

You will see continued improvement in the lawn for four to five months after the renovation. To keep a lawn healthy and to prevent problems from re-occurring, you will need to follow a regular, continuous lawn care program.

Maintaining A Lawn (Complete Annual Lawn Care Program)

Early Spring

- Soil test if it is your **first year** maintaining the lawn, take a soil test to determine the condition of the soil. Then apply applications as needed to correct any soil deficiencies.
- Pre-emergent crab grass control plus a balanced, slow release fertilizer application.

Spring

- Weed control application.
- Surface insect control (as needed).

Late Spring

- Balanced, slow release fertilizer with micronutrients.
- Surface insect control and weed control (as needed).
- Disease control (as needed).

Early Summer

- Surface insect control and weed control (as needed).
- Post-emergent crab grass control (as needed).
- Disease control (as needed).
- (Optional) Pre-emergent grub control application.

Summer

- Balanced, slow release fertilizer.
- Surface insect control (as needed).

- Post-emergent wild grass control (as needed).

- Disease control (as needed).

Late Summer/Early Fall

- Spot seeding, renovations, repairs (as needed).

- Post-emergent grub control and surface insect control (as needed).

- Disease control (as needed).

Fall

- Balanced, slow release fertilizer.

- Weed control (as needed).

Late Fall/Early Winter

- Limestone (depending on the area of the country you live in).

- Winterizing fertilizer application.

Note: The applications above are for a **Complete** Annual Lawn Program. A Basic Lawn Program is used more often. A Basic Lawn Program should include fertilizer, weed and insect control applications. Anything else needed would be an additional charge. A Budget Lawn Program would include only fertilizer and weed control applications. A Reduced Pesticide Program would only apply pesticides as needed when an active problem is found in the lawn. An Organic Program uses only organic fertilizers and no pesticides. Each customer will be different by having a Complete, Basic, Budget,

Reduced Pesticide and Organic Lawn Program. By offering all the programs above, you will have a good program for everyone.

PREPARING THE GROUND FOR A NEW LAWN
(CHAPTER 24)

Before establishing a new lawn area, the ground must be prepared correctly. Stones and debris will need to be raked up and removed from the ground. The ground must have the correct slope so that water flows away from the house or building and not up against it and to keep the entire property as dry as possible. Any holes or uneven areas will need to be filled in. Topsoil and soil amendments should be added to improve the soil. Roto-tilling of the soil would also be very helpful. However, roto-tilling is rarely done because it requires too much labor and time. Therefore we will not discuss roto-tilling.

Tools and Equipment
You will need the following tools and equipment to prepare the ground for a new lawn. A small tractor with a landscape rake, wheelbarrows, shovels, picks, metal bow rakes, and grading rakes.

Work Procedures
- *If there are any unwanted weeds or wild grass growing in the area, they should be removed. If you scrap the tops of the weed off, you will not kill the root system and the weed will grow back. Spraying the weeds with a chemical will work best. Use a product such as Round-up Pro. Round-up Pro will kill the entire weed and you will be able to seed two weeks after you have*

sprayed. Spray the weeds and wild grass 14 days before you start preparing the ground. Then after the ground has been prepared, you can install the seed immediately.

- Take a soil test. By taking a soil test, you will know what nutrients the soil is lacking. Then you can apply the correct type of application so the soil has all the nutrients needed to establish a lawn. A soil test should be taken a few weeks before preparing the ground.

- Rake up any large debris. Use a tractor with a landscape rake or rake the debris into piles by hand. Pickup the piles of debris and remove them. Only rake up and remove the large debris, do not remove the smaller pieces of debris.

- The ground must have the correct slope so water flows away from the house and off the property. Using the bucket on a tractor, try to remove some of the high spots on the ground. Then use that dirt to adjust the slope or fill in any holes or low spots. Additional soil may be needed to raise up any low areas or to get correct slope. Spread the soil with the tractor bucket and rough grade it with the landscape rake. Then finish grade the area by hand.

- After the correct grade is established, you should top dress the entire area with a high quality topsoil or organic matter. Many landscapers do not top dress the ground. The results will be a poor quality lawn that may have ongoing problems. For a professional job, top-dress the entire area before installing the lawn.

- When top dressing the area, you will be spreading a thin layer of high quality soil over the ground. A layer of approximately 1 or 2 inches of soil will be beneficial and economical. If the existing ground is extremely poor, a thicker layer of soil should be installed. Topdressing should also be used to smooth out any imperfections on the ground. Use a tractor bucket and landscape rake to spread the soil. Then finish grade the area by hand.

Note: For best results, only top dress when weather conditions have been dry. Top dressing with wet soil on wet ground is almost impossible.

Optional: Roto-tilling and grading is the best way to prepare the ground for a new lawn. But this procedure is not done often because of the large amount of time and labor involved. Core aeration is a good option because it will remove plugs of soil from the existing ground. Top dress after you core aerate the ground, then the topsoil will be able to incorporate with the existing ground. Then the ground will be more suitable for root development.

- Shortly after the ground has been prepared, the seed or sod will need to be applied.
- Applications such a fertilizer and lime will be applied when we install the seed or sod.

INSTALLING SEED OR SOD
(CHAPTER 25)

Installing a Lawn with Seed

Establishing a lawn from seed is the most economical way to create a new lawn. Seed grown lawns will require more time and effort to become established. But once they are established, they are often stronger than a lawns made from sod. Seeds come in a variety of different mixtures such as: Full Sun, Sun and Shade, or Dense Shade. You can install a mixture that will meet the specific conditions of each job.

In most regions of the country, the best time to start a lawn from seed is in the **early** fall. In the early fall, the ground is still warm which helps speed up the germination process. The air is cool during the night. The cool air helps the soil stay moist for a longer period of time. The seed must remain moist or it will not germinate. When a lawn is established in the fall, it has more time to develop a strong root system before stressful summer conditions arrive. Early spring is the next best time to start a lawn from seed. Never try to establish a lawn during the summer.

Tools and Equipment

After the ground has been prepared, you will need the following tools and equipment to install a lawn with seed. Wheelbarrows, plastic leave rakes, rotary spreader, a drop spreader, a hand spreader, a clean five gallon bucket for seed, a lawn roller, and a utility knife.

You should wear gloves and a dust mask and consider wearing kneepads and a back support.

Prepare the ground as we discussed in the previous chapter. After the ground has been prepared, follow the procedures below for best results.

- Apply the seed or sod immediately after top dressing the area. After top dressing, the soil will be loose and the roots will be able to establish easily. If the area was not top dressed with soil, you will have to loosen the soil surface. Never seed or sod onto hard compact soil.
- Choose the correct type of seed for the conditions at each specific job.
- Only use high quality seed.
- Read the label on the seed and find out the recommended amount of seed required for your job. You will need to measure the area to determine the square feet. Then you will be able to purchase the correct amount of seed for your job.
- To determine the square feet of a property, measure the length and width of the front, back and sides of the property. Separately calculate each area.

For example:

Front property:	100 feet × 50 feet =	5000 square feet
Back property:	100 feet × 25 feet =	2500 square feet
Right side:	55 feet × 25 feet =	1375 square feet
Left side:	70 feet × 10 feet =	700 square feet
Total of property:		9575 square feet

Round off the number 9,575 sq. ft. would be rounded off to 10,000 sq. ft. Now you can purchase enough seed to establish a new lawn that is 10,000 square feet in size.

Always purchase a little extra seed. You will need extra seed so that you can apply it generously and so that you have some extra to spot seed any areas that did not grow.

- Apply an application of starter fertilizer. Starter fertilizer is used to help establish the root system of seed and sod. Always check the recommendation on the bag of starter fertilizer. **Never apply any more than recommended.** If you apply more than recommended, you may burn out the new seed or sod because the fertilizer application is too strong for the young tender roots.
- A soil test should have been taken a few weeks before starting the job. Apply the correct type of application as recommended by the soil test. If fertilizer is needed to correct a soil deficiency, the nutrients may be available in the starter fertilizer. Be careful not to apply too much fertilizer or the seed or sod can get damaged and will not grow.

- We will discuss over-seeding since over-seeding is the best way to establish a lawn when the ground has no existing lawn and is only soil.

- Apply seed to all the edges of the new lawn area. Use a hand spreader or put seed into a clean bucket and spread it by hand. Be careful not to get any grass seed into the landscape beds or other areas where grass is not wanted. The seed must be applied evenly and at the correct rate. Avoid applying the seed too heavy or too light. Avoid clumps of seeds on the ground. Apply the seed at least two feet wide from all the edges. The edges can also be seeded by using a drop spreader. A drop spreader will spread the seeds close to the edges without getting the seeds into the landscape beds. Adjust the spreader to the correct rate and you will be able to spread seed around the edges quickly and easily.

- After the edges have been completed, use a rotary spreader to spread seed on the larger areas of the property. A rotary spread will spread seed approximately 6 to 8 feet wide in one pass. A drop spreader will spread seed approximately three feet wide in a pass. Adjust the spreader to the correct rate. When applying the seed, walk at the same speed throughout the entire area. By walking at the same speed, the seed will be applied evenly. Slightly overlap the seed when making each pass with the spreader.

- Cover the entire area with hay. The hay will help hold moisture around the seed and it will help prevent damage to the new seed from a heavy rainfall. It will also help discourage birds from eating the new seeds. Put the bails of hay into wheelbarrows to move them around the property. Spread the hay by hand as **evenly** as possible. If there is a slope or area that will get a lot of run off from a rainfall, apply more hay to protect the area.

- Then you will need to roll the entire area. By rolling the area, you will push the seeds into the soil. The seeds must make good contact with the soil or they will not grow. Fill the lawn roller with water and roll the entire area.

The correct instructions must be followed after the seed has been installed or poor results will occur. Read the following information, then make sure the customer is fully aware of these instructions and what they need to do to get the seed established.

- Watering of entire area must be done as needed in order to keep seed, sod, and soil moist at all times.
- Lawn areas must remain moist for 4 to 8 weeks to insure proper germination and root development. Seeds germinate at different time periods; continue to water up to 8 weeks for best results. After an 8-week period, water generously at least twice per week throughout the remaining year.
- **Do not** discontinue watering when some green up is noticed.
- Make sure to allow the lawn and ground to completely dry before mowing. To accomplish this you should not water the day before mowing. The first 4 to 8 mowings should be done very carefully since the grass has not matured, and root system is not fully developed. Keep the mower height on highest setting possible.

- Try and keep people and pets off new lawn area for 4 to 8 weeks, or damage and poor results will occur.

- Regular scheduled fertilizer applications should be applied starting approximately 30 days after seeding.

- Do not apply pesticides to your new lawn area until approximately 12 weeks after germination, carefully read the label on any lawn products you may apply.

- Additional spot seeding of new lawn areas may be needed to insure a beautiful thick lawn. Spot seed as soon as possible after first seeding is approximately 75% established; this will also help avoid a weed problem.

Installing a Lawn With Sod

Installing sod provides the customer with an instant lawn. The lawn will look thick and healthy immediately, and after a few weeks, it will be rooted into the existing soil. Most sod is established from Kentucky Bluegrass. Bluegrass will do well in a sunny location and do poorly in shady conditions. Sod is usually only available in the Bluegrass type of grass. If the job site conditions are not sunny, it may be better to seed the area.

Sod comes in strips of approximately eight feet long by two feet wide. Sod is sold by the square foot. Measure the square feet of your job to determine how much sod you will need. Buy 5 to 10% more to allow for cuts and wasted pieces. Prepare the ground as we discussed in the previous chapter. After the ground has been prepared, install the sod in the following way.

- You can order sod from your local garden center or you can purchase sod directly from a sod farm if there is one in your area. The sod pieces will be rolled up and put on a pallet. Once you get the pallets of sod, the sod must be removed from the pallets and installed. If the sod is left of the pallet for a long period of time, it will get damaged or die.

- Apply fertilizer and nutrients as we discussed on the previous page.

- Remove the rolls sod from the pallet. Place them into a wheelbarrow and lay them near the area where you will start working. Keep the sod rolled up until you are ready to install it.

- As always, organize the job. One person should be removing the sod from the pallet while the second person lays the sod. Remember to organize each job before you start and again during the job if needed. As a landscape professional, you must always think of ways to do the job the easiest, fastest and safest.

- Lay the first row of sod end to end along the straight edge of a walk, driveway, and road or landscape bed. If there is no straight edge to work from, set up a string in between two stakes. Start the first row of sod using the string as a guide.

- Make sure each piece of sod is fit tightly against each other and is installed straight. The pieces of sod should not have any high spots. The entire piece of sod should be making contact with the ground.

Stager each row of sod so the center of the piece of sod covers the joint of the sod pieces below it.

- Be careful when working on top of the sod that you just installed. Some landscape professionals use pieces of wood to work on. Then they do not damage the sod that was just installed. Move the wood forward as you work.
- Use a sharp utility knife to cut any curves or small pieces. Try to keep each piece of sod as large as possible. Small pieces will move very easily.
- After the sod has been installed, use the lawn roller to roll the entire area. Roll the area in two different directions. Rolling the sod will ensure good contact between the roots of the sod and the existing soil.
- After the sod has been installed, give the entire area a heavy watering. Then follow the watering recommendations given early in this chapter.

La Guía Completa De Instrucción Bilingüe Del Césped Y Paisaje

Edición Española E Inglesa

CONTENIDO

INTRODUCCIÓN

Bienvenido a la guía completa de instrucción bilingüe del Céspedy Paisaje. Esta guía de instrucción profesional utilza los procedimientos de trabajo más recientes y efectivos. Mejorará en grande el conocimiento y habilidad de cada individual que este envuelto en el cuidado del césped y paisaje. Esta guía profesional es un recurso que debe ser obetenido pro los dueños de casas. Cada tema se compone en instrucciones de paso-por-paso y es fácil y entendible al leerló.

Después de leer esta guía, su trabajo sera disfrutable, fácil de completar, y terminará más rápidamente y correctamente. Usted reducirá el riesgo de herida a usted mismo y a otros. Usted reducirá el riesgo de herida a usted mismo y a otros. Usted reducirá el daño no deseado a la propiedad en la que usted trabaja y a la maquinaria que usted utiliza. Utilize esta guía para leer acerca de un tema seleccionado antes de empezar el tipo de trabajo o lea el libro completo para mejorar su conocimiento lo cual ayudará a que liegue a ser un profesional del paisaje.

Gracias especiales a Claudia Diaz y Banner Rosales por traducin esta guía correctamente al idioma hispano. Ulilizando las palabras más comunes, esta guía bilingüe ha probado ser un ganador con el lector hispano.

Sinceramente,

InfoExchange Inc.

Bryan Monty

Presidente

LIMPIEZA DE PRIMAVERA
(CAPÍTULO 1)

La limpieza de primavera es la limpieza de hojas, palos, astillas y de escombros de basura que han soplado en una propiedad sobre los meses de invierno. La limpieza de primavera debe hacerce durante la primavera temprana tan pronto en cuanto el suelo este lo suficientemente seco para trabajar en el. Este servicio se debe hacer antes que el césped necesite su primer corte. Las hojas, palos, astillas y escombros de basura serán más fáciles de limpiar mientras el césped este corto y todavía inactivo del invierno.

Usted necesitará el equipo siguiente para hacer una limpieza de primavera.
- Un soplador de tierra
- Un soplador de muchila.
- Rastrillos.
- Carpeta.
- Barril grande del paisaje.

Usted debe ponerse:
- Guantes.
- La protección de los oídos.
- Los lentes de seguridad, pantalones largos, y botas de trabajo al usar cualquier equipo de potencia.

Sopladores de Tierra

Los sopladores de tierra es un soplador que sopla los escombros de basura a través del suelo. Tiene más potencia que un soplador de muchila y se debe usar en áreas grandes del césped. Hay un (chute) en el soplador de tierra que se usa para ajustar el flujo de aire. Si hay hojas atascadas en el césped, ajusta el (chute) para que más aire sople hacia el césped. Si hay sólo escombros de basura de superficie, ajusta el (chute) para soplar a través de la superficie del césped. Siempre tenga cuidado cuándo ajusta el (chute) del soplador.

Apaga la máquina primero y **nunca** ponga las manos adentro del (chute). Cuándo trabaja en hojas pesadas, la abertura del frente del soplador de tierra se puede atascar con hojas. Cuándo esto suceda, apaga la máquina y quita las hojas a mano. **Nunca** Limpie esta abertura cuándo la máquina está encendida.

El soplador de tierra no debe ser utilizado en las camas del paisaje; es muy poderoso y soplará pajote (mulch) o tierra fuera de la cama. Usted también puede dañar las plantas muy fácilmente con un soplador de tierra, así que tenga cuidado adonde usted usa esta máquina.

La mayoría de los sopladores de tierra usan gas regular. Llene el tanque de gas en el remolque o la calle mientras el motor está fresco. Los sopladores de tierra utilizan aceite motriz más rápido que cualquier otra máquina. Verifique el nivel del aceite de motor **dos o tres veces por día**. Cerciórese que tenga aceite de motor extra con usted antes que usted vaya al sitio del trabajo.

Sopladores de muchila

El soplador de muchila es una máquina de 2 ciclos. Use el soplador de muchila en camas de paisaje, las aceras y las áreas más pequeñas de la propiedad.

Rastrillos de Hoja

Traiga unos cuantos rastrillos para que si uno se rompe, usted tenga unos extra. Tenga cuidado mientras está usando rastrillos, no empuje hacia abajo duro en el asidero de madera si no se romperá. Verifique sus rastrillos y se cerciora que la parte que rastrilla no este desgastada. Cuándo las orillas del rastrillo se desgastan, no trabajarán apropiadamente y es tiempo para usar un rastrillo nuevo.

Carpetas y Barriles de Paisaje

Durante el sevicio de limpieza de primavera, traiga ambos una carpeta y un barril del paisaje. Usted debe usar el barril del paisaje para recoger palos, astillas y montones pequeños de escombros de basura. Si los escombros no están demasiado pesados, vacíe su barril en la carpeta. Después cuándo la carpeta está llena, hace un viaje a la área de descarga de basura. No sobrellene la carpeta o el barril porque luego no podrá moverlo.

También tenga cuidado de no rasgar la carpeta al estirarla a través de un objeto agudo. Unas cuantas personas serán necesarias para halar una carpeta llena. El trabajo en equipo siempre resulta mejor.

La limpieza de Primavera (Procedimientos del Trabajo)
Cuándo usted hace una limpieza de primavera, siempre es muy importante trabajar con su compañero en equipo. ¡El trabajo será más fácil y obtendrá resultados más rápidamente cuándo usted trabaja en equipo!

Siempre lleve puestos los guantes, lentes de seguridad y protección de oídos al usar cualquier equipo de poder. Acabamos de hablar acerca del equipo necesitado para la limpieza de primavera, así que ahora lleguemos al trabajo.

Comienze caminando la propiedad con el barril del paisaje y recoga cualquier palos y astillas. Los palos no pueden ser soplados para juntarlos así que deben ser recogidos primero. Si hay muchos palos pequeños, use un rastrillo para hacer los montones de palos a través de la propiedad, y después los recoge. Después que todos los palos hayan sido recogidos y descargados en la basura, usted está listo para empezar a soplar las camas del paisaje. Ponga el gas del soplador y pongase su equipo de seguridad. También, traiga un rastrillo y carpeta con usted. Comienze en las camas del paisaje contra la casa. Sople los escombros de basura fuera del área de césped. Tenga cuidado con el soplador de muchila alrededor de la casa y plantas. **Usted quiere soplar las hojas y escombros de basura pero no el pajote (mulch)**

ni la capa superior de tierra. Limpie cualquier escombros de basura que se atascó adentro o debajo de las plantas.

Cuándo escombros de basura se atascan y no pueden ser soplados fácilmente con un soplador de muchila, usted tiene que usar un rastrillo. Que un compañero tome un rastrillo y levante las ramas más bajas de la planta mientras usted usa el soplador. Usando un rastrillo junto con un soplador obtendrá el trabajo más rápidamente y más fácilmente. Primero rastrille levemente a través de la cama para aflojar los escombros de basura, entonces los escombros de basura se soplarán más rápido y más fácil y la cama del paisaje se mirará profesionalmente limpia.

Después que las camas han sido sopladas en el césped, recoja los escombros de basura pesados con un rastrillo y carpeta y lo descarga en su camión o en una área de la propiedad adonde se descarga la basura. Limpie cualquier otras camas del paisaje en la propiedad de la misma manera.

Después que todas las camas sean limpiadas, use el soplador de tierra junto con un soplador de muchila o un rastrillo para limpiar las áreas de césped. Trabajen juntos como un equipo. Trabajen juntos de aquí para allá a través del césped. Use el soplador de muchila para cualquier rincón, esquinas, las orillas, las colinas o áreas pequeñas. Dondequiera que el soplador de tierra tenga dificultad.

Use un soplador de muchila o el rastrillo para ayudar aflojar los escombros de basura atascados en el césped. Trabaje a unos pocos pasos enfrente del soplador y afloje los escombros de basura. Entonces el soplador de tierra podrá limpiar fácilmente los escombros de basura una vez que se han aflojado.

Mientras trabaja de aquí para allá, usted comenzará a hacer un monton de escombros de basura corriendo en medio del área de césped. Cuándo este monton de escombros de basura empieza a construirse, comenzará a obtener difícultad para moverse. Pare sus máquinas y recoja los escombros de basura pesados con un rastrillo y carpeta. No hay necesidad de soplar los escombros de basura en un montón de basura ordenado ya que usted no ha terminado de limpiar el césped. Simplemente estire la carpeta enfrente del monton de escombros de basura y lo rastrilla hacia la carpeta. Ahora usted está listo para comenzar a soplar otra vez.

Una vez que usted está a las orillas del área de césped, recoja los escombros de basura restantes y lo acarrea lejos. Use un soplador de muchila y el rastrillo para hacer un montón final para ser recogido. Si usted trabaja en una propiedad donde usted puede soplar los escombros de basura en un área arbolada, limpia el césped para que usted termine por el bosque entonces usted puede soplar los escombros de basura del césped hacia el bosque. Limpie todas las aceras, plataformas, patios, piscinas, y el camino de entrada. **Cierre y ponga bajo llave cualquier portón o puertas** y ahora usted ya ha terminado con la limpieza de primavera.

Siga los procedimientos del trabajo de la limpieza de primavera como nosotros acabamos de discutir y cada trabajo llegará a tener resultados rápidamente y fácilmente lo más posible y cuando usted haya terminado, el trabajo se mirará magnífico! Algunas compañías también desierban y bordean las camas del paisaje durante la limpieza de primavera. Para aprender acerca de la desierba y bordear, acude a las próximas secciones en esta guía titulados la Eliminación de hierba y Bordear Camas de Paisaje.

Instrucción y consejos de Seguridad de la limpieza de primavera

- Mantenga todas las máquinas seguramente abrochadas en el remolque o en el camión durante el transporte.
- Siempre lleve puestos los lentes de seguridad, pantalones largos, botas de trabajo, y protección de oídos cuándo utilize cualquier máquina sopladora.
- Siempre trabajen juntos. El trabajo en equipo obtiene resultados más fácilmente y rapidamente.
- Primero recoja los palos, astillas con un rastrillo y el barril. No sea perezoso y trate de soplar los palos juntos.
- Mire alrededor de la casa por cualquier pozos de ventana, si están sucios, limpie los escombros de basura a mano.
- Afloje los escombros de basura en las camas de paisaje con un rastrillo, después sople los escombros de basura fuera con un soplador de muchila.

- Primero afloje los escombros de basura en el césped con un soplador de muchila o el rastrillo, después termine usando un soplador de tierra.

- Un compañero de trabajo debe empujar el soplador de tierra detrás del área que acaba de ser aflojada. Después **todos** los escombros de basura serán quitados y el césped se mirará profesionalmente limpio.

- Busque por áreas mojadas en la propiedad durante la limpieza de primavera. Mantengase lejos de alguna área mojada con la máquinaria pesada.

- Mantenga manos y pies lejos de todas partes móviles de todas las máquinas.

- Apaga la máquina y tenga cuidado cuándo ajuste el (chute) en un soplador de tierra.

- Apaga los sopladores para desatascar las hojas del área del ventilador.

- Llene todas las máquinas en el remolque o en la calle, no en el césped.

- Llene las máquinas antes de que usted empieze a trabajar cuando el motor está fresco.

- Cerciórese que las tapas del gas esten rectas antes de apretarlas.

- No sobre apriete la tapa de gas si no usted romperá el sello y goteará.

- Verifique el nivel de aceite motriz en los sopladores de tierra por lo menos dos veces al día.

- ¡¡Siempre piense en la seguridad primero!!

CORTARDO EL CÉSPED (LAWNMOWING)
(CAPÍTULO 2)

Hay muchas máquinas diferentes usadas en cortar el césped. Hablaremos acerca de la mayoría de las máquinas comúnmente usadas. Ellas son la caminata atrás 21", 36" y 48" cortacésped. La razón por la cual nosotros las llamamos 21", 36" o 48" es porque eso es cuán lejos la máquina cortará. Un cortacésped de 21" se utiliza para cortar los pedazos pequeños de césped. Un cortacésped de 36" se debe utilizar en áreas de césped pequeñas hasta áreas de césped medianas. Y el cortacésped de 48" trabaja mejor en las áreas más grandes del césped. Para hacer un trabajo bueno, esté seguro de usar la cortadora de césped del tamaño correcto para cada área diferente de césped.

Preparando la Máquinaria de Cortacésped antes del dia de trabajo

Antes de usted comenzar su día de trabajo, usted necesitará verificar sobre unas pocas cosas en todos los cortacéspedes que usted estará utilizando. **En una base diaria:**

- Verifique el nivel de aceite para cerciórarse que haya suficiente aceite en el motor. Si el motor corre sin suficiente aceite, el motor se podria dañar o ser destruido. Verifique el nivel de aceite cuando la máquina está en tierra plana. Busque la marca del aceite en la varilla graduada del nivel de aceite y llene el aceite a esta marca. **No llene demasiado; también mucho aceite puede dañar o destruir el motor.**

- Verifique todas las llantas para cerciórarse que tengan suficiente presión de aire. Si le parecen bajas, las llena con aire, entonces las verifica usando un chequeador de aire de la presión! Todas las llantas deben tener la misma presión de aire o la máquina cortará desigual y será más duro de controlar. Si usted mira en la llanta, allí estará escrito cuánta presión de aire la llanta debe tener, tal como 30psi. Siga esta información para mejores resultados.

- Verifique cualquier cinturón y la polea para cerciórarse que esten limpios y en buen estado.

- Verifique y cerciórese que nada este flojo en la máquina.

- Si, la máquina no está trabajando correctamente, no utilize la máquina y digalé a alguien que está a cargo inmediatamente.

- Cerciórese que la plataforma del cortacésped esté limpia y la cuchilla esté aguda, de otro modo la máquina no cortará la hierba fácilmente. Una cuchilla lánguida (sin filo) romperá la hierba, y causará daño al césped. Con una plataforma sucia, será difícil reunir los recortes de hierba y sin un recolector de hierba, el césped se agrupará en vez de extenderse hacia afuera uniformemente en el césped. Afile las cuchilla y limpie debajo de la plataforma del cortacésped una vez a la semana para mejores resultados.

- Cerciórese que también el recolector de hierba este limpio. Si los agujeros del recolector de hierba estan atascado con hierba seca, el recolector no trabajará y hará su trabajo más difícil. Limpie los recolectores de hierba con un cepillo de alambre siempre que afile las cuchilla y limpie la plataforma del cortacésped.

- Antes de que usted arranque la máquina, esté seguro de verificar que haya suficiente gas en el tanque de gas. Nunca llene el tanque de gas en el césped y nunca llene el tanque de gas cuando el motor esté caliente. La mayoría de las máquinas tienen un tanque grande de gas que usted puede llenar en la mañana y no tendrá que volver a llenarlo otra vez por unas cuantas horas.

- La última cosa que se debe verificar es la altura del cortacésped. En otras palabras, cuán alto el césped se cortará. El cortacésped debe cortar el césped a una altura de aproximadamente 2-1/2". En el verano, cuando hay calor, levante la plataforma del cortacésped para cortar en lo más alto. Cuándo el césped se corta más alto, no se fundirá fácilmente del tiempo caliente del verano. Es mejor dejar la altura del cortacésped en el nivel correcto y cortar todas las propiedades a este nivel. Sin embargo, algunos clientes pueden insistir en que ellos quieren su césped cortado más alto o más bajo. Si esto sucede entonces usted tendrá que ajustar la altura del cortacéspedes antes y después de ese trabajo.

- **Cerciórese que todas las máquinas de cortacéspedes corten a la misma altura.** Cada máquina tiene las colocaciones diferentes. Por ejemplo: Su máquina 36" y 48" pueden estar activadas en el grado numero del corte 3 para cortar a una altura de 2-1/2", pero su máquina 21" puede estar activada en el grado número del corte 4 en obtener la misma altura de 2-1/2".

Después que usted ha verificado todas las máquinas como nosotros acabamos de discutir, usted está listo para trabajar. Primero haga un chequeo visual del área del césped que usted cortará. Recoga cualquier objeto que esté en el césped tal como ramas, juguetes, basura, una manguera del jardín, etc. Sí hay cualquier persona en el área del césped, cerciórese que ellos salgán del área antes de que usted empieze a trabajar. Entonces escoja la máquina correcta para el área de césped que usted necesita cortar.

Piense en la manera más fácil de cortar el área del césped. En la mayoría de los casos, usted correrá la máquina a través del área más larga del césped para que usted no tengá que girar la máquina tan a menudo. Cualquier tamaño de máquina que usted esté usando, la propiedad debe ser verificada visualmente y resolver la manera más fácil de cortar el área. Obviamente cuándo usted regresé a la misma propiedad la siguiente semana, usted sabrá la mejor manera de cortar el césped sin pensarlo. Después de unos cuantos meses, usted necesitará cambiar el patrón/modelo de cortar, utilizando el segundo patrón/modelo de cortar más fácil. **Cambiar el patrón/modelo cada unos cuantos meses será saludable para el césped.**

Operando Un Cortacésped 21"
Arranque la máquina y gire la válvula reguladora para que el motor corra a su velocidad máxima. Corriendo el motor a su velocidad máxima, el cortacésped será capaz de cortar el césped más fácilmente. Algunos cortacéspedes 21" son auto-propulsado, mientras que otros usted los tiene que empujar. Si usted está utilizando un cortacésped auto-propulsado, ajuste la velocidad. Si usted está cortando un área

que es plana, usted puede correr la velocidad rápida, pero si usted está cortando en una colina o cuesta, usted debe bajar la velocidad.

Corra primero el cortacésped alrededor de la orilla exterior del área que usted está cortando. Después corra la máquina a través del césped, hacia adelante y hacia atrás en el patrón/modelo que usted planeó durante el chequeo visual. Usted debe cortar en una línea recta. Gire la máquina alrededor y corte el área de al lado que usted acaba de cortar. Si usted está utilizando un cortacésped auto-propulsado, suelte el mecanismo impulsor y gire el cortacésped alrededor manualmente. Mientras hace el próximo paso, usted debe traslapar levemente la máquina sobre el área que acaba de ser cortada. Haciendo un traslape leve usted no perderá ningun corte del área del césped.

Una vez que el recolector de hierba está lleno, estacione el cortacésped en la tierra llana y apaga el motor. Cuándo usted vacíe fuera el recolector de hierba, quite cualquier hierba que esté estorbando el (chute) de la máquina. Una vez más, **siempre** cerciórese que la máquina esté **apagada** y espera por lo menos un minuto hasta que la cuchilla pare de girar antes de limpiar alrededor del área del (chute). El (chute) sólo se atascará si la hierba está muy mojada o si usted sobre llenó el recolector de hierba.

Si usted está cortando un área que llenará más de un recolector de hierba, esté seguro de traer consigo un barril de hierba del paisaje al área donde usted está trabajando. Vaciar los recolectores llenos de hierba en el barril, después cuándo usted acabe de cortar el área, usted necesitará hacer solamente un viaje para vaciar la hierba.

Operando UN 36" o 48" Cortacéspedes

Ahora que usted sabe como usar el 21", usted puede cortar las áreas más grandes de la propiedad con la máquina 36" o 48". La máquina 36" o 48" se deben llenar de gas y prepararse como discutimos previamente y el área de césped debe ser verificada visualmente como discutimos previamente. Cuándo se utiliza un 36" o 48" **siempre** traiga consigo un barril de hierba para vaciar adentro el recolector de hierba. Con la mayoría de las máquinas, usted puede poner el barril enfrente de la máquina y empujarlo al área que usted está cortando.

Nota: Algúnas máquinas pueden operar levemente diferente a lo que describó abajo.

La mayoría de las máquinas operan en la siguiente manera.

- Con las palancas del control de mano fuera el cortacésped se mueve hacia **adelante**.
- Hale las palancas del control de mano hasta medio adentro, y el cortacésped estará en **neutro**.
- Hale las palancas del control de mano completamente adentro y el cortacésped **parara**.
- Hale en la palanca derecha para **girar a la derecha** y la palanca izquierda para **girar a la izquierda**.

Antes de arrancar la máquina, cerciórese que los asideros del control esten cerrados y el freno de estacionamiento está activado para que la máquina no empieze a moverse cuándo usted la arranca.

Los Procedimientos operadores:

- Arranque el cortacésped.
- Ponga la máquina en la velocidad correcta, y entonces suelte el freno de estacionamiento.
- Una vez que el freno de estacionamiento se suelta, aumente la válvula reguladora para que el motor corra a su velocidad máxima.
- Sí usted está en un área de césped, emplee las cuchillas.
- Ponga sus manos en las palancas del control de mano y suelte lentamente las palancas. La máquina empezará a moverse.
- **Nunca** deje ir las palancas del control de mano si no usted perderá el control del cortacésped.

Una persona inexperta tomará un día o dos en llegar a ser familiarizado con el funcionamiento del cortacésped. Recuerde de nunca dejar ir las palancas del control de mano mientras la máquina está moviendose. Para detener la máquina, simplemente hale en ambas palancas. Una vez que usted llegue a ser familiarizado con el cortacésped y cada propiedad, los trabajos llegarán a ser mucho más fácil de completar.

En la mayoría de los trabajos, usted podrá andar alrededor del camino de entrada o calle para entrar en el área del césped. Sin embargo, si usted no puede, usted tendrá que llevar el cortacésped sobre el bordillo de la siguiente manera.

Cuándo pasa por una bordillo:

- Cerciórese que las cuchillas esten apagadas y baje la válvula reguladora.
- Ponga la máquina en neutro.
- Empuje hacia abajo en los manerales para levantar las ruedas delanteras sobre la curba entonces empuje la máquina hacia adelante para que las ruedas posteriores esten al lado del bordillo.
- Levante la parte posterior de la máquina mientras que empuja hacia adelante, coloque la máquina hacia abajo una vez que las ruedas posteriores hayan pasado la curba.

Una vez que usted pase la curba y esté en el área del césped que será cortado, ajuste la válvula reguladora y la velocidad de impulsión como sea necesario. Entonces arranque las cuchilla del cortacésped y usted está listo para trabajar.

Los Procedimientos de Cortar el Césped:

Primero corte alrededor de la orilla exterior del área del césped. Si no hay gente alrededor, deje el recolector de hierba afuera mientras hace el primer corte en el área del césped. Posicione el cortacésped para que los recortes de césped soplen adentro del área del césped y no adentro de las camas, la calle ni el camino de entrada. Cuándo usted acabe por donde usted comenzó, apaga las cuchilla, ponga el freno de estacionamiento, y entonces conecta el recolector de hierba. Ahora haga el primer paso a través del área de césped, gire la máquina alrededor y continúe con el próximo paso.

Cuándo gire un cortacésped 36" o 48", Hale las palancas del control de mano a la posición neutro entonces usted podrá girar manualmente la máquina alrededor. Utilice su peso corporal para ayudar a girar la máquina, y nunca deje ir los asideros. Levemente usted puede emplear una rueda de afuera para ayudar a hacer una vuelta. No cierre la rueda de adentro mientras gira. la rueda cerrada se dará vuelta a su lugar y dañará el césped. Siempre evite cerrar las llantas o girar las llantas mientras gira.

Recuerde de traslapar levemente sobre el área que acaba de ser cortada para que así usted no pierda ninguna área. Trate de mantener la máquina cortando en una línea recta; esto le dará al césped una apariencia profesional cuándo usted haya terminado. Hale levemente lo necesario en cada palanca del control de mano para ayudar a mantener la máquina cortando en una línea recta. Cuándo usted llegue a un árbol o cama del paisaje, camine alrededor con el recolector de hierba en el **exterior** de la cama del árbol o paisaje. De esta manera usted no dañará nada con el recolector de hierba. Camine alrededor de la cama entera, y entonces continúe cortando con el patrón/modelo de una línea recta en ambos lados de la cama. Entonces usted obtendrá un trabajo con una apariencia profesional cuándo usted haya terminado.

Cuándo usted comienze a ver grupos pequeños de hierba caer fuera del recolector de hierba, es hora de vaciar el recolector.

- Estacione la máquina en tierra llana.
- Detenga la máquina y las cuchillas.
- Emplear el freno de estacionamiento.
- Disminua la válvula reguladora.
- Vaciar el recolector de hierba.
- **Siempre mantenga sus manos y pies lejos del área de la cuchilla aunque esten apagadas.**

Si grupos de hierba de un recolector lleno se han derramado sobre el césped, detenidamente recoga la hierba a mano después corra el cortacésped sobre esa área otra vez para recoger los recortes restantes, si no utilize un soplador de muchila para desmenuzar los grupos de hierba.

Una vez que usted haya acabado de cortar un área del césped, corra el cortacésped alrededor del borde exterior del área de césped otra vez para darle una apariencia profesional. En un área más grande del césped, o en una propiedad que no es mantenida perfectamente, este último paso no se puede necesitar.

Cortacéspedes de Correas y Hidráulico (Máquina de Faja y Hidráulico)
Cortacésped de Correas (Máquina de Faja)

Una caminata estandárd atrás del cortacésped es conducida por fajas. Las fajas corren de la transmisión a las ruedas. Hay algunos problemas con el cortacésped de fajas. Tal como:

- Cuándo las fajas y poleas llegan atascarse con tierra o recortes del césped, el cortacésped llegará a ser difícil o imposible de operar.

Nota: Inspeccione las fajas y las poleas en una base regular. Si usted ve tierra o recortes de césped en el <u>interior</u> de las fajas o en las poleas, los limpia inmediatamente. Usted tendrá que utilizar un destornillador plano de cabeza para limpiar en el <u>interior</u> de las fajas y la polea. Siempre apaga la máquina antes de limpiar las fajas y las poleas.

o Cuándo las fajas llegan a mojarse, el cortacésped llegará a ser difícil o imposible de operar.

Nota: Mantenga el cortacésped y las fajas secas. Permanecer lejos de las áreas mojadas.

- Cuándo las fajas estan viejas, el cortacéspedes llegará a ser difícil o imposible de operar. Las fajas se deben reemplazar tan pronto estan gastadas. Si el cortacésped es utilizado en una base regular, reemplace las fajas una vez al año.

Cortacésped Hidráulico (Máquina Hidráulica)

Un Cortacésped hidráulico tiene una bomba hidráulica que conduce las ruedas en vez de fajas. Operando un cortacésped de caminata-atrás hidráulica es levemente diferente al operar una de fajas.

Procedimientos Operadores de un Cortacésped Hidráulico:

- Permita las palancas del control de mano completamente hacia afuera y el cortacésped irá hacia **adelante**.

- Hale las palancas del control de mano hasta la mitad y el cortacésped estará en **neutro**.

- Levemente hale en las palancas del control de mano y el cortacésped **parara**.

- **Hale las palancas del control de mano completamente adentro y la máquina no parará. Por el contrario irá hacia atrás.**

Después que usted aprenda cómo operar el cortacésped hidráulico, debera ser más fácil y menos cansado para usted operar uno de fajas. *Sin embargo, un cortacésped hidráulico puede despedazar la hierba muy fácilmente cuándo gira, así que sea cuidadoso.* Cuándo usted tiene que cortar debajo de un árbol o un área dificil de alcanzar, usted no tendrá que halar manualmente la máquina para sacarla hacia afuera. Por lo contrario usted halará las palancas del control de mano completamente hacia adentro y la máquina se saldrá hacia atrás.

Las bombas hidráulicas se deben mantener muy bien, o podria ocurrir daño que sería grave y caro.

- Siempre mantenga las bombas hidráulicas llenas correctamente. Chequee La bomba hidráulica una vez a la semana.

- La bomba Hidráulica tiene un tanque separado de aceite que debe ser llenado al nivel correcto y requiere un tipo especial de aceite.

300

No Use aceite motriz regular y **No** Sobre llene el tanque de aceite de la bomba hidráulica.

- Cambie el aceite y los filtros en una base regular y **no opere la máquina si usted detecta un escape de aceite de cualquier pieza de la máquina.**

Cortacésped de Montar/Cabalgar

Cortacésped de cabalgar funciona básicamente lo mismo al del Cortacésped de caminata detrás excepto que usted se sienta y cabalga sobre el mientras corta. Las palancas del control serán diferentes, que una caminata detrás del Cortacésped. Cada marca diferente de cortacéspedes de cabalgar funcionará levemente diferente.

Nota: Cerciórese que usted entienda claramente todas las palancas del control antes de que usted comienze a operar cualquier Cortacésped de cabalgar.

La mayoría de cortacéspedes de cabalgar cortarán 48" o más grande por lo tanto usted sólo debe usar los cortacéspedes de cabalgar en áreas abiertas grandes de césped. **Permanezca lejos de áreas pequeñas o áreas inclinadas.** Algúnos Cortacéspedes de cabalgar pueden tener un segundo motor usado para el sistema de la aspiradora (vacuum). Si el motor esta lleno de tierra (mounded) en el lado de cabalgar, permanezca en alerta si no usted puede destruir el motor o dañar la propiedad al tropezar con algo.

Los procedimientos de cortar son casi igual al del Cortacésped de caminata detrás que acabamos de discutir. Siga estos procedimientos y una vez que usted llegue a familiarizarse con el Cortacésped de cabalgar que usted está usando, usted será capaz de cortar rápidamente áreas grandes de césped sin cansarse de la constante caminata.

Instrucciónes de cortar el Césped y Consejos de Seguridad
Cortar el césped será diferente en cada propiedad. Cada propiedad tendrá terreno y problemas diferentes con los cuales usted necesitará tratar. La información preparada abajo le ayudará a mejorar su habilidades para cortar el césped. Cuándo usted comprenda cómo tratar con diferentes condiciones, terreno, y problemas, su trabajo llegará a ser más fácil y siempre con una apariencia profesional. Usted estará más seguro hacia usted mismo y otros. Un Cortacésped es una pieza de equipo peligrosa. **Siempre piense en la seguridad primero!**

- Siempre lleve puestos los lentes de seguridad, pantalones largos y botas de trabajo cuándo opera un cortacésped.
- Cuándo estacione un cortacésped por **cualquier** razón, apaga las hojas, baje la válvula de admisión, y utilice el freno de estacionamiento.
- No estacione un cortacésped en una colina ni en una cuesta porque la máquina puede moverse o rodarse, aún con el freno puesto.
- No use ninguna máquina cuando gente o mascotas están en el área en la cual usted quiere trabajar.

- Mantenga las manos, los pies, y todas las partes del cuerpo lejos de alguna parte móvil de cualquier máquina a menos que la máquina este **apagada.**

- **No despedaze áreas de césped por cerrar o girar las llantas!**

- Si las llantas del cortacésped estan dañando al césped por correr sobre el mismo puesto semana tras semana. Mueva el cortacésped para que las llantas no corran otra vez sobre esa área dañada.

- Levante la máquina para prevenir dejar caer en un agujero o parte baja la llanta. Si una llanta cae en un agujero, causará daño al césped y puede causar daño a la máquina.

- Mire hacia adenlante y permanezca en alerta cuando corta.

- No permita que recortes de hierba vuelen hacia las camas del paisaje, contra una casa, adentro de piscinas, ni en coches cercanos.

- No golpee los postes de correo, árboles, cercas, piedras, ni curbas con el cortacésped.

- Trabaje detenidamente y cuidadosamente en céspedes mojados. Dejé cualquier área de césped si esta muy mojada para la máquina.

- Si un área de césped esta muy mojada para el cortacéspedes, use una podadora de cuerda para cortar el área. Si está extremadamente mojado, dejé las áreas completamente hasta la semana siguiente cuando las condiciones esten secas.

- No llene de gas a las máquinas en el césped. Llénelos en el remolque o calle cuando el motor esta frio.

- Siempre traiga consigo un barril del paisaje cuándo recoja el césped.

- Corte más despacio cuándo hay bordes en el césped, si la hierba esta mojado o alto, o cuándo corta en una cuesta.

- Corra la válvula de admisión del motor a su máximo y siempre corra el cortacésped en el cambio de velocidad correcto.

- Evite dejar cúalquier grupo pesado de hierba sobre el césped. Utilice un soplador de muchila para separar cualquier grupo pesado de hierba.

- No utilice un Cortacésped 36" donde se debe usar 21". Siempre escoja el cortacésped correcto para el área que usted esta cortando.

- Visualmente chequee, inspeccione y planee cómo usted cortará antes que usted comienze.

- Mueva todo los juguetes, mangueras, etc. del área de césped antes de cortar.

- Después de cortar, siempre cierre y ponga bajo llave cúalquier portón!

- Mantenga en buenas condiciones todo el equipo.

- No deje recolectores de hierba ni barriles de paisaje llenos de césped por la noche.

- El equipo de seguridad en las máquinas **debe** ser usado. No desconecte ni deje de usar el equipo de seguridad.

- Ponga los conos de emergencia alrededor de su camión y remolque en cada sitio de trabajo tan pronto se estacione. Use por lo menos dos conos de emergencia.

- Cuándo estacione un camión en una colina, gire las ruedas dentro de la curba para que no rode hacia abajo del camino si el freno de estacionamiento falla.

- Verifique el remolque antes de conducir hacia el próximo trabajo para cerciórarse que todo está cargado correctamente.

- No esparza herramientas y equipo alrededor del área de estacionamiento y propiedad en la cual usted trabaja. Ponga las herramientas y equipo de regreso en el camión o remolque tan pronto usted termine de usarlos. ¡Sea organizado!

- Ponga todas las herramientas y equipo de regreso donde pertenecen. De esta manera estarán en el mismo lugar todo el tiempo y serán fácil de encontrar la próxima vez que alguien necesite algo.

- Condusca el camión al limite o bajo el límite de velocidad.

- En su camión, mantenga todo los espejos retrovisores ajustados correctamente. Siempre utilize estos espejos cuando conduce.

- ¡Permanezca en alerta! No corra las llantas del remolque hacia las curbas. Haga las vueltas anchas para evitar correr las llantas hacia las curbas.

- No utilize ninguna máquina que este dañada o que no está trabajando bien.

- ¡Siempre **piense**…sea listo y actue **profesional**!

- Organize cada trabajo. Piense acerca de cómo usted puede hacer el trabajo más fácil y quien lo hará **antes** qué usted comienze, luego trabajen juntos. El trabajo en equipo es la mejor manera de trabajar y terminar un buen trabajo.

- Chequee cada propiedad antes de que usted se vaya. Chequee que todas las áreas del césped estén cortadas y podadas correctamente. Cerciórese que todos los portones esten cerrados y que todas las herramientas y equipo sean guardados. Haga una nota si hay cúalquier problema en la propiedad.

- Digale a su jefe o capataz acerca de cúalquier problema que usted haya encontrado en la propiedad o con las máquinas.

- Si usted no comprende **completamente** cuando su capataz o su jefe discute un trabajo, por favor digales que usted no entiende.

- No trate de hacer algo sí usted no está **100% seguro** acerca de lo que usted hace.

- Por favor sea honesto, trabaje duro, listo, y seguro.

- Siempre piense en la seguridad primero.

RECORTAR CON CUERDA Y LIMPIEZA DE ESCOMBROS
(CAPÍTULO 3)

Podar con Cuerda

Podar con cuerda se hace para cortar las áreas donde el cortacésped no puede alcanzar. Tal como: alrededor de árboles, camas de paisaje, cercas, aceras y caminos de entrada. Todo las podadoras de cuerda son muy similares. Unas cuantas cosas para recordar acerca de estas máquinas son:

- Esté seguro de usar gas de 2 ciclos, no gas regular. El gas de 2 ciclos es gas y una mezcla de aceite.

- Antes de llenar la máquina, agite el bote del gas para que el gas y el aceite siempre estén mezclados.

- Llene la máquina antes de que usted empieze a trabajar cuando el motor esté frio.

- Enrosque cuidadosamente la tapa del gas. Cerciórese que la tapa del gas sea puesta firmemente. Entonces aprietelo, pero no lo sobre apriete si no usted romperá el sello dentro de la tapa. Después la tapa de gas goteará.

- Cuándo llene la cabeza de la podadora con cuerda, cerciórese que todas las partes dentro de la cabeza de la podadora se mantengan limpio. Si hay tierra dentro de la cabeza de la podadora, no trabajará apropiadamente.

- Cuándo se usa una podadora de cuerda, la cuerda debe extenderse aproximadamente 6 pulgadas fuera de la cabeza. Si la cuerda es más corta o más larga, la podadora no trabajará apropiadamente.

- Hay dos tipos diferentes de cabezas de podadoras. Un tipo soltará más cuerda cuándo usted golpea el fondo de la cabeza en el suelo. El otro tipo soltará más cuerda cuándo usted baja la velocidad del motor y luego aumenta la velocidad del motor y más cuerda saldrá.

- Algunas máquinas tendrán una cortadora de cuerda en el protector de seguridad que cortará la cuerda a la longitud correcta. Pero si usted mueve al protector de seguridad, no trabajará. Sí la podadora no tiene un cortador de cuerda, tenga cuidado no deje mucha cuerda hacia fuera.

- Siempre deje al protector de seguridad en la podadora. Ajústelo adonde le parezca mejor a usted pero nunca lo quite. Una podadora sin el protector de seguridad puede tirar piedras a más de 50 mph en todas las direcciones.

- Siempre lleve puestos los lentes de seguridad, pantalones largos y botas de trabajo cuando opere una podadora de cuerda.

Operadorando una Podadora de Cuerda (String Trimmer)

Cuándo usted enciende una podadora de cuerda, hay dos maneras diferentes de usar la podadora. La primera manera usted debera de mantener la podadora para que la cuerda esté horizontal con el suelo. Esta es la misma manera que la cuchilla de un cortacésped corta. Esto se debe hacer alrededor de árboles, los postes de buzón, cercas, y áreas pequeñas que fueron dejadas por el cortacésped. Corte el césped alto a la misma altura del césped que acaba de cortar. **Sea muy cuidadoso de no tocar ningún árbol, cercas, etc. con la cuerda.** La podadora de cuerda causará daño grave a los árboles, cercas, etc. si usted viene cerca y los toca.

La segunda manera es sostener la podadora de modo que la cuerda corte vertical (arriba y abajo). Ésta es la misma manera que una cuchilla de borde corta. Esta manera se debe utilizar por senderos, los caminos de entrada, y a lo largo de las camas del paisaje que tienen una orilla. Mucha gente incurre en la equivocación de cortar estas áreas con las cuerdas en un ángulo de 45-grados, ésto es incorrecto. Cuándo usted recorta en un ángulo de 45 grados, usted estára cortando el césped a un punto muy bajo. Entonces, luego bajo cualquier condición atmosférica caliente, la hierba se volverá marrón y morirá en estas áreas. El cortar en 45-grados no se recomienda en ninguna situación.

Cuando poda, comienze en un extremo de la propiedad y trabaje hacia el otro final. Intente cortar alrededor de las aceras y camino de entrada primero. Entonces un compañero de trabajo puede soplar la acera y camino de entrada si usted sigue podando. Tenga cuidado de no excederce en cortar. Cuándo poda en las aceras y los caminos de entrada, no haga el espacio entre la acera y el césped más grande que 1 pulgada. Podar estas áreas ligeramente o quincenalmente. Muchas áreas en la propiedad pueden ser cortadas quincenalmente, por ejemplo las camas de paisaje, aceras, y el camino de entrada. Durante los meses del verano, usted debe también reducir el recorte de cuerda.

No recorte ninguna áreas demasiado baja o las áreas del césped se volverán marrón y morirán. Mientras trabaja en una propiedad con la podadora de cuerda, examine visualmente el césped entero.

Puede haber áreas donde los cortacéspedeses hayan cortado desigual. Utilize la podadora para arreglar estas áreas. Recorte cualquier punto alto obvio para igualar el césped.

Quite cualquier mala hierba grande que esté creciendo fuera de la calle o en el camino de entrada. Intente no golpear ninguna piedras sucitas al hacer esto.

Nunca opere podadoras de cuerdas cuando hay gente en el área donde usted está trabajando. Si usted tiene que cortar a lo largo de un camino con muchos coches, corra la podadora a una velocidad minima de motor, y recorte con la cuerda en la posición horizontal. Esta es la manera más segura de recortar. Recuerde de siempre pensar acerca de la seguridad cuándo se usa cualquier equipo de potencia.

Limpieza de los escombros de basura
La limpieza de basura de las aceras, caminos de entradas y las plataformas es el último paso de progresión a un servicio de cortar el césped. Recomendamos el uso de un soplador de muchila. Un soplador de muchila es una máquina de 2-ciclos.

Cuándo usted soplé las aceras, comienze en la puerta del frente. Corra el motor **lentamente** y soplé el área de la puerta del frente. Cerciórese que esta área se deje muy limpia ya que esta es una área que muchas personas verán. Después que el área del frente ha sido soplada, limpie el camino del frente. Una vez que usted esté lejos de la puerta del frente, usted puede aumentar la velocidad del motor para terminar el trabajo más rápidamente. Intente soplar los escombros de ambos lados del camino. Si hay muchos escombros, **no sople** los escombros sobre el césped que se acaba de cortar; no lo sople en las camas de paisaje. Sople los escombros pesados en un monton, después recoga el monton y llevese los escombros.

Después de que termine de hacer el camino del frente, camine alrededor de la parte posterior y hace igual. Mientras que recorre alrededor de la propiedad, haga una inspección visual de la propiedad. Busque por cúalquier recortes pesado de la hierba dejados en algún lado en el césped o en las camas de paisaje. Si es así sople estas áreas para que no quede ningún recorte de hierba pesado sea dejado dondequiera. Si la propiedad tiene una piscina, limpie esta área lentamente y cuidadosamente para que así usted no sople ningún escombro de basura en la piscina.

Al limpiar las plataformas o patios, soplé cuidadosamente cualquier mueble al aire libre después de que se haya hecho el área del patio. Tenga cuidado de no destruir ninguna mazeta o cualquier otra cosa pequeña en el patio. Soplé cualquier estera al aire libre y si lo mueve cuándo usted lo sopló, los endereza después.

Después que el traspatio esté limpio, cerciórese que cualquier portón este cerrado. Cerciórese que cada portón se cierra y este cerrado con picaporte o este bajo llave cerrado. Los niños y las mascotas pueden ser heridos o pueden morir si ellos llegan a los lugares donde ellos no deben estar. Recuerde que todos los portones necesitan estar siempre cerrados bajo llave.

El camino de entrada es la última cosa que usted necesita limpiar. Intente soplar el camino de entrada a un área donde usted puede desacerse de los escombros tal como un desaguadero de alcantarilla o área arbolada. Si el camino de entrada esta bastante limpio, usted puede soplar los escombros de ambos lados del camino de entrada. Si el camino de entrada esta muy sucio, usted puede necesitar hacer los escombros en una pila, entonces recoge la pila y se los lleva. Tenga cuidado cuándo trabaja alrededor de algún coche estacionado. Después que usted termine de soplar alrededor del coche, sople él mismo coche para mantenerlo limpio. Si usted sopla cualquier césped en el camino mientras estaba cortando, Cerciórese de soplar el área del camino así como también el camino de entrada. Tenga cuidado y mantengase alerta del tráfico que se acerca mientras usted está en la calle. Cuándo limpia caminos de entrada muy grandes o parqueos de estacionamiento grandes, un soplador de tierra conseguirá hacer el trabajo mejor.

Instrucción y Consejos de Seguridad de la podadora de cuerda y limpieza de escombros

- Siempre lleve puestos los lentes de seguridad, pantalones largos y botas de trabajo cuándo trabaja con una podadora de cuerda o sopladores.

- Mantenga la línea de podar en la longitud correcta. Si la cuerda es demasiado corta o larga, no trabajará correctamente.

- No trabaje cerca de otra gente.

- Sea extremadamente cuidadoso cuándo trabaje con coches cercanos. Corra la máquina en una velocidad minima en la posición horizontal.

- Mantenga la cuerda de cortar lejos de piedras o de escombros flojos.

- No golpee árboles, los buzones, etc. con la cuerda de cortar.

- Mantenga el césped alto a lo largo de las curbas y los caminos de entrada o se fundirá durante el tiempo caliente.

- Mantenga el espacio entre senderos y césped no más grande que 1 pulgada.

- Busque por áreas en el césped donde el cortacésped cortó desigual. Entonces mezcle estas áreas con el cortador de cuerda.

- Mantenga manos y pies lejos de todas las partes móviles de las máquinas.

- Llene todas las máquinas en el remolque o la calle, no en el césped.

- Llene todas máquinas antes que usted empieza a trabajar cuándo el motor está fresco.

- No sobre apriete la tapa de gas o se romperá la tapa y el sello goteará el gas.

- Cerciórese que la tapa de gas esté directamente puesta antes que usted lo aprieta.

- No sople escombros de basura pesados adentro de las camas de paisaje o en el césped que acaba de ser cortado.

- Corra el soplador a una velocidad minima cuándo sople cerca de la casa, piscina, patio, o coches.

- Todas los portones necesitan estar cerrados y bajo llave siempre.

- Mantenga todas las máquinas seguramente abrochadas en el remolque o el camión.

- Nunca quite el protector de seguridad de la podadora (trimmer).

- ¡¡¡Siempre piense en la seguridad primero!!!

ELIMINACIóN DE HIERBA
(DESERBANDO A MANO)
(CAPÍTULO 4)

La eliminación de hierba a mano es la eliminación de hierbas no deseadas de las camas de paisaje. Usted quitará estas hierbas usando las manos o una herramienta manual. La eliminación de hierba de las camas del paisaje debe ser hecho en una base regular para mantener una propiedad que se vea lo mejor. Cuándo quite las hierbas no deseadas, usted necesitará las herramientas siguientes:

- Una herramienta manual para ayudar a cavar el sistema de raíz de la hierba. Hay muchos tipos diferentes de herramientas manuales usadas para la eliminación de hierba. Algunas herramientas son simplemente un (shaft) de metal con unos cuantos puntos en la orilla. Otras herramientas se parecen a un piocha pequeño o una excavadora pequeña. Usted tendrá una variedad de diferentes herramientas manuales disponibles.
- Usted necesitará un barril del paisaje o una carretilla para reunir las hierbas.
- Usted también necesitará un par de guantes para proteger sus manos.

Deserbando a mano (los Procedimientos del Trabajo)
Comience quitando las hierbas en una orilla de la propiedad y trabaje hasta la otra orilla del paisaje. Traiga el barril del paisaje y una

315

herramienta manual y **esté seguro de llevar puesto los guantes**. Hay muchos tipos diferentes de hierbas. Algunas de ellas son tóxicos y si usted no lleva los guantes puestos, usted esta buscando problema. Las hierbas tóxicas le dejarán con un sarpullido malo. Algunas personas son más sensible a estas hierbas e incluso pueden terminar en el hospital si ellos hacen contacto con estas hierbas. Cuándo quite las hierbas, tenga cuidado también de no tocar las hierbas con sus brazos o su cara y tenga cuidado de tocarse usted mismo con los guantes que usted lleva puesto.

Antes que usted empieze a deserbar un área, verifique que lo que usted quitará es una hierba **y no una flor o perenne (perennial).**

Perenne (Perennial) son flores que crecen año tras año. Están llegando a ser muy populares pero el problema es que muchos de ellos se parecen a una hierba mala por cierta parte del año. Así que este alerta, y si usted no está seguro acerca de lo que usted esta mirando, siempre es mejor no cortarlo. Las (Perenials) son costoso y usted puede causar mucho daño si usted los quita. ¡Así que sea cuidadoso!

Es mucho más fácil remover la hierba cuando la tierra esta húmeda. Trate de tomar ventaja de los días lluviosos o los pocos días próximos después de una lluvia para remover las hierbas. Cuándo usted remueve la hierba de una tierra seca, es casi imposible quitar el sistema entero de raíz de la hierba. **Cuándo usted deja un pedazo** del sistema de raíz en la tierra, la hierba crecerá de regreso en unos pocos días y usted tendrá que hacer el trabajo otra vez.

Cuándo usted agarra una hierba para quitarla, la agarra lo más bajo al suelo posible. Luego la arránca lentamente. Si la hierba se saca con las raíces, usted ha hecho el trabajo correctamente. Pero si la hierba es dura de sacarla, tome su herramienta manual y deberá cavar para aflojar la tierra alrededor de la hierba. Después arránquela lentamente y deberá salir con las raíces. No saque las hierbas rápidamente si no usted romperá las raíces y no quitará el sistema entero de raíz. Entonces la hierba crecerá de regreso en unos pocos días y usted tendrá que hacer el trabajo otra vez.

Todo las hierbas son diferentes. Algunas se pueden sacar muy fácil porque tienen un sistema superficial de raíz. Otras son muy duras de remover porque tienen un sistema de raíz muy profunda. Con alguna experiencia, usted llegará a familiarizarse con las hierbas que son más fáciles y cuales son más difíciles de remover. Mientras este haciendo la eliminación de hierba, usted encontrará que algunas hierbas son pequeñas y duras de agarrar. Usted puede dejar estas pequeñas hierbas allí y regresar siete días después para removerlas cuando esten más grandes. También puede rocíarlas con un rocío quimico. Un rocío quimico deberá ser aplicado solamente por un aplicador con lisencia. Discutiremos el control químico de eliminación de hierba en la próxima sección de esta guía de entrenamiento.

Algunos tipos de hierbas siempre crecerán bajo al suelo y son casi imposible de remover a mano. En este caso, si usted no esta calificado para rocíar, usted necesitará usar una herramienta manual. Una herramienta que baje hacia abajo en la tierra y remueva la hierba y la mayor parte de las raíces. Si las hierbas pequeñas continúan regresando y usted no puede rocíarlas con una sustancia química, usted necesitará poner una capa de pajote (mulch). Una capa pesada de pajote (mulch) parará cúalquier hierba de crecer.

Hace algunos años, me encontré con una hierba que crecia baja y que era casi imposible de detener. Primero nosotros la arráncamos, después la rocíamos muchas veces con sustancias químicas.
Un mes más tarde la hierba regreso. Yo la rocíe correctamente con muchos diferentes sustancias químicas y ninguno funciono. La hierba siempre regreso un mes más tarde. Terminamos poniéndo una tela de paisaje con un cuarto de pulgada de capa de pajote (mulch) y la hierba nunca regreso. Discutiremos acerca de cómo cubrir con pajote (mulch) más adelante en esta guía de entrenamiento.

Mientras usted desierba, esté seguro de mirar a los arbustos! Muchas personas no miran a los arbustos. Si usted ve algo creciendo fuera de un arbusto, lo quita. Siga la cima de la hierba y la arránca con las raíces para que usted no tenga que hacerlo otra vez la siguiente semana.

Las hierbas que se quitan de las aceras, caminos de entrada, y patios son generalmente fracasos si se quitan sin un rocío químico. Usted puede tratar de sacarlos, pero usted generalmente no sacará las raíces. También sacar las hierba de un sendero a mano toma demasiado tiempo. Usted puede cortar las cimas de las hierbas con una podadora de cuerda (string trimmer), pero crecerán de regreso. El rocío químico puede ser la única manera de matar permanentemente las hierbas.

Para quitar las hierbas tóxicas tal como hiedra de veneno o de roble, primero corte la parte de la vid de la hierba cercana a la tierra. Después use un rocío químico y rocíe las hojas y el área que usted cortó. Protéjase cuándo corta una vid o la planta tóxica. Tire cúalquier guante que hizo contacto pesado con plantas tóxicas.

Una vez que usted haya terminado deserbando a mano una propiedad, usted necesitará desacerse de las hierbas que usted acaba de quitar. Mantenga las hierbas en un montón compacto pequeño y los descarga lo más lejos posible porque las hierbas se secarán y cualquier semillas de hierba pueden soplar de regreso a la propiedad, creando otro problema. Cubra las hierbas con hojas o recortes de césped si usted los va a dejar en el sitio de trabajo.

Instrucción y consejos de Seguridad Deserbando a mano

- Siempre lleve puestos los guantes cuándo desierba a mano.
- Si usted esta inseguro si usted esta removiendo una hierba o una flor. Detengase y preguntele a alguien.
- Tenga cuidado de las hierbas tóxicas tal como hiedra de veneno o de roble.

- Agarre la hierba lo más bajo posible y las hala lentamente para que el sistema de raíz se remueva junto con la hierba.

- Utilize una herramienta manual para aflojar la tierra alrededor de las raíces si la hierba es dura de remover.

- Recuerde que usted debe quitar las raíces o la hierba crecerá de regreso.

- Tome provécho del tiempo humedo y haga la eliminación de hierba durante este tiempo.

- Si las hierbas continuán creciendo de regreso, un rocío químico debe ser utilizado o aplicar una tela de paisaje y pajote (mulch) sobre el área del problema.

- Siempre piense en la seguridad primero.

LA ELIMINACIÓN DE HIERBA (ROCÍO QUÍMICO) (CAPÍTULO 5)

La eliminación química de hierba se hace para controlar hierbas en áreas que son difíciles de remover a mano. El rocío de sustancia química de hierbas también se puede hacer para controlar el crecimiento de hierbas más pequeñas a más grande y de extenderse. Si es hecho correctamente, rocíar puede ahorrar tiempo y hacer un trabajo profesional de parar el crecimiento de hierba. Rocíando las hierbas correctamente matará el sistema entero de raíz de las hierbas que hara imposible que crescan de regreso. Sin embargo, si el rocío de químicos no se hace correctamente, problemas graves pueden ocurrir. Tal como, dañar o matar las plantas del paisaje, dañando o matando áreas de césped y crear un problema grave de salud a nosotros mismos y a todos alrededor de nosotros.

La mayoría de los estados requieren que usted sea licenciado como un applicator de pesticide u operario para aplicar hierba el control legalmente. Cerciórese gue es permitido legalmente y apropiadamente aplicar hierba el control antes de trabajar en cualquier sitio del trabajo. Siempre siga todo la lay requerido por su estado.

No aplique control químico de hierba de ninguna manera, forma o manera si usted no esta licenciado y entrenado. Leyendo este capítulo de nuestra guía de entrenamiento es su primer paso.

El equipo del Rocío de sustancias químicas

El equipo usado para rociar hierbas es bastante sencillo. Un tanque de rocíar de muchila o de mano, guantes de goma, botas, un respirador y lentes de seguridad.

Tanque de Rocíador de muchila

Este tipo de tanque de rocíador trabaja muy bien y es comúnmente usado. El tanque de rocíador de muchila generalmente aguanta tres galones de mezcla. Algo más pequeño no es recomendado porque si no usted tendrá que parar a mezclar la sustancia química y el agua con demasiada frecuencia.

El tanque de rocíador de muchila tiene dos correas y es llevado en los hombros y espalda. Cuándo abra y cierra la tapa, tenga cuidado para cerciórarse que el sello de goma (seal/gasket) en la tapa sea puesta correctamente en su lugar.

Apriete la tapa seguramente, pero no sobre apriete si no usted romperá el sello y la tapa goteará. Cuándo la tapa comienza a tener fugas, la sustancia química llegará a su ropas, cuello y espalda. No utilize el rociador si la tapa gotea.

Puede haber un filtro debajo de la tapa de recolectar cúalquier escombros de basura antes de que entre al tanque. Utilize este filtro y no lo quite. El filtro a veces hace dificil para poner la tapa correctamente en su puesto por eso algunas personas lo quitan. ¡No quite el filtro! Usted sólo creará más problemas. En el fondo del tanque esta la bomba y una bomba de brazo para darle la presión correcta de rocío. Entonces hay una manguera que conecta la bomba a la pistola del rociador. Puede haber otro filtro en la pistola o antes de la boca del rocío. Mientras este usando este rociador, usted usará un brazo para controlar la bomba de brazo para darle la presión correcta de rocío y usted usará su otro brazo para aguantar la pistola del rociador.

Antes de ir a un sitio de trabajo, cerciórese que todos los filtros esten limpios. También, cerciórese que todas las conexciones de manguera esten apretadas y seguras. Después cerciórese que la punta del rociador este limpia y los rocíos correctos. Que los filtros estén en su lugar para detener cúalquier basura de llegar atascarse en la punta del rociador. No hay nada peor que mezclar la sustancia química y después llegar al sitio de trabajo y tener la punta atascada cada cuantos minutos. Siempre limpie y verifique el rociador antes de usarlo.

Tanque Rocíador de mano

El tanque rocíador a mano es básicamente lo mismo que el de muchila excepto que tiene una bomba y el asidero encima del rociador. Usted tiene que parar de trabajar y poner el rociador abajo en el suelo cada vez que usted tiene que bombearlo. Con el de muchila usted puede bombear y rocíar al mismo tiempo.

El Equipo de seguridad

Lleve puestos el equipo apropiado de seguridad, un respirador, lentes, guantes de goma y botas de goma.

Respirador

Hay dos tipos de respiradores que usted puede utilizar. El primer tipo es una máscara de goma con dos cartuchos de filtro. Cuándo usted respira el flujo de aire pasa por los cartuchos del filtro. Hay una válvula en la parte de la goma de la máscara donde usted exhala. Cerciórese que los cartuchos esten marcados para pesticidas y los reemplaza como se recomienda por fabrica. Usando el respirador de goma con los cartuchos correctos es la manera disponible más segura de protegerse de respirar la niebla del rocío de sustancia química.

El segundo tipo de respirador es una máscara de papel. La máscara de papel es más pequeña y más fácil de llevar. La máscara **debe** estar marcada para el uso con nieblas de rocíos. La máscara correcta de papel reducirá la cantidad de niebla de químicos que usted respira, pero no parará 100% de ello. La máscara se debe deshechar después que se usa unas pocas veces. Ambas máscaras necesitan mantenerse lo más limpias posible. Manténgalas en el frente de su camión; envuélvalos con una toalla de papel limpia en cada uso.

Cuando se usa un rocíador de muchila, usted debe estar usando una presión baja y debe estar aguantando la punta del rocíador más o menos de 6 a 12 pulgadas del suelo. Cuándo se usa correctamente, hay muy poca desviación de la niebla del rocío de sustancia química. Por lo tanto la máscara de papel es muy comúnmente usada con un rocíador de muchila o rocíadores de mano.

En adicion a llevar puesto un respirador, usted debe llevar puestos los lentes de seguridad, guantes de goma (marcados para el uso con sustancias químicas), y botas de goma. Las botas de trabajo de cuero no se recomiendan porque llegarán a ser saturadas con la niebla del rocío de sustancia química y penetrará las botas si un derrame de rocío de químicos ocurre.

Mezcla de Sustancias Químicas

La mezcla de químicos se necesita hacer muy cuidadosamente.

- Siempre lleve puesta la protección de seguridad cuándo este haciendo la mezcla. La sustancia química es muy fuerte antes de ser mixta con agua; por lo tanto la protección de seguridad es muy importante mientras este mezclando.
- Haga su mezcla en el suelo donde no hay objetos alrededor que puedan crear un problema.
- No se distraíga de cualquier cosa que este sucediendo alrededor de usted mientras usted esta mezclando si no usted puede hacer un error grave.
- No haga mezcla si hay algún niño, mascotas o actividades en el área.

- Mezcle el primer tanque al comienzo del día en el garaje. Entonces si después se necesita, mezcle los tanques restantes en el sitio de trabajo.

- Use sólo una copa de medida para el control químico de hierba. Marque la copa y no la use para otra cosa más.

- Haga otra marca en la copa de medida por la cantidad del producto que usted usa para hacer un tanque lleno. De esta manera usted no se olvidará.

Por ejemplo, si usted usa un tanque de tres galones y usted necesita mezclar (tres onzas por galón), usted necesitará un total de (nueve onzas para mezclar un tanque lleno). Marque la copa de medida a nueve onzas. Usted debe marcar también los galones en el tanque del rocío para que sean fáciles de ver y leer.

- Trate de usar la misma sustancia química durante todo el año de esta manera mezclar será fácil de recordar.

- Use un producto de buena calidad ese matará todos los tipos diferentes de hierbas, también césped, la hiedra de veneno, vides silvestres, y la maleza que crece baja. La mayoria de productos nuevos no se esparcirá ni se rezumará en la tierra. Ellos tendán una sustancia pegagosa química para que el producto permanezca en la hierba y no se lave después que este seco por unas pocas horas. Después de rocíar el producto, usted puede volver en dos semanas y la tierra estará libre de químicos. Usted puede plantar semilla o ajardinar las plantas sin ningún problema. Siempre lea la etiqueta completamente antes de usar algún producto químico. Las instrucciones variarán basado en cada aplicación diferente.

- Permanezca lejos de productos viejos tal como Asesino de Vegetación (Vegetation Killer). Este producto matará toda clase de vegetación hasta por un lapso de un año. La tierra estará contaminada por un lapso de un año. Bajo condiciones de lluvia recia, la sustancia química puede esparcirse a otras áreas que matará lo que sea en su sendero y la sustancia química es muy tóxica.

- Permanezca con los mejores productos. Lea y entienda completamente la etiqueta y usted no debe tener ningún problema.

Siempre, cerciórese de entender completamente todo acerca del producto que usted esta usando. Haga preguntas si usted no esta 100% seguro acerca de la sustancia química, de cómo utilizarla, de lo que hace, y cuales son los peligros de usarlo.

Mezclando un Tanque de Rocío de Tres Galónes

- Para mezclar su tanque de tres galones, llenelo con un galón de agua primero. Después agregue la sustancia química medida.

- Llene la copa medidora con agua y lo descarga en el tanque unas pocas veces hasta que la copa medidora este limpia, después agrega más agua para llegar a la marca de tres galones en el tanque de rocío.

- Sí hay un filtro a la cabeza del tanque, no lo quite. Recolectará cúalquier escombros de basura antes de que entren al tanque y causen un problema.

- De vuelta a la tapa del tanque pero no la sobre apriete si no usted romperá el sello de goma en la tapa.

- Agite el tanque por 30 segundos a un minuto.

- Rinse el exterior del tanque si se necesita.

- Ponga el contenedor de químicos y la copa medidora en un lugar seguro, bajo llave y asegurados en una caja de herramientas es mejor. Cerciórese que el contenedor químico este seguro y que no se invertirá ni se derramará.

- Asegure el tanque del rocío atrás en el camión o el remolque. El tanque debe ser almacenado alto para que los niños no puedan alcanzar el tanque.

Rociando la hierba en el sitio de trabajo

- Una vez que usted está en el sitio de trabajo, póngase su protección de seguridad, agite el tanque un poco más y usted está listo para rocíar.

- Las áreas que usted rociará deben ser deserbadas a mano primero. Quite cúalquier hierba que este más grande que una pulgada; quite también hierbas que están cerca de arbustos, árboles, raíces expuestas, o áreas duras de rocíar.

- Cerciórese que no haya gente ni mascotas alrededor cuándo usted este rocíando.

- Empieze en un extremo de la cama del paisaje y trabaje hacia el otro extremo. Mientras usted este caminando, cubra un área de más o menos seis pies de ancho. Camine de atrás hacia delante alcanzando más o menos tres pies en cada lado de usted. Camine a través de la cama igual a cómo uste camina cuándo corta un césped. Mantenga una línea recta cuando camina de atrás hacia delante. Usando este método, usted no perderá ninguna hierba ni rocíara ninguna hierba dos veces.

- La desviación del rocíador es causado por sobre bombear que es un error muy común y puede causar muchos problemas.

- **No sobre bombee el tanque** o el rocío saldrá demasiado rápido. Cuándo el rocío sale demasiado rápido, hará mucho exceso de niebla y se desviará en áreas indeseables La niebla del rocío llegará a su cara, y se desviará a cúalquier plantas en el área. Si la niebla del rocíador químico hace contacto con cúalquier planta, causará graves daños o la muerte a la planta.

- Sólo bombee el tanque lo suficiente para que el rocío salga lentamente. Tomará un poco de práctica para obtener la presión correcta del rocíador.

- Sobre-bombiando sucede mayormente en los rocíadores de muchila.

- Aguante la punta del rocíador más o menos de 6 a 12 pulgadas del suelo. Haciendo esto usted hará buen contacto con las hierbas. El rocío estará muy cerca del suelo y no podrá desviarse demasiado distante.

- También aguante la punta del rocíador lejos de usted mismo para que su ropas no se empape de la sustancia química.

- Rocíe la hierba para que se cubra completamente con el rocío. Una vez que la hierba este cubierta, pare de rocíar. No hay necesidad de empapar la hierba o la tierra alrededor de las hierbas.

- La hierba absorberá la sustancia química por sus hojas. Una vez que la sustancia química es absorbida por las hojas, la hierba morirá incluyendo el sistema de raíz.

- Sin embargo, sí la hierba no se rocía completamente, no puede morir; cubra 100% de la hierba.

- Cuándo usted este rocíando, permanezca lejos de todas las otras plantas. Permanezca lejos de charcos, corrientes, o corrientes de agua. Permanezca lejos de alguna superficie de raíz expuesta de un árbol o arbusto.

- Cuándo usted ha terminado con una área, Limpie sus pies en tierra seca. Sí hay un poco de sustancia química debajo de sus botas y usted camina en un área del césped, usted matará el césped por la sustancia química.

- Sí hay condiciones de mucho viento, es mejor que usted no rocíe.

- Sí hay una lluvia venidera, no rocíe. La mayoría de las sustancias químicas requieren más o menos unas cuatro horas de tiempo seco antes de una lluvia o la sustancia química no trabajará.

- La mayoría de sustancias químicas tomarán de 7 a 10 días para matar la hierba. Unas pocas hierbas que son duras de matar pueden tomar una segunda aplicación.

- Haciendo una mezcla química más fuerte no hará un mejor trabajo. Si la mezcla química es demasiado fuerte, usted quemará la cima de la hierba. Entonces la sustancia química no sera absorbida en la hierba, el sistema de raíz no morirá y la hierba volverá en unas pocas semanas. Nunca agregue sustancia química extra, solamente siga las instrucciones de mezclar recomendadas.

- Dependiendo del estado en que usted vive, usted tendrá que poner las banderas de notificación de aplicación de pesticidas en las áreas rocíadas.

Esté seguro que usted entiende y siga los procedimientos que acabamos de discutir y siga las instrucciones de etiqueta de la sustancia química o usted puede crear problemas graves. Una vez que usted entiende todas las instrucciones y rocíe correctamente, usted tendrá excelente resultados en el control de hierbas no deseadas.

Instrucciones y Consejos de seguridad del Rocío de sustancia Química

- Sí usted no esta entrenado y no esta 100% seguro acerca de lo que usted esta haciendo, no utilice el rocío químico. La mayoría de los estados también requieren que usted tenga licensia para aplicar rocío de sustancia químicas.
- Lleve puestos los lentes de seguridad, guantes, respirador, botas de goma y una ropa de mangas largas cuando mezcla.
- Siempre lea y entienda cada etiqueta antes de usarlo.
- Sea muy cuidadoso cuándo mezcla la sustancia química con agua.
- No mezcle cerca de otra gente ni mascotas. Evite las distracciones cuándo mezcla.
- Cerciórese que el tanque se mezcle completamente.

- La mayoría de los rocíadores tienen filtros en algún lugar de la pistola del rocío o manguera y a la cabeza del tanque. Mantenga estos filtros limpios y los verifica a menudo; no los quite.

- No sobre apriete la tapa del rocíador. Verifique para cerciorarse que el sello de goma este siempre en buen estado.

- No use cúalquier rocíadores si no trabajan apropiadamente. Todo el equipo debe estar al 100% a la orden del trabajo o no se debe usar.

- Lave completamente las copas medidoras, contenedores de químicos y rocíadores.

- Mantenga las sustancias químicas bajo llave.

- Mantenga el rocíador seguro y de cuatro a cinco pies del suelo en su vehículo.

- No rocíe cerca de la gente o de mascotas. Evite las distracciones cuándo está rociando.

- Lleve puesto el equipo apropiado de seguridad mientras está rociando.

- No rocíe durante las condiciones del tiempo ventoso.

- No aplique también mucha presión de bomba mientras está rociando. Un rocío de presión baja sale tosco y no se desvia. Un rocío de presión alta sale en un rocío fino y se desvia.

- Tenga cuidado cuándo rocia cerca de flores, plantas y áreas de zona de raíz. Estas áreas deben ser limpiadas deserbandolas a mano.

- Aguante la punta de la boca del rocío 6-12 pulgadas del suelo.

- Sí la punta del rocío se atasca, limpielo con un cuchillo o con un cepillo de alambre pequeño. Si esto no trabaja, toma la punta aparte y lo limpía bajo agua.

- Nunca sople la punta del rocíador con su boca.

- Sí la punta continúa atascandose, enjuague el rocíador entero y los filtros.

- Siempre piense en la seguridad primero.

BORDEAR CAMAS DE PAISAJE
(CAPÍTULO 6)

Bordear camas de paisaje se hace para detener el césped de crecer en el área de las camas de paisaje. Mantiene las camas bien definidas y da al paisaje una vista de mantenimiento profesional. Usted necesitará tener una máquina que bordea, una pala espada, una piocha, y una carretilla. Cuándo crea camas nuevas de paisaje, usted necesitará una pistola de pintura para marcar donde irán las camas nuevas.

La Máquina que Bordea

La máquina que bordea es una máquina que tiene una hoja de metal. La hoja gira muy rapidamente en una dirección vertical. Cuándo la hoja se baja hacia abajo, cortará en el suelo. La mayoría de las máquinas de bordear tienen motores de 2 ciclos. La hoja debe estar en buen estado o si no hará un trabajo pobre. Verifique la condición de la hoja y la cambia cuando se desgaste. Nunca use la máquina si no tiene un protector de seguridad y siempre lleve puestos los lentes de seguridad cuando opera esta máquina.

(Spada) Pala Plana

La pala plana es un tipo de pala. La parte del fondo de la pala no es puntuda, pero es plana. Esta pala sólo se debe usar para bordear camas. La parte plana de la pala quedará en el corte que usted hizo con la máquina que bordea. O, sí usted no tiene una máquina que bordea, usted puede cortar en el suelo con la pala plana (spade).

Piocha

Piocha es una herramienta que tiene muchos propósitos. Sí usted tiene que remover hierba o tierra dura de las camas, será más fácil usar un piocha.

Las Carretillas

La carretilla se usara para recoger cúalquier césped o tierra que necesite ser deshechado después de bordear.

Pistola de Pintura

Una pistola de pintura es una herramienta que se usa para hacer las marcas en las áreas de césped o en el área de las camas. Tiene un asidero largo y se arrolla en una rueda. Halando el disparador a la cabeza del asidero, la pintura se rociará en el suelo. Se usa cuándo se crea camas nuevas de paisaje o se puede usar para re-formar una cama existente.

Bordear Camas de Paisaje (los Procedimientos del Trabajo)
Re- bordeando Camas Existentes

Primero discutiremos re-bordear camas existentes de paisaje. Las camas de paisaje deben ser re-bordeadas una vez al año. Antes de que usted arranque la máquina que bordea, camine lentamente por el área que usted está a punto de bordear. *Busque contra la casa o el edificio por la caja donde todos los alambres de utilidad van. Si hay una cama de paisaje en esa área, esté seguro de ser extra cuidadoso en esa área. Use una pala y bordee esa área cuidadosamente a mano. Los alambres y los tubos deben estar enterrados 6 pulgadas de profundo pero en muchos casos, estan sólo unos pocas pulgadas bajo el suelo y pueden ser cortados al usar una máquina de bordear.* Busque por algo que pueda ser dañado por la hoja que bordea o por algo que pueda dañar la hoja en la máquina que bordea. Tal como:

- Alambres para luces.
- Sistema de tubería y regadera.
- Sistema de las cabezas de regadera.
- Alambres de Cable de Television y de telefonos.
- Alambres electricos.
- Piedras grandes

Otra cosa de tener cuidado es de la cerca invisible del perro. Esto es un alambre enterradó unas cuantas pulgadas en el suelo. Rodea la propiedad entera. El perro lleva puesto un collar especial y siente un golpe electrico cuándo viene cerca del alambre. Sí usted ve un perro en la propiedad, preguntele al cliente si ellos tienen una cerca invisible. Cerciórese que el cliente marque claramente donde esta el alambre o si no usted no puede hacer el trabajo de bordear.

Una vez que usted está enterado de todo lo que usted necesita evitar en la propiedad, Inspeccione de nuevo el área que usted está a punto de bordear. ¿Hay algunas áreas de las camas de paisaje que necesitan ser mejoradas o ser expandidas? La orilla de las camas de paisaje deben correr lisamente y deben tener una buena forma. Sí hay áreas que se miran mal, ahora es el tiempo de mejorarlas.

Antes de bordear, preguntese a usted mismo las siguientes preguntas.

- ¿Hay allí algun área donde la cama necesita ser cortada más grande?
- ¿Hay allí algun área que usted puede reformar para que se vea mejor?

Piense acerca de esto y haga el cambio sí es necesario. No re-bordee exactamente en la vieja orilla existente, no sé ve bien. Sí se necesita, use una pistola de pintura para re-formar la cama de esta manera usted tendrá una marca para seguir.

Habrá algunos trabajos donde las camas **no** necesiten ser mejoradas ni reformadas. Entonces usted puede simplemente correr la hoja de bordear a lo largo del contorno existente. Cuándo las camas no necesitan ser mejoradas, corte **lo menos posible** de la orilla de la cama. Entonces habrá poco césped y tierra para ser removidos y recogidos.

Arranque la máquina de bordear y corra el motor a su velociad máxima y entonces haga el corte. Corte aproximadamente de 2 a 3 pulgadas en el suelo. Sí usted esta cortando a traves del césped, corte aproximadamente 2 pulgadas debajo de la capa del césped. Empuje la máquina mientras corre el motor a su velocidad máxima. Deje cúalquier área donde hay piedras, cabezas de regadera, etc o donde pueden haber alambres enterrados. Re-forme cúalquier áreas de camas que necesiten ser mejoradas.

Ahora que la orilla ha sido cortada, usted está listo para usar su (spade) pala o piocha. Empuje la (spade) pala en la ranura que usted acaba de cortar. Después levante y quite la tierra o el césped de **el interior** de la cama de paisaje. Quite todo el césped y hierbas dentro del área de la cama de paisaje, cerca de la orilla que acaba de ser cortada. Mantenga una orilla recta y aguda donde la hoja de bordear cortó en el suelo.

La pala plana (spade) es la herramienta más comúnmente usada para bordear. La pala plana (spade) trabaja bien si usted esta quitando cantidades pequeñas de tierra o césped.

Si usted tiene que quitar mucho césped, y hierbas, o si la tierra esta muy dura, una piocha trabajará mejor. Utilize la parte ancha dela piocha, cave hacia abajo y levante el césped. Utilize piocha en la misma dirección que la orilla fue cortada. Usted debe ser capaz de remover la tierra y el césped y dejar el borde bien cortado.

Después que la orilla se ha cortado (dug out), usted necesita recoger el césped o la tierra que se quitó. **Trate de dejar la mayor parte de la tierra en la cama**. Si hay algún pedazo grande de césped con tierra en ellos, agite el césped para que la mayor parte de tierra se caiga y regrese a la cama. Recoga el césped, hierbas, piedras, etc y pongalas en su carretilla. En la mayoría de los casos, es más fácil recoger el césped, etc con sus manos. Después que el césped, etc ha sido limpiado, el trabajo esta terminado. En algunos trabajos, usted puede quitar también hierbas de la cama entera de paisaje mientras esté bordeando. Después usted quizás cubra con pajote (mulch) las camas. Discutiremos como cubrir con pajote (mulch) en el próximo capítulo de esta guía de entrenamiento.

Bordear Camas Nuevas de Paisaje

Bordear camas nuevas de paisaje se hace casi lo mismo excepto que la nueva cama es marcada primero con pintura de marcador. Después usted corta a lo largo de la línea marcada y quita todo lo que este dentro de la nueva cama.

Bordear Anillos de Árbol

Los anillos del árbol son camas circulares pequeñas alrededor de árboles ornamentales. Ellos protegen a los árboles del cortacésped y podadoras de cuerda. Ellos ayudan también a proteger el sistema de raíz durante condiciones calientes y frías del tiempo.

Para bordear un anillo existente de árbol, primero verifique para ver si la forma existente se ve bien y lo ajusta si se necesita. Después use los mismos procedimientos que acabamos de discutir. Asi como el árbol crece más grande, el anillo del árbol se debe hacer también más grande.

Aumente el tamaño de los anillos del árbol como sea necesitado, generalmente cada dos o tres años el anillo se debe hacer levemente más grande.

Para bordear un **nuevo** anillo del árbol:

- Haga una marca donde usted quiere la orilla que este.

- Use un pedazo de lazo; envuélvalo flojamente alrededor del tronco del árbol.

- En la otra punta del lazo, ate una lata de pintura de marcador.

- Usted debe poder mecer el lazo alrededor del árbol.

- Ajuste la lata de pintura para que pueda hacer una marca donde usted quiere.

- Mientras que usted mece el lazo alrededor del árbol, rocía la pintura en el suelo. Esto le dará un círculo parejo agradable alrededor del árbol y el trabajo se mirará profesional.

Bordeando Aceras y Patios

Sí una propiedad no se ha mantenido, puede tener césped que crece en las aceras o en el patio. Al utilizar la máquina de bordear, corra la hoja contra la orilla exterior del sendero o patio. Después, quita cúalquier césped o tierra que está en el camino o patio. Debe haber un espacio pequeño entre el césped y un sendero o patio. Recuerde de buscar por cúalquier alambres, tubos, etc. antes de bordear.

Bordear de camas de paisaje se debe hacer una vez al año. La primavera es el mejor tiempo del año para hacer el trabajo ya que el suelo es generalmente suave y fácil de trabajar. Bordear en duro, o tierra seca es muy difícil y no se debería hacer si es posible. Las orillas se deben mantener con una podadora de cuerda durante el servico de cortar el césped. Aguante la podadora de cuerda para que la cuerda corte vertical hacia abajo en la orilla existente. Esto se debe hacer más o menos cada dos semanas y mantendrá la propiedad con una vista magnífica.

Instrucción y Consejos de Bordear Camas de Paisaje

- Siempre lleve puestos los lentes de seguridad con la máquina de bordear.
- Siempre verifique el área que usted bordeará antes que usted hage el corte. Busque las líneas de cable y teléfono, iluminación de luces, tubos de regadera, piedras y otros problemas. Corte estas áreas cuidadosamente a mano.
- Si la forma de la cama o del anillo del árbol no es perfecta, lo arregla cuándo usted haga la nueva orilla. No siga la misma forma si no se mira bien.
- Haga su corte lo más cercano posible a la vieja orilla. Entonces habrá menos tierra y césped de quitar y el trabajo será mucho más fácil.
- Mantenga las manos y pies lejos de todas las partes móviles de las máquinas.
- Llene las máquinas en los remolques, no en el césped.
- No sobre apriete la tapa de gas si no usted romperá el sello y goteará
- Mantenga todas las máquinas seguras abrochadas en el remolque o camión.
- No quite ningún protector de seguridad.
- ¡¡¡¡¡Siempre piense en la seguridad primero!!!!!

CUBRIR CON PAJOTE (MULCH) LAS CAMAS DE PAISAJE
(CAPÍTULO 7)

Cubrir con pajote (mulch) se hace por muchas razones diferentes. Primero ayudará a proteger las plantas de paisaje. A través del año, una capa de pajote (mulch) ayudará a sostener el agua y humedad alrededor del área de la zona de raíz de las plantas. Las plantas del paisaje podrán sostener el agua por más largo tiempo, permanecer más saludable, y podrán resistir mejor las condiciones secas del tiempo. Durante el invierno, el pajote (mulch) ayudará a proteger el sistema de raíz de plantas de las condiciones malas del tiempo. Las plantas con pajote (mulch) alrededor de ellas serán más saludables y tendrán una mejor oportunidad de sobrevivencia durante las condiciones de tensión. El pajote (mulch) reducirá la cantidad del crecimiento de hierba en las camas de paisaje. Las hierbas crecerán muy rápidamente y serán duro de controlar en una cama sin pajote (mulch). El pajote (mulch) ayudará también a prevenir la erosión de tierra. Sin pajote (mulch), la tierra en las camas de paisaje comenzará a lavarse con una lluvia pesada. El pajote (mulch) comenzara a descomponerse después de unos cuantos años y lentamente se volvera tierra. La tierra será rica en orgánicos y algunos nutritivos se añadirán a las camas de paisaje. Otra razón para cubrir con pajote (mulch) es porque se mira magnífico y le da a las camas una limpia, vista profesional.

Hay muchos tipos diferentes de pajote (mulch) disponible. Los pajote (mulch)s serán diferentes en colores, la materia y el costo.

Permanezca lejos de usar los pajote (mulch)s muy baratos. La mayor parte de los pajote (mulch)s muy baratos tienen basura en ello, tal como viejos escombros de basura, (pallets) o madera podrida o contaminado con sustancias químicas. Estos pajote (mulch)s baratos y bajos de calidad pueden hacer más daño que bien. He visto plantas de paisaje que mueren por usar un pajote (mulch) de una pobre calidad contaminado. Sí hay algún químico en el pajote (mulch), y se lava en la tierra durante una lluvia, habrá daño grave hecho a la tierra y plantas existentes. Cerciórese que usted este obtienendo su pajote (mulch) de una compañía segura y acreditada. Verifique el pajote (mulch) a través del año y cerciórese que este todo el año en una buena calidad.

A veces un suministrador tendrá un cuadro muy grande de pajote (mulch) y ya para el tiempo que lleguen al fondo del montón, el pajote (mulch) puede ya haber comenzado a descomponerse. Entonces usted tendrá pajote (mulch) que ya a comenzado a volverse tierra. Si el pajote (mulch) tiene alguna tierra en ello, no se debe usar.

El pajote (mulch) debe estar compuesto de varios pedazos molidos de madera, sin ninguna tierra en la mezcla. ¿Cómo controlará el pajote (mulch) hierbas si ya hay tierra en el pajote (mulch)? Algunos suministradores le venderán cúalquier cosa, así que sea cuidadoso.

343

Inspeccione el pajote (mulch) que usted está comprando a través del año.

El pajote (mulch) es comprado generalmente por la yarda cúbica. Una yarda es una medida que es 3 pies por 3 pies por 3 pies, en la forma de un cubo o cuadrado. Cuándo se vende, se descargará en su camión con un tractor de balde. Usted puede medir la cama del camión que usted esta usando para determinar cuánto pajote (mulch) cabe en el.

Si la cama de su camión es:

- 9 pies largos por 6 pies anchos por 3 pies altos (multiplica $9 \times 6 \times 3 = 162$ pies cuadrados).
- Una yarda cúbica es $3 \times 3 \times 3$ (un total de 27 pies cuadrados).
- Divide 162 por 27, que totaliza 6 yardas.
- Si se llenó al nivel, el camión aguantará un total de 6 yardas.

Tipos de Pajote (mulch)

Ahora vamos a hablar acerca de los diferentes tipos de pajote (mulch) que están disponibles. Hablaremos acerca de la mayoría de los pajote (mulch)s populares y comúnmente usados. Dependiendo en qué parte del país usted este trabajando, usted puede usar un pajote (mulch) que nosotros no hemos discutido. Tal como en los estados Sureños hay muchos árboles de pino. La gente en esta área del país usan las semillas de pino como un pajote (mulch) ya que es fácil de juntarse y vender. Pero recuerde que todo los pajotes (mulch) hacen básicamente la misma cosa. Protegen las plantas, protegen el suelo de la erosión, ayudan a prevenir el crecimiento de hierba, y se mira magnífico.

Empezaremos discutiendo el pajote (mulch) más barato en costo y calidad y trabajaremos hasta lo mejor.

Astillas de Madera del Campo (Playground Wood Chips)

Las astillas de madera del campo de juegos son astillas de madera que son muy limpias. No hay palos pequeños, hojas, ni escombros de basura en las astillas de madera del campo. Son usados en su mayor parte alrededor de áreas de juego de niños. Una capa de 3" a 4" mantendrá a los niños de ensuciarse y será más seguro que caer en el suelo duro. Las astillas de madera del campo están disponibles en la mayoría de los centros de jardín.

El Pajote (mulch) de Madera Dura (Hardwood Mulch)

El pajote (mulch) de madera dura se compone de diferentes tipos de madera dura. Se muele dos veces para que sea más fino que las astillas de madera y es generalmente de color marrón. El pajote (mulch) de madera dura es muy popular porque no es demasiado caro y se mira bastante atractivo. Tenga cuidado cuándo compra pajote (mulch) de madera dura. A veces el fabricante molerá escombros de construcción y otra basura en este tipo de pajote (mulch). Inspeccione el pajote (mulch) y sí usted encuentra alguna basura en ello, no lo use.

Algunos tipos de pajote (mulch) de madera dura tendrán un olor malo en ellos. El olor puede durar por unas cuantas semanas. El pajote (mulch) de madera durará más o menos por un año. Después de un año se mirará viejo y comenzara a descomponerse. Cuándo se usa pajote (mulch) de madera dura, usted debe dar a las camas de paisaje

345

una capa de aproximadamente 1 a 2-1/2" por año. El pajote (mulch) de madera dura se puede comprar en la mayoría de los centros de jardín o directamente del fabricante para obtener el mejor precio.

El Pajote (mulch) de Raíz (Root Mulch)

El pajote (mulch) de raíz es un pajote (mulch) de color oscuro marrón/negro.El pajote (mulch) de raíz se hace de troncones del árbol y se envejece para volverse en un color oscuro.El pajote (mulch) de raíz durará más o menos de uno a dos años antes de que se necesite volver a llenarse de nuevo. El pajote (mulch) de raíz se vende en la mayoría de los centros de jardín y costará un poco más que el pajote (mulch) de madera dura.

Pajote (mulch) de Madera Dura Colorado (Colored Hardwood Mulch)

El Pajote (mulch) de madera dura colorado ha llegado a ser popular en los últimos pocos años. Este producto es colorado para que se mire café rojizo. El color permanece en el pajote (mulch) por un año o más. Casi no hay decadencia del color. La mayoría de los otros pajote (mulch)s se destiñen después de unos pocos meses. Cerciórese que el cliente tenga una muestra de cualquier pajote (mulch) de color antes de que usted haga algún trabajo.

Algunas personas les gusta el color blanco y otras personas no lo encuentran atractivo. También los pajote (mulch)s colorados variarán levemente en colores. Esté seguro de comprar todo el pajote (mulch) necesario para un trabajo de las mismas reservas porque el próximo montón puede que no sea del mismo color exacto. El producto está disponible en la mayoría de los centros de jardín pero es bastante costoso.

El Pajote (mulch) de (Hammermill) (Hammermill Mulch)

El pajote (mulch) de (Hammermill) es un pajote (mulch) de alta calidad que está disponible en diferentes sombras de marrón. Cuándo el pajote (mulch) de (Hammermill) se hace, sólo la mejor madera de calidad se utiliza. El pajote (mulch) es molido en pedazos que son levemente diferentes en el tamaño. El pajote (mulch) de (Hammermill) durará más largo tiempo que el pajote (mulch) de Madera Dura. Otra cosa buena del pajote (mulch) (Hammermill) es que no huele mal. Muchos de los pajote (mulch)s de madera dura tienen un mal olor por una o dos semanas. Un olor malo le puede dar un cliente infeliz. El pajote (mulch) (Hammermill) necesitará ser reabastecido de nuevo en uno a dos años. El pajote (mulch) (Hammermill) no se usa tan frecuentemente como el pajote (mulch) de Madera Dura por causa de su costo. (Hammermill) generalmente cuesta más o menos dos veces más que el pajote (mulch) de Madera Dura. El pajote (mulch) (Hammermill) está disponible en todos los centros de jardín. Si se compra en una cantidad grande, se puede comprar directamente del fabricante.

El Pajote (mulch) de Cedro (Cedar Mulch)

El pajote (mulch) de cedro es el mejor pajote (mulch) que usted puede comprar. Es de color café rojizo y es hecho de árboles de cedro. La madera de cedro durará más que las demas maderas. No se descomponera tan rápidamente como los otros pajotes (mulch). Sin embargo el color se desteñirá más o menos al mismo tiempo que la mayoría de los otros pajote (mulch)s. El pajote (mulch) de cedro es magnífico para usarlo alrededor de la base de una casa. Más o menos por un mes el cedro tendrá un olor bueno. El pajote (mulch) de cedro es el único pajote (mulch) que los insectos evitarán evadir. Los insectos no harán un hogar en el cedro y ni siquiera aún les gusta caminar a través de ello.

Sí usted tiene un cliente con un problema de hormiga o comején, el pajote (mulch) de cedro es el pajote (mulch) de usar. El costo del pajote (mulch) de cedro es su único punto malo. Su costó es de tres veces más que el Pajote (mulch) de Madera Dura (Hardwood Mulch).

Las herramientas Necesarias Para Cubrir con pajote (mulch)

Usted necesitará las siguientes herramientas cuándo cubra con pajote (mulch):

- Una carretilla de tamaño muy grande y una regular.
- Una horquilla (pitchfork) de tamaño muy grande y uno regular.
- Un rastrillo del arco de metal.
- Un rastrillo de hoja.
- Una pala plana.
- Un soplador de muchila.
- Un camión de descarga o alguien que entregue el pajote (mulch) al sitio de trabajo.

Esté seguro de traer la cantidad correcta de herramientas al sitio de trabajo. Si usted trabaja como una tripulación de dos personas, usted necesitará dos carretillas, dos horquillas (pitchforks) y dos rastrillos. Sí usted trabaja como una tripulación de tres personas, trae tres de cada una de las herramientas. Es incompetente e improductivo tener una tripulación de tres personas trabajando con sólo uno o dos carretillas y compartir un rastrillo de metal y una horquilla. Aunque usted trabaje como un equipo y no usa todas las herramientas a la misma vez, siempre es mejor tener herramientas de reserva en el sitio de trabajo.

Carretillas

La carretilla de tamaño muy grande debe tener las ruedas dobles y ser capaz de aguantar más o menos el doble de cantidad que una carretilla de tamaño regular. La carretilla de tamaño regular se debe usar cuándo usted necesita caber en áreas pequeñas entre las plantas, árboles, o cercas. Trabajará también mejor cuándo usted trabaja en una colina. Cualquier tamaño de carretilla que usted use, cerciórese que las llantas tengan suficiente presión de aire. El trabajo será dos veces más duro si usted empuja una carretilla repleta con una llanta que esta media inflada. Siempre mantenga una bomba de aire en su camión; Después cuándo usted este en el sitio del trabajo y usted ve una llanta baja, usted puede arreglar el problema y no tiene que sufrir todo el día.

Horquillas (Pitchforks)

Las horquillas se usan para recoger el pajote (mulch). Una horquilla grande trabaja mejor cuándo llena las carretillas del montón de pajote (mulch). Una horquilla de tamaño más pequeño con un un asidero largo trabaja mejor cuándo usted toma pajote (mulch) de la carretilla y la pone en las áreas dificíles de alcanzar. También se puede usar a comenzar a esparcir los montones de pajote (mulch) que se han descargado a través de una cama de paisaje.

Rastrillos, Pala y el Soplador de muchila

Un rastrillo del arco de metal se debe usar para esparcir los montones de pajote (mulch). Algunas personas terminan esparciendo el pajote (mulch) con el rastrillo de metal, mientras que otras personas usan el rastrillo plástico de hoja para terminar. Cuando use un rastrillo de plástico usted puede levemente rastrillar cualquier área que no esta perfectamente pareja. Esto le dará una mirada profesional. El rastrillo de hoja, pala de plenicie, y el soplador de muchila son todos usados para limpiar un área donde un mónton de pajote (mulch) se descargó, tal como una área de camino de entrada o calle. Usted debe rastrillar también o soplar cualquier pajote (mulch) que se derramo en cúalquier áreas de césped.

Camión de Descarga

Usted necesitará un camión de descarga para llevar el pajote (mulch) al sitio de trabajo. El camión de descarga que usted usa debe tener la presión de aire correcta en las llantas y necesita una carpeta para cubrir la carga de pajote (mulch). Usted necesita tener la presión de las llantas correctas en su camión porque si una llanta tiene menos aire que las otras, el camión se inclinará cuándo se cargue. Esto pondrá aún más énfasis en la llanta baja y el camión se puede dar vuelta sí se inclina demasiado mientras se conduce. Sí, le puede acontecer a usted. Verifique la presión aérea antes de que el camión sea cargado. Usted necesitará una carpeta para cubrir el pajote (mulch) cargado en el camión. El camión necesita tener una carpeta y el rodillo encima del cuerpo de descarga. Usted no debe recoger pajote (mulch) ni otros suministros sin una carpeta. Usted obtendrá una multa por la policía si usted es sorprendido conduciendo un camión cargado sin un carpeta sobre la materia.

Llevando el Pajote (mulch) al Sitio de Trabajo

Usted necesitará tener el pajote (mulch) entregado al sitio de trabajo con su camión de descarga o por el centro local de suministrador o por el centro de jardín. La mayoría de los (landscapers) recogen su pajote (mulch) con el camión de descarga de su compañía. Cuándo usted recoge el pajote (mulch) en su propio camión, usted puede descargar los montones en la mejor ubicación en el sitio de trabajo. Usted puede trabajar también directamente del camión si el trabajo es por sólo una camionada o menos. Sí usted tiene un trabajo muy grande de pajote (mulch) de 50 o más yardas, usted debe considerar tenerlo entregadó en un camión grande directamente del fabricante. El costo del pajote (mulch) siempre cuesta menos cuándo se compra a granel directamente de la compañía que hace el pajote (mulch). A veces puede ser más fácil de terminar el trabajo si usted trabaja de muchos montones pequeños mientras otras veces puede ser mejor trabajar de un solo montón grande. Piense y planee cada trabajo antes de que usted tenga el pajote (mulch) entregado.

Generalmente cuándo usted tiene una cantidad grande de pajote (mulch) entregado, ha sido descargadó al lado dela calle. Cuándo descargue pajote (mulch) en el lado dela calle, usted debe seguir algunas reglas.

- *Usted siempre debe poner los conos de emergencia en ambos lados del montón para poner claramente sobre aviso a todo el tráfico que se acerca.*
- *Usted necesitará remover todo el montón dela calle al final del día o usted puede obtener una multa de la policía.*
- *Algunas calles con mucho tráfico requerirán un permiso para descargar pajote (mulch) en ellos.*

El jefe o capataz hacen generalmente la discusión acerca de recoger o entrega del pajote (mulch). Sin embargo, todos deben darle a cada trabajo pensamiento y luego discutirlo uno con otros sobre la mejor manera de hacer cada trabajo para que el trabajo sea hecho de la manera más fácil y efectiva que sea posible. **Siempre busque las maneras de hacer cada trabajo más rápido, más fácil y mejor.**

Un Trabajo Típico de Pajote (mulch)

Cada trabajo de pajote (mulch) será diferente y requerirá una cantidad diferente de pajote (mulch). El trabajo que estaremos discutiendo necesitará un total de 50 yardas. Un acuerdo se ha hecho con el cliente para esparcir 50 yardas de pajote (mulch) en su propiedad. Es una propiedad grande con camas en muchas áreas diferentes de la propiedad. Un camión grande puede entregar el pajote (mulch) pero sera duro de trabajar de ese montón ya que sólo se puede descargar en la calle. Así que usted recogerá y entregará el pajote (mulch) al sitio del trabajo usted mismo. Cinco carretadas de 10 yardas cada una le dará el total de 50 yardas.

Cada Trabajo Necesita Ser Explicado y Organizado

Antes de comenzar cúalquier trabajo, **todos** deben saber cuánto pajote (mulch) se usará, donde necesita ser esparcido y cúalquier otros detalles acerca del trabajo. Antes de que usted empieze a trabajar, todos deben caminar juntos el sitio de trabajo y discutir lo que se debe hacer exactamente. El trabajo irá mucho más fácil y más rápido cuando todos sepan exactamente lo qué se debe hacer.

Sí usted esta inseguro acerca de lo qué se debe hacer en un sitio de trabajo, haga preguntas hasta que usted este 100% seguro. Después que usted camina y discute el sitio de trabajo, usted necesita organizarse.

Todos los tipos diferentes de trabajos del paisaje necesitan ser explicados y organizados antes de que usted empieze a trabajar. Esté enterado que usted tendrá que reorganizar cada trabajo unos cuantas veces a través del dia de trabajo.

En el trabajo que discutimos, usted debe hacer algún trabajo en las camas de paisaje antes de que usted pueda esparcir el pajote (mulch).

Usted ha decidido que dos trabajadores desherbarán y bordearán las camas mientras otro trabajador recoge y entrega el pajote (mulch) al sitio del trabajo.

Recogiendo y Entregando el Pajote (mulch)

Cuándo usted llega al suministrador del pajote (mulch), apoya la parte posterior del camión de descarga hasta el montón del pajote (mulch). De esta manera si algún pajote (mulch) se sale de la parte posterior del camión mientras se está cargando, bajará detrás cerca del montón. Una vez el camión este cargado, suba sobre el camión con un rastrillo de metal o pala y anivela el montón.

Empuje los puntos altos de pajote (mulch) a las áreas bajas y limpía cualquier pajote (mulch) en la puerta posterior del camión. Estire la carpeta sobre el pajote (mulch) y amarra la carpeta hacia abajo. La carpeta debe venir encima de la puerta posterior del camión (tailgate).

Mientras conduce de regreso al sitio de trabajo, condusca cuidadosamente ya que el camión está cargadó. Mientras está conduciendo con pesor en el camión, usted debe ir más lento serca de curvas e ir más despacio cuándo viene a una parada. **Antes** de que usted llegue al sitio de trabajo, piense acerca del mejor lugar para descargar el pajote (mulch) o dónde seria mejor estacionarse sí usted va a trabajar del camión. Hable con su colaboradores para decidir donde es el mejor lugar o lugares. Hay una orden básica obvia de mantener. Traiga el pajote (mulch) lo más cerca posible de las camas que usted cubrira con pajote (mulch).

En el trabajo que discutimos, usted necesitará un total de 50 yardas que es un total de cinco carretadas. Después de planear y organizar este trabajo, usted ha decidido descargar tres carretadas en el rincón del camino de entrada cerca del garaje. Este pajote (mulch) cubrirá todas las camas alrededor de la casa y el traspatio. Después usted descargará una carretada en la calle. La última carretada no se descargará. Usted trabajará del camión y usted usará la última carretada para cubrir con pajote (mulch) las ultimas pocas camas distantes de la propiedad.

Usted necesitará retroceder en el camino de entrada con el camión. Antes de retroceder en el camino de entrada:

- Llame a un colaborador para ayudar.

- Su colaborador se necesitara para dirigirlo a usted y pueden necesitarse para dirigir el tráfico si usted trabaja en una calle con mucho tráfico.

- Sí usted trabaja en una calle con mucho tráfico, usted debe tener a dos colaboradores que lo dirijan a usted. Una persona debe estar en el camino de entrada y la otra persona necesita estar en la calle para detener cualquier tráfico que se acerca si es necesario.

- Espere hasta que no haya tráfico que se acercan en el sitio, entonces comienze a retroceder hacia el camino de entrada.

- Mire por los espejos traseros para ver la **curva** del camino de entrada

- Metase dentro del camino de entrada y salgase de la calle tan pronto sea posible.

- Si un carro viene mientras usted está retrocediendo, su colaborador necesita alzar su mano hacia arriba para hacer un signo de un alto. Él debe alzar su mano hacia arriba rapido para que el conductor del carro pueda ver claramente y entender qué hacer antes de acercarse a usted. Usted quizás también debe considerar en comprar banderas rojas para alzarlas hacia arriba porque son mucho más visible.

- **Vigile las curvas mientras retrocede.** Sí usted frota contra cualquier curva con el camión cargado, usted dañará o destruirá la llanta. Conduciendo con una llanta dañada es muy peligroso porque la llanta puede explotar y puede causar que el camión se de vuelta.

- Aún si el camino de entrada es fácil de retroceder, usted debe siempre debe tener alguien dirigiendolo. Los niños, perros, gatos, herramientas, juguetes, la iluminación del paisaje y bordillos crearán un problema grave si son golpeados.

- Nunca retroceda en un camino de entrada sin alguien que este dirigiendolo a usted.

Descargando el Pajote (mulch)

- Siempre estacione el camión en tierra plana dura y fije siempre el freno de estacionamiento.

- No levante el cuerpo de descarga sí el camión no se estaciona a nivel.

- Siempre de una mirada a lo qué está arriba de usted. Alejese de ramas de árbol y alambres.

- Dese a usted mismo espacio para mover el camión hacia adelante. Deje más o menos 15 pies de espacio para que usted pueda mover el camión mientras descarga.

- Una vez que el pajote (mulch) esté fuera, ponga la descarga abajo inmediatamente.

- Nunca conduzca con el cuerpo de descarga arriba.

- Una última cosa para recordar es nunca deberá bloquear el área del camino de entrada ni garaje a menos que haya hablado primero con el dueño de la propiedad para cerciorarse que esta bien. Trate lo más posible de dejar el camino de entrada y garaje abiertos, por si alguien necesita entrar o salir, puedan hacerlo. Si usted debe bloquear el camino de entrada, siempre pregunte primero.

Procedimientos del Trabajo Cubriendo con Pajote (mulch)

Ahora que la primera carga de pajote (mulch) se descarga, un trabajador irá a recoger la próxima carga mientras los otros dos trabajadores empiezan a cubrir con pajote (mulch). Ya que el trabajo es bastante grande, usted debe tener tres carretillas en el sitio del trabajo. Ponga las tres carretillas al lado del montón de pajote (mulch).

Comienze tomando pajote (mulch) del área que salió del camión de ultimo. De esta manera usted hará el montón más pequeño y cuando la próxima carga de pajote (mulch) venga, se puede descargar casi en el mismo lugar, descargando lo más cerca posible en un mismo lugar será más fácil de limpiar el área cuando usted haya terminado.

Organice el trabajo, una persona debe estar llenando las carretillas mientras el otro debe estar empujando las carretillas y descargandolos en las camas. Usando tres carretillas, siempre habrá una carretilla llena para empujar y una carretilla para llenar. No habrá tiempo perdido esperarando por una carretilla.

Antes de que usted comienze descargando el pajote (mulch) en las camas, cerciórese de saber cuán profundo el pajote (mulch) debe estar en cada trabajo. Algunos trabajos requerirán sólo una leve cubierta de pajote (mulch), mientras que otros trabajos requerirán una profundidad de dos o tres pulgadas. Las camas de paisaje deben tener más o menos de dos a tres pulgadas de pajote (mulch). Sí las camas tienen todavía pajote (mulch) del año previo, usted sólo necesitará poner otra pulgada. Sí no hay ningún pajote (mulch), usted necesitará poner por lo menos dos pulgadas; sin embargo, esto depende de lo que el cliente pagará. **Todos deben saber cuán profundo la capa de pajote (mulch) se debe esparcir y saber cuánto pajote (mulch) se puede usar en cada trabajo.** Si un trabajo necesita ser completado con 10 yardas y usted no termina con 10 yardas creará un grave problema. **¡Siempre entienda la cantidad de pajote (mulch) que se puede usar y la profundidad aproximada de pajote (mulch) que se debe esparcir antes de que usted empieze cada trabajo!**

El trabajo que usted está trabajando actualmente requerirá más o menos 1-1/2 a 2 pulgadas de pajote (mulch). Comienze descargando los montones de pajote (mulch) a través de la cama del paisaje. Trate de espaciar los montones de manera que cuando sean esparcidos, el pajote (mulch) estará más o menos de 1-1/2 a 2 pulgadas profundas. Esto tomará un poco de práctica. Siempre será mejor poner hacia abajo un poco **menos** de pajote (mulch) al principio. Una vez que usted esparció el pajote (mulch) y si usted necesita un poco más, usted siempre puede traer otra carretilla para terminar. Pero si usted descarga los montones muy cerca, el pajote (mulch) será esparcido grueso y usted no terminará el trabajo con la cantidad de pajote (mulch) que se requiere.

Cuando se usa una carretilla de tamaño grande, usted puede descargar montones pequeños en unos pocos lugares diferentes. Es mejor hacer unos pocos montones pequeños en vez de un sólo montón grande. Después los montones serán más fáciles de esparcir. Si hay algún área angosta donde no puede caber una carretilla grande, use la más pequeña. Sea muy cuidadoso de no chocar con la carretilla ningún arbusto. Usted romperá las ramas y las ramas se volverán marrón y morirán. Sí la carretilla más pequeña es todavía demasiado grande para caber en el área angosta, use una horquilla (pitchfork).

Una horquilla regular con un asidero largo trabaja mejor. Saque el pajote (mulch) fuera de la carretilla y lo esparce en las áreas angostas duras de alcanzar. Usted debe usar también la horquilla para tirar pajote (mulch) debajo de plantas que son difíciles de alcanzar. **Cerciórese de poner pajote (mulch) debajo de cada planta**. cuando usted está cubriendo con pajote (mulch) alrededor de (ground cover plants), una horquilla trabaja mejor. Llame a un colaborador para que lo ayude; uno de ustedes debe levantar las ramas para que el otro pueda tirar pajote (mulch) debajo de la planta.

Continúe trabajando en equipo con un trabajador llenando las carretillas mientras que el otro descarga los montones en las camas. Cuándo las cama de paisaje sean cubiertas con montones de más o menos hasta la mitad, un trabajador necesita comenzar a esparcir los montones. El otro trabajador entonces llenará, empujará, y descargará más montones en la cama sólo.

Para esparcir los montones de pajote (mulch), use un rastrillo del arco de metal. Si los montones son grandes y duros de esparcir con el rastrillo de metal, use una horquilla primero para esparcir los montones. Sí mientras esparce el montón, usted encuentra áreas donde usted necesita un poco más de pajote (mulch), llame a su colaborador para que descargue un poco más de pajote (mulch) donde sea necesario.

Cuándo usted esparce pajote (mulch) contra una casa, cerciórese que el pajote (mulch) no toque el entablado. El entablado es hecho de madera, vinilo, o aluminio y el pajote (mulch) nunca deben ser puestos contra ello. El pajote (mulch) sólo se debe poner contra la base de la fundación que es concreta. Deje por lo menos una pulgada de espacio entre el pajote (mulch) y el entablado. Sí la cama es más alta que el entablado, use una pala y cave un área para que usted pueda comenzar una pulgada debajo del entablado.

Entonces el resto de la cama de paisaje debe inclinarse lejos de la casa y base para que la lluvia se corra lejos de la casa.

Mientras usted esparce el pajote (mulch) a través de la cama, trate de rastrillarlo para que las camas sean lisas y parejas cuándo usted haya terminado. Sí hay algunos puntos bajos en las camas, agrega un poco más de pajote (mulch) para llenar los lugares bajos. Sí hay lugares altos, ponga menos pajote (mulch) en ellos. Una vez que todo el pajote (mulch) se esparce uniformemente a través de la cama, da una inspección final a la cama para cerciórarse que todas las áreas se cubren uniformemente. Entonces usted puede querer usar un rastrillo plástico de hoja para rastrillar levemente el pajote (mulch) una última vez. Un rastrillo plástico de hoja trabaja bien para gradúar levemente el pajote (mulch).

En el trabajo que discutimos, usted ahora tiene las tres carretadas de pajote (mulch) descargadas en el rincón del camino de entrada cerca del garaje, que se usa para cubrir con pajote (mulch) alrededor de la casa y el traspatio. Usted tiene también un camión lleno de pajote (mulch) para usar en los extremos del camino de entrada cerca de la calle. Usted necesitará descargar esta carga del camión al lado de la calle para que el camión pueda recoger la quinta y final carga de pajote (mulch). Pero usted no descargará esa cuarta carretada hasta que usted acabe de trabajar alrededor de la casa.

Nunca descargue un montón de pajote (mulch) en el lado de la calle hasta que usted esté listo para trabajar de ese montón. Si usted descarga un montón grande, cerciórese que usted tiene suficiente tiempo durante el día para remover completamente el montón de la calle antes del fin del día. Siempre use los conos de emergencia cuándo descarga o se estaciona al lado de cualquier calle.

Ahora que usted tiene a tres trabajadores en la propiedad, usted debe cerciórarse que todos esten organizados todavía. Aunque usted no esté a cargo, sí usted piensa en una manera más fácil de terminar el trabajo, haga una sugerencia a su jefe, capataz o colaborador en lo qué pueden trabajar mejor. **Siempre** permanezca alerta y piense acerca de la mejor manera de completar cada trabajo. Vigile y aprenda de colaboradores con experiencia y haga sugerencias sí usted ve una mejor manera de completar el trabajo.

Después que re-organiza el trabajo, usted ahora tiene tres carretillas cerca del montón de pajote (mulch). Un trabajador está llenando las carretillas, el segundo trabajador está empujando y descargando los montones pequeños a través de las camas, y la tercera persona está esparciendo los montones. Sí muchos montones se construyen en las camas, cambien posiciones.

Dos personas deben esparcir y una persona llenar y empujar las carretillas a las camas. Si el pajote (mulch) se esparce y más montones se necesitan. Cambie de regreso a tener sólo una persona esparciendo. Hable uno con el otro acerca del trabajo a través del día para que todos sepan qué hacer y no se cometa ningún error. Entonces el trabajo irá lo más rápidamente y fácilmente posible.

Ahora que usted ha terminado de cubrir con pajote (mulch) alrededor de la casa y el traspatio, usted necesita limpiar el área de camino de entrada donde el montón de pajote (mulch) estaba. Use primero un rastrillo del arco de metal, de vuelta al rastrillo y use la parte posterior del rastrillo para empujar el pajote (mulch) en un montón. Después use un rastrillo plástico de hoja. Recoja el pajote (mulch) con una pala plana. Después que usted haya recogido todo con una pala, sople el área con un soplador de muchila.

Después camine alrededor de las camas de paisaje que acaban de ser cubridas con pajote (mulch). Recoja cualquier pajote (mulch) que se derramo en el césped,aceras, etc., entonces sople estas áreas. Verifique para cerciórarse que todas sus herramientas están fuera del área de la propiedad que acaba de terminar. Mantenga todas sus herramientas juntas para que nada se pierda. Entonces como siempre, cerciórese que cúalquier portón esté bajo llave antes de que usted salga del área.

Ahora que usted está listo para cubrir con pajote (mulch) los exteriores de las camas del camino de entrada y necesita estacionar el camión al lado de la calle, verifique el tráfico que se acerca y tenga a lguien que lo dirija si es necesario. Una vez que el camión esté estacionado donde usted quiere descargar el pajote (mulch), ponga los conos de emergencia. Usted necesita usar dos o tres conos de emergencia para que el tráfico tenga bastante advertencia de que hay algo en el lado del camino. Ponga un cono aproximadamente diez pies

363

lejos del montón. Luego ponga otro cerca de veinte pies retirado. Use conos de emergencia aunque usted esté trabajando en una calle con poco tráfico. Hay muchos conductores malos en el camino y si un accidente sucede cerca de su montón de pajote (mulch), usted y su compañía serán culpados. Sí los conos de emergencia son utilizados correctamente, habrá pequeño o ningún problema sí un accidente ocurre. Sí los conos de emergencia no son utilizados y un accidente ocurre, usted y su compañía serán culpados.

Antes de descargar, verifique por algún alambre o ramas peligrosas. Cerciórese también que el camión esté estacionado en tierra firme. Cuándo trabaja cerca de cualquier camino, usted siempre necesita tener cuidado del tráfico que se acerca. Organice el trabajo y termine el trabajo.

Su última carretada de pajote (mulch) no se descargará. Trabaje el pajote (mulch) directamente del camión cuándo le sea posible. Si usted trabaja en un trabajo que necesita sólo una carretada de pajote (mulch) o menos, o cuándo usted trabaja en su última carretada, deje el pajote (mulch) en el camión. De esta manera si usted tiene algún pajote (mulch) extra, no se descargará en el suelo. Usted no tendrá que limpiar tanto y usted puede manejar alrededor de diferentes áreas de la propiedad cuándo el pajote (mulch) está en el camión.

En el trabajo que discutimos, usted tiene algunas camas en diferentes áreas alrededor del exterior de la propiedad. Será más fácil de estacionar el camión en diferentes áreas del camino para que usted esté lo más cerca posible de estas camas, siempre use los conos de emergencia.

Cuándo usted trabaja del camión, esté parado en la puerta posterior (tailgate) y remueva la primera mitad del montón de pajote (mulch). Después que la mitad del pajote (mulch) esté fuera del camión, cierra el (tailgate) y levanta el cuerpo de descarga. Levántelo hasta que el pajote (mulch) del frente se caíga a la parte posterior del camión, entonces baje el cuerpo de descarga hacia abajo. Ahora usted puede alcanzar fácilmente el resto del pajote (mulch) y usted no tiene que caminar de aquí para allá en el camión para poner el pajote (mulch) dentro de las carretillas.

Recuerde de organizar y planear cada parte de cada trabajo. Entonces su trabajo resultará magnífico y usted habrá terminado el trabajo lo más rápidamente y fácilmente posible.

Instrucción y Consejos de cómo Cubrir con Pajote (mulch)

- Piense acerca de cada trabajo y lo organiza antes de que usted comienze y reorganice como sea necesario a través del dia de trabajo. Trabaje junto como un equipo.
- Todos deben entender qué se necesita hacer y cuánto pajote (mulch) puede ser utilizado en cada trabajo antes de empezar a trabajar.
- Mantenga suficiente presión de aire en las llantas del camión cuándo conduce con una carga llena de pajote (mulch).

- Anivele el pajote (mulch) en el camión, limpie las puertas posteriores y use la carpeta.

- Mantenga suficiente presión de aire en las llantas de las carretillas y la carretilla será más fácil de empujar.

- Cuándo usted ponga las horquillas en el suelo o en el camión, mantenga las puntas mirando hacia abajo.

- Mantenga las llantas de las carretillas lejos de las horquillas.

- Mantenga las llantas del camión lejos de las curbas o de algo que pueda dañar las llantas. Especialmente cuando el camión está cargadó.

- Siempre estacionese en tierra plana cuándo descarga el pajote (mulch). Mire hacia arriba de usted para ver cúalquier alambre, ramas de árbol, etc.

- Siempre utilize los conos de emergencia.

- Siempre organice y piense en la seguridad primero.

PODAR ARBUSTOS Y ÁRBOLES DE ORNAMENTAL
(CAPÍTULO 8)

¿Por qué Podar es Necesario?

- *Podar arbustos y árboles ornamentales se necesita para mantener las plantas saludables y que semiren mejor.*

- *Sí usted no poda las plantas en una base regular, crecerán fuera de control, crecerán en uno al otro, llegarán a ser insalubres, inactractivas y morirán prematuramente.*

- *El podar correctamente aumentará completamente la salud y vida de las plantas. Las plantas producirán más flores o frutas y tendrán hojas y ramas más coloridas.*

- *Podar reducirá el riesgo del daño durante condiciones pesimas tal como condiciones extremas del tiempo, o durante el ataque de insectos o enfermedad.*

- *Podar es hecho para controlar completamente el tamaño de la planta y para dirigir la planta a crecer una cierta manera.*

- *Podar es hecho también para quitar de las plantas ramas enfermas o dañadas.*

Saber que Podar y Cuándo Podar

Como un profesional del paisaje, usted debe saber como podar correctamente los muchos tipos diferentes de arbustos y de árboles ornamentales. Los arbustos variarán en tamaño y forma, de una (ground cover) baja a un árbol de hoja perenne grande (evergreen) de 15 pies de diámetro, de un (weeping) a una planta vertical, de un árbol de hoja perenne (evergreen) a una planta de hojas caducas (deciduous plant). Los árboles ornamentales son árboles pequeños que crecen más o menos de 25 a 30 pies de altura y tienen generalmente flores. Cúalquier árboles que son más grande de 25 a 30 pies se consideran árboles de tamaño completo y una compañía de árboles debe podar estos árboles, no una compañía de paisaje.

El mejor tiempo para podar la mayoría de las plantas es durante los meses del verano o poco después que las plantas han florecido. Por julio y agosto, la mayoría de las plantas ya han florecido y tienen mucho crecimiento nuevo en ellos de la primavera. Cerca del 70% del crecimiento de una plantas acontece durante la primavera y los meses tempranos del verano.

Así que al podar en el verano tarde, usted no tendrá nuevo crecimiento adicional de la planta después que usted la corte. La planta mantendrá su forma de corte hasta la próxima primavera.

Sí usted poda demasiado tarde en el año, tal como en el otoño, las plantas que florecen pueden no tener suficiente tiempo para crecer nuevos capullos para la próxima temporada de primavera. Los capullos son de donde las flores vienen. Entonces sí usted poda demasiado tarde y quita los capullos, las plantas no pueden florecer en la siguiente primavera. Sí usted poda temprano en la primavera, usted quitará los capullos que apenas están listos para florecer y la planta parecerá que necesita ser podada otra vez más tarde en la temporada. Permanezca con un horario de podar durante el verano a menos que sea una situación especial.

La mayoría de arbustos y árboles ornamentales necesitan ser podados en una base anual. Sí usted se salta un año o dos, habrá dos o tres años de crecimiento nuevo en la planta y no puede ser posible podar la planta a su tamaño original. Sí no es mantenida por unos cuantos años, el centro de la planta puede comenzar a morir. La falta del flujo de aire y luz del sol al centro de la planta causará que los insectos y enfermedad dañen el centro de la planta. Entonces, no será posible podarla a su tamaño original ya que no habrá nada vivo en el centro de la planta, sólo ramas muertas marrones. Nota: nunca pode una planta hasta las ramas muertas marrones en el centro de la planta. Quitando todo el crecimiento verde de las ramas, usted dañará o destruirá la mayoría de las plantas.

Podando cada año, usted evitará este problema, la planta se mirará mejor y vivirá mucho más tiempo.

Las Herramientas y Equipo Necesario

Usted necesitará las siguientes herramientas para podar arbustos y árboles ornamentales.

- Podadoras de Poder, (una de tamaño pequeño y una de tamaño grande).
- Podadoras de Poder de Alcanze Extendido (Extended reach power trimmers).

- Tijeras (Hedge) (Hedge Shears).
- Una Motosierra Pequeña (Small Chain Saw).
- Un Serrucho (Hand Saw).
- Tijeras Manuales (Hand Shears).
- Tijeras Grandes (Loppers).
- Una combinación de sierra de poste/loppers (Pole Saw).
- Una escalera (Step Ladder).
- Rastrillos (Rakes).
- Un barril del paisaje (Landscape Barrel).
- Una carpeta (Tarp).
- Un soplador de muchila (Backpack Blower).
- Usted necesitará también el rocío de abeja y avispa en caso de que usted encuentre un nido de abeja.
- Alcohol para limpiar las herramientas.

Podadoras de Poder

El uso de las podadoras de poder es común cuándo se podan los arbustos. Hay dos hojas en la podadora de poder. Las hojas tienen nudos y cerrojos atravesandolos para mantenerlos juntos. Los nudos y cerrojos se deben apretar para que no haya ningún pequeño espacio entre las hojas. Si hay un espacio, usted obtendrá un corte malo. Sin embargo, si los cerrojos están demasiado apretados, las hojas no se podrán mover. Cerciórese que las hojas se ajusten correctamente. Las hojas necesitan también ser afiladas, si las hojas no estan afiladas, usted obtendrá un corte malo y tendrá problemas al podar. Verifique el espacio y el filo de las hojas después de cada trabajo y las repara si es necesario.

Después de cada trabajo, usted debe limpiar las hojas usando un trapo con alcohol para limpiarlos. Durante los meses del verano, hay muchas enfermedades activas en los arbustos que usted esta podando. Enjuagando las hojas, usted quitará cualquier enfermedad y usted no esparcirá la enfermedad a la próxima propiedad. Cuándo usted está en el sitio de trabajo y ve un arbusto que se mira bastante enfermo, enjuaga las hojas después de que usted poda y **antes** de podar los otros arbustos. Enjuague todas las otras herramientas tal como tijeras manuales, sierras, (loppers) o las sierras de poste sí han tenido contacto con alguna planta enferma y después de cada trabajo.

Las podadoras de poder usan gas de 2 ciclos. Llene el tanque de gas antes de cada trabajo en su camión, no en el césped ni camas. Cuándo aprieta la tapa de gas, cerciórese que este puesta correctamente antes de que usted la enrosca. Tenga cuidado también de no sobre apretarla sí no usted romperá el sello dentro de la tapa.

Cuándo usted rompe el sello, el gas goteará. Sí hay escapes de gas en las plantas que usted esta podando, habrá lugares muertos por todas partes de las plantas. Sí hay escapes de gas de la tapa o de cúalquier otro lugar, detengase inmediatamente y no use la máquina.

Las podadoras de poder son muy peligrosas, sí usted toca las hojas con sus brazos o piernas usted causará herida grave a usted mismo.

¡Tenga cuidado y permanezca en alerta! Es mejor tener dos podadoras de poder de diferentes tamaño; una con una hoja de tamaño regular de más o menos 2 pies de largo para podar plantas de tamaño pequeño a tamaño mediano, la otra con una hoja de longitud lo más larga posible, 3 o 4 pies largos. Úselo para arbustos, cercados, y árboles de hoja perenne (evergreen) grandes o difíciles de alcanzar.

Podadoras de Poder de Alcance Extendido (Extended Reach Power Trimmer).

Las podadoras de poder de alcance extendido están ahora disponibles. Estas máquinas tienen las hojas montadas a un final del (shaft) y el motor montado en el fondo del (shaft). El (shaft) es más o menos de cinco a seis pies de largo y las hojas pueden ser ajustadas a diferentes angulos de cortar. Mushos equipos de fuerza de los fabricantes tienen una podadora de cuerda donde la cabeza puede ser fácilmente removida y la podadora de poder puede ser montada en su lugar. La máquina es también de peso liviano y es fácil de trabajar con ello. Las podadoras de poder de alcance extendido harán muchos de los trabajas más seguros ya que usted no tendrá que ir tan frecuentemente arriba y abajo en una escalera. Yo recomiendo altamente el uso de podadoras de poder de alcance extendido.

Arrancar las podadoras de poder puede ser a veces un problema. Todas las máquinas arrancarán levemente diferente. Sin embargo, la mayoría de las máquinas arrancan más fácil usando estos procedimientos.

Utilize primero el (choke) de la máquina con la válvula reguladora (throttle) solamente hasta la mitad. Cuándo la máquina se escuche como que si ya arrancó, apaga el (choke) y aplica la válvula reguladora más o menos de la mitad hasta tres cuartos de la dirección abierta y la máquina debe arrancar. El error que mucha gente hace es que sostienen la válvula reguladora completamente y aplican también demasiado gas o dejan el (choke) demasiado tiempo. Esto inundará el motor y después la máquina no arrancará. Siempre también tenga cuidado de no aplicar demasiado gas o usted tendrán un problema.

Todas las máquinas arrancarán diferentemente. Una vez que usted encuentra la manera más fácil de arrancar una máquina, **repita ese proceso cada vez que usted necesite arrancarla**. Una vez que la máquina este tibia, arrancara más fácil y usted probablemente no tendrá que usar el (choke). Los lentes de seguridad, protección de oídos y guantes se deben llevar puestos al usar esta máquina.

Tijeras (Hedge) (Hedge Shears)

Las Tijeras (Hedge) manuales cortan similarmente a las podadoras de poder. Tienen una hoja cortante larga de aproximadamente dos pies de longuitud.

Motosierra Pequeña (Small Chain Saw)

- Antes de usar la motosierra, cerciórese que la cadena no esté floja. La cadena nunca debe estar floja; debe quedar ajustado alrededor de la barra. Tan pronto la cadena se afloja un poco, detengase y pare de usarla y la ajusta. No sobre apriete la cadena si no usted fundirá la cadena, la barra y el motor. **Siempre** mantenga las herramientas necesarias para apretar la cadena dondequiera que usted vaya con la motosierra.

- Usted también necesitará verificar la cadena para cerciorarse que siempre esté afilado. Si la cadena se desafíla después de un trabajo, **cerciórese** que usted le diga a alguien a cargo para tenerlo afiladó **antes** de ir al próximo trabajo.

- Una motosierra usa gas de 2 ciclos y tiene otro tanque usado para la barra y el aceite de la cadena. Siempre llene ambos tanques juntos; cuándo usted llena el gas, llene el aceite también. Si usted se queda sin la barra y aceite de cadena, aceite de motor se puede usar también.

  Traiga la barra y aceite de cadena o el aceite de motor dondequiera que usted vaya con la motosierra. Al usar la motosierra sin el aceite destruirá la barra y la cadena.

- Los lentes de seguridad, protección de oídos y guantes se deben llevar puestos al usar esta máquina.

Tenga cuidado cuándo arranca la motosierra. Las motosierras tienen el mismo problema como las podadoras de poder, se inundan muy fácilmente. Una vez que el motor se inunda con gas, la máquina no arrancará. Aplique el (choke) con la válvula de admisión cuidadosamente y usa el mismo procedimiento de arrancar como discutimos con las podadoras de poder.

Cuándo se usa una motosierra, cerciórese que siempre esté parado en una posición equilibrada. Mantenga la cadena lejos de su cuerpo y sólo corte ramas pequeñas. Las ramas grandes están bajo presión y pueden quebrarse repentinamente. Las ramas grandes deben ser quitadas por un profesional de árbol no por un paisajista.

Cuándo corta ramas pequeñas, usted quiere hacer un corte parejo, corte paralelo. Haga primero un corte pequeño en el fondo de la rama, después corte de la cima. La razón por la cual usted hace primero el corte pequeño en el fondo es para cortar por la corteza, así que cuándo la rama cae, la corteza no se pela. Sin el corte del fondo, la rama puede caer y pelar la corteza. Si la corteza se pela de las áreas que usted no quiere quitar, se mirará muy malo y inprofesional. Los insectos y enfermedad pueden infectar estas áreas del árbol donde no hay corteza. Si usted deja un trocon, córte y empareja a la rama más grande.

La mejor manera de cortar una rama y evitar peladura (descorteza) es haciendo un corte doble. Primero corte la rama como acabamos de discutir pero deja el troncon más o menos un pie de largo. Entonces hace un corte parejo cuándo quita los pedazos más pequeños.

Cuándo usted hace un corte, no empuje la sierra muy duro, sólo ponga presión ligera en la sierra. Si usted empuja muy duro, usted tendrá dos problemas.

- Primero usted estará cortando muy rápido, cuándo usted corta demasiado rápido las astillas de madera se atascan en la sierra.

Esto causará que la sierra trabaje mal o deje de trabajar por las astillas atascadas en la máquina.

- Segundo, usted quizás golpee otra rama, corte en la tierra, golpee una piedra, o se tropieze y pierda su equilibrio cuándo usted atraviese la rama y la sierra este libre.

Usted necesita poner una presión pequeña en la sierra cuándo usted está cortandó, después mitiga la presion cuándo ya usted casi atraviese la rama.

El problema más comun que tiene un paisajista ha sido que cuándo usa motosierras han tocado tierra o piedras con la cadena. La cadena sólo puede cortar madera. Una vez que toca tierra o una piedra, llegará a perder su filo y no cortará. Un profesional del árbol usará la misma motosierra toda la semana porque ellos tienen cuidado de sólo cortar madera. Usted puede hacer lo mismo si usted trata.

Serrucho (Hand Saw)

Un serrucho se puede usar en vez de una motosierra. Es mucho más seguro y no se rompera como una motosierra. Pero usted tendrá que trabajar más duro y cada trabajo tomará más tiempo para ser terminado. Sí usted cortando sólo unas pocas ramas, use el serrucho. Mantenga un serrucho en su camión, entonces si su motosierra se descompone, usted siempre puede terminar el trabajo usando su serrucho.

Tijeras Manuales (Hand Shears)

Las tijeras manuales se usan para cortar ramas pequeñas. Las tijeras manuales no se deben usar para cortar algo más grande que ¾ de una pulgada. Si usted trata de cortar algo más grande, sus tijeras manuales se pueden romper. Las tijeras manuales sólo se deben usar para cortar madera. Una vez que la hoja en la tijera manual se desafila, trabajarán muy mal y no deben ser usadas. Use una piedra de afilar para afilar la hoja de las tijeras manuales unas cuantas veces al año. No afile la hoja en una afiladora de molino (grinding wheel).

Cuándo usted poda los arbustos y árboles, las tijeras manuales siempre se deben mantener con usted; en su muchila o en un estuche que se engancha en su cinturón. **Nunca** ponga un par de tijeras manuales en el suelo. Se pueden perder muy fácilmente. Póngalas de regreso en su estuche cuando usted no las use. Las tijeras manuales son costosas y es la herramienta más fácil de perder. Haga un lugar en su camión donde las tijeras manuales siempre deben estar. Entonces no se perderan y siempre podran ser encontradas sin malgastar ningún tiempo.

Tijeras Grandes (Loppers)

Los (Loppers) son como tijeras manuales muy grandes. Cortarán ramas de ½ a más o menos 2 de grueso. Use las tijeras grandes (Loppers) para quitar ramas que son demasiado grandes para la podadora de poder o las tijeras manuales. Las tijeras grandes (Loppers) también trabajan bien en ramas que no son estables.

Algunas ramas se mueven demasiado para usar una sierra; las tijeras grandes (loppers) trabajarán mejor en ramas inestables.

Combinación de Sierra de Poste y Tijeras Grandes (Pole Saw and Loppers)

Una siera de poste con tijeras grandes (loppers) es la próxima herramienta que usted necesitará. Una sierra de poste es usada para podar las ramas duras de alcanzar de un arbusto grande o un árbol pequeño. La mayoría de las sierras de poste son de más o menos 8 pies de largo y se pueden extender hasta 16 pies. Con una sierra de poste, usted puede cortar ramas o usar las tijeras grandes (loppers) para cortar las ramas.

- Si la rama que usted tiene que quitar es estable y no se mueve alrededor, use la sierra para quitarlo.
- Si la rama es inestable y se mueve alrededor, ponga la rama en las tijeras grandes (loppers), entonces hale el lazo que esta conectado a la sierra de poste. Halando el lazo usted abrirá y cerrará las tijeras grandes (loppers).
- Cerciórese que usted esté bien equilibrado cuando esté usando una sierra de poste. No trate de alcanzar una rama que esté muy demasiado lejos o usted se puede caer. Sea especialmente cuidadoso cuándo esté trabajando en una escalera.
- Cuándo la hoja de la sierra de poste no corta fácilmente, reemplazela. Nunca trate de trabajar con una sierra de poste que tenga la hoja desafilada, es muy peligroso, cansado, y el trabajo tomará el doble del tiempo que debe ser.

Escalera de Paso

Usted necesitará una escalera de paso cuándo poda arbustos y árboles ornamentales. Una escalera de paso se abre y no tiene que descansar en nada como una escalera regular. Usted la puede abrir, la coloca en tierra firme y sube a la escalera. Es mejor tener dos escaleras de dos tamaño diferentes; una pequeña que es fácil de recoger y de mover alrededor entre los arbustos y una más grande que se debe usar para arbustos altos y árboles ornamentales.

Las escaleras estan hechas de madera o de aluminio. Las escaleras de madera son muy peligrosas porque se pueden deshacer cuando son más viejo. Si usted usa una escalera de madera, inspecciónela antes de cada trabajo. Sí no es estable, o sí alguna parte se mira débil o se ve desgastadó, no la use. La mayoría de gente usa las escaleras de aluminio porque son más fuertes y duran mucho más tiempo. Pero las escaleras de aluminio también se pueden romper; por eso es buena idea de abrirla y inspeccionarla antes de cada uso.

Siempre cerciórese que la escalera sea estable antes de trabajar en ello. Si usted está trabajando en cualquier tipo de cuesta o terreno desigual (no parejo), tenga un colaborador que sostenga la escalera mientras usted trabaja en ello. Mientras trabaja en una escalera de pasos, no use los últimos pasos. Habrá una notificación cerca de la cima de la escalera que le dirá no ir más alto. No desatienda esta nota, pararse en la cima de una escalera es muy peligroso y puede causar graves heridas al caerse.

Otro Equipo Necesario

Usted necesitará un soplador de muchila, unos cuantos rastrillos, un barril del paisaje y una carpeta para limpiar los escombros de basura. Traiga por lo menos dos rastrillos. Traiga un barril para que usted pueda poner escombros de basura en el barril cuándo limpia áreas duras de alcanzar. Extienda la carpeta y descarga los barriles llenos en la carpeta. Entonces con la ayuda de unos pocos trabajadores, descarga la carpeta llena de escombros de basura en su camión o en el lugar de descarga de la propiedad. Después que usted limpie, use un soplador de muchila para soplar juntos los escombros de basura más pequeños y para soplar cualquier escombros de basura que se atasco en los arbustos que usted apenas acaba de podar.

Cuándo poda, traiga consigo los lentes de seguridad, protección de oídos, y guantes. Usted necesitará también el rocío de abeja y avispa. Mantenga la lata del rocío cerca del área en donde usted trabaja, entonces si usted choca con un nido de abeja usted no estará indefenso. Los nidos de abejas son muy comunes durante los meses del verano. Traiga consigo un contenedor de alcohol y un trapo. Sí usted poda un arbusto en el sitio de trabajo que está pesadamente enfermo, enjuaga sus herramientas antes de podar los otros arbustos saludables.

También después de cada trabajo, enjuaga las hojas de cualquier herramienta que fue usada para matar cúalquier enfermedad que ha hecho contacto con la hoja. De esta manera usted no traerá la enfermedad a otra propiedad. Tome un minuto y enjuague las herramientas después de cada trabajo.

Antes de conducir al sitio de trabajo, cerciórese que usted tenga todo el equipo de herramientas y seguridad cargado en su camión y asegurado. Cerciórese que su podadoras de poder o motosierra no se den vuelta o se deslizen alrededor en el camión. Sujete la escalera y cualquier otra cosa más que quizás pueda moverse.

Organizando e Inspeccionando el Trabajo

Una vez que usted llega al sitio de trabajo, sea organizado.

- Con una tripulación de dos personas, ambos pueden podar hasta que esten cerca de la mitad del trabajo. Entonces una persona debe continúar podando mientras que la segunda persona rastrilla los escombros de basura. Con una tripulación de tres personas, dos personas deben podar mientras la tercera rastrilla los escombros de basura.

- Llene de gas todo su equipo de poder en el camión. Sí usted se queda sin gas durante el trabajo, regrese al camión para llenar de gas. Recuerde de sólo apretar levemente las tapas de gas en las máquinas, sí usted sobre aprieta la tapa, usted romperá el sello dentro de la tapa de gas y el gas goteará. Traiga todas sus máquinas y herramientas a la propiedad, cerca de donde usted estará trabajando. Cuándo todo esté cerca de usted, usted no tendrá que caminar de aquí para allá al camión cada vez que usted necesite una máquina o una herramienta diferente.

Antes de que usted comienze a podar, es importante caminar alrededor de la propiedad e inspeccionar los arbustos, árboles y discutir exactamente qué se necesita hacer. Cada trabajo será diferente y tendrá cosas diferentes que se necesita hacer. Antes de podar, mire individual a cada arbusto y árbol ornamental y se imagina cómo usted lo podara para hacer que se mire mejor.

La identificación de planta es importante cuándo poda. Cada planta crece diferentemente; algunas crecen lento; algunas crecen rápido; algunas tienen flores y otras no. Algunas plantas que pierden sus hojas son llamadas caducas (deciduous). Otras plantas permanecen siempre verdes todo el año y son llamadas los árboles de hoja perenne (evergreens). Sí usted no es familiarizado con las plantas que usted está a punto de podar, cerciórese que alguien con conocimiento camine el sitio del trabajo con usted. Discuta todas las plantas y cómo podar cada planta de la manera correcta. **Nunca pode arbustos ni árboles a menos que usted esté 100% seguro acerca de lo qué se debe hacer**. El podar incorrecto puede hacer más daño que bueno. Cada planta puede requerir un método diferente de podar. Ahora vamos hablar acerca de los diferentes métodos de podar.

Recortando Arbustos de Paisaje (Shearing of Landscape Shrubs)
(Shearing) es cuándo usted recorta reduje la superficie exterior de una planta usando la podadora de poder o las tijeras (hedge). Usted creará una superficie exterior, uniforme y lisa en la planta. (Shearing) es recortar todas las ramas exteriores de la planta. Haciendo esto, usted

382

alentará el exterior de la planta a crecer más grueso. El crecimiento nuevo aumentará en el exterior de la planta, creando un esqueleto exterior denso. Cuándo recorta (shearing) año tras año una planta, el interior de la planta morirá lentamente porque no puede obtener suficiente luz del sol ni flujo de aire. El recortar (shearing) traerá rápidamente una planta hacia abajo en tamaño pero le dejará con una planta insalubre que fácilmente se infectaria con el problema de insectos y enfermedades. Los insectos y enfermedades les gusta el interior de un arbusto recortado ya que hay poca luz del sol o flujo de aire. En general recortar (shearing) creará una planta pobre de salud y acortará la vida de la planta. El recorte de (Shearing) las plantas se deben hacer raramente. El recorte (Shearing) trabaja bien en algunos cercados o en plantas ornamentales o plantas esculturales.

Desgraciadamente, muchas compañías de paisaje a través del país recortan casi todas las plantas que ellos tienen que podar porque es la manera más rápida y más fácil. Los dueños de la compañía necesitan explicar a sus clientes la manera correcta de podar. Deberian cobrar correctamente para que el trabajo pueda ser hecho de la manera correcta.

Afinar (Thinning) Arbustos del Paisaje

Afinar es la mejor manera de podar los arbustos pero se tomará la mayor parte del tiempo. Trate de retratar cómo usted quiere que la planta se mire antes de que usted comienze a podar. Use las tijeras manuales, encuentre las ramas que sobresalen de la planta. Alcance en la rama en el centro de la planta, entonces corteló con sus tijeras manuales. Continúe podando las ramas más largas. Usted estará reduciendo el tamaño de la planta mientras que esta abriendo para permitir que el sol y el aire alcanzen el interior. Trate de no cortar cúalquier rama que dejará grandes espacios abiertos en la planta. A veces tendrá que cortar sólo la mitad de la rama.

Cuidadosamente quite unas cuantas ramas más viejas de la planta. Esto alentará las ramas más nuevas a crecer saludables y fuertes. Sea muy cuidadoso cuándo quita ramas viejas; cuando usted quita ramas más viejas, siempre debe haber una rama más joven para crecer en su lugar.

Busque por cúalquier ramas que esten dañadas de enfermedad o insectos y las quita.

No quite más del 25 a 30% de la planta. Sí usted quita el 30% de una planta y está todavía demasiado grande, usted debe esperar hasta el próximo año para quitar el resto.

Usted puede tener que usar las tijeras grandes (loppers) para las ramas más grandes. No use una motosierra porque usted puede golpear y dañar las ramas que usted quiere mantener. Después que quite las ramas selectas y afina la planta, usted puede necesitar levemente podar la superficie exterior de la planta. Pode el exterior de la planta sí usted quiere reducir más el tamaño o para reparar un arbusto mal formado. Afinar puede ser hecho a todas las plantas del árbol de hoja perenne (evergreen) y las plantas caducas (deciduous). Entonces esto nos trae al próximo método de podar, recortando y afinando (shearing and thinning).

Recortando (Shearing) y Afinando (Thinning) Arbustos de Paisaje

Mire primero cada planta y la retrata en su mente de cómo esa planta se debe mirar cuándo usted acabe de podarla. Mire para ver si hay algún área de la planta que necesita tener algo más o menos quitado. Sí una planta debe ser redonda, pero tiene un lugar plano en ello, no corte el lugar plano. Permita que esa área crezca de regreso y la planta tendrá la forma correcta el año siguiente. Usando su podadora de poder o las tijeras (hedge) muy **levemente**, corte y forme el exterior de la planta. Después de recortar **levemente** y formar el exterior de la planta, usa sus tijeras manuales para **afinar** la planta. Cuándo afine una planta:

- **Quite ramas selectas por todas partes de la planta.**
- **Agarre las ramas y las quita del interior de la planta.**
- **Trate de quitar las ramas viejas pero sea cuidadoso cuándo quita las ramas que son grandes o usted dejará la planta con un hoyo abierto grande en ello.**
- **No deje ningún tocón cuándo usted corte las partes de una rama.**
- **Siempre corte la rama para que haya más joven, rama más pequeña dejada para crecer en su lugar.**
- **Nunca quite más del 25 – 30% de las ramas de una planta en una podada.**

- Cuándo usted acabe de afinar una planta, **el exterior de la planta se debe mirar formado pero flojo y velloso para que el sol y el aire puedan alcanzar el centro de la planta**. Cuándo afina una planta usted quita parte del interior y exterior de la planta. El crecimiento nuevo entonces sucederá en ambos en el interior y exterior de la planta. Así es como una planta saludable debe crecer. Cortando levemente y luego afinando es una buena manera de podar y terminar el trabajo rápidamente y correctamente. Sin embargo, este método no se debe usar en todas las plantas.

La Renovación de Podar Arbustos de Paisaje (Renewal Pruning)
Renovación se hace para mejorar la salud y la apariencia general de una planta vieja. Por la renovación, usted puede transformar una planta grande, fea, y sobre crecida en una mejor planta más pequeña saludable y con mejor apariencia. Renovación de podar sólo se debe hacer a algunas plantas, en su mayor parte a las plantas caducas (deciduous). Lo qué usted debe hacer es quitar todas las ramas más viejas de la planta y permitir que las ramas menores nuevas crezcan. Nunca quite más del 30% de la planta en una podada. Corte las ramas por la base de la planta. Use las tijeras manuales, tijeras grandes (loppers) o un serrucho.

Tenga cuidado para no cortar ni dañar cúalquiera de las ramas menores cuando quita las viejas. Sí usted ha quitado el 30% de las planta más grandes y ramas más viejas, y hay todavía hay más para podar, usted tendrá que esperar hasta el año siguiente. Este proceso puede tomar hasta tres años para quitar completamente todas las ramas más viejas mientras permite a las ramas menores crecer. El resultado final valdrá la espera y lo dejará con una planta que se mirará bien y que permanecerá saludable por muchos más años.

Podar Arboles Ornamentales

Los árboles ornamental son árboles que crecen aproximadamente 25 a 30 pies en altura. Pueden ser los árboles de hoja perenne (Evergreen) o (Deciduous). Primero explicaremos podar de árboles (Deciduous) tal como (Flowering Dogwood) Floreciendo el Cornejo, (Cherry) Cereza, (Plum Trees) o árboles de Ciruela.

Antes de podar, un árbol una inspección visual para averiguar los problemas con el árbol. Después visualise en su mente lo que usted hará para corregir estos problemas y mejorar el árbol. Mire el tronco principal del árbol, después mira las ramas principales que forman el árbol. Éstas son las ramas que usted quiere mantener y permitir que crezcan. Entonces mire para **quitar** lo siguiente:

- Quite las ramas chupadoras (sucker). Las ramas del chupador son ramas muy jóvenes y nuevas que crecen rápidamente alrededor del tronco del árbol y las ramas principales.
- Quite ramas que se cruzan uno al otro o frotan juntas.
- Quite ramas que están creciendo en la dirección equivocada. Todas las ramas deben estar creciendo del centro del árbol. Quite cualquier rama que esté creciendo en el centro del árbol, o que esté creciendo directamente hacia arriba.

- Quite ramas principales que están creciendo muy cerca del uno al otro. Quite ramas que crecen muy cerca del uno al otro o encima de uno del otro.

- Quite ramas que tienen una horcajadura (crotch) de ángulo **estrecho** ya que crecerán más débiles que las ramas con una horcajadura (crotch) de ángulo ancho. Una horcajadura (crotch) con ángulo estrecho es cuándo las ramas crecen en la forma de una V. Una horcajadura (crotch) con ángulo ancho es cuándo las ramas crecen en la forma de una L. Una horcajadura (crotch) con ángulo ancho es mejor.

- Quite ramas que esten dañadas de insectos o enfermedad.

- Quite ramas que esten agrietadas o dañadas.

- Quite ramas muertas o agonizantes.

Cuándo poda, comienze del fondo del árbol y trabaje hasta la cima del árbol. La mayor parte de podar se puede hacer con una sierra de poste y con tijeras grandes (loppers). Primero úselo en la longitud de ocho pies, luego lo extiende cuándo usted trabaje más alto en el árbol. Sin embargo, usted puede necesitar otras herramientas para terminar el trabajo, tal como tijeras manuales, tijeras grandes manuales (loppers), un serrucho o una motosierra.

Cuándo quita ramas más pequeñas, haga un corte parejo. No deje ningún tocón después de quitar la rama. Haga un corte rápido a traves de la rama usando las tijeras (loppers). Haciendo un corte rápido, las tijeras (loppers) no será pellizcado ni atascado cuándo la rama comienze a caer.

Cuándo se usa un serrucho, sostenga la rama con una mano mientras corta con la otra para evitar que se caiga y se pele la corteza por el corte. Cuándo corta ramas más grandes, haga un corte pequeño a traves de la corteza en el fondo de la rama luego corte de la cima. Para ramas más grandes, haga los cortes dejando un tocón. Permita la caída de la rama grande y entonces quite el tocón dejando un corte parejo.

Cuándo pode del centro a la cima del árbol, usted debe usar una sierra de poste/loppers. Primero trabaje del suelo, después cuándo usted empieze a trabajar más alto en el árbol, usted tendrá que usar una escalera de paso. Sí el árbol es bastante grande, usted también debe ser capaz de subir dentro del árbol para alcanzar más ramas para podar. **Sólo** suba dentro del árbol sí el árbol es lo suficientemente grande para sostener su peso. Cuándo esté usando la escalera, cerciórese que la escalera sea segura o que usted tiene a alguien que sostenga la escalera mientras usted trabaja. Mientras poda, usa las tijeras grandes (loppers) en el poste primero ya que harán un corte rápido y la corteza no se pelará. Si las ramas son demasiado gruesas use la sierra. Haga un corte pequeño en el lado del fondo de la rama, luego corte de la cima. Mientras usted esté trabajando en la escalera o dentro del árbol, llegará a ser más difícil de ver todas las ramas que necesitan ser podadas. Tenga a alguien que le ayude del suelo a indicarle qué se debe hacer.

Después que usted haya podado todas las ramas dentro del árbol, usted puede necesitar reducir el tamaño completo del árbol.

La mejor manera de reducir el tamaño completo del árbol es localizar las ramas grandes que se extienden fuera de la forma del árbol. Quite estas ramas de adentro del árbol. Usted estará afinando las ramas exteriores para reducir el tamaño y permitir que el sol y el flujo del aire alcancen el interior. Entonces después de afinar, usted debe cortar cúalquier rama exterior más pequeña si es necesario. La forma exterior del árbol debe tener una apariencia natural y suelta.

Sólo quite 25 al 30% de las ramas de un árbol, sí se necesita podar más después que el 30% de las ramas han sido quitadas, espere hasta el año siguiente. Los árboles de hoja perenne (Evergreen) se deben podar usando el método de cortar y afinar que discutimos más temprano.

Limpieza

Para limpiar usted necesitará un rastrillo, un barril del paisaje, una carpeta, un soplador de muchila y un par de tijeras manuales. Comience levemente rastrillando los recortes de los arbustos. Sí hay alguna rama grande atascada en el arbusto, las quita a mano. Después que usted rastrilla y quita los recortes de los arbustos, usted podria encontrar alguna rama que fue dejada durante usted podaba. Mantenga un par de tijeras manuales con usted por sí encuentra alguna rama que se habia sido dejada mientras usted podaba, usted puede recortarlas. Después que usted ha limpiado los recortes de los arbustos, rastrille los escombros de basura y los reune en unos montones pequeños alrededor del área de la cama del paisaje. Rastrille levemente para que usted no quite el pajote (mulch) mientras limpia. Algunos recortes muy pequeños no podrán ser rastrillados. Dejelos en la cama y usted los soplará con un soplador de muchila más tarde. Después que haga muchos montones, ponga los montones de basura en un carpeta o en un barril del paisaje y los descarga en su camión o en el área de descarga en la propiedad.

Después que usted haya recogido los montones de escombros de basura, use el soplador de muchila para soplar los arbustos y después sople levemente el área de la cama.

Es importante quitar la mayor parte de los recortes de los arbustos. Después de unos pocos días, los recortes se volverán marrónes y sí no son quitados apropiadamente, habrá recortes marrónes adentro y alrededor de los arbustos. Esto se mirará inprofesional.

El área de la cama se debe soplar muy levemente para que usted no quite ningún pajote (mulch) ni la capa superior. Es importante dejar cada trabajo lo más limpio posible. Antes de que usted salga, camina el sitio del trabajo e inspecciona el trabajo que usted acaba de hacer. Cerciórese que todas sus herramientas y equipo estén limpios y sean puestos de regreso en su camión.

Instrucción y Consejos de Seguridad al Podar

- Lleve puestos el equipo de seguridad como sea necesario, tal como los lentes de seguridad, la protección de oídos y guantes.

- Siempre entienda **claramente** qué se debe hacer **antes** de que usted comienze a podar.

- **Siempre es mejor quitar un poco menos que demasiado. Una vez que usted quite demasiado de una planta, se llevará años para que crezca de regreso. En algunos casos, usted puede causar daño permanente.**

- Siempre tenga cuidado cuando usa podadoras de poder. Manténgalas lejos de su cuerpo mientras las utiliza.

- Tenga cuidado cuándo trabaja en cualquier tipo de escalera. Cerciórese que la escalera esté en tierra llana sólida. Asegurese de tener a alguien que sostenga la escalera mientras que usted trabaja cerca de la cima. No utilice los últimos pasos de una escalera de pasos.

- Durante el verano y el otoño temprano, esté en alerta por las abejas. Sus nidos pueden estar en la tierra o en los arbustos y árboles o en el apartadero de una casa.

- No sobre apriete la tapa de gas o usted romperá el sello y causará que la tapa tenga agujero y tendrá fugas de gas.

- No pode con una tapa de gas que tiene fugas.

- Siempre llene las máquinas en el camión o en el remolque, no en el césped.

- Mantenga todas las herramientas afiladas, limpias y cuidadas.

- Mantenga todas las máquinas y latas de gas seguramente abrochadas en el remolque o camión.
- ¡¡Siempre piense en la seguridad primero!!

LIMPIEZA DE OTOÑO
(CAPÍTULO 9)

El servicio de limpieza del otoño es para quitar las hojas, palos y escombros de basura de áreas del césped y cama. La limpieza de otoño de hojas sucederá de septiembre a diciembre dependiendo del área del país en que usted vive. Las limpieza de hojas será más fácil si usted hace unas cuantas visitas a cada propiedad durante la temporada del otoño. Si las hojas se dejan en un área del césped por un largo período de tiempo, dañarán o matarán el césped. También, las hojas se atascarán en el césped que hara que la limpieza sea aún más duro. Trate de hacer visitas cada 7 a 14 días para hacer limpiezas del otoño. Durante el otoño temprano, comienze a cortar los céspedes que usted mantiene levemente bajos de lo normal. Haciendo esto, será más fácil de quitar las hojas durante la limpieza.

El equipo necesitado durante la limpieza de otoño es básicamente el mismo equipo que usted usa durante la limpieza de primavera. Usted necesitará el siguiente equipo para hacer una limpieza de otoño:

- Un soplador de tierra.
- Un soplador de muchila.
- Rastrillos.
- Una carpeta.

- Un barril grande del paisaje.

  Usted debe llevar puestos:

- Guantes.
- **Protección de oídos.**
- Lentes de seguridad.

Soplador de Tierra

El soplador de tiera es un soplador que sopla escombros de basura a través del suelo. Tiene más poder que un soplador de muchila y se debe usar en áreas grandes del césped. Hay un (chute) en el soplador de tierra para ajustar el flujo de aire. Sí hay hojas atascadas en el césped, ajuste el (chute) para que más aire sople **hacia abajo** en la superficie del césped. Si sólo hay escombros de basura a través de la superficie, ajusta el (chute) para soplar a través de la superficie del césped. Siempre sea cuidadoso mientras ajusta el (chute) del soplador. Apaga la máquina y nunca ponga las manos dentro del (chute). El soplador de tierra no se debe usar en camas de paisaje. Es demasiado poderoso y soplará pajote (mulch) o tierra fuera de la cama.

La mayoría de los sopladores de tierra usan gas regular. Llene el tanque de gas en el remolque o la calle mientras el motor esté fresco. **Verifique el aceite de motor (engine oil) dos o tres vez por día.** Cerciórese que tenga aceite extra de motor con usted antes de que usted vaya al sitio del trabajo.

Soplador de Muchila

El soplador de muchila es una máquina de 2 ciclos que usa una mezcla de gas y aceite para correr. Use el soplador de muchila para camas de paisaje, las aceras y áreas más pequeñas de la propiedad. Tenga cuidado para no dañar nada con el soplador en su espalda. Mientras usted trabaja en camas de paisaje, contra una casa, es fácil de retroceder y golpear en la casa, árbol o arbusto y causar daño. Tenga cuidado cuándo usted esté trabajando cerca de una casa, carros, árboles y arbustos.

Rastrillos

Traiga unos cuantos rastrillos al sitio del trabajo por si uno se rompe, usted tiene un extra. No empuje hacia abajo duramente en el asidero de madera sí no lo romperá. Verifique sus rastrillos y cerciórese que la parte que hace el rastrillar no esté desgastadó. Cuándo las orillas del rastrillo se desgasta, no trabajará apropiadamente y es tiempo para un nuevo rastrillo.

Carpetas y Barriles

Traiga ambos una carpeta y un barril del paisaje. Cada propiedad requerirá algo diferente. Use el barril del paisaje para recoger palos y montones pequeños de escombros de basura. Vacíe su barril en su camión o en la carpeta. Entonces cuando la carpeta esté llena, la trae a su camión de descarga o al área de descarga en la propiedad. No sobre llene una carpeta ni el barril sí no usted no podrá moverlo. Tenga cuidado para no rasgar la carpeta estirandola a través de un objeto afilado.

Aspiradora de Hoja (Leave Vacuum)

Una aspiradora de hoja es una máquina opcional usada durante la limpieza de hoja del otoño. Una aspidora de hoja es una máquina que chupa hojas y escombros de basura por medio de una una manguera grande que es más o menos de 12 pulgadas anchos y 20 pies de largo. Una vez que las hojas atraviesan la manguera, atraviesan un ventilador que gira muy rápidamente. Cuándo las hojas atraviesan este ventilador, se rompen aparte. Después las hojas salen de un (chute). El (chute) ira adentro de la parte de atrás del camión. Su camión necesita estar sellado con una carpeta de malla (mesh tarp) para que las hojas que soplan hacia el camión no se puedan escapar. La carpteta necesita estar aseguradamente conectada al camión. Usted debe usar una carpeta de malla para que el aire pueda escapar a través de la carpeta pero las hojas no puedan. Las hojas rotas vendrán al camión con la presión, esto permitirá que usted duplique la cantidad normal de hojas que cabe en su camión. La mayoría de las aspiradoras de hoja se montan en la puerta posterior (tailgate) del camión y algunas son montadas en un remolque. La aspiradora que es montada en la puerta posterior (tailgate) es mejor porque usted puede retroceder fácilmente el camión en caminos de entrada o en áreas duras de alcanzar.

Usted necesita tener el (chute) del escape de la aspiradora de hoja montado cerca de la cima del camión. Teniendo el (chute) montado a la cabeza del camión, usted puede llenar el camión a la cima. Una vez que el camión esté llenado hasta la cima, afloja la carpeta y arrastrela adentro del camión. Trate de empujar las hojas hacia abajo con su cuerpo. Haciendo esto, usted puede empujar las hojas abajo unos cuantos pies y entonces caberán más hojas en su camión.

La mayoría de las aspiradoras también recogerán recortes de césped y palos pequeños. Sin embargo, permanezca lejos de los palos grandres ya que estos se atascaran en la manguera. Permanezca lejos también de piedras flojas; recogiendo piedras dañará o destruirá la máquina en un corto período de tiempo.

Cuándo recoga hojas mojadas, la máquina se puede también atorar muy fácilmente. No fuerce demasiadas hojas mojadas en la manguera a una sola vez. Escuche el motor y las hojas que entran al camión. Sí el motor suena extraño y no hay hojas entrando al camión, usted tiene una traba. También sí usted afloja el poder de la aspiradora de la manguera, usted puede tener una traba. **Detenga** la máquina y quite la manguera, entonces limpia el ventilador, manguera y el (chute) del escape. Limpiar la máquina de una traba toma mucha tiempo y no es fácil. Así que trate de usar las aspiradora de hojas correctamente para evitar este problema.

Hay dos maneras de usar la manguera de la aspiradora de hoja. La primera manera deberá usar los asideros de la manguera, mueva la manguera de aquí para allá a través de un montón de hojas. La segunda manera deberá poner la manguera en el suelo y rastrillar las hojas hacia la manguera; ambas maneras trabajan bien. Uno o dos trabajadores deben operar la máquina; no hay necesidad de tener más de dos trabajadores utilisando la aspiradora de hojas. Sin embargo, una vez que el camión está completamente lleno y listo para ser descargado, usted necesitará por lo menos dos trabajadores fuertes para levantar la máquina de la puerta posterior (tailgate) del camión.

Siempre lleve puestos la protección de oídos y ojos cuándo se utilise esta máquina. Verifique el tanque de gas antes de arrancar la máquina y sólo llene el tanque de gas cuándo el motor esté fresco. **Recuerde de verificar el nivel del aceite motriz por lo menos dos veces por día.**

Ahora que hemos discutido todo el equipo utilisado para la limpieza del otoño, permita discutir cómo hacer el trabajo correctamente y eficientemente.

Completando un Trabajo de limpieza de Otoño

Como cada trabajo del paisaje, usted necesita planear y organizarse antes de que usted comienze a trabajar. Cuándo usted llegue al sitio del trabajo, todos deben echar una mirada a lo qué se debe hacer. Entonces discuta cómo se hará el trabajo y quíen usará qué máquina. Trabajen juntos como un equipo para obtener el trabajo hecho. Después que usted ha determinado la mejor manera de hacer el trabajo, llene de gas sus máquinas, verifica el aceite motriz (por lo menos dos veces por día), póngase su equipo de seguridad y usted está listo para comenzar. Cerciórese que no hay gente en el área donde ustedes trabajarán. Sí hay gente en el área que usted quiere trabajar, pidales que se marchen mientras usted trabaja. Sí esto no es posible, es mejor írse y deberá volver al sitio del trabajo en otra vez cuando el área esté libre de gente. Nunca opere algúna máquinaria de poder cerca de otra gente.

En el principio de la temporada del otoño, empieze limpiando solamente las áreas de césped. Cuándo usted limpia las áreas de cama de paisaje, usted quitará parte del pajote (mulch). Por lo tanto es mejor limpiar las camas del paisaje sólo dos o tres vez durante el otoño.

Cuándo usted limpia solamente las áreas de césped, será más fácil de simplemente cortar y embolsar el césped para reunir una **leve** cubierta de hojas. Recuerde de cortar el césped levemente más bajo de lo normal durante el otoño. Entonces será más fácil de soplar las hojas en la próxima visita de limpieza.

Cuándo las hojas comienzan a llegar a ser más pesados, Será demasiado difícil o imposible de embolsarlas. Ahora usted necesitará usar los sopladores para limpiar el césped.
- Primero utilise un soplador de muchila y limpie un área más o menos de cinco pies alrededor de las orillas del área de césped.
- Entonces otra persona debe poner el soplador de tierra en esta área limpiada. Empieze a caminar y soplar de aquí para allá a través

del césped utilisando un soplador de tierra y un soplador de muchila. Mueva unos cuantos pies adelante con cada paso a través del césped.

- Sí hay alguna cama de paisaje en el área del césped, vaya alrededor de ellas usando el soplador de muchila. Nunca use un soplador de tierra en una cama del paisaje ya que soplará el pajote (mulch) o la capa superior fuera de la cama y en el césped.

- Continúe trabajando de aquí para allá a través de la propiedad. Una vez que las hojas llegan a ser difíciles de soplar, haga un montón, después rastrilla el montón de hojas a una carpeta y las acarrea lejos. Continúe soplando y limpia el área de césped.

- Omita limpiar todas las áreas de cama de paisaje. Pero **no** sople hojas a las camas cuándo usted esté limpiando el césped. Esto hará la limpieza de las camas muy difícil en el futuro. Se Mirará desordenado y no es una manera profesional de limpiar el césped.

- Después que el área del césped esté limpia, usted puede necesitar cortar el césped o puede ser posible omitir el corte hasta la próxima visita. Sí usted no regresará a ese trabajo de 10 a 14 días y el tiempo está todavia tibio, será mejor para usted cortar el césped o el trabajo le será muy difícil en la próxima visita.

Limpiando la Propiedad Entera

En su próxima visita, debe ser tiempo de limpiar la propiedad entera inclusive las camas. No espere demasiado tiempo para limpiar las camas del paisaje. Sí las hojas se ponen demasiado pesado y llueve, las camas serán muy duras de limpiar.

Usar un soplador de muchila, limpia todos los arbustos y la cama del paisaje. Mientras un trabajador sopla el área de arbustos y cama, un segundo trabajador debe ayudar a mover las hojas con un rastrillo.

Dondequiera que las hojas se construyan y se hacen pesado, rastrillelas. Las hojas se atascan entre ramas y bajo arbustos. Utilise el rastrillo para levantar las ramas de los arbustos o de (ground covers) plantas de cubierta de suelo mientras que un colaborador sopla los escombros de basura.

Cuándo usted trabaja en una cama del paisaje, tenga cuidado para no dañar ninguno de los arbustos ni árboles pisandolos mientras usted limpia. Tenga cuidado cuándo camina hacia atrás con un soplador de muchila, usted puede apoyarse en un arbusto o árbol y terminar rompiendo las ramas o dañar la casa. Un soplador de muchila se extiende casi dos pies lejos de su espalda, así que sea cuidadoso.

Mientras sopla, no permita que ninguna hoja se acumule cerca del ventilador del soplador de muchila. Hay un espacio pequeño entre el área acolchada que se monta a su espalda y el ventilador. Durante la limpieza de hoja, esta área puede llegar a ser atascada con hojas. Cuándo el área se atasca, el soplador perderá poder y daño al motor ocurrirá. Es muy dificil darse cuenta si hay algún problema ya que usted no puede ver el área cuándo usted utiliza el soplador. Así que vigilese el uno al otro durante la limpieza, y sí usted nota este problema, notifique a su colaborador inmediatamente.

Apaga la máquina y quite las hojas a mano, o ponga la máquina atascada en estado de parado (idle) y utilizando otro soplador de muchila, sople las hojas atascadas en la máquina. Nunca meta su mano en el área para quitar las hojas mientras la máquina está encendida. Algunos sopladores más nuevos vienen con una cubierta sobre esta área para prevenir este problema.

Continúe trabajando juntos como un equipo soplando y rastrillando las hojas de las camas. **Tenga cuidado** para no soplar demasiado duro en el pajote (mulch). Trate de mantener el pajote (mulch) en las camas y no las sople al césped. Después que usted ha limpiado el área de la cama, usted puede necesitar soplar levemente la casa o edificio, especialmente cuándo trabaja en condiciones polvorientas. Mire a la casa y las ventanas y si usted ve una capa de tierra, sóplelas. Sí alguna ventana está abierta, notifica al dueño de casa para cerrarlas antes de que usted empieze a trabajar. Sí esto no es posible, sopla muy lentamente y usa un rastrillo para limpiar el área para que así no sople tierra y polvo a la casa. Una vez que las camas esten limpiadas, limpie el área de césped unos cuantos pies para que el soplador de tierra pueda comenzar en esta área. Entonces comienze a limpiar el área de césped de la misma manera como nosotros discutimos más temprano.

Usted tendrá que usar una carpeta para recoger y acarrear las hojas más a menudo cuando las hojas están más pesadas. Usted acarreara las hojas a un área de descarga en la la propiedad o los tendrá que poner en su camión.

Si usted descarga las hojas en un área arbolada en la propiedad, hale la carpeta lo más distante posible en el bosque para que las hojas no se vean fácilmente y no soplen de regreso al área que usted limpió. Tenga cuidado de no rasgar la carpeta cuando la estire por el bosque. Recuerde después que usted descarga, esparcir los montones para que no sean notables. Sí usted sopla las hojas en una línea de bosque, los pone lo más lejos posible o si no se soplarán de regreso. Utilize un soplador de muchila o rastrillo para esparcir las hojas y reducir la altura de las hojas cuándo las sopla en alguna área arbolada. Cuándo descarga en un área arbolada, tiene cuidado que usted no llene ninguna corriente de agua o áreas donde el agua corre durante una lluvia.

Si usted está quitando las hojas de la propiedad y acarreandolos a su camión, hay dos maneras de llevar las hojas a su camión a mano o utilizando una aspiradora de hoja. Cuándo usted pone las hojas en su camión a mano.

- Primero quite el remolque del camión.
- Ponga los conos de emergencia alrededor del remolque, entonces estaciona el camión lo más cerca posible del área de la propiedad en la cual usted trabaja.

- Sí hay muchas hojas, usted las tendrá que poner en una carpeta. Poner las hojas en un barril del paisaje tomará demasiado tiempo.

- Una vez que usted tiene las hojas sopladas en un montón y entonces las rastrilla a una carpteta, ata juntos los dos rincónes de atrás de la carpeta. Entonces agarra los otros dos rincónes del frente y hala la carpeta arriba hacia la parte posterior del camión.

- Sí usted está trabajando sólo, usted tendrá que utilizar una carpeta pequeña. En la mayoría de los casos habrá dos o tres personas que trabajan juntos. Utilize una carpeta más grande cuándo usted está trabajando con una tripulación más grande; la carpeta más grande obtendrá el trabajo más rápido y más fácil. Ate los dos rincónes de atrás de la carpeta juntos, tenga a una persona agarrando cada rincón del frente, entonces subase al camión y hale la carpeta de hojas mientras la tercera persona levanta y empuja de atrás. Con el trabajo en equipo, usted puede obtener muchas hojas en su camión rápidamente.

- Después de descargar las hojas en su camión, camine arriba y abajo encima de las hojas. Trate de comprimirlas para que pueda caber lo más posible en su camión.

- Siempre cubra las hojas con una carpeta antes de conducir. Debe haber una carpeta y un rodillo montados en su camión. Cubra las hojas aunque el camión sólo esté medio lleno. Sí alguna hoja se sale mientras conduce, usted puede obtener una multa de la policía.

La otra manera de obtener las hojas en su camión es utilizando una aspiradora de hoja. La aspiradora de hoja será montado atrás de su camión o puede ser montada en un remolque pequeño. Cuándo se utiliza una aspiradora de hoja, usted tendrá probablemente que halar el remolque del paisaje con un segundo vehículo. Las aspiradora de hoja y la carpeta de malla se deben montar apropiadamente en su camión o sí no usted tendrá problemas consecutivamente mientras utiliza la máquina. La carpeta debe cubrir completamente la parte de atrás de su camión. No puede haber ninguna apertura pequeña sí no las hojas se escaparán por la apertura cuándo usted utilize la máquina. Una carpeta de malla se debe usar para que el flujo de aire pueda escapar por la carpeta pero no las hojas.

Verifique el nivel del gas y aceite motriz antes de cada vez que usted utilize la aspiradora de hoja. Utilize las luces en el camión mientras opera la aspiradora de hoja. Sí usted trabaja cerca de la calle, cerciórese que usted tenga los conos de emergencia afuera por todas partes del área en la cual usted trabaja. Utilize luces y conos de emergencia siempre aunque usted esté trabajando en un área con poco tráfico. Antes de que usted empieze a usar la máquina, ponga todas las hojas juntas en un montón. Cree un montón en un área que es más fácil de alcanzar con su camión. No ponga los montones de hoja en caminos de entrada o donde sea área donde hay muchas piedras. También, no bloquee el camino de entrada con montones de hoja.

Una tripulación de dos personas trabaja mejor cuándo utiliza la aspiradora de hoja. Una persona para sostener la manguera mientras la otra persona rastrilla las hojas cerca de la manguera de la aspiradora, o para retroceder el camión hacia el montón como sea necesitado. Trabaje más lento cuándo limpia con la aspiradora hojas mojadas y no forze demasiadas hojas en la aspiradora a la misma vez para evitar que la aspiradora se atore. Así como lo discutimos más temprano, recuerda de evitar utilizar la aspiradora para limpiar piedras y cúalquier ramas que sean más grande de un pie en longitud. Cuándo el camión está completamente lleno, suba al camión debajo de la carpeta. Empuje las hojas hacia abajo con su cuerpo y entonces usted podrá hacer caber más hojas en el camión.

Condusca cuidadosamente cuándo el camión este cargado y asegurese que tenga la cantidad correcta de aire en las llantas del camión. Nunca ponga cargue el camión cuándo las llantas esten bajas de aire.

Visita Final Limpieza de Otoño

Después que la mayor parte de las hojas han sido limpiados de cada sitio del trabajo usted está haciendo su última visita del año, puede ser más fácil de reunir las hojas con un cortacésped otra vez. Primero sople las camas por última vez. Recoja los escombros de basura de las camas sí es demasiado para el cortacésped de recoger. Sí hay algunos palos en el césped o camas, los recoge y los pone en un barril. Mire contra la casa para ver cualquier pozos de ventana, si están sucios, limpie los escombros de basura a mano. Después corte el césped con la bolsa para reunir una leve cubierta de hojas. Si hay hojas pesadas en el césped, usted necesitará limpiarlos como acabamos de discutir antes del corte final. Esto le dará a la propiedad una vista profesional durante el invierno.

Trabajando en Condiciones de mucho viento

Durante el otoño, puede haber días cuándo el viento hace la limpieza de hoja difícil o casi imposible. Obviamente si usted está en la temporada temprana del otoño o la temporada tarde del otoño, y usted esté sólo recogiendo las hojas con el cortacésped, usted no tendrá ningun problema. Durante los días de mucho viento, usted debe darse cuenta que usted no puede hacer un trabajo perfecto. Su meta debe ser de quitar las hojas pesadas y entonces regresar en una o dos semanas después para hacer un mejor trabajo.

Antes de que usted empiece a trabajar, trate de encontrar en cuál dirección el viento sopla, después sopla las hojas en la dirección que el viento está soplando. Algunos días esto trabajará, otros días esto no funcionara. A veces los vientos soplan en muchas direcciones diferentes que hacen la limpieza aún más duro o imposible. Mientras limpia durante condiciones de mucho viento, recoga las hojas más a menudo que lo usual. Si usted recoge las hojas en una carpeta o barril rápidamente, no se podrán soplar de regreso al área que acaba de limpiar. Trate de vigilar y aprender acerca de cada propiedad. Algunos casas serán siempre más ventosos que otros. En un día de mucho viento, escoja las propiedades que tienen generalmente menos viento.

No pierda tiempo. Sí usted ha tratado lo mejor de usted en un día de mucho viento y es casi imposible de obtener algo hecho, piense acerca de algunos otros trabajos que se pueden hacer, tal como: la conservación del equipo o un trabajo pequeño del paisaje o tomese el dia libre.

Instrucción y Consejos de Seguridad de Limpieza de Otoño

- Siempre lleve puestos **la protección de oídos** porque usted puede causar daño permanente a sus oídos del ruido fuerte de los sopladores. También lleve puestos otro equipo de seguridad tal como los lentes de seguridad y guantes.
- Piense acerca de cada trabajo y organicese antes de que usted comienze.
- Trabajen juntos como un equipo.
- Llene las máquinas con gas en el remolque cuando el motor esté fresco.
- No sobre apriete las tapas de gas.
- Verifique el nivel del aceite motriz por lo menos dos veces por día.
- Mantenga las manos y pies lejos de todas las partes móviles de las máquinas.
- Tenga cuidado cuándo ajusta el (chute) en el soplador de tierra.

- Apaga el motor para desatrancar (unclog) las hojas de un soplador.

- Mantenga las máquinas abrochadas aseguradamente en su remolque o el camión.

- Siempre piense en la seguridad primero.

ESCOGER Y MANEJO DE LA MATERIA DE PLANTA

(CAPÍTULO 10)

Escoger y manejo de la materia de planta se debe hacer cuidadosamente y correctamente o la planta que está a punto de instalar **no puede sobrevivir**. La materia de planta es muy costosa y reemplazarlo después que lo ha instalado es una pérdida grave para todos. Siguiendo unos pocos procedimientos sencillos del trabajo, usted estará escogiendo exitosamente, estará manejando y estará instalando la materia de planta que crecerá saludable y se mirará hermoso por muchos, muchos años.

Preparandose para Escoger y Recoger la Materia de Planta del Semillero

Prepararando una Lista de Planta y Seleccionando un Semillero

Antes de hacer una visita a su sermillero local, usted necesita crear una lista de todas las plantas que usted necesita. Procure agrupar juntos unos cuantos trabajos pequeños para que cuándo usted visite el semillero usted pueda obtener el material de planta necesaria para unos cuantos trabajos diferentes todo en una visita. Su lista debe tener los nombres de las plantas, la cantidad que usted necesita y los tamaños que usted necesita. Una vez que la lista está preparada, alguien necesitará llamar al semillero local para saber si las plantas que usted necesita están disponibles. No desperdicie su

411

tiempo conduciendo hacia el semillero local sí usted no está seguro acerca de lo que ellos tienen en su almacen.

Usted debe negociar con unos cuantos diferentes semilleros locales. Escoja los mejores tres semilleros locales en su área. Entonces aprenda acerca de cada semillero; por ejemplo: Un semillero puede tener siempre una selección grande de árboles mientras que otro semillero puede tener siempre una selección grande de plantas más pequeñas. Entonces usted sabrá a quién llamar para la materia de planta que usted necesita.

Preparar Su Camión y el Remolque

Una vez que usted está listo para recoger el material de planta, escoge el camión y/o el remolque correctos para la materia que usted obtendrá. El camión y el remolque necesitan estar perfectamente limpios de cúalquier gas o aceite. Sí usted derramo gas o aceite en su camión o en el remolque, ponga hacia abajo una carpeta sólida antes de cargar cúalquier materia de planta.

Usted necesitará también una carpeta de malla para cubrir las plantas durante el transporte. Cubriendo las plantas, usted las protegerá de que sean dañadas de la tensíon del viento o del tiempo calido. La carpeta que usted usa para cubrir la materia de planta debe ser de malla para que el aire pueda fluir a traves de ello y que las plantas puedan respirar.

Nunca use una carpeta sólida para cubrir el material de planta. El semillero debe suministrale a usted con lazo para sujetar cúalquier planta; sin embargo, es una buena idea mantener un lazo en su camión para situaciones de emergencia. Verifique la presión de aire de las llantas en su camión y el remolque antes de cargar el material de planta. Cuándo usted llega al semillero busque por alguien para que lo ayude inmediatamente. Siempre escoja y carque los árboles y arbustos más grandes primero, después usted puede hacer caber las plantas más pequeñas en medio de las más grandes. Las plantas más grandes ayudarán apoyar las plantas pequeñas y ayudarán a manternerlas de circular mientras usted conduce.

Las Opciones de entrega

A veces, puede ser mejor no tomar las plantas en el mismo día que usted las inspecciona y las compra. Dependiendo de su situación de trabajo, puede ser mejor etiquetar las plantas y recojerlas el día que usted las estará instalando.

El material de planta debe ser movida lo menos posible y debe ser regada con agua en una base regular. No traiga las plantas al garaje o sitio de trabajo si usted no las instalará inmediatamente.

Si usted necesita un número grande de plantas, usted debe considerar tener las plantas entregadas. La mayoría de las veces será más fácil y más barato pagar por una entrega en vez de conducir de aquí para allá al semillero local todo el día. El jefe o capataz en su compañía debe tomar esta decisión.

Etiquetando el Material de Planta

Cuándo está etiquetando el material de planta haga **doble** etiqueta para cada planta. Entonces habrá menos oportunidad de que otra persona quite la etiqueta de su planta y ponga su etiqueta en una planta diferente. La doble etiqueta trabaja mejor cuándo se usa una etiqueta regular con el nombre de su Compañía cello y luego envuelve la planta con un pedazo de marcador de cinta plástica de color. Usted necesitará traer el marcador plástico usted mismo. Manténgalo en su camión a lo largo del año.

Inspeccionando La Materia de la Planta

Obviamente usted quiere escoger las plantas más saludables y las que se ven mejor. Así que usted necesita tomarse unos cuantos minutos para inspeccionar cada planta antes de comprarla. **Nunca compre el material de planta sin inspeccionarlo primero.** Recuerde que la persona que trabaja en el semillero local es una persona de ventas y puede venderle cúalquier planta aunque tenga problemas. Como un profesional del paisaje, usted sólo debe comprar las plantas que son de buena calidad y estan en buen estado. No escoja por nada menos.

Inspeccionando y Escojiendo Árboles

La primer cosa que usted debe hacer es mirar la forma completa del árbol. Escoja un árbol repleto con muchas ramas saludables. Las ramas deben estar creciendo en la forma correcta. Evite escoger árboles con unas pocas ramas o ramas que crecen irregular. Será muy duro encontrar árboles o arbustos que tienen los cuatro lados perfectos. Sí tres lados del árbol se ven bien y el cuarto lado tiene un **leve** problema, usted todavía puede usarlo. **Usted siempre debe instalar árboles o arbustos para que el lado peor no esté frente al lado del área que es muy visible.**

Después que usted escoge un árbol con una buena forma, usted debe inspeccionar también lo siguiente:

- Inspeccione la condición de las hojas y las ramas. Las hojas deben tener un buen color y deben ser firmes y vertical. Evite los árboles que tienen un color débil o las hojas hundidas o ramas. Evite árboles con hojas o ramas marrones. Corra su mano encima de las ramas y sí muchas agujas se caen, el árbol es débil y tiene tensíon. De una mirada alrededor la bola de raíz, y sí muchas hojas se han caído, evite escoger ese árbol.

- Inspeccione las hojas, ramas por cúalquier signo de insectos o enfermedad. Sí hay cúalquier insecto o enfermedad en el árbol, evite escoger ese árbol.

- Inspeccione el tronco del árbol. El tronco debe ser recto y saludable y tener una corteza sin daño. Evite los árboles con un tronco torcido. Evite los árboles que tienen una corteza partida o dañada.

- Inspeccione el tamaño de la bola de raíz. Sí el árbol es bastante grande y tiene una bola de raíz pequeña, no puede sobrevivir. A veces usted encontrará árboles donde la bola de raíz parece pequeña comparada con el tamaño del árbol. Sí la bola de raíz se cortó demasiado pequeña, muchas de las raíces han sido quitadas. Esto pone el árbol en una condición de tensíon. Sólamente escoja árboles donde la bola de raíz iguala el tamaño del árbol. Evite los árboles donde la bola de raíz parece demasiado pequeña.

- Inspeccione la bola de raíz para cerciórarse que no ha sido dañado. Después de mirar el tamaño de la bola de raíz, busque por cúalquier daño. La mayoría de las bolas de raíz vienen en una jaula de metal (balled y burlapped). Algunos árboles más pequeños pueden venir en un contenedor plástico. Verifique la condición de la arpillera y evite la arpillera que es vieja y que empieze a pudrirse. **Sin embargo, si el árbol se mira fuerte y saludable y tiene raíces que crecen por la arpillera vieja se puede envolver con una arpillera nueva y ser usada sí la bola de raíz esta sólida y no está dañada.**

- Escoja un árbol con una bola de raíz **sólida**. La tierra de la bola de raíz **no** debe ser rompida ni aflojada. Evite los árboles con la arpillera podrida, o con una bola de raíz que no esté sólida. También evite los árboles con perforaciones grandes en la bola de raíz.

- Escoja un árbol que tiene el tronco **centrado** en la bola de raíz. No escoja el árbol sí el tronco no está en el centro de la bola de raíz.

- Usando las manos, agarre por el tronco del árbol más o menos de cuatro pies arriba de la bola de raíz. Entonces mueva el tronco de aquí para allá. Sí el tronco parece muy flojo y no está conectado sólidamente a la bola de raíz, se puede dañar. Evite escoger ese árbol.

- Trate de escoger árboles crecidos sobre árboles que crecen en un contenedor plástico. Los árboles que son (balled y burlapped) son generalmente más fuertes y más fáciles de instalar.

- Sea extra cuidadoso cuándo hay sólo unos pocos árboles dejados para escoger. Generalmente los últimos árboles de un puñado son los que tienen problemas.

Inspeccionando y Escojiendo Arbustos

- Otra vez, mire primero la forma completa del arbusto. Cerciórese que por lo menos tres lados del arbusto se vean bien y que el cuarto lado tenga sólo un problema leve.

- Inspeccione el color de la planta y verifica la condición de las hojas o ramas.

- Inspeccione las hojas, y ramas por cúalquier signo de insectos o enfermedad. Sí hay cúalquier insecto o enfermedad en el arbusto, evite escoger ese arbusto.

- Inspeccione la base del arbusto de donde el tronco o ramas crecen y cuidadosamente mueva el tronco o las ramas. Sí el tronco o las ramas se sienten flojas y no están aseguradas a la bola de raíz, evite escoger ese arbusto.

- Verifique el tamaño del arbusto comparandolo con la bola de raíz. Sí la planta es muy grande comparada con la bola de raíz, el arbusto puede estar bajo tensíon. Sólamente escoja las plantas donde el tamaño de la bola de raíz iguala el tamaño del arbusto.

- Cerciórese que el arbusto se centra en la bola de raíz o contenedor. Una planta que no se centra no ha sido quitada del suelo correctamente. La bola de raíz fue cortadó desigual; esto causará el énfasis de tensíon adicional a la planta.

- Verifique la bola de raíz envuelta (burlapped) o contenedor plástico. Cerciórese que no haya sido dañado en ninguna manera. Si se dañó, evite escoger ese arbusto.

- Otra vez, sea extra cuidadoso cuándo hay sólo unos pocos arbustos dejados para escoger. Generalmente las últimas pocas plantas de un puñado son los que tienen problemas.

Inspeccionando y Escojiendo (Ground Covers y Perennes Perennials)

- (Perennials) son las plantas que regresan año tras año. Se van inactivas y generalmente no son visibles durante el tiempo de invierno. Después vuelven durante la temporada creciente. Usted debe escoger los (perennials) durante la temporada creciente. Evite escoger (perennials) cuándo están inactivas ya que usted no podrá saber sí la planta está fuerte y saludable o pequeña y débil.

- Mire al color de la planta. Escoja las plantas con un color fuerte, esto indica que la planta está saludable.

- Cerciórese que las hojas, ramas crezcan vertical. Evite las plantas con hojas, ramas doblegadas .

- Inspeccione la planta por cúalquier signo de insectos o enfermedad y evite la planta sí usted encuentra cúalquier problema

- Cerciórese que el contenedor de la planta y la tierra en el contenedor no hayan sido dañados en ninguna manera.

- Otra vez sea extra cuidadoso cuándo hay sólo unas pocas plantas dejadas para escoger, ya que generalmente las últimas pocas plantas de un puñado son los que tienen problemas.

Inspeccionando y Escojiendo Flores y Bulbos

Las Flores anuales

Las flores anuales crecen sólo durante el tiempo calido y morirán cuándo sean expuestas a temperaturas heladas. Por lo tanto, son plantadas cada año (anualmente). Deben ser plantadas en la primavera después que haya pasado la última oportunidad de helada o las temperaturas heladas. Entonces crecerán hasta que el tiempo frío regrese en el otoño.

Cuándo escoja flores anuales:
- Cerciórese que el color de las hojas sea fuerte, no débil y desteñido.
- Cerciórese que las hojas crecen vertical; no doblegadas (sagging).
- Escoja las plantas que tienen sólo unas pocas flores o ninguna flor. Entonces tendrán un tiempo más largo para florecer cuándo sean instalados.
- Escoja las flores que son de un tamaño bueno. **No demasiado grande, pero no demasiado pequeñas**. Las flores pequeñas son duras de instalar y pueden morir muy fácilmente.
- Escoja las flores que no tienen ningún tipo de daño a ellas ni al contenedor en las que crecen.
- Busque por problemas de insectos o enfermedad.

- Sí hay una selección pequeña de flores de las cuales debe escoger, y no estan en buen estado, no las compre.

Los Bulbos (Bulbs)

Un bulbo es una flor inactiva. Es pequeña en tamaño y generalmente semejante a la forma de una cebolla. Los bulbos son perennes (perennials); que son plantados en el suelo y producen una flor por unas pocas semanas cada año. Entonces se van inactivo hasta el próximo año.

- Cuándo escoja bulbos individuales, aguante cada bulbo en su mano. Entonces busque por algún lugar suave en el bulbo. Los lugares suaves son áreas dañadas en el bulbo. El bulbo debe ser firme y no debe tener ningún lugar suave.
- Sí usted está comprando una caja de bulbos, abre la caja y verifica los bulbos. Sí la mayor parte de los bulbos están en buen estado, usted puede comprar la caja. Sí usted encuentra muchos bulbos dañados, no los compre.
- No compre los bulbos a menos que usted los vaya a sembrar brevemente después. Sí usted tiene que almacenar los bulbos, manténgalos en un lugar fresco y seco.

El manejo del Material de Planta

Siempre que una planta se quita del suelo, transportada a un semillero, descargada y colocada en el suelo, será puesta bajo tensíon y tiene una oportunidad de morir. Como un profesional del paisaje, usted debe estar enterado de esto. Para reducir el riesgo de que las plantas mueran, usted debe manejar todo el material de planta correctamente y manejar las plantas lo menos posible. Su meta es de llevar el material de plantas del semillero local al sitio de trabajo e instalarlo correctamente en el suelo, sin agregarle algún énfasis de tensíon adicional a la planta.

Levantando y Moviendo el Material de Planta

- Asi como acabamos de discutir, maneje y mueva todo el material de planta lo menos posible.

- **Nunca** recoja o mueva la planta agarrandola de las ramas o del tronco.

- Solamente agarrela de la bola de raíz para levantarla o mover la planta. Sí la planta está en un contenedor plástico, agarre el contenedor para levantar o mover la planta. Sí la bola de raíz de la planta está envuelta en la arpillera debe haber también una jaula de metal envuelta alrededor de la arpillera. Agarrelo del metal de la jaula para levantar o mover la planta.

- Evite dejar caer las plantas y evite el manejo áspero de las plantas. Dejando caer las plantas, usted puede romper la bola de raíces y causar que la planta muera.

- No trate de mover una planta que está demasiado pesada para usted. Utilice un carrito de árbol o una máquina para mover las plantas grandes.

Cargando el Material de Planta

Inspeccione y escoja el material de planta más grande primero. Después que las plantas grandes sean cargadas, inspeccione y escoja las plantas más pequeñas. Entonces las plantas más pequeñas se pueden colocar en medio de las más grandes y no serán dañadas.

Cargando Material Grande de Planta (Árboles y Arbustos Grandes)

- Asi como acabamos de discutir, cargue el material de planta más grande primero.

- Antes de cargar los árboles generalmente es mejor atar las ramas. Atando las ramas, usted reducirá el riesgo de daño al árbol y usted tendrá más espacio en su camión o remolque. El empleado del semillero local debe suministrarle a usted con lazo y ayudarlo atar los árboles.

- Planee la mejor manera de cargar los árboles y las plantas grandes. Planeándolo, usted estará habil para hacer caber más en su camión y remolque.

- Evite doblar las ramas de las plantas.

- Si las ramas frotan en algo como la parte posterior de su camión, utilice alguna arpillera para proteger las ramas.

- Trate de mantener todo el material de plantas acostada para que no se mueva a causa del viento cuándo usted conduce. El viento pone bajo tensíon a la planta y puede dañarla o matarla.

- Después que los árboles y los arbustos grandes sean cargados, cerciórese que no se moverán durante la transportación. Sí hay alguna posibilidad de que quizás se muevan, atelos hacia abajo. Sí la materia grande de plantas se mueve durante el transporte, puede crear un problema grave. Cerciórese que todo esté asegurado.

- Toda el material de planta se debe cubrir con una carpeta de malla de respirar. La carpeta protegerá las plantas del daño del calor y del viento durante el transporte.

Cargando Plantas más Pequeñas

Sí usted tiene las plantas grandes cargadas en su camión y remolque, usted puede colocar generalmente las plantas más pequeñas en medio de las más grande. Entonces las plantas más grande ayudarán apoyar las más pequeñas. Sí esto no es posible o sí usted sólo esta comprando plantas pequeñas, usted los tendrá que agrupar juntas. Agrupando las plantas pequeñas juntas, ayudará a que una al otro se apoyen y será menos probable que se muevan. Una vez que todas las plantas se cargan, las cubre con un carpeta de malla de respirar. Cerciórese que la carpeta esté sujetado seguramente y usted estará listo para conducir hacia el sitio de trabajo.

Durante el transporte, condusca lentamente. Evite las paradas repentinas o aceleración rápida. Condusca lentamente y constante y sus plantas estarán en buen estado cuándo usted llegue al sitio de trabajo.

INSTALACIÓN DE ÁRBOLES Y ARBUSTOS
(CAPÍTULO 11)

Antes de instalar cúalquier material de planta, se debe hacer una investigación para asegurarse que la planta es mejor acomodada en la ubicación escogida. El sol, sombra, tierra mojada o seca, los problemas de venado y el diseño del paisaje todo debe ser planeado antes de comprar e instalar cúalquier material de planta. Después que la planta correcta se ha escogido para la ubicación, se debe espaciar apropiadamente. Debe haber suficiente espacio para permitir que la planta pueda crecer a su tamaño normal. Después que usted inspeccione y escoge el material de planta saludable, deben ser instalados correctamente para que pueda crecer fuerte y saludable y vivir una vida larga. Asi como un profesional del paisaje, usted es responsable de instalar todo el material de planta correctamente para que no muera prematuramente.

Investigación nueva ha mostrado que muchos de los métodos estándares de plantar que han sido usados por muchos años han pasado de moda. Ahora hay mejores maneras probadas de instalar el material de planta, que le dará a la planta la mejor oportunidad de crecer fuerte y saludable y una vida larga.

Usted necesitará las siguientes herramientas y equipo cuándo instale árboles, arbustos, (ground covers) cubiertas del suelo, (perennials), flores y bulbos. Un carrito del árbol, una carretilla, palas, una piocha, y un rastrillo de arco de metal, un rastrillo de hoja, una horquilla, tijeras manuales, pala manual, una piocha manual (hand sized pick), un cuchillo de utilidad, y un soplador de muchila.

Lleve puestos las botas de trabajo y guantes. Sí usted se agacha o levantar demasiado, usted debe llevar puesto proteccion de rodillas y un soporte de espalda.

Instalando Arboles en Bola y Envueltos (Balled and Burlaped)

- Traiga los árboles sobre a la ubicación donde se instalarán. **Nota:** Maneje los árboles muy cuidadosamente. Use un carrito de árbol o máquina para mover los árboles. Nunca use el tronco de árbol ni ramas como un asidero. Sólo tomele de la bola de raíz para mover un árbol.
- Antes de empezar a cavar, los árboles deben ser espaciados correctamente y claramente marcados **exactamente** dónde deberán ser instalados. **Nota:** El dueño o el capataz deben ser los responsables en espaciar la marca exactamente dónde los árboles deberán ser instalados. **Nunca** instale cúalquier material de planta sí usted no está 100% seguro de la ubicación correcta.
- La bola de raíz del árbol se debe colocar muy cerca de donde se instalará. Luego cuándo usted ha terminado de cavar el hoyo, la bola de raíz puede ser colocada cuidadosamente en el hoyo.
- Cave el hoyo dos veces más de ancho que la bola de raíz pero no más profundo que la profundidad de la bola de raíz. Sí usted no tiene una cinta métrica, mide la bola de raíz con el asidero de una

pala. Tome el asidero con la mano y lo usa como un palo de medir.

- Verifique la anchura y profundidad de la bola de raíz y lo compara al hoyo que usted está cavando. Recuerde **dos veces** de ancho pero no más profundo que la profundidad de la bola de raíz. Cave el hoyo más ancho por encima para que el hoyo tenga una forma de platillo.

Usando el método viejo de plantar, usted cavaría también la profundidad dos veces más profundo y luego llenaria el hoyo con tierra. El problema con ese método es que esa tierra se asentará causando que el árbol se hunda más profundo en el hoyo. Las raíces nuevas pueden ser arrancadas cuándo el árbol se asienta.

- Cuándo la bola de raíz se pone en el hoyo, la cima de ello debe ser levemente más alto que el suelo existente. Sí usted cava el hoyo demasiado profundo, llenelo con tierra y **firmemente apretelo** hacia abajo.
- **Afloje** los lados y el fondo del hoyo con un piocha o una pala.
- **Vuelva a verificar el tamaño del hoyo una última vez. Es muy importante tener la profundidad exacta.** Sí usted pone un árbol pesado en el hoyo y el hoyo es demasiado profundo usted creará un trabajo adicional para usted mismo y es posible que usted no pueda levantar la bola de raíz de regreso del hoyo.
- Una vez que usted esté 100% seguro que el hoyo está correcto, unas cuantas personas deben tomar de la bola de raíz. Agarre de la jaula de metal o de los lazos envueltos alrededor del árbol. Nunca

use el tronco del árbol para levantar ni mover el árbol. Cuándo usted la agarre, cerciórese también que usted pueda soltarla rápidamente y fácilmente o usted puede lastimarse cuándo usted ponga la bola de raíz en el hoyo.

- Cuidadosamente levante la bola de raíz en el hoyo. **No deje** caer la bola de raíz en el hoyo. Permita que se deslize lentamente en el hoyo, entonces lo para arriba y lo mueve al centro del hoyo. Sí usted no puede deslizar la bola de raíz en el hoyo, trate de darle **vuelta** mientras empuja y estira al moverlo unas pocas pulgadas a la vez, entonces permita que deslize lentamente en el hoyo.

- Después de posicionarlo al centro del hoyo, gira el árbol para que el mejor lado del árbol esté frente al área más visible. Entonces cerciórese que el árbol este recto. Sí necesita, agrega alguna tierra debajo de la bola de raíz hasta que el árbol esté parado perfectamente derecho.

- Después que el árbol se posiciona correctamente y usted no lo tiene que mover más, desata todo el lazo y lo pela, (burlap) la arpillera y jaula de metal lo mejor posible.

- Llene el hoyo con tierra. Haga una mezcla que use más o menos el 50% de tierra que usted quitó del hoyo y 50% de la capa superficial del suelo. **Esté seguro de mezclarlo completamente cuándo usted llena de regreso el hoyo.** Evite poner piedras de regreso en el hoyo.

Investigación nueva ha probado que una planta es capaz de crecer mejor en una locación nueva sí las raíces pueden establecerce en la tierra existente. El método viejo de plantar es de cavar un hoyo y llenarlo con 100% de capa superficial del suelo. El problema es que una vez que las raíces nuevas crecen y pasen el área de la capa superficial del suelo es posible que no puedan crecer en la tierra existente. Por lo contrario círculan alrededor de la capa superficial del suelo. Esto causa que el árbol muera prematuramente.

- **Después que el hoyo este medio lleno de regreso, verifique para cerciórarse que el árbol esté todavía recto**, entonces **levemente** apriete la tierra debajo alrededor de la bola de raíz. Entonces llene de regreso la parte restante del hoyo y **levemente** presione la tierra cuándo usted ha terminado.

La mayoría de las plantas no necesitan ser abonadas cuándo están siendo instaladas. Las plantas son alimentadas en el semillero local. Al aplicarle demasiado abono puede dañar o matar la planta. La mayoría de las plantas no necesitan un abono hasta su segundo año de haber sido instalado. Sí usted escoje abonarla cuándo esté plantando, sólo use un producto organico de desolver lento.

- Después que el árbol se ha instalado, pode cúalquier rama rota, también pode cúalquiera rama que esté colgando bajo o fuera de lugar. **Solamente** pode unas pocas ramas del árbol; no sobre pode.
- Corte un anillo del árbol alrededor del árbol sí se ha plantado en un área de césped.
- Construya un anillo de tierra unas pocas pulgadas de alto alrededor de la parte exterior de la bola de raíz. Esto ayudará a

traer agua a la bola de raíz y previene que el agua se corra de la superficie.

- Aplique dos o tres capas de pulgada de pajote (mulch) alrededor de la bola de raíz. **Mantenga el pajote (mulch) lejos del tronco del árbol.**

- Sí el árbol es muy pesado o está localizado en un área expuesta a mucho viento o área comercial, se debe estacar. Cuándo usted estaca un árbol, cerciórese que las ataduras sean dejadas flojas para que el árbol pueda crecer. Después de un año quite las estacas y las ataduras.

Para estacar un árbol:

Use 2x2 postes de madera o de cercas de 4 a 6 pies de altura dependiendo del tamaño del árbol. Use dos o tres estacas para sostener cada árbol, espacielos uniformemente alrededor del árbol. Martille la estaca en el suelo al lado de bola de raíz. Martille las estacas en la tierra existente dura y no en el área que ha sido desenterrada durante la plantaba. Martille la estaca abajo aproximadamente 1-1/2 pies de profundo. Ate el árbol a las estacas. Usar las ataduras plásticas nuevas hechas para estacar árboles trabaja mejor. O sostiene el árbol de la manera vieja usando un alambre a tráves de un pedazo de manguera de jardín para proteger la corteza del árbol. Siempre deje las ataduras flojas alrededor del tronco de árbol, luego hala cada atadura para apretarla y la envuelve alrededor de cada estaca para sostener el árbol.

- Riegue completamente el árbol y cerciórese que el dueño del árbol nuevo comprenda claramente las responsabilidades de regar. Dé a su cliente una hoja de información que le explica para cómo cuidar de sus plantas nuevas. Vea el ejemplo en la página siguiente.

Instrucciones Importantes para las Plantas instaladas del Paisaje
Las plantas instaladas están libres de enfermedades e insectos, están sanas y viable en tiempo de la instalación.

Será únicamente la responsabilidad del comprador de proporcionar el cuidado y la protección adecuados para las plantas después de la instalación. **Por favor siga las instrucciones abajo:**

- Cerciórese que las plantas obtengan el agua adecuada. Rieguelos dos veces a la semana durante el primer mes. Sí las temperaturas están sobre los 80 grados, rieguelos tres vez por semana. (Una lluvia ligera no se considera un regar apropiado. Sí hay una cantidad buena de lluvia, eso se puede considerar como un regar).
- Riegue las plantas en la mañana o en la noche temprana (en la mañana es preferida). Riegue el área de la zona de raíz, no las ramas. Con una manguera del jardín, riegue cada planta por aproximadamente un minuto, entonces repite el proceso. Para plantas o árboles más grande, ponga una manguera del jardín en la bola de raíz. Entonces permita que el agua corra lentamente por aproximadamente 5-10 minutos por planta. Sí usa un sistema de la irrigación, cerciòrese que todas las plantas se cubren y que el área de la zona de raíz obtenga suficiente agua. **El agua debe penetrar**

la superficie y empapar el sistema de raíz de las plantas. Sí usted usa una manguera de absorber, verifique el área después de correr la manguera por una una hora.

- En el otoño reduzca el regar a una vez a la semana hasta la ultima semana de octubre.

- Por los años siguientes, comienze a regar por lo menos una vez a la semana en cuanto las temperaturas alcancen los 80 grados.

- Sí las plantas no son 100% resistentes al venado, los protege en los meses de invierno con malla o rocío.

- Después que las plantas han sido instaladas por un año, es un tiempo bueno de alimentarlas. (No las alimente más temprano.)

- Siempre mantenga una capa de pajote (mulch) alrededor de planta de aproximadamente 2" de grueso.

- Avísenos sí usted ve cúalquier problema tal como hojas descoloridas que se inclinan o sí ve las hojas cayéndose de la planta.

Con el cuidado apropiado sus plantas del paisaje aumentarán en el tamaño, belleza y valor. Por favor llame sí usted necesita más información. Gracias por su negocio y goze su paisaje.

Instalaciòn de Arbustos con la bola de raiz envuelta (Balled y Burlaped)

Los arbustos envueltos de la bola de raiz (balled y burlaped) se instalan básicamente de la misma manera que los árboles envueltos de la bola de raiz. Permite brevemente repasar los procedimientos correctos de instalar un arbusto:

- Maneje los arbustos cuidadosamente; use un carrito de árbol o carretilla para moverlos. Nunca recoga los arbustos por las ramas, sólo recogalos o los mueve agarrandolos de la bola de raíz.
- Traiga los arbustos adonde serán instalados.
- Antes de que usted empieza a cavar **cerciórese** que los arbustos se han espaciado y marcados correctamente.
- Cave un hoyo de forma de platillo dos veces más ancho que la bola de raíz. No cave la profundidad más profundo.
- Mida la profundidad de la bola de raíz y la profundidad del hoyo. Esté 100% seguro que el hoyo es del tamaño correcto.
- La cima de la bola de raíz debe ser plana o levemente más alta que el suelo existente.
- Levemente afloje la tierra en el fondo y los lados del hoyo y entonces ponga detenidamente el arbusto en el hoyo.
- Posicione el arbusto para que el lado mejor esté frente al área más visible. Entonces cerciórese que el arbusto esté sentado recto. Sí necesita, agrega alguna tierra debajo de la bola de raíz hasta que el arbusto esté recto.
- Remueva el lazo y la arpillera del arbusto lo más posible. Use un cuchillo de utilidad para cortarlo. No perturbe la bola de raíz mientras quita el lazo y arpillera.
- Llene el hoyo con tierra. Use aproximadamente 50% de tierra existente y 50% de tierra nueva y **Esté seguro que esté mezclada completamente cuándo llene el hoyo.**
- Después que el hoyo esté medio lleno, cerciòrese que el arbusto esté todavía recto entonces aprieta levemente la tierra abajo

alrededor de la bola de raíz. Llene el resto del hoyo y levemente presione la tierra otra vez. No rompa ninguna rama cuándo presiona la tierra alrededor del arbusto.

- corte las ramas rotas, también pode cúalquier rama que esté colgando fuera de lugar. **Sólo** corte unas pocas ramas del arbusto, no sobre corte.

- Haga un anillo de tierra alrededor de la parte exterior de la bola de raíz.

- Aplique una capa de 2-3 pulgadas de pajote (mulch) alrededor del arbusto y riegue el arbusto.

Instalar Arboles y Arbustos (Crecido en Contenedores Plásticos)

Sí sus árboles o los arbustos que crecen en un contenedor plástico, hay algunos procedimientos diferentes a seguir cuándo los instala.

- Para evitar dañar la planta, recojalos o muevalos sólo por el contenedor.

- Traiga las plantas a la ubicación donde serán plantadas. Cerciórese que las plantas sean espaciadas correctamente y marcados exactamente donde deberán ser instalados.

- Remueva cúalquier raíz que crece fuera de los hoyos en el fondo del contenedor, sí estas raíces no se quita, usted no podrá quitar la planta del contenedor. Siempre verifique el fondo del contenedor primero.

- Riegue la tierra y el sistema de raíz dentro del contenedor. Regándolo será más fácil de deslizar fuera del contenedor y la tierra permanecerá junta mejor que sí la tierra está seca.

- El hoyo debe ser, medido y preparado de la misma manera como nosotros discutimos usar una planta envuelta de la bola de raiz (balled y burlaped).

- Despacio y cuidadosamente remueva la planta del contenedor plástico. Sí la planta es muy pequeña, usted podrá girar la planta al revés entonces su ayudante puede quitar el contenedor plástico. Sí la planta es demasiado grande, colocarlo en su lado y hala detenidamente el contenedor.

- Sí la planta es difícultosa para removerla del contenedor plástico, haga dos o tres cortes al contenedor con un cuchillo afilado.

Algúnas plantas crecidas en contenedores se romperán muy fácilmente. Para ayudar a prevenir que la tierra se rompa, moje la tierra, entonces la maneja muy cuidadosamente y tan pocamente frequente posible. Las plantas del contenedor pueden tener raíces que crecen y circulan alrededor de la superficie exterior de la bola de raíz. Use un cuchillo, corte toda la masa de raíces por todas partes de la planta. Haciendo esto, las raíces serán re-dirigidas para que puedan crecer al exterior en vez de crecer en circular alrededor como que sí estuvieran aún en el contenedor.

- Posicione la planta correctamente en el hoyo y entonces llena con tierra. corte, cubre con pajote (mulch) y riega como discutimos más temprano.

Instalar Arboles y Arbustos (Raíz Descubierta)

Las plantas descubiertas de la raíz no se usan frecuentemente; sin embargo, son económico y aún son usadas a veces. Las plantas descubiertas de la raíz son exactamente eso, descubiertas de la raiz sin tierra alrededor de ellas. Algunos consejos al instalar las plantas con raíz descubierta son:

- Mantenga el sistema de raíz húmedo o mojado todo el tiempo. Sí el sistema de raíz se seca, la planta no puede sobrevivir. Plántelos inmediatamente después de comprarlos.

- Después que el hoyo ha sido cavado, medido y preparado, ponga la misma tierra en el hoyo. Entonces cuidadosamente ponga el sistema de raíz de plantas encima de la tierra. Ajuste la planta a la posición y altura correcta.

- Posicione la planta al mismo nivel como creció en el semillero local.

- Mueva la tierra en medio del sistema de raíz a mano. Tenga cuidado para no dañar las raíces, y evite tener aire embolsado. Las raíces deben tener buen contacto con la tierra.

- Cuidadosamente llene el hoyo y entonces aprieta levemente la tierra alrededor de la planta.

- Sí hay alguna rama dañada, las corta todas. Cubra con pajote (mulch) y rieguelas completamente.

INSTALANDO (GROUNDCOVERS, PERENNES, PERENNIALS) FLORES Y BULBOS (BULBS) (CAPÍTULO 12)

Instalando (Groundcovers)

Un (groundcover) es una planta que crecerá a nivel bajo, en una masa densa que cubre el suelo. Después que un (groundcover) se ha establecido, requerirá un mantenimiento minimo y se mirará hermoso. Para un trabajo profesional, instale las plantas de (groundcover) usando los procedimientos siguientes.

- Para mejores resultados y para un establecimiento rápido del (groundcover),es mejor preparar el área de cama antes de que usted instale las plantas. Para preparar un área de cama de paisaje para plantar, invierte la tierra con una pala o un (roto-tiller). Quite cúalquier hierba, piedras y escombros de basura no deseados. Sí la calidad de la tierra existente es pobre, la mejora con una capa de tierra nueva y o turba de musgo.

- Sí usted no prepara la cama del paisaje como nosotros acabamos de discutir, usted tendrá que cavar un hoyo separado para cada planta. Este método trabajará pero las plantas de (groundcover) tomarán mucho más largo tiempo para establecerse ya que la tierra puede estar dura y compacta en medio de cada planta.

- Las plantas (groundcover) generalmente vienen en una bandeja, la bandeja se llama plano (flat). Cada plano tendrá tierra en ello y tendrá de 50 a 100 plantas pequeñas. Cuándo usted quita cada planta del plano, vendrá sin ninguna tierra alrededor de ello entonces será una planta de raíz descubierta. Los (groundcovers) más grandes vendrán en contenedores pequeños. Con contenedores de plantas crecidas, habrá tierra alrededor de las raíces y deben ser instalados de la misma manera como un arbusto crecido en un contenedor.

- Espaciar la planta es muy importante. La mayoría de las plantas se instalan aproximadamente 8 a 10 pulgadas aparte. Se pueden instalar más cerca para un establecimiento más rápido o espaciarlo cortara además en el costo del trabajo. Evite el espaciamiento de las plantas por más de 12 pulgadas. Las plantas (groundcovers) crecidas en contenederos son más grandes y pueden ser espaciadas más aparte. Verifique la etiqueta y la recomendación de espacio antes de instalarlos. *Para instalar las plantas de (groundcover) rápidamente, espacie y cave todos los hoyos primero y después instale las plantas.*

- Sí la cama del paisaje se ha invertido y preparado para las plantas, será fácil de instalar. Use una pala manual o una piocha pequeña para hacer un hoyo pequeño. Cerciórese que los hoyos sean espaciados apropiadamente. Entonces instale una planta en cada hoyo y presione levemente la tierra alrededor de cada planta con sus manos.

- Sí la cama del paisaje no se preparó, los hoyos serán más duro de cavar. Sí la tierra esta muy pobre, mezcle un poco de capa de tierra nueva o de musgo pantanoso (peat moss) pequeño cuándo planta. Esparce la capa de tierra nueva o de musgo pantanoso (peat moss) sobre el área de cama primero. Entonces cuándo usted instala las plantas, mezcle junto algo de la capa de tierra nueva y tierra existente.

- Las plantas crecidas (groundcovers) deben ser manejadas y instaladas de la misma manera que los arbustos crecidos en contenedor. Por favor refiérase al capítulo anterior donde esto se discutió.

- Una vez que las plantas son instaladas, aplique una capa de pajote (mulch) para ayudar a mantener las plantas de secarse y prevenir el crecimiento de hierba. Aplique una capa de pajote (mulch) cada año hasta que el (groundcover) se establezca completamente.

- Riegue las plantas nuevas el día que fueron instalados y después en una base regular.

- Un **liviano** abono equilibrado se puede mezclar en el área de cama cuándo está plantando, entonces no aplique abono hasta un año después.

Instalando Perennes (Perennials)

(Perennials) son las plantas que vuelven año tras año. Perecen hacia el suelo después de cada temporada creciente. Entonces se quedan inactivas en el suelo hasta el año siguiente. (Perennials) vienen en dos maneras diferentes; raíces descubiertas o en un contenedor pequeño. Los (perennials) crecidos en contenedor son muy común. Sí usted está instalando varios tipos diferentes de (perennials) en una cama de paisaje, será mejor preparar la tierra en la cama antes de que usted instale las plantas. Sí usted sólo instala unas pocas (perennials) a través de diferentes áreas del paisaje, sería mejor cavar un hoyo separado para cada planta.

Instalando Perennes (Perennials) Crecidos (en Contenedor)

Los (perennials) crecidos en contenedores deben ser manejados y instalados de la misma manera que los arbustos crecidos en un contenedor. Permite repasar los procedimientos de plantar:

- Maneje la planta por el contenedor no por las hojas ni ramas.
- Traiga las plantas a la ubicación donde serán instaladas. Cerciórese que las plantas se han espaciado y marcado correctamente exactamente donde serán instalados.
- Remueva cúalquier raíz que crece fuera del fondo del contenedor.
- Riegue la tierra y el sistema de raíces dentro del contenedor.
- Cave y prepara los hoyos para las plantas. Cave dos veces más ancho pero no más profundo que la bola de raíz de las plantas. Afloje levemente la tierra en el fondo y lados del hoyo. Verifique para cerciòrarse que la profundidad está correcto. La cima de la bola de raíz de las plantas debe ser plana o levemente más alta con el suelo cuándo sea instaladó.
- Voltee la planta al revés, aguante su mano sobre la cima de la raíz de la bola de raíz y agarra la planta [araqie deslize hacia fuera.
- Usando un cuchillo, hace unos pocos cortes alrededor de la bola de raíz. Esto alentará las raíces a crecer hacia afuera en vez de circular alrededor de la bola de raíz.
- Posicione la planta en el hoyo y entonces llene con tierra. Presione levemente en la tierra alrededor de la planta.

439

- Aplique una capa de pajote (mulch) alrededor de la planta y la riega.

Instalando Perennes (Raiz Descubierta)

- Mantenga el sistema de raíz húmedo todo el tiempo. Almacene las plantas en un área fresca y oscura. Evite almacenarlos no más largo tiempo que un día o dos. Instálelos lo más pronto posible.
- Diseñe y prepara los hoyos para las plantas.
- Ponga alguna tierra dentro del hoyo. Entonces ponga cuidadosamente el sistema de raíz de plantas encima de la tierra. Ajuste la altura de la planta para que no esté demasiado profundo ni demasiado alto.
- Ponga más tierra alrededor del sistema de raíz con sus manos. Presione levemente en la tierra y raíces. Evite tener cúalquier embolsamiento de aire. Las raíces deben tener buen contacto con la tierra.
- Aplique una capa de pajote (mulch) y agua.

Instalando Flores (anual)

Las flores anuales dan el color al paisaje; generalmente florecen por un período largo de tiempo. Sin embargo, no pueden sobrevivir ninguna temperatura fría. Por lo tanto, son plantados en la primavera después de la ultima helada y vivirán hasta la primer helada del otoño. Unos pocos tipos de flores anuales pueden sobrevivir una helada, pero la mayoría no pueden. Como hemos discutido más temprano, escoge las flores anuales que no son demasiado pequeñas pero también no demasiado grandes de tamaño. La mayoría de las flores anuales vienen en plano (flat). Un plano (flat) es una bandeja que aguanta plantas pequeñas tal como las flores anuales o plantas (groundcovers). Cuándo compra un plano de flores anuales, generalmente hay otra bandeja pequeña dentro del plano. Esta bandeja más pequeña tiene compartimientos individuales. Cada célula tendrá una flor. Los planos varían en el tamaño; un plano mediano tendrá acerca de 48 flores.

Trate de instalar flores inmediatamente después que usted los compra. Sí usted las tiene que almacenarlas por unos pocos días, manténgalos regandolos en una base diaria. Sólo riéguelos temprano en la a.m. o en la tarde p.m. Regar durante las horas calientes y soleadas del día puede causar daño a las flores tiernas. Procure mantener las flores en un área con sombra hasta que sean plantadas.

Para instalar las flores anuales:
- Marque y escoja las áreas donde ustedes plantarán. Verifique la etiqueta para seguir los requisitos. La mayoría de las flores anuales se espacian acerca de 12 pulgadas aparte.
- Prepare la tierra en el área de plantar. Invierta la tierra para que la tierra se afloje y las raíces podrán crecer fácilmente. Sí la tierra es muy pobre, vuelque alguna tierra nueva de buena calidad y/o turba de musgo.
- Para mejores resultados, gire algún alimento de planta (abono) en la tierra. **Cerciórese** que el alimento de la planta que usted usa

este marcado para flores anuales y **no haga** de sobre aplicar el abono o usted causará más daño que bien.

- Usando una pala manual, hace un hoyo dondequiera que usted va a instalar una flor. Espacie los hoyos como es recomendado en la etiqueta. No espacie más aparte de lo recomendadó.

- Riegue las célula, entonces gire la célula al revés y la flor debe salir. Sí la flor no sale, empuja el fondo de la célula para ayudarlo a salir. Tenga cuidado de no dejar caer las flores cuándo salgan. Trabaje cerca del suelo cuándo quita las flores. **Nunca** hale la flor para tratar de quitarla de la célula.

- Una vez que la flor esté fuera, mira el sistema de raíz, sí hay un sistema masivo de raíz, usted necesitará romper suavemente las raíces para ayudar a las raíces a crecer en la tierra cuándo sean plantados. Use sus manos y rompa suavemente el fondo del sistema de raíces o use un par de tijeras manuales para cortar en la masa de raíces.

- Ponga la flor en el hoyo; tenga cuidado para no plantarlo demasiado alto ni demasiado profundo. Entonces empuje la tierra alrededor de la bola de raíz de las flores y presiona levemente en la tierra.

- Aplique una capa de pajote (mulch) y riega el área entera.

Instalando Bulbos (Bulbs)

La mayoría de los bulbos son vendidos y plantados durante el otoño. Entonces florecerán la siguiente primavera y regresaran año tras año. Para instalar bulbos, siga estos procedimientos.

- Escoja sólo los mejores bulbos; evite bulbos que tienen lugares suaves en ellos. Mantenga los bulbos en un área fresca seca hasta que sean plantados.
- Planee y marca las áreas donde usted los plantará.
- Cerciòrese que usted sepa cuán profundo el bulbo se debe plantar. Algunos bulbos necesitan 8 pulgadas de profundidad, mientras que otros deben ser sólo 3 pulgadas de profundidad. Lea la etiqueta y entienda exactamente cuán profundo el bulbo necesita estar. Verifique también la etiqueta para ver cuán lejos aparte los bulbos deberán ser distanciados.
- Prepare el área de plantar. Sí usted planta muchos bulbos muy juntos en un área pequeña, usted debe invertir la tierra en esa área.
- Sí usted planta los bulbos en áreas diferentes a través del paisaje, será mejor cavar un hoyo individual para cada bulbo. Quite cúalquier piedra y mejora la tierra sí se necesita.
- Después que los hoyos estén todos preparados, usted está listo para plantar. Inspeccione los bulbos para cerciòrarse claramente que comprende qué es la cima y qué es el fondo del bulbo. En el lado del fondo, usted puede ver generalmente el sistema de raíz.
- No ponga abono ni comida de hueso en el hoyo con el bulbo.

No utilize comida de huezo cuándo instale los bulbos. La comida de huezo atrae animales y algunos animales comerán los bulbos sí los encuentran en el suelo. Los bulbos pueden ser abonados levemente en la primavera temprana antes o después que han florecido. Esto ayudará a que puedan crecer más grande y florecer más el siguiente año.

- Después que usted ha determinado el lado del fondo de los bulbos, coloque uno en cada hoyo individual, empuje hacia abajo levemente en el bulbo para que haga contacto bueno con la tierra en el fondo del hoyo. Entonces llena el hoyo con tierra, cubre con pajote (mulch) el área para un trabajo profesional.

- Ya que los bulbos son inactivos cuándo son instalado. No necesitarán ser regados.

Recuerde que como un paisajista profesional, usted está en control de cómo y cuán saludable la planta crecerá. Instalando todo el material de planta cuidadosamente y correctamente, usted ayudará hacer un hermoso, duradero paisaje. Usted necesita dar a usted mismo y a su compañía una buena reputaciòn y ganar el respeto de otras personas que noten su buen trabajo.

INSTALANDO CAMAS DE PAISAJE Y PRUEBA DE TIERRA
(CAPíTULO 13)

Muchas camas del paisaje se bordean simplemente por fuera en una tierra existente y pobre de calidad. Después que las plantas se instalan en la cama pero no pueden crecer saludables ni fuerte. Las tierras duras o las tierras cubiertas de arena pueden ser mejoradas mezclando y volviendo la capa de tierra del suelo a buena calidad con la materia orgánica. Al instalar profesionalmente una cama nueva del paisaje o al mejorar una cama existente usted creará un ambiente para que toda la materia de planta pueda crecer saludable y fuerte.

Usted necesitará las siguientes herramientas y equipo al instalar o al mejorar una cama del paisaje. Una máquina de bordear, unas cuantas carretillas, palas, piochas, rastrillo de arco de metal, una pala plana, una pistola de pintura, cinta métrica, un soplador de muchila, y un (roto-tiller) (opcional).

Usted debe llevar puesto las botas y guantes y considerar llevar puesto almohadillas en las rodillas y un cinturón de apoyo de espalda mientras esté trabajando.

Instalando Camas del Paisaje

El primer paso necesario sería de escoger la forma de la cama nueva. Generalmente cuándo las camas se hacen alrededor de una casa variarán en el tamaño de 5 pies a 25 pies. El jefe o el capataz necesitarán diseñar las camas del paisaje basada en esa propiedad y basado en lo qué será plantado en las camas. Una vez que la forma se determina, una pistola de pintura se usa para marcar la forma de la cama nueva en el suelo. Sí usted trabaja de un cianotipo (blue print) use una medida de cinta y haga marcas de medida. Después que las marcas de medidas se hacen, conecte las marcas con la pistola de pintura para darle la forma de la cama nueva. La forma debe tener las líneas y las curvas libres y con corrientes que fluen y no debe tener ninguna irregularidad.

Después que las líneas se establecen en el suelo, cerciórese que no hay nada que puede ser dañado en el área de cama tal como alambres eléctricos, cabezas de regadera, etc. Marque cúalquier cosa que usted encuentre para que usted no cave en esa área.

Ahora arranque la máquina de bordear y corte a lo largo de la línea marcada como se discutió en el capítulo previo. Entonces quite todo del interior de la cama tal como césped, hierbas, etc, y entonces se deshace de los escombros de basura.

Después que las camas nuevas se han bordeado y han sido limpiadas, usted necesitará agregar tierra y alimentos nutritivos a las camas. Las camas del paisaje deben ser levantadas por lo menos 5 pulgadas de alto. Agregue una capa de tierra de buena calidad para levantar las camas. Como un profesional de paisaje, usted debe agregar también musgo pantanoso (peat musgo), estiércol o algún tipo de materia orgánica tal como (compost). Usted puede agregar también un equilibrado abono granulado en este tiempo. Esto aumentará los alimentos nutritivos disponibles en la tierra. *Nota:* Una prueba de tierra se recomienda antes de mejorar cúalquier área de la camas de paisaje. Entonces las enmiendas correctas de tierra se pueden agregar. Una prueba de tierra se discutirá luego en este capítulo.

Después que las camas son levantadas con la correcta capa de tierra, usted necesitará volver esta mezcla hacia abajo en la tierra existente. Esto se puede hacer manualmente usando una piocha y una pala o utilizando una máquina (roto-tiller). Cúalquier que usted use, es importante cavar hacia abajo por lo menos un pie profundo en la tierra existente y completamente mezclarlo con las enmiendas nuevas de capa de tierra.

Muchos paisajistas agregan simplemente unas pocas pulgadas de tierra encima de la tierra existente. Esto no es profesional y es un trabajo de pobre calidad. Las plantas del paisaje no podrán crecer más grande en estas condiciones pobres de tierra.

El próximo paso después de mejorar e invertir la cama del paisaje es de formar y graduar la cama. Sí la cama que usted instala está alrededor de una casa o edificio, cercióre se que las camas se inclinan lejos de la casa. Entonces durante una lluvia la mayor parte del agua correra lejos de la casa. Mantenga la línea de tierra más o menos de cuatro a cinco pulgadas lejos de cúalquier entablado (siding) de la casa. Deje dos a tres pulgadas para el pajote (mulch). Entonces debe haber aún todavía un espacio en medio de la cama de paisaje y el entablado (siding).

La tierra y el pajote (mulch) sólo deben hacer contacto con la parte concreta de la casa y **nunca** tocar el entablado (siding). Use un rastrillo del arco de metal para formar y graduar la cama. Sepáre los pedazos grandes de tierra cuándo gradua la cama. Aunque usted trabaje en una cama del paisaje que está lejos de la casa aún debe inclinarse levemente hacia abajo.

Ahora que la cama recien instalada de paisaje esta completa. Está listo para que las plantas sean instaladas y para que sea cubierta con pajote (mulch) tan pronto como sea posible. El pajote (mulch) ayudará aguantar la tierra en su lugar y a prevenir que se lave lejos en una lluvia pesada. Ayudará también a prevenir el crecimiento de hierba y a proteger las plantas del paisaje.

Prueba de Tierra

Una prueba de tierra se debe hacer cuándo:

- Las plantas establecidas son débiles y no saludables aún después que usted ha aplicado un abono equilibrado.
- Para mejorar la condición de tierra antes de instalar la materia nueva de planta, semilla o sardo (sod).

La Prueba de tierra

Para tomar una prueba de tierra, quita primero la capa de encima de pajote (mulch) u hojas de la cama del paisaje. Entonces usando una pala manual o herramienta especial para quitar muestras de tierra, cava hacia abajo por lo menos seis pulgadas de profundo y pone la tierra dentro de una bolsa. Repita este proceso por lo menos seis vez y tome las muestras a través de diferentes áreas de la cama del paisaje. Entonces mezcle completamente los pedazos de tierra juntos en la bolsa y los trae a un laboratorio de prueba de tierra.

Una prueba de tierra puede ser hecha por su Servicio Cooperativo Local (generalmente esta forma parte de un colegio agrícola) o por un laboratorio privado de prueba-de-tierra. Los resultados incluirán: Nitrógeno, Fósforo, Potasio, pH de Tierra, contenido Orgánico, y Micronutritivos.

- El nitrógeno, Fósforo y el Potasio son los tres alimentos nutritivos mayores que toda planta la necesita. Sí uno de estos elementos está bajo, habrá un problema. Los resultados de la prueba de tierra indicarán cúalquier problema.

- PH de tierra. Aunque todos los otros alimentos nutritivos estén disponibles en la tierra, no pueden ser capaces de ser absorbido por la planta sí el nivel de pH de tierra está inexacto. PH de tierra nivela la distancia de 1 a 14 y un nivel entre 6.0 y 7.5 trabajo mejor. El nivel entre 6.0 y 7.5 es llamado Neutral. **Algo debajo de 6.0 es llamado tierra Acidica (Acidic soil); algo encima de 7.5 es llamado Alcalino (Alkaline).** Teniendo el nivel correcto de pH, la planta será capaz de absorber todos los alimentos nutritivos en la tierra y llegar a ser más saludable y más fuerte. Para ajustar el nivel de pH de tierra a neutral:

- Cuándo la tierra es Acidica (Acidic), aplica la piedra caliza para **aumentar** el pH.

- Cuándo la tierra es Alcalina (Alkaline), aplica azufre para **disminuir** el pH.

Contenido orgánico—La prueba de tierra deberia dejar también que usted sepa cuánta materia orgánica hay en la tierra. Entonces usted puede agregar orgánicos tal como, musgo pantanoso (peat moss), estiércol (manure) o (compost) para mejorar la tierra.

Alimentos Micro Nutritivos—Los Micronutritivos son alimentos nutritivos secundarios que la planta necesita. Los que incluyen Calcio, Magnesio, Hierro y otros alimentos nutritivos. Micronutritivos son muy importantes y usted debe agregar micronutritivos a la tierra sí se necesita.

INSTALANDO TELA DE PAISAJE
(CAPÍTULO 14)

La tela de paisaje se usa para detener el crecimiento de las hierbas en las camas del paisaje. Se puede usar para detener un problema existente de hierba o para prevenir el crecimiento de las hierbas en el futuro. Al instalar la tela de paisaje reducirá la cantidad de mantenimiento de conservación necesaria para mantener las camas de paisaje libre de hierba. La tela se puede usar también debajo de piedra decorativa. Cuándo se instala debajo de piedra decorativa, ayudará a prevenir que las piedras se hundan dentro del suelo y ayudará a prevenir el crecimiento de hierba. La tela de paisaje se hace para que el agua y aire pueda penetrar la tela pero que las hierbas no puedan. Es muy importante que el sistema de raíz de las plantas existentes en la cama del paisaje puedan obtener fácilmente agua y aire. Sí las plantas tienen problema para obtener agua o aire, llegarán a tener tensiòn, ahogadas, no saludables, y pueden morir. Siempre use una tela de buena calidad que esta hecha específicamente para camas de paisaje. Nunca use cúalquier otro tipo de producto.

Usted necesitará una cinta métrica y un cuchillo agudo cuándo instala tela de paisaje.

Instalando Tela de Paisaje (Procedimientos del Trabajo)

- Antes de instalar cúalquier tela de paisaje, cerciórese que la cama esté gradúada correctamente. Cerciórese que la cama se inclina de la casa. Rastrille cúalquiera lugar alto o bajo en la cama y agrega tierra adicional sí se necesita.

- Sí los perennes (perennials) son plantados en la cama del paisaje, cerciórese que todos esten marcados claramente para que usted no sobre instale tela sobre ellos. También sí hay áreas grandes usadas para plantar flores anuales, marca estas áreas y las deja abiertas. Pero sí el áreas de flores anual son pequeñas, será fácil de cortar las formas después que la tela se instale.

- Después que las camas se han graduado y han sido marcadas, usted necesita tomar una medida áspera de las camas para determinar cuánta tela usted necesitará. Entonces escoja la mejor manera de instalar la tela. La tela viene en rollos de 50 a 100 pies de largo. La anchura de la tela puede estar dondequiera de 3 a 10 pies de anchos. Escoja un tamaño que se acomoda mejor para su trabajo cuándo instala la tela. Usted quiere mantener los pedazos lo más grande que sea posible.

- La tela se instalará más fácil y rapidamente cuándo dos personas trabajan juntos. Una persona debe sostener un extremo de la tela en su lugar mientras que la segunda persona desenrolla la tela a través de la cama del paisaje. Entonces usando un cuchillo agudo corta la tela a la longitud correcta.

- Cuándo coloca cada pedazo de tela, cerciórese que lo traslapa con el pedazo que está en el suelo. Después que unos cuantos pedazos se han puesto hacia abajo, usted necesitará asegurarlos para evitar

452

que se muevan. Usted puede usar piedras o ladrillos grandes. Ponga las piedras en la tela para aguantarlos hacia abajo. Camine cuidadosamente para que usted no mueve la tela. Después que usted pone pajote (mulch) o piedra decorativa encima de la tela, usted puede quitar las piedras. Las grapas de paisaje se pueden usar también. En una superficie plana, las grapas no se necesitan, pero sí usted está instalando tela en una cuesta o donde hay una corriente pesada de agua, instala las grapas y los deja enel lugar. Las grapas necesitan ser martilladas dentro del suelo con un martillo.

- Corte alrededor de todas las plantas que están en la cama del paisaje. Usted puede instalar la tela debajo de las ramas de las plantas hasta el tronco. Cuándo esté haciendo algún corte difícil, utilize su cinta métrica para marcar la tela correctamente y evitar cometer errores.

- Despues que la tela se instala, aplica pajote (mulch) o piedra decorativa en la cima. **Sea muy cuidadoso para no mover la tela cuándo usted descarga y esparce el pajote (mulch) o piedra. Usted tendrá que trabajar detenidamente y cuidadosamente para evitar un problema.** Ahora usted puede quitar cúalquiera de las piedras o ladrillos que usted puso sobre la tela para ayudar aguantarla en su lugar.

Nota: Discutiremos de cómo cubrir con pajote (mulch) y piedra decorativa en el próximo capítulo en este manual.

La tela de paisaje trabaja muy bien, especialmente cuándo se usa con piedra decorativa. El problema con pajote (mulch) es que comenzará a descomponerse y entonces creará una capa pequeña de tierra sobre la tela. Después de unos pocos años, las hierbas comenzarán a crecer en esa capa pequeña de tierra.

INSTALANDO PIEDRA DECORATIVA
(CAPÍTULO 15)

La piedra decorativa se usa en las camas de paisaje en vez de pajote (mulch). La piedra decorativa se puede usar en áreas pequeñas de una cama junto con pajote (mulch) o se puede usar por sí mismo. Piense cuidadoso en el color y tamaño de piedra que se usará y donde en el paisaje lo instalará. Cuándo la piedra decorativa se escoge, diseñada y instalada correctamente, agregará variedad y belleza al paisaje.

Las herramientas que usted necesitará para instalar piedra decorativa incluirá lo siguiente:

- Carretillas.
- Palas.
- Rastrillo de arco de metal.
- Soplador de muchila.
- Un camión de descarga (una puertita en la compuerta es opcional (chute of the tailgate).

Usted necesitará también las herramientas necesarias para instalar la tela de paisaje. La tela de paisaje siempre se debe instalar antes de cubrir la cama con piedra decorativa. La tela ayudará a prevenir que las piedras se asienten en el suelo y ayudará a prevenir que las hierbas crescan.

Calculando el Suministro de Trabajo

Antes de comprar la piedra, las camas del paisaje se deben medir para que usted pueda determinar la cantidad exacta de piedra que usted necesitará. La medición y determinación de la cantidad de suministros necesitados es hecha generalmente por el jefe o el capataz; sin embargo, es bueno que todos sepan. Este método se puede usar también para determinar cuánto pajote (mulch) o tierra se necesita para cubrir un área.

Siga estos pasos para determinar cuánta materia se necesita para un área:

Ejemplo 1

- Mida la longitud y la anchura de la cama del paisaje. Esta medida le dará los pies cuadrados de la cama. Por ejemplo: (40 pies × 8 pies = 320 pies cuadrados.)
- Determine cuán profundo usted quiere que la piedra, pajote (mulch) o tierra estén. En este ejemplo nosotros permaneceremos dos pulgadas de profundo.
- Piedra, pajote (mulch) y tierra son vendidos por la yarda cúbica. Una yarda cúbica es una medida de 3 pies por 3 pies por 3 pies. Esta medida está en la forma de un cuadrado o cubo. Multiplique esto junto y usted obtendrá (3 × 3 × 3 = 27 pies cuadrados) para 1 yarda cúbica.
- Ahora usted debe cambiar **la altura** del cubo de pies a pulgadas. 3 pies = 36 pulgadas.

- Usted quiere que la piedra esté 2 pulgadas de profundo entonces divida las 36 pulgadas (la altura de la yarda cúbica) por 2 (o 2 pulgadas). Por lo tanto 36 ÷ 2 = 18. (Usted obtendrá 18 capas, 2 pulgadas de grueso.)

- Ahora multiplique **la anchura** y **profundidad** del cubo ($3 \times 3 = 9$ pies cuadrados).

- Multiplique 18 por 9 pies cuadrados = 162 pies cuadrado por yarda. En una profundidad de 2 pulgadas usted cubrirá 162 pies cuadrado **por yarda**.

- La cama del paisaje que usted quiere cubrir es de 320 pies cuadrados. En una profundidad de 2 pulgadas usted cubrirá 162 pies cuadrado por yarda.

- Ahora divida 320 ÷ 162 = 1.975 yardas.

- Un total de 1.975 será necesitado para cubrir el área de 320 pies cuadrados con 2 pulgadas de piedra.

Vamos a repasar otro ejemplo. Sin embargo, esta vez no explicaremos todo en detalle.

Ejemplo 2:

- El área de la cama es de 50 pies $\times$ 4 pies = 200 pies cuadrados.

- Usted necesita la materia 3 pulgadas de profundo.

- Divide la altura de una yarda cúbica por 3 (o 3 pulgadas). 36 pulgadas ÷ 3 pulgadas = 12.

- La anchura $\times$ la profundidad de una yarda cúbica es ($3 \times 3 = 9$ pies cuadrados).

- Multiplique $12 \times 9 = (108$ pies cuadrados por yarda en 3 pulgadas de profundo)
- Ahora divida $200 \div 108 = 1.851$ yardas.
- Usted necesitará 1.851 yardas para cubrir el área 3 pulgadas de profundo.

La piedra, pajote (mulch) y la tierra son vendidos por la yarda por eso redondea todos los números calculados.

El ejemplo # 1: 1.975 yardas (compra 2 yardas).
El ejemplo # 2: 1.851 yardas (compra 2 yardas).

Instalando Piedra Decorativa (Procedimientos del Trabajo)
Después que usted ha determinado cuánta piedra se necesita para su trabajo, usted estará listo para recoger la piedra. Obviamente un camión de descarga será mejor para recoger y entregar la piedra. Sin embargo, sí usted sólo necesita una cantidad pequeña, un camión de palangana (pickup truck) se puede usar también. Cúalquier vehículo que usted use siga las siguientes instrucciones para evitar problemas.

- Verifique la presión de las llanta del camión antes de cargar el camión. Nunca lo cargue sí las llantas están bajas de aire.
- Cerciórese que el camión esté limpio de cúalquier escombros de basura para que la piedra permanezca limpia.

- No sobrecargue el camión, las piedras son muy pesadas. Usted tendrá que hacer unos cuantos viajes sí usted necesita mucha piedra.

- Mantenga las piedras lejos de la puerta posterior (tailgate) y limpia todas las piedra de la puerta posterior (tailgate) del camión. Sí las piedras se caen de su camión mientras usted conduce, las piedras pueden causar daño a otro carro.

- No golpee ninguna curva ni otros objetos con las llantas.

- Condusca lentamente y cuidadosamente y siempre piense en la seguridad primero.

Una vez que usted llega al sitio del trabajo, estacione el camión lo más cerca posible del área donde usted esté trabajando. Estacionese en tierra plana y use el freno de estacionamiento. Sí usted usa un camión de descarga, cerciórese que no hay alambres ni ramas encima del camión. Usted necesitará levantar el cuerpo de descarga para que seá más fácil de remover las piedras del camión. Evite dejar caer las piedras afuera, algunas piedras pueden dañar un camino de entrada y será mucho más duro de recoger las piedras del suelo.

Organice el trabajo, camine a trávez de la propiedad y discuta lo qué se debe hacer. Todos deben saber exactamente lo qué se hará **antes** de que usted empieze a trabajar. Sí usted está inseguro acerca de lo qué será hecho, haga preguntas.

Antes de instalar la piedra decorativa en las camas del paisaje, usted necesitará instalar la tela del paisaje. La tela del paisaje se debe usar debajo de toda las piedras decorativas, aunque las áreas sean muy pequeñas. (La instalación de Tela de paisaje se explicó en el capítulo previo).

Después que la tela del paisaje se instala, usted estará listo para cubrir la cama con la piedra. Sí usted usa un camión de descarga, levanta el cuerpo hasta la mitad, entonces las piedras serán más fáciles de mover con pala hacia afuera. Algunos camiones de descarga tienen una puertecita (chute) en la puerta posterior (tailgate), ponga una carretilla debajo del (chute) y usted podrá llenarlo rápidamente y fácilmente. Tenga cuidado de no sobrellenar las carretillas porque si no serán muy difíciles de empujar. Cerciórese que también las llantas de la carretilla tengan abundancia de aire.

Generalmente un trabajador llenará las carretillas mientras que el segundo trabajador las empuja y descarga las piedras afuera en la cama. Usted necesitará por lo menos dos carretillas para que una se llene mientras la otra es empujada hacia la cama. Cuándo descarga las piedras en la cama encima de la tela, descarga las piedras **lentamente** para que usted no mueva la tela.

Haga los montones pequeños a través de la cama. Tenga cuidado para no descargar las piedras muy juntas. Después que la cama está llena hasta la mitad con montones de piedra, un trabajador debe comenzar a esparcirlos. Use un rastrillo del arco de metal para esparcir los montones. **Tenga cuidado cuándo esparce las piedras sobre las terminaciones de la tela. Sí usted no es cuidadoso, usted moverá la**

tela y empujará las piedras debajo de la tela. Una vez que usted tiene una capa de piedra sobre la tela, será más fácil de esparcir las piedras restantes.

Las piedras decorativas se esparcen generalmente acerca de 2-1/2 pulgadas de profundidad. Esta profundidad trabaja bien para piedras pequeñas. Cuándo instala piedras grandes, usted tendrá que ir más profundo. Como una orden general, usted no debe poder ver ninguna tela a tráves de la piedra. Las piedras grandes serán más difíciles de instalar. Son más duros de recoger con una pala y más duro de esparcir con un rastrillo de arco de metal. A veces puede ser más fácil de esparcirlos a mano.

Sí usted usó piedras o ladrillos para sujetar la tela del paisaje, mientras esté cubriendolo con la piedra decorativa los quita y llena las áreas como sea necesitado. Inspeccione el trabajo, limpie sus herramientas y usted ha terminado.

INSTALANDO SISTEMAS BÁSICOS DE DESAGÜE
(CAPÍTULO 16)

Los sistemas básicos del desagüe se instalan para llevar agua de un lugar a otro. Los sistemas del desagüe ayudarán a mantener áreas importantes del paisaje secas y utilizable. Discutiremos un sistema de desagüe de canal primero. Los tubos del desagüe se instalan alrededor de la base de una casa para reunir toda el agua de los canales y entonces lo trae afuera a la calle. Al instalar un sistema de desagüe de canal alrededor de una casa, usted mantendrá el área más seca y ayudará a prevenir que la base de la casa sea empapada de agua y que se rezuma en el sótano. El segundo tipo de sistema de desagüe que discutiremos ayudará a secar las áreas mojadas en una propiedad y ayudará a bajar un nivel alto de agua. El tercer tipo de sistema de desagüe que discutiremos secará las áreas mojadas, ayudará a bajar el nivel alto de agua y a reunir agua de la superficie que fluye sobre el suelo.

Usted necesitará las siguientes herramientas y equipo cuándo instale un sistema básico de desagüe.

- Carretillas (wheel barrels).
- Palas (shovels), piochas (picks), rastrillo de metal del arco (metal bow rakes).
- Cinta métrica (tape measurer), serrucho para el plástico de PVC (hand saw for PVC plastic).

- Un nivel regular (standard level) y un nivel de línea (line level), cuerdas y estacas (string and stakes).

- Cuchillo (knife).

- Pistola de pintura (paint gun).

- Marcador Negro (black marker pen).

- Soplador de Muchila (backpack blower).

- Camión de descarga (dump truck).

- La máquina excavadora es opcional (back-hoe machine is optional).

El equipo de seguridad para considerar:

- Guantes (gloves).

- Rodilleras (knee pads) .

- Cinturón de Soporte de espalda (back support belt).

Instalando un Sistema de Desagüe de Canal

antes de comenzar algún trabajo manual, usted necesitará planiar el trabajo. Mire primero todo los canales (downspouts) que se estén bajando de la casa. Escoja la mejor manera de conectar todos estos canales (downspouts). Los tubos que conectan los canales (downspouts) se instalará hacia arriba **contra** la base de la casa. Entonces unos pocos tubos correran fuera de la casa y traerán el agua a la calle, un área arbolada o no usada de la propiedad, o a un pozo seco.

- *Cerciórese que los tubos del desagüe que está instalando no dirigan el agua a la propiedad del vecino.*
- *Sí usted está dirigiendo agua fuera en la calle, usted necesitará un permisode la ciudad (township) de dónde está trabajando.*
- *Llame a la compañía local de utilidad para marcar todos los alambres y tuberia de utilidad enterrados y verifica con el dueño de la casa para discutir la ubicación de otros alambres, líneas de regadera, etc. antes de que usted planee un diseño de sistema de desagüe.*

Planee el frente, atrás y los lados de la casa. La mejor situación sería de tener sólo dos tubos corriendo fuera de la casa; uno en el frente y uno atrás. Sin embargo, esto no será posible en cada casa. Algunos trabajos requerirán que cuatro tubos corran fuera de la casa, uno en el frente, uno atrás, y un tubo en cada lado. Trate de evitar usar dobleces agudas y planee instalar las conexiones cada 50 pies a través del sistema para que puedan ser limpiadas sí es necesitado.

Después que usted ha escogido la mejor manera de instalar el tubo, usted estará listo para comenzar el trabajo:

- Usando una pistola de pintura, marca las áreas donde todos los tubos se instalarán. Mida todas las áreas marcadas, entonces usted sabrá exactamente cúanto tubo comprar. Hay dos tipos diferentes de tubo plástico que usted puede usar. La primer clase se llama (ADS). Es de cuatro pulgadas de ancho, viene en un rollo de 100 pies y es flexible. El problema con este tubo es que se asentará en alguna área desigual en el fondo de la zanja que usted está cavando. Sí el tubo se asienta en un lugar bajo, el agua tendrá problema de fluir a tráves de ello y el lugar bajo puede causar un atasque.

El segundo tipo de tubo se llama PVC. Es un tubo duro de plástico que no es flexible. Viene generalmente en longitudes de 10 pies y es también 4 pulgadas de ancho. Se puede poner en una zanja que no es perfectamente lisa y no se hundirá en ningun lugar bajo. Las dos tuberías pueden ser cortadas a cúalquier longitud y varios tubos de ajuste (fittings) están disponible paraellos. El tubo plástico duro de PVC le dará un mejor trabajo de calidad.

- Cava una zanja contra la base de la casa. Comience en el canal (downspout) que será el **primero** para ser conectado al tubo. Cave la zanja acerca de 6 pulgadas de ancho y acerca de 6 pulgadas de profundo.

Mantenga el fondo de la zanja suave y lo más parejo posible. No quite también mucha tierra del fondo de la zanja. Sí usted quita también mucha tierra, usted tendrá que llenar la zanja otra vez para levantarlo hacia arriba, entonces la tierra llenada puede asentarse lo cúal puede causar que el tubo se mueva. Sí el tubo se mueve, el agua no puede ser capaz de fluir hacia fuera.

- Incline la longitud entera de la zanja para que baje por lo menos 1-1/4 de pulgadas a una longitud de diez pies de tubo o 1 pie para cada 100 pies. Para medir la cuesta, usted necesita usar un nivel. Coloque el nivel encima del tubo para tomar una medida. Después que el primer pedazo de tubo es instalado en la cuesta correcta marca la ubicación de la burbuja en el nivel. Entonces utilice el nivel marcado para instalar correctamente el resto de los tubos.

- Usted tendrá que instalar los codos (elbows) o los agustes (tee-fittings) para conectarlo al canal (downspouts). Hay otra conexión que se instalará encima del codo o agustes (tee-fittings) que se conectarán al canal.

- Cuándo esté conectando los tubos, codos, o los ajustes (tee-fittings) o los adaptadores de canal juntos, limpie el tubo utilizando una solución de limpiar de plástico PVC. Entonces aplique el pegamento plástico PVC a ambos lados del tubo y apriete las dos piezas juntos. Evite respirar los vapores del limpiador o el pegamento y evite hacer contacto con ellos.

- Algunos pedazos de tubo tendrán que ser cortados a una cierta longitud. Antes de cortar el tubo, hace una medida exacta y marca el lugar exacto que el tubo necesitará ser cortado. Utilize una marcador negro para hacer una marca. Utilize un serrucho con una hoja de metal (ridged), o utiliza un serrucho que es hecho para cortar plástico PVC. Haga el corte lo más recto posible a tráves del tubo.

- Después que el tubo se ha instalado alrededor de la base de la casa, usted necesitará cavar y instalar los tubos que llevarán el agua lejos de la casa. Estas líneas se deben mantener lo más recto posible. Muchas secciones largas de tubería son necesitadas para ser instaladas, puede ser más fácil de cavar la zanja con una máquina pequeña de excavar (back-hoe). Ya que el tubo está inclinado 1-1/4 pulgadas de profundo por cada 10 pies de longitud, la zanja tendrá que ser más profunda cada vez que usted se aleje más del punto de partida.

- Para medir la cuesta en una longitud recta larga de la zanja utiliza una cuerda y un nivel de línea. Áspero (rough) la zanja y tiene cuidado para no cavar demasiado profundo. Entonces ponga la cuerda en el fondo de la zanja dónde está la profundidad correcta **(este punto será donde el último pedazo de tubo se instaló)**. Martille una estaca (espigón) en el suelo y ate la cuerda en la estaca. Corra la cuerda debajo de la longitud de la zanja y martille una segunda estaca en el suelo y ate la cuerda a ello. Conecte el nivel de la línea al centro de la cuerda. Ajuste la cuerda al extremo distante hasta que lea el nivel. Entonces mueva la cuerda hacia abajo al extremo distante para obtener la cuesta correcta.

Por ejemplo:

Sí la zanja es de 100 pies de largo, el extremo distante de la línea necesita ser 1 pie más bajo que el punto de partida. Sí la zanja es de 50 pies de largo, la línea se debe bajar 6 pulgadas. Sí la línea no se puede bajar porque la zanja no es lo suficiente profundo, quite lo necesario de tierra.

Nota: Sí usted hace mucho trabajo de desagüe, usted puede querer alquilar o comprar un tránsito de agrimensores o nivel de laser. Estas herramientas harán el trabajo mucho más fácil.

- Su tubo puede descargar en la calle, sí es el caso, esté seguro de obtener un permiso y seguir los requisitos de la civdad (township).

Sí el tubo no se descarga en la calle, puede correr a un área arbolada o no usada de la propiedad o en a un pozo seco (drywell).

* Después que el tubo es instaladó, llene de nuevo la zanja y termine de gradúar todas las áreas de la superficie.

Un pozo seco (drywell) es un área donde el agua corre y luego se rezume en el suelo. Un pozo seco (drywell) es acerca de 4 pies de profundo y llenó con piedra o una inserción plástica. Los pozos secos no trabajarán, sí usted tiene un suelo de nivel alto de agua. Verifique los requisitos y permisos dela ciudad (township) antes de instalar pozos secos (drywells).

Sistema subterráneo de Desagüe

El segundo tipo de sistema de desagüe que estaremos discutiendo ayudará a secar áreas mojadas en una propiedad y ayudará a bajar un nivel alto de agua. La tabla de agua es el nivel en el cual el agua del suelo corre debajo de la superficie del suelo.

Para instalar este tipo de sistema, usted tendrá que usar tubo plástico perforado de PVC que es 4 pulgada por 10 pies largos. Es el mismo tubo que usamos para instalar el sistema de desagüe de canal excepto que este tubo tendrá hoyos en el. El tubo se instalará a través de áreas mojadas de la propiedad.

Instalando un Sistema Subterráneo de Desagüe

- Escoja el sistema de desagüe, donde lo comenzará y donde el agua se descargará. Recuerde de tener todas las utilidades etc. marcado antes de que usted diseñe el sistema. Recuerde también que el tubo necesitará inclinarse por lo menos 1-1/4 de pulgada por diez pies o 1 pie por 100 pies de longitud. Trate de evitar usar las dobleces agudas en el sistema y escoja instalar las conexiones limpias cada 50 pies a través del sistema para que puedan ser limpiadas sí se necesita.

- Después que el sistema se ha planeado y ha sido marcado, usted puede comenzar a cavar la zanja. Cave la zanja aproximadamente ocho pulgadas de ancho y comience con una profundidad de aproximadamente 12 pulgadas de profundo.

Trate de instalar el tubo (drainpipe) lo más profundo posible pero recuerde que el fin del desagüadero tendrá que ser más profundo que el punto de partida. En algunos trabajos, puede ser mejor comenzar en el punto más bajo (el cuál debe ser el fin del desagüadero) y trabaje hacia atrás hasta el punto más alto (o el comienzo del desagüadero). Al instalar el tubo lo más profundo posible, usted bajará la tabla de agua del suelo y secará la mayoría del área. Los hoyos en los tubos se colocan en el fondo de la zanja. Entonces así como ascende arriba el agua del suelo, desembocará en los hoyos y fluira al fin del sistema del desagüe.

- Cave la zanja acerca de dos pulgadas más profundas de donde usted quiere que el tubo sea instalado. El fondo de dos pulgadas se llenarán con piedra. El tubo se instalará con (¾ de pulgada) de piedra limpia por todas partes. Esto ayudará de atracción de más agua dentro del tubo.

- Antes de instalar la piedra, usted necesitará colocar tela de paisaje en la zanja. Corte la tela para que sea capaz de envolver alrededor del tubo con dos a tres pulgadas de piedra alrededor del tubo. La tela se instala para mantener la tierra fuera de las piedras y tubo. La tela que solamemte cubre el tubo está también disponible. Es más rápido y más fácil de usar, pero cuesta más dinero. Instalar la tela alrededor de la piedra y el tubo es mejor.

- Cerciòrese que la zanja tiene la cuesta correcta. Entonces instale la tela del paisaje a través de la longitud de la zanja.

- Después que la tela se instala, llena el fondo de la zanja con aproximadamente dos pulgadas de piedra. Trate de mantener la piedra a la misma profundidad a través de la zanja, entonces gradúa la piedra con un rastrillo del arco de metal.

- Después que la capa de piedra se gradúa en el fondo de la zanja, comienze a instalar el tubo. Instale el tubo para que los hoyos estén hacia abajo. Usted tendrá que verificar cada pedazo de tubo con un nivel para cerciòrarse que está inclinado correctamente. Sí la cuesta no es correcta, usted necesitará agregar o quitar piedra hasta que el tubo esté en la cuesta correcta.

- Corte y pega todos los tubos como nosotros discutimos más temprano. Cuándo todos los tubos se instalen, agrega más piedra en los lados y la cima del tubo. Debe haber acerca de dos pulgadas de piedra alrededor de la cima, fondos y los lados del tubo.

Nota: Tiene cuidado para no cavar la zanja muy ancho. Mantenga la anchura de la zanja no más grande que ocho pulgadas. Sí la zanja es demasiado ancha, usted malgastará tiempo y los materiales llenándolo con piedra.

- Envuelva la tela sobre la cima de la piedra y el tubo. Entonces llena de regreso la zanja con tierra. Tenga cuidado para no permitir ninguna tierra entre la tela porque si no entrará en el sistema de desagüe. Usted necesitará acerca de 6 pulgadas de tierra encima de la piedra para que el césped pueda crecer.

- El sistema debe acabar (o descargarse) dentro de un área no usada de la propiedad, en la calle o el desagüe localizado en la calle, o en un pozo seco.

- Planiando y luego instalando un sistema subterráneo de desagüe como nosotros acabamos de discutir, usted puede convertir un área mojada del suelo en un pedazo utilizable de la propiedad.

Hay otra manera de instalar un sistema subterráneo de desagüe, que requerirá trabaj menos, pero no trabajará así de bien como el tipo que acabamos de discutir. Usted instalaría el sistema de la misma manera pero usted no pondría piedra alrededor del tubo. Esto reducirá el trabajo y el costo del trabajo pero reducirá también la calidad del trabajo.

Instalando un Sistema Subterráneo de Desagüe (Abierto)
El tercer tipo de sistema de desagüe que discutiremos ayudará a secar áreas mojadas y ayudará a bajar una tabla alta de agua y a reunir agua

de superficie que fluye sobre el suelo. Este sistema del desagüe es diseñado y instalado de la misma manera como el sistema subterráneo de desagüe que acabamos de discutir **excepto** que la zanja no es llenada de regreso con tierra. En lugar de ello será llenada de regreso con piedra hasta que la piedra se anivele con el suelo. Al llenar la zanja con piedra en vez de tierra, cúalquier agua de superficie caerá fácilmente en el desagüadero. Instale este tipo de desagüadero dondequiera que hay un problema con el fluye del agua de superficie sobre el suelo. Las piedras decorativas se pueden instalar encima del desagüadero para que se mire mejor en el paisaje.

Combinando los Tipos Diferentes de Sistemas de Desagüe

Cada propiedad en la cuál usted trabaje tendrá problemas diferentes de desagüe. Habrá muchos trabajos que requerirán unos cuantos tipos diferentes de sistemas de desagüe para resolver los problemas en la propiedad. Los tres tipos de sistemas de desagüe que discutimos se pueden combinar uno con el otro sí se necesita.

Planiando y instalando un sistema de desagüe correctamente, usted será capaz de mejorar una propiedad cambiando un área inutilizable mojada en un pedazo utilizable seco de la propiedad, usted ayudará también a prevenir que el agua dañe un hogar o un edificio y aumenta el valor de la propiedad.

INSTALANDO LADRILLO DE LOSA EN ACERAS, PATIOS Y CAMINOS DE ENTRADA (CAPÍTULO 17)

Ladrillos de losa son hechas por hombres usadas para aceras, patios y caminos de entrada. Son semejantes a los ladrillos viejos de moda excepto que duran más tiempo y están disponible en muchos colores y diferentes formas. Las piedras de losa han llegado a ser muy populares y como un porfesional de paisaje, usted debe saber cómo instalarlos correctamente. Cuándo es instalada correctamente, un trabajo de piedra de losa debe durar para siempre. Sin embargo sí son instalados incorectamente, se hundirán y le deja con un trabajo pobre de calidad y un cliente no feliz. Sí usted sigue las instrucciones en este capítulo, su trabajo de piedra de losa debe durar una vida.

Las Herramientas y Equipo Necesarios

Usted necesitará las siguientes herramientas y equipo para instalar una acera básica, patio o camino de entrada. Carretilla, palas, piochas, un rastrillo de metal, un rastrillo que gradúa, una escoba, una cinta métrica, una pistola de pintura, un nivel regular y un nivel de línea, cuerdas y estacas, un martillo de caucho, un pedazo recto de madera, (2) 1 diámetro de pulgada de tubería que son acerca de 10 pies de largo, un vibrante de plato (tamper), una sierra de albañilería para cortar las piedras de losa, y una excavadora (opcional).

El Equipo de Seguridad Necesitadó:

Guantes, lentes de seguridad, una máscara de polvo, rodilleras, y un cinturón de apoyo de espalda.

Instalando una Acera de Ladrillo de Losa
Escogiendo los ladrilloa, el Modelo y la Disposición

El primer paso para instalar ladrillos de losa es escoger la piedra correcta, el modelo y la disposición del trabajo; esto es hecho generalmente por el jefe o el capataz de su compañía.

- Hay muchos tipos diferentes de ladrillos de losa que variarán en colores y la forma. Cuándo escoge un color y la forma, le trae un folleto al cliente, la mayoría de los folletos mostrarán todos los colores diferentes y formas disponibles. Los folletos deben estar disponibles de su comerciante local de piedra de losa. Después que un color y la forma se han escogido del folleto, traiga unas cuantas muestras de ladrillo de losa al cliente para que el cliente entienda claramente cómo los ladrillos de losa se mirarán.

- El modelo es la próxima cosa para escoger y confirmar con el cliente. Los modelos se muestran también en el folleto. El modelo es la manera que las piedras de losa son instaladas. Pueden ser instalados rectas o en un ángulo. Algunos trabajos más grandes pueden tener dos a tres diferentes modelos. Permita que el cliente sepa que el costo del trabajo variará basado en el modelo que se escoge.

- La disposición del trabajo necesitará también ser planiado. La anchura, longitud y la forma necesita ser determinada. Un trabajo con muchas curvas requerirá muchos cortes, haciendo el trabajo más difícil y caro. Mientras que una disposición de trabajo que es recta será más fácil de instalar y menos caro. Durante el proceso de la disposición, usted tendrá que determinar también sí el área tiene la cuesta correcta. Sí la cuesta no está correcta, usted tendrá que cambiar la cuesta excavando el área. Durante el proceso de la disposición, busque los alambres o los tubos enterrados en el área. Sí usted no está 100% seguro de donde están enterradas las utilidades, llame por teléfono a la compañía de utilidad para que ellos los puedan marcar. También, cerciórese qué el dueño de la propiedad le avise de cúalquier otro peligro tal como, tubos de regadera o alabres de luz del paisaje. Sí en el futuro quizás la iluminación se instale, planee en instalar un tubo plástico de PVC por la base del trabajo para que los alambre entonces puedan ser instalados por el tubo y en ambos lados del trabajo.

Después que los ladrillos, el modelo y la disposición han sido confirmados, usted estará listo para comenzar el proceso de la instalación.

El Proceso de Instalación
Nota: Siempre verifique las recomendaciones exactas de los fabricantes antes de instalar ladrillos de losa.

La Disposición (Layout)
Mida y marque el área donde la acera, se instalará. Usted necesitará que la materia prima esté aproximadamente un pie más grande en

ambos lados de la caminata. Al instalar la materia prima más grande que la caminata prevendrá que las orillas de la caminata se muevan y se asienten. Use una cinta métrica y una pistola de pintura para medir y marcar el área. No haga ninguna excavación hasta que todo esté marcado claramente.

La Excavación

Una base apropiadamente instalada es un procedimiento muy importante cuándo instala ladrillo de losa. La materia prima para las aceras, debe ser de cuatro a seis pulgadas de profundo. Entonces agregue tres pulgadas a la base de la profundidad para determinar la profundidad total de la excavación requerida. Las tres pulgadas adicionales son excavadas para tener en cuenta el polvo del ladrillo de losa que se instalarán encima de la materia prima. La materia prima debe componerse de (0 a ¾ de pulgada) piedra. Usted necesitará excavar un total de nueve pulgadas para la caminata que discutimos.

Para quitar la tierra, utilice una pala y piocha. Ponga la tierra en una carretilla y se deshace de ello. En algunos trabajos, usted puede necesitar usar esta tierra para re-gradúar, rellenar un área cerca de la caminata o en otra parte en la propiedad. Sí usted necesita excavar una cantidad grande de tierra, será más fácil y más rápido usar una excavadora. Verifique la profundidad del área excavada con su cinta métrica. Trate de mantener el fondo del área excavada parejo y mantiene los lados del área rectos. Rastrille el fondo del área excavada para que esté lo más parejo posible. Entonces comprima el suelo con su vibrador de plato (tamper). Esto comprimirá algunas áreas suaves en el suelo antes de que usted agregue la materia prima (base material)

Materia Prima (Base Material)

Sí usted trabaja en un área humeda, una tela especial del paisaje se debe instalar en el fondo del área excavada. La tela hará la base más fuerte y prevendrá qua la materia prima (base material) se rezuma/filtre en la tierra existente. Su suministrador local de ladrillo de losa podrá recomendarle y suministrarlo con la tela correcta.

Después que la tela se instala, usted puede comenzar a llenar el área con la materia prima. Otra vez, la materia prima (base material) debe componerse de (0 a ¾ La pulgada) piedra. Instale una capa de cuatro pulgadas, entonces rastrilla el nivel de piedra y comprime la materia con su vibrador de plato (tamper). (Nunca instale más de 4 pulgadas de la materia prima (base material) la materia sin graduar y comprimirlo primero.) Moje la materia prima (base material) con agua y haga varios pases sobre el área con el (vibrador) (tamper). Entonces agregue dos pulgadas más de materia prima (base material), nivela y repite el proceso. Verifique el área con un nivel en varios lugares para cerciorarse que la materia prima (base material) esté nivelada y lo mismo a través de la acera entera.

Bordear

El fabricante de ladrillo de losa lo suministrará con un borde especial que deberá ser usado con su ladrillo de losa. La mayoría de los pedazos de borde son hechos de plástico. Son flexibles para que puedan ser instalados fácilmente alrededor de alguna área curva y vienen generalmente en longitudes de 12 pies. Las estacas se martillan por el borde y dentro del suelo para sujetarlos en su lugar. La mayoría de los fabricantes de piedra de losa recomiendan instalar el plástico que bordea encima de la materia prima (base material).

Instale el plástico que bordea en **un lado** de la materia prima (base material). Usando las estacas de 10 pulgadas, instale una estaca cada dos pies. Comenzando del plástico que bordea que usted acaba de instalar, disponga una sección pequeña de piedra de losa a través de la caminata en el modelo que usted estará usando. Entonces tome una medida de un lado de la caminata al otro. Use esa misma medida para medir y marcar áreas a lo largo del lado opuesto de la caminata. Entonces instale el borde en estas marcas.

Colocación del Material (Setting Material)

La (setting material) es el material en el cuál las piedras de losa se pondrán encima de ello. El polvo de la piedra o de la arena concreta se deben usar para poner la materia. Esparza una capa de colocación de material de 1 a 1-1/2 de pulgada encima de la materia. Riegue la materia de colocación (setting material) con un rastrillo de metal. Para propósitos de desagüe, debe haber una inclinación de dos por ciento en la materia de colocación (setting material). La inclinación del dos por ciento permitirá que la lluvia fluya fácilmente sobre la acera. El dos por ciento igualará al ¼ pulgada por pie. Por lo tanto, sí su sendero es de tres pies de ancho, la inclinación de un lado de la caminata al otro lado debe ser de ¾ de pulgada. La inclinación siempre debe inclinarse **lejos** de una casa o edificio. Algunos trabajos pueden tener ya un inclinación que permite que el agua fluya fácilmente lejos de las piedras de losa.

Sí el plástico que bordea se ha instalado, usted puede usar el borde como una guía para terminar de graduar la materia. Usted necesitará usar un pedazo recto de madera. Haga un corte en ambos extremos de la madera para que descanse en el borde pero quede también dentro del borde. Ajuste el corte para que usted obtenga también la correcta inclinación en la materia de colocación (setting material). Esto tomará una práctica pequeña pero es fácil después que usted lo haga un par de veces. Después que la colocación de materia se ha graduado apropiadamente, tiene cuidado para permanecer lejos del área. La colocación de materia (setting material) no se comprime hasta después que los ladrillos de losa se han instalado.

La Instalación de Ladrillos de Losa

Coloque los ladrillos de losa hacia abajo en el modelo que usted ha escogido. Comience el modelo en el área más ancha de la acera. Generalmente esto sería en el área del frente o la puerta trasera. Comience instalando una sección pequeña de losas. Verifique el modelo y el ángulo de ladrillos para estar seguro que está correcto antes de que usted continue trabajando. Detenidamente camine en la losa que usted instaló, trabaje hacia adelante, siempre trabajando encima de la losa que usted acaba de instalar. Para obtener una distribución constante del color y textura, se recomienda que usted escoja ladrillos de losas de más de una paleta a la vez.

Como siempre, usted debe tener el trabajo organizado siempre. Cuándo instala la losa, una persona los debe instalar mientras que la segunda persona escoge la losa de la paleta y los coloca dónde serán más fácil de alcanzar para la persona que los instala.

Los ladrillos de losa se fabrican con espaciadores de lado. Los espaciadores de lado mantendrán un espacio de 1/8 de pulgada entre cada losa. Cuándo usted termine de instalar la losa, la arena se barrerá en estos espacios para ayudar a sujetar la losa junta. Cuándo usted coloca cada losa hacia abajo, suavemente lo coloca contra la último losa. Busque el espacio de 1/8 de pulgada en medio de las losas. Sí el espacio entre las losas es más grande de 1/8 de pulgada, no han sido instalados correctamente. Alguna personas levemente golpean con un martillo de caucho suavemente después de ponerlas correctamente. Mientras instala las losas, verifica el modelo para cerciórarse que no esta cambiando ni moviendose en la dirección equivocada. En trabajos más grande, usted puede instalar una cuerda, entonces usted puede usar la cuerda como una guía para mantener su modelo recto y correcto. Instale todas ladrillos de losa sólidas primero. Deje un espacio abierto donde la losa necesitará ser cortado.

Cortando los Ladrillos de Losa

Mida y marque todas las losas que necesitan ser cortado. Hay dos tipos de sierras que se puede usar para cortar las piedras. Una sierra de mesa o una sierra de mano. Ambas sierras deben tener una hoja especial que se debe usar sólo para cortar piedra. Corte los ladrillos para que tenga un espacio de 1/8 de pulgada en todos los lados del ladrillo, entonces los ladrillos quedarán fácilmente en su espacio. Nunca fuerce una losa en su espacio; sí no queda fácilmente, usted debe cortar un poco más. Cuándo corta las losas, usted hará mucho polvo. El agua se puede usar para ayudar a controlar el problema de polvo. Siempre lleve puestos los lentes de seguridad y una máscara de polvo cuándo corta la losa.

Estabilizando los Ladrillos de Losa

Después que usted ha acabado de instalar todo la losa, usted necesitará estabilizar la losa usando un vibrante de plato (tamper). Este procedimiento apretará la losa hacia abajo en la materia de colocación (setting material) y nivelará la superficie de la acera. Para mejores resultados, corra el vibrante de plato sobre la losa dos o tres vez en ambas direcciones. Los ladrillos de losa se asentarán en la colocación de materia (setting material) por 3/8 de pulgada.

Después que usa el (vibrador) de plato (tamper), usted necesitará esparcir la arena sobre la losa. La arena llenará los espacios de 1/8 de pulgada entre los ladrillos de losa. Use una escoba para cepillar la arena sobre la caminata. Agregue más arena hasta que todos los espacios se llenen. Una vez que todos los espacios se han llenado con la arena, corra el vibrador sobre el área otra vez. El vibrador ayudará a que la arena se asiente en los espacios. Agregue más arena a cúalquier espacio que no están llenados completamente. Repita este proceso hasta que todos los espacios estén llenados y la arena no se asentará más. Remueva el exceso de arena de la superficie de la caminata, y entonces humedezca el área con agua para estabilizar la arena aún más.

Instalando un Patio o Camino de entrada con Ladrillo de Losa

Nota: Siempre verifique las recomendaciones exactas del fabricante antes de instalar ladrillo de losa.

Un patio o camino de entrada se instala casi lo mismo que una caminata con excepción de unos pocos cambios. Estos cambios incluirán:

- El área se debe excavar más profundo, ya que la base de la materia necesitará ser más profundo. Siga las recomendaciones en el diagrama.

Acera:	Profundidad aproximadamente	6 pulgadas
Patio:	Profundidad aproximadamente	8 pulgadas
Camino de entrada:	Profundidad aproximadamente	12 pulgadas

- Nivele y comprime cada cuatro-pulgadas de la base de la materia (base material).
- Fije la inclinación correcta en la materia prima (base material), no en la colocación de materia (settiing material).
- Cuándo nivele la colocación del material, las áreas grandes se tendrán que graduar en secciones. Coloca dos tubos que son de una pulgada en el diámetro y aproximadamente 10 pies de largos. Espacíelos aproximadamente seis pies aparte. Los tubos se deben colocar en la materia prima (base material). Entonces llene entre

los tubos con la materia de colocación. Entonces usar una tabla que esté perfectamente recta, ponga la tabla encima de los tubos. Arrastre la tabla hacia usted para graduar la materia de colocación. Agregue o quite la materia como sea necesitado. Después que el área se ha graduado, quita cuidadosamente los tubos y los mueve a la próxima sección. Los espacios que se dejaron de los tubos serán llenados a mano cuándo instale los ladrillos.

- Una cuerda debe ser establecida y usado como una guía cuándo instala ladrillos. Trabajando con una cuerda, usted ayudará prevenir que el modelo se mueva mientras instala los ladrillos en un área grande.

Nota: Antes de intentar completar un trabajo grande complicado, usted debe obtener experiencia de completar trabajos menos complicados y más pequeños. Cada trabajo le dará a usted más experiencia y confianza. Entonces cada trabajo será hecho más fácil y más rápido y tendrá una vista profesional .

INSTALANDO PAREDES DECORATIVAS DE PIEDRA

(CAPÍTULO 18)

Las paredes decorativas se usan para sujetar las cantidades pequeñas de tierra y agregan belleza al paisaje. Una pared de piedra decorativa recorrerá en la altura de 6 pulgadas a una altura máxima de 2-1/2 de pies. Sí la pared es más de 2-1/2 pies de alto, se considera una pared estructural. Una pared de piedra decorativo y una pared estructural se instalan casi lo mismo excepto que la pared estructural requerirá algunos refuerzos adicionales (estaremos discutiendo sólo paredes decorativas de piedra).

Los tipos de Paredes

Hay muchos tipos diferentes de paredes de piedras, nosotros discutiremos los más populares.

Sistema de Pared Pre-fabricada

Sistemas de pared pre-fabricada ha llegado a ser muy popular en los últimos años. Son bloques hechos que están disponible en varios colores y formas. Son hechos de material semejante al ladrillo de losa. No se agrietarán ni se descarvarán cuándo sean viejos. Los bloques son bastante sencillos de instalar y no requieren ningún mantenimiento una vez que son instalados. Los bloques prefabricados estan tomando el lugar de paredes de madera. Las paredes de madera durarán 40 años luego la pared necesitará ser reemplazada. Los bloques de pared pre-fabricados durarán una vida.

Pared de Piedra

Hay muchos tipos diferentes de pared de piedra. Las piedras variarán en colores, textura y la forma. Las paredes de piedras son básicamente planicie en su forma y se instalan sin usar ningún cemento. Las paredes de piedras vienen de la tierra y le darán al paisaje una vista natural. Cuándo son instaladas correctamente, un trabajo con pared de piedra debe durar una vida.

Pedrejónes (boulders) de Paisaje

Los pedrejónes naturales o hechos se usan también para hacer paredes decorativas o colocadas separadamente a través del paisaje. Hay muchos tipos diferentes de pedrejónes de donde escoger. Los pedrejónes siempre agregan belleza cuándo son escogidos y colocados en el paisaje correctamente.

Las Herramientas y Equipo

Usted necesitará las siguientes herramientas cuándo instale cúalquier tipo de pared de piedra decorativo.

- Las carretillas, un carrito de árbol, palas, piochas, un rastrillo de metal, una escoba, una cinta métrica, una pistola de pintura, un anivelador, cuerda, un martillo de caucho, un vibrador de mano (tamper), una sierra de albañilería, un martillo (sledgehammer), y un cincel de albañilería.

El equipo de seguridad:

- Los guantes, lentes de seguridad, una máscara de polvo, rodilleras, y un cinturón de apoyo de espalda.

Instalando Bloques de Pared Pre-fabricados

- El primer paso para instalar una pared decorativa deberá escoger el tipo correcto, el color y el tamaño del bloque entonces planea la disposición de la pared. Esto es hecho generalmente por el jefe o el capataz.

- Mida y marque el área donde la pared se instalará. Marque cúalquier utilidad que está enterrado cerca de la pared. **Nunca** comience a excavar hasta que usted esté 100% seguro que nada está enterrado debajo del área donde usted estará trabajando.

- Excave una zanja de aproximadamente 12 pulgadas de ancho por 6 pulgadas de profundo. Comience a excavar donde la parte más **baja** de la pared se instalará. Esto será el punto del área de suelo más bajo. El fondo de la zanja debe ser plano, parejo y compacto. Cerciórese que el fondo de la zanja se comprima bien. Use un vibrador de mano para comprimir la tierra sí es necesario.

- Instale aproximadamente 2-1/2 de pulgadas (0 a ¾ de pulgada) de piedra en la zanja. Rastrille y nivele la piedra lo más posible, entonces comprime la piedra con un vibrador de mano esto sera la base de la pared. Instale otra ½ pulgada de piedra y lo rastrilla hasta que lo nivele. Verifique la materia prima (base material) con un nivel cada pocos pies. La longitud entera de la materia prima (base material) debe ser parejo antes de instalar cúalquiera de los bloques de pared. No comprima la última ½ pulgada de la materia prima (base material).

- Instale la primera fila de bloques de pared. Nivele cada bloque de lado a lado, del frente hacia atrás para apoyarlo con el próximo bloque. Use un martillo de caucho para ayudar nivelar los bloques.

Nota: Sí usted está instalando una pared en una cuesta desigual, usted tendrá que excavar, emparejar e instalar la primera fila de bloques (comenzando en el punto más bajo). Entonces excave y empareje para instalar las siguientes filas hasta que los bloques sean instalados alrededor en la forma de la pared.

- Al instalar la primera fila de bloques de pared se debe hacer correctamente ya que todos los otros bloques se colocarán encima de la primera fila.
- Cuándo instale la segunda fila de bloques, coloca el bloque hacia abajo para que el centro del segundo bloque cubra el espacio de los bloques de abajo. La mayoría de los bloques de pared tendrán una punta extra detrás, el lado del fondo del bloque. Deslice los bloques hacia adelante hasta que la orilla haga contacto con los bloques de abajo.
- El procedimiento es bastante fácil después que usted obtenga una pequeña práctica. Sólo la primera fila necesita ser nivelada. Después que la primera fila se nivela correctamente, todas las otras filas de encima no necesitan ser niveladas.

- Llene de regreso cada fila de bloques con ¾ de pulgada de piedra. La piedra se instala atrás de la pared para propósitos de desagüe para mantener el agua lejos de la pared. Instale ¾ de pulgada de piedra aproximadamente un pie de ancho y la misma altura como la pared. Entonces llene de regreso el área restante con tierra.

- (Opcional.) Cuándo usted fije la fila primera de bloques, un bloque especial (tapa) se puede instalar. La (tapa) bloque le dará al trabajo una mejor vista. Los bloques de la tapa necesitarán ser asegurado con un adhesivo concreto.

Instalando la Pared de Piedra

La pared de piedra es un tipo natural de piedra. Las piedras se instalan sin ningún cemento. Las piedras se colocan encima de uno del otro. Los pedazos más pequeños de piedra se ponen en los espacios entre las piedras más grandes y detrás de la pared. Esto ayudará hacer la pared estable. Al instalar pared de piedra tomará un tiempo más largo que instalar los bloques de pared pre-fabricados, y requerirá más habilidad. Leyendo las instrucciones de abajo y trabajando en el sitio de trabajo, usted ganará el conocimiento y la experiencia y llegará a ser un profesional después de unos pocos trabajos.

- **Escogiendo las Piedras**—Las paredes de piedras vendrán generalmente en un paleta. La paleta se cubre con alambre para tener las piedras juntas. Busque una paleta que tiene los mejores pedazos calibrados. Escoja una paleta que tiene el promedio de piedras en su mayor parte plano calibradas. Evite las piedras que son muy pequeñas, muy grandes o redondas en el tamaño. Estas piedras serán muy difíciles para trabajar y harán su trabajo más duro. Cuándo cargue una paleta de piedras en su camión, se cerciórese que las llantas tienen suficiente presión de aire. Cerciórese que el freno de estacionamiento está activado antes que cargue la paleta. Coloque la paleta en el centro del camión y **asegure la paleta** para que no se deslize cuándo usted maneja. Maneje cuidadosamente y no acelere ni frene demasiadamente rápido.

- **La Disposición**—Mida y marque el área donde la pared se instalará.

- **La Excavación**—Excave una zanja de aproximadamente 12 pulgadas de ancho por cuatro pulgadas de profundo. Comience excavando donde la parte más baja de la pared se instalará. La zanja necesitará ser nivelada. Después de excavar, cerciórese que el fondo de la zanja se comprime bien. Use un (vibrador) de mano para comprimir la tierra sí es necesario.

- **La Materia Prima** —Llene la zanja con (0 – ¾ de pulgada) de piedra. Instale aproximadamente dos pulgadas de piedra en la zanja. Rastrille y nivela la piedra lo más posible, entonces comprime la piedra con un (vibrador) de mano. Instale otra ½ pulgada de piedra y lo rastrilla y nivela. Verifique la base de materia con un nivel cada pocos pies. La longitud entera de la materia prima debe ser pareja antes de instalar la pared de piedra. No comprima la última ½ pulgada de la materia prima (base material).

Nota: Sí usted está instalando una pared en una cuesta desigual, usted tendrá que excavar, emparejar e instalar la primera fila de bloques (comenzando en el punto más bajo). Entonces excave y empareje para instalar las siguientes filas hasta que los bloques sean instalados alrededor en la forma de la pared.

- **Instalando las Piedras**—Instale la primera fila de piedras en la materia prima (base material). Cuándo instale las piedras, ponga el mejor lado de la piedra frente al exterior de la pared. Cada fila de piedras se debe centrar encima del espacio de las piedras de abajo. Use los pedazos más pequeños de piedra para ponerlos en los espacios entre las piedras hasta que esté seguro y no se mueva. Use un nivel para mantener las piedras y la pared recto. Ya que las piedras son irregulares, será difícil de obtener una medida exacta del nivel. Use el nivel para obtener una medida aproximada. Algunos de los pedazos más grande de piedra se pueden partir y reducidos en el tamaño usando un martillo y un cincel de albañil.

- **Llenar de Regreso**—Después que unas pocas filas de piedra se han instalado, llene de regreso la pared con (¾ de pulgada) de piedra. Usando sus manos o una pala, llene los espacios entre las piedras detrás de la pared. Entonces agregue piedra a una anchura de 6 a 12 pulgadas detrás de la pared. La piedra ayudará a sostener la pared y mantendrá el agua lejos de la pared. **Llenar de regreso es muy importante.** Muchos paisajistas no profesionales se saltan este paso y sólo llenan de regreso con tierra. Entonces la tierra se asienta y las paredes comienzan a caerse hacia atrás. Para hacer un trabajo profesional, siempre llene de regreso con (¾ de pulgada) de piedra.

- **El Paso Final**—trate de encontrar pedazos buenos de piedra que se miran bien para terminar la pared. Ponga estos pedazos aparte mientras usted construye la pared. Habrá muchos pedazos pequeños de piedra que sobraran. Utilize algunos de ellos para llenar los espacios más grandes del frente y detrás de la pared. Use algún pedazo pequeño inutilizable para llenar detrás de la pared. Guarde cúalquier pedazo bueno para su próximo trabajo.

Instalando Pedrejónes (boulder) del Paisaje

Los pedrejónes son piedras grandes, generalmente natural. Sin embargo, algunos son hechos. Hay muchos tipos diferentes de pedrejónes. Ellos variarán en colores, forma y la textura. Los pedrejónes agregarán belleza al paisaje cuándo son escogidos e instalado en las áreas correctas. Los pedrejónes se pueden colocar juntos para crear una pared con una vista natural.

Los pedrejónes se pueden colocar también separados en el paisaje, y luego plantas se pueden instalar alrededor de ellos. Como siempre, el jefe o el capataz deben hablar con el cliente y confirmar el tipo de pedrejónes que se usarán y donde los pedrejónes se instalarán. Después que el trabajo ha sido confirmado con el cliente, usted estará listo para trabajar.

- Los pedrejónes se venden generalmente separadamente. Escoja pedrejónes que son grandes, pero no demasiado grandes sí no usted no podrá moverlos a menos que usted use algún tipo de maquinaria. No sobrecargue su camión y maneje cuidadosamente al sitio del trabajo.

491

- Una vez que usted está en el sitio del trabajo, marca las áreas donde los pedrejónes se instalarán.

- Sí usted no usa maquinaria para mover los pedrejónes, hay dos maneras de moverlos manualmente.

La primera manera deberá usar una carretilla de tamaño grande. Ponga una carretilla contra la parte posterior del camión. Mientras una persona sostiene la carretilla, deslice el pedrejón del camión y dentro de la carretilla.

- La segunda manera deberá descargar fuera los pedrejónes. **Cerciórese que esté descargando los pedrejónes en un área que no obtendrán daño.** Después que los pedrejónes se han descargado en el suelo, use un carrito de árbol para mover cada pedrejón a su lugar en el paisaje. Antes de mover los pedrejónes en el paisaje, preparan un área para cada pedrejón. Cave un área para que el pedrejón no se mueva cuándo sea puesto en su lugar. Los pedrejónes se instalan generalmente para que sean enterrados parcialmente en el suelo. Sea muy cuidadoso cuándo mueve los pedrejónes. Mantenga las manos y los pies lejos de la parte inferior del pedrejón. Trabaje junto cuándo mueve y posicione cada pedrejón.

- Después que las áreas se han preparado, escoja el mejor lado del pedrejón y ubique el mejor lado adelante. Entonces llene de regreso con tierra y pajote (mulch). Esto le dará al paisaje una vista natural. Los pedrejónes deben parecer que forman parte del paisaje y que siempre han estado allí. Piense de la mejor manera de posicionar cada pedrejón antes de que usted lo instale y su trabajo se mirará magnífico cuándo usted termine.

OPERANDO DIFERENTES TIPOS DE EQUIPOS DE APLICACIÓN

(CAPITULO 19)

Nota: Por favor, este advertido que su equipo de aplicaciòn puede trabajar levemente diferente de lo que es describido en esta guía de instrucciòn.

Esparcidores

Hay dos diferentes tipos de esparcidores de césped que se usan para aplicar el abono, la semilla de césped y otras materias secas. El esparcidor de césped más comùnmente usado se llama esparcidor rotorio (rotary spreader). El segundo tipo de esparcidor de césped se llama esparcidor de gota (drop spreader).

Esparcidor Rotorio

El esparcidor rotorio esparce la materia en un arco ancho. La materia puede ser esparcida de 6 a 10 pies de lejos en una pasada. Este tipo de esparcidor debe ser usado en las áreas grandes de césped. El operario del esparcidor necesita ser muy cuidadoso. Si el esparcidor rotorio no es usado apropiadamente, la materia se esparcira dentro de las camas del paisaje, caminos de entrada, aceras, etc. Tal como un profesional, usted debe operar el esparcidor para que la materia sea esparcida **uniformemente** solamente en las áreas del césped.

Antes de usar el esparcidor, usted necesitara inspeccionarlo. Si el esparcidor no trabaja apropiadamente, usted puede obtener resultados muy pobres o daños muy graves al área del césped. En una base **diaria** usted debe inspeccionar lo siguiente.

- Cerciorese que el esparcidor siempre este completamente limpio. El rotor que gira y esparce la materia se debe verificar muy a menudo. Se atascara con materia rápidamente. Si esta materia no se limpia, el esparcidor no trabajará correctamente.

- Verifique las llantas para cerciorarse que esten ambas llenas con aire. Si las llantas estan bajas en aire, el esparcidor será dificil de operar.

- Engrase todas las partes moviles del esparcidor.

- Busque por alguna parte dañada o floja en el esparcidor. Si usted encuentra un problema, reparelo antes de usar el esparcidor.

Tal como un profesional del cuidado del césped su esparcidor debe tener una cubierta. La cubierta cubre la cima del esparcidor y prevendrá que la materia se descargue si el esparcidor se volco. La cubierta también protegera la materia de las condiciones mojadas del tiempo.

Un deflector se debe instalar en su esparcidor. El deflector se monta en el lado del esparcidor. Cuando el deflector se usa, la materia no se distribuira en un lado del esparcidor. El deflector se debe usar alrededor de aceras, caminos de entrada, camas de paisaje y áreas pequeñas de césped. Esto prevendra que la materia llegue a los lugares no deseados.

Habra una palanca del control de mano a la cabeza del esparcidior cerca de los asideros. Esta palanca es usada para abrir y cerrar el flujo de materia. Comezara o parara la materia de esparcirse en el césped. Hay también una palanca de tasa que es usada para ajustar la cantidad de materia que es usada. La palanca de tasa tiene letras o nùmero seleccionado luego la materia saldra a la cantidad correcta. Si libera la cantidad incorrecta de materia, usted obtendra resultados muy pobres y causara daños muy graves al área de césped.

Siempre lea y comprenda la etiqueta en el producto que esta utilizando. Todos los productos del cuidado de césped tienen una etiqueta. La etiqueta le dara instrucciones, advertencias, y medida (rates) recomendados que la materia se debe aplicar. La etiqueta dara la medida para algunos tipos diferentes de esparcidores. Por lo tanto, usted debe saber el nombre de la marca del esparcidor que esta utilizando.

Al lado de la marca del nombre del esparcidor habra una recomendación de la cantidad (rate) de aplicación. Esta cantidad sera una letra o nùmero. Después que usted sabe la medida de aplicación, ajuste el esparcidor a la letra o nùmero recomendado. Asegurese de apretar la perilla en la tasa o la palanca puede moverse y cambiar el sitio de medida mientras usted este trabajando.

Los esparcidores profesionales vienen con un medidor (gage) manual. Al usar este medidor (gage), usted obtendra el esparcidor más exacto.

El medidor (gage) de calibracion mide los hoyos en el fondo del esparcidor que libera la materia. Para ajustar el esparcidor al pie de la letra o el nùmero, luego inserte el gage dentro de cada hoyo en el esparcidior. Ajuste los hoyos hasta que el gage de calibracion quede comodo, entonces aprieta la perilla en el gage para cerrar la palanca en su sitio escogido.

Usted debe llevar siempre puestos botas, pantalones largos que cubren la parte de encima de sus botas, una camisa de manga larga, guantes, lentes y un respirados o mascara de polvo (si es recomendada en la etiqueta del producto). Si usted estara usando el esparcidor a lo largo del dia, usted debe considerar en llevar puesto algun tipo de mascarilla de polvo aunque la materia que este usando no sea peligrosa.

Operando un Esparcidor Rotorio

- Antes de operar un esparcidor, inspeccione el esparcidor y ajustelo al sitio de la tasa (rate) recomendado como acabamos de discutir. Pongase todo su equipo de seguridad y usted esta listo para comenzar el trabajo.

Siempre lea y comprenda la etiqueta del producto antes de aplicar el producto en el área del césped. Cada producto tendra diferentes instrucciones a seguir. Resultados pobres y daños muy graves pueden ocurrir si usted no sigue las instrucciones de etiqueta en cada producto.

- Antes de llenar el esparcidor con materia, cerciorese que las palancas de control de mano esten cerradas. Si no lo estan, la materia se vertira por medio del esparcidor hacia el suelo.

- El esparcidor siempre debe ser llenado en tierra plana. Luego si la materia se derrama, puede ser muy fácilmente limpiado. Nunca llene el esparcidor en las áreas del césped.

- Debe de haber una malla dentro del esparcidor. La malla se usa para atrapar algun pedazo grande o irregular de materia antes que se atasque en el fondo del esparcidor. Limpie la malla cuando se empieze a llenar con escombros. Siempre use la malla y no opere el esparcidor sin ella.

- Si usted esta usando el esparcidor en tierra plana o en una cuesta leve, usted puede llenar el esparcidor completamente. Pero si usted usa el esparcidor en una cuesta escarpada, usted solo debe llenar el esparcidor ¾ de manera entera. Un esparcidor lleno puede volcarse muy facilmente en una cuesta escarpada. Tambien, el esparcidor lleno sera muy dificil de empujar en una cuesta escarpada. Llenarlo ½ o ¾ de lleno es recomendado.

- Despues que usted ha llenado la materia en el esparcidor, ponga la cubierta encima del esparcidor. Verifique el deflector si esta cerrado en su sitio. Si el deflector si no esta cerrado en su sitio, puede comenzar a moverse. Si se mueve, creara un grave problema mientras usted este operando el esparcidor.

- Visualmente inspeccione el área de césped que va aplicar el abono. No debe haber gente, niños, mascotas, juguete en el área de césped. Recoga alguna cosa que este en área de césped.

- El área de césped debe estar también limpia. Si el césped tiene muchas hojas, palos, escombros, la aplicación de abono no trabajará correctamente. Si el césped tiene muchos escombros, seria mejor regresar despues que el césped sea limpiado.

- Una vez que el área de césped esta limpio, planee la mejor manera de empujar un esparcidor sobre el césped. El esparcidor necesita ser empujado en una linea recta lo mas posible. Tambien, escoge un modelo donde no tendra que girar el esparcidor alrededor muy a menudo.

- Siempre procure de comenzar en una orilla recta tal como la curba de la calle, camino de entrada, acera. Si no hay orillas rectas de donde comenzar, empuje el esparcidor en una linea recta a traves del area de césped. Use el primer paso a traves del césped como una guia, entonces hago todo el resto de los pasos de la misma direccion.

- Despues que usted ha escogido el modelo a seguir, usted necesitara escoger una velocidad caminante. Su velocidad debe ser aproximadamente de 3 mph. Esto es un promedio de velocidad que caminara; no tan rápido, pero no tan lento.

- Es muy importante que usted empuje el esparcidor a la misma velocidad caminante a traves de todo el área del césped. Al empujar el esparcidor a la misma velocidad a traves de todo el área de césped, usted aplicara la materia uniformemente y profesionalmente. Si usted camina a diferentes velocidades, la materia se aplicara diferentemente. Esto causara pobres resultados o daños graves al área de césped.

Empujando el esparcidor a la misma velocidad en una cuesta escarpada o en un área de césped pequeña puede ser difícil. Permanezca en alerta y solamente empuje el esparcidor a una velocidad.

Cuando usted empuja un esparcidor a la velocidad correcta (aprox 3mph), el material se esparcira en la anchura y tasa correcta. Usualmente la materia se esparcira aprox 4 pies en ambos lados del esparcidor. Esto le dara una suma de 8 pies tratada de césped para cada paso que camina en 3 mph. Si usted camina lento, la anchura de la materia sera menos que los 8 pies y la materia sera aplicada muy pesada. Si usted camina rápidamente, la anchura de la materia sera mas de 8 pies y la materia sera aplicada muy leve. Siempre empuje el esparcidor a la misma velocidad caminante a traves de todo el área entera de césped o si no obtendra pobres resultados o daños graves pueden ocurrir.

- Posicionese usted mismo en un esparcidor para que usted este listo para hacer el primer paso a traves del césped. Posicionese para que usted este a unos pocos pies atrás del área que usted tratará.

- Comienze a caminar hacia delante. Dentro de unos pocos pasos, usted debe estar empujando el esparcidor en la velocidad correcta. Entonces abra rápidamente la palanca para dejar la materia afuera.

- Mientras usted esta empujando el esparcidor a lo largo del primer paso a traves del césped, busque en ambos lados del esparcidor para ver exactamente que tan lejos la materia esta siendo esparcida.

- Cuando usted llegue cerca del fin del primer paso, no se detenga. Continue caminando a la velocidad correcvta. Si la materia esta siendo esparcida 4 pies en frente del esparcidor, usted necesitara cerrar la palanca para detener la materia aproximademente 4 pies antes del de la pasada.

- Despues que el primer paso es hecho, posicione el esparcidor para el proximo paso. Usted debe **levemente traslapar** la materia con cada paso que usted paso. Por esto usted debe **siempre** vigilar que tan lejos la materia esta siendo esparcida.

- Antes de cada paso, recuerde que usted necesitara comenzar unos cuantos pies mas atrás o al lado del área que usted quiere tratar.

- **Si usted comienza el esparcidor encima del paso que usted va hacer, usted no curbrira el área en la cual usted esta parado. Por lo tanto, usted debe comezar el esparcidor unos cuantos pies atrás del punto de partida. Recuerde que todas las áreas que usted esta tratando deben recibir la misma cantidad de materia.**

- Cuando usted abre y cierra la palanca para dejar la materia comenzar o parar, el esparcidor debe siempre estar moviendo a la velocidad correcta. Una vez que el esparcidor este moviendose a la velocidad correcta y posicionado correctamente, usted debe usar esta palanca rápidamente. También al fin de cada pasada, la palanca debe cerrarse rápidamente.

- **La palanca le permite a la materia salir y debe tambien ser usada como una palanca de emergencia. Si usted golpea un hoyo en el césped y el esparcidor se detiene, rápidamente**

cierre la palanca. Cuando usted tiene un problema o dificultad, cierre la palanca inmediatamente. Al cerrar la palanca inmediatamente, usted prevendra que la materia se descargue sobre el césped.

- Continue haciendo cada pasada a traves del césped como acabamos de discutir. Si hay árboles o camas de paisaje en el área de césped, detenga el esparcidor. Luego comienze el esparcidor en el otro lado del árbol o cama de paisaje. **nunca empuje el esparcidor sobre un área de césped que ha sido ya tratado, usted estaria aplicando la materia a una tasa doble de la tasa de recomendación. La mayoria de las materias causaran daño al césped si se le aplica abono en demasia a lo que la tasa recomienda.**

- Cuando trata las áreas pequeñas, usted puede necesitar usar un deflector. El deflector dentendra la materia de salir de un lado del esparcidor. Use el deflector en todas las áreas pequeñas o estrechas de césped. Nunca esparsa materia dentro de las camas de paisaje, aceras, caminos de entrada. Use el deflector para un trabajo profesional.

- Cuando usa el esparcidor, recuerde de siempre vigilar la materia. Vigile que tan lejos se esta esparciendo y si se esta esparciendo uniformemente. A veces, la materia se puede atascar en el esparcidor o el esparcidor no puede trabajar correctamente. Si usted ve un problema, detenga el esparcidor. Entonces remueva la materia del esparcidor. Limpie y inspeccione el esparcidor y llenelo de nuevo con materia y trate otra vez.

- Algunos profesionales les gusta hacer la primer pasada alrededor de la orilla exterior del área que esta siendo tratada. Y luego hacen directamentos los pasos adelante y atrás a traves del área. De cualquier manera que usted escoga, asegurese que todas las áreas de césped esten siendo tratadas uniformemente.

Limpieza

Después que usted ha terminado de aplicar la aplicación de abono del césped, usted necesitara limpiar cualquier material que este en los caminos de entrada, acera, calle. Si usted aplica la aplicación de césped correctamente, no debe haber materia en estas áreas. Usted necesitara un soplador de muchila o un soplador de mano para limpiar la materia.

Cuando limpie el área de materia, debe soplar la materia uniformemente. **No** sople la materia en un montón o en un solo área. Al soplar la materia en un monton el área de césped que hace contacto con ella morirá. El área puede también contaminarse de la materia pesada. **Siempre sople la materia uniformemente.** Si hay una materia **pesada** en un área no deseada, no la sople. Use una escoba y barra en un monton, y recojala con una pala y remueva la materia pesada del área del sitio de trabajo.

Esparcidor de Gota

El esparcidor de gota es el segundo tipo de esparcidor utilizado para aplicar materias secas. Es usado para areas muy pequeñas de césped. También puede ser usado para aplicar semilla de césped y otras materias a lo largo de las orillas de un área de césped ya que el esparcidor aplica la materia exacta.

Los esparcidores de gota vienen en diferentes anchuras. La mayoría de los esparcidores de gotas son mas o menos de cuatro pies de ancho. La materia se derramara haca abajo. Por lo tanto, si el esparcidor es de cuatro pies de anchura, la materia sera esparcida a una anchura de cuatro pies.

Antes de usar el esparcidor de gota, necesitara inspeccionarlo de la misma manera que usted inspecciona a un esparcidor rotorio.

- Cerciorese que el esparcidor siempre este completamente limpio.
- Verifique las llantas para cerciorarse que ambas esten llenas con aire. Si las llantas estan bajas de aire, el esparcidor sera dificil de operar.
- Mantenga todas las partes moviles del esparcidor engrasadas.
- Busque por alguna parte dañada o floja en el esparcidor. Si usted encuentra un problema, reparelo antes de usar el esparcidor otra vez.

El esparcidor de gota tendra una palanca de control en la cima del esparcidor, cerca de los asideros. Esta palanca es usada para abrir y cerrar el flujo de materia. El esparcidor de gota tendra tambien una tasa (rate gage) que es usada para ajustar la tasa de materia que esta siendo liberada. La palanca de control de mano y la tasa trabajaran basicamente igual como en un esparcidor rotorio.

Siempre lea la etiqueta del producto para determinar la tasa de aplicación correcta. Ajuste la tasa como sea necesario antes de aplicar alguna materia.

Equipo de Seguridad

Un esparcidor de gota es más seguro que un esparcidor rotorio porque la materia es liberada muy cerca del suelo y no se desviara. Sin embargo, debe aun llevar puestos los pantalones largos, botas, camisa de mangas largas, y guantes. También, lleve puestos los lentes de seguridad y un respirador y una mascarilla de polvo si es recomendado en la etiqueta del producto.

Operando un Esparcidor de Gota

- Antes de operar un esparcidor de gota, inspeccionelo y ajustelo al sitio de tasa recomendado como acabamos de discutir. Pongase el equipo de seguridad y esta listo para trabajar.
- Cerciorese que la palanca de control este cerrada, entonces llene el esparcidor con materia.
- Visualmente inspeccione el área de césped donde usted va aplicar la aplicación. El área debe estar limpia y no debe haber gente, niños, mascotas en el área.
- Planee la mejor manera de empujar el esparcidor sobre las áreas de césped. Entonces opere el esparcidor de gota de la misma manera que el esparcidor rotorio. La unica diferencia es que la materia va solamente a ser esparcida fuera cuatro pies de anchura por cada pasada.

Esparcidor de Mano

Un esparcidor de mano es usado para tratar las área en ciertos lugares del césped. El esparcidor de mano es usado con más frecuencia cuando se trata ciertos lugares (spot seeding). Esparcira la semilla rápidamente y uniformemente. Estos esparcidores son aguantados a la altura de la cintura en frente de su cuerpo. Los esparcidores solamente aguantaran una pequeña cantidad de materia. Algunos esparcidores de mano pueden tener una correa que va alrededor de su cuerpo. La correa ayudara a soportar el peso del esparcidor cuando esta lleno. En el fondo del esparcidor hay un rotor. Hay un asidero que hara que el rotor gire. El asidero esta localizado en un lado del esparcidor. Hay tambien una palanca que comenzara y detendra el flujo de materia del esparcidor y la tasa (rate gage) para ajustar la cantidad de materia que sale.

Antes de utilizar su esparcidor de mano

- Asegurese que este limpio y mantenido.
- Asegurese que este trabajando correctamente.
- Lleve puestos ropas protectiva y equipo de seguridad como sea necesario.
- Ajuste la tasa (rate gage) como sea necesario.
- Inspeccione las áreas que usted esta a punto de tratar. El área debe estar limpia y preparada para la aplicación.

- Ponga una mano en la palanca encender/apagar (on/off) para que usted pueda rápidamente y fácilmente encender o detener la materia de salir del esparcidor.

Cuando usa el esparcidor, siempre gire el asidero a una velocidad constante. Comienze girando el asidero, entonces abre la palanca encender/apagar (on/off). Vigile que la materia salga del esparcidor y caiga sobre la tierra. Camine lentamente alrededor del área que usted quiere cubrir. Cierre la palanca encender/apagar (on/off) lo más pronto cuando haya terminado.

Usar un esparcidor de mano tomara un poco de practica. Una vez que usted ya sabe como operarlo, usted puede rápidamente y profesionalmente tratar las áreas seleccionadas del césped.

Esparcidores de Tanque

Un esparcidor de tanque es un esparcidor grande que es utilizado para aplicar una aplicación de liquido al área de césped o a los arbustos y árboles ornamentales.

Como un profesional, usted debe usar un solo tanque rociador para las aplicaciones de césped y un segundo tanque rociador para los arbustos y árboles ornamentales solamente. Los tanques rociadores de césped son generalmente usados para aplicaciones de liquidos para matar la hierba. Aunque usted limpie el tanque rociador, siempre habra residuos quimicos dejados dentro. Si usted trata arbustos y árboles ornamentales con el mismo tanque rociador con el cual usted aplico liquido para matar la hierba, algo del residuo quimico puede salirle a los arbustos que usted esta tratando. Si un residuo quimico de matar hierba hace contacto con los arbustos o árboles ornamentales, daño grave puede ocurrir. Por lo tanto, es mejor mantener tanques rociadores para aplicaciones de césped solamente y tanques rociadores para arbustos y árboles ornamentales.

Los tanques rociadores son montados en la parte posterior del camion. El tanque que aguanta las materias de liquido variara en tamaño. La mayoria de tanques aguantara entre 100 y 300 galones de materia liquida. Hay algunas marcas en los tanques que indican cuantos galones hay en el tanque. generalmente hay una marca por cada 20 galones. Es muy importante que usted pueda leer facilmente cuantos galones hay en el tanque para que pueda mezclar la materia y agua correctamente.

Todos los tanques rociadores tienen una tapa encima del tanque. Esto es donde usted vierte la materia quimica y agua en el tanque. debe haber un filtro de malla montado debajo de la tapa. El filtro de malla detendra cualquier basura de llegar a dentro del tanque y que se atasque. Debe haber tambien un enlace montado encima del tanque.

Usted conectara una manguera a este enlace para llenar el tanque con agua. Este enlace mantendra un espacio entre la manguera y el tanque. el espacio prevendra que la materia liquida fluya de regreso dentro de la manguera. Este enlace es requerido por la ley en la mayoria de los estados.

Nunca ponga la manguera dentro del tanque. debe haber siempre un espacio entre la manguera y el tanque.

Hay un marco de metal que sostendra el tanque, motor, bomba y manguera. La mayoria de los tanques rociadores tienen el motor y bomba montados en la parte baja del marco. Entonces la manguera del tanque y el riel de manguera son montados arriba del motor y bomba. Hay un boton de empujar, el cual girara el riel de manguera, la manguera debe ser sacada manualmente, pero regresará por un motor electrico. Cuando concluya la manguera, guie la manguera para que termine lo mas cerca posible juntos.

El motor es generalmente un motor de 4 ciclos que utiliza gas regular. Verifique el nivel del aceite de motor en una base diaria. La bomba se presurizara la materia liquida para que pudea ser rociada de la manguera. Cuando usa el tanque rociador, encienda la bomba a una presion baja. Entonces lentamente aumente la presion de la bomba. Los tanques tienen dos filtros. Uno montado debajo de la tapa y el segundo filtro montado entre el tanque y la bomba. Asegurese que estos filtros sean mantenidos limpios.

Inspeccionando y Preparando el Tanque Rociador
Antes de usar su tanque rociador, debe ser inspeccionado.

Es muy importante inspeccionar el tanque rociador en una base diaria. Daño muy grave puede ocurrir si el tanque rociador se rompre y materia liquida se derrama en el sitio de trabajo.

En una base diaria, inspeccione lo siguiente:

- Llene el tanque de gas mientras el motor esta fresco. Verifique el nivel de aceite de motor.

- Verifique el filtro montado entre el tanque y la bomba. Limpielo si tiene suciedad. Para limpiar el filtro, pongase un par de guantes y lentes de seguridad. El tanque debe ser vaciado o debe cerrar las valvulas para detener el liquido de fluir del tanque. Destornille el filtro, entonces traiga el filtro a una llave de manguera y saque la basura del filtro. Antes de instalar el filtro, ponga una capa de grasa en los hilos del tornillo. La grasa prevendra que el sea atascado y sera facil de quitar la proxima vez que usted lo limpie. Cuidadosamente enrosque de regreso el filtro y aprietelo levemente a mano.

- Remueva la tapa y inspeccione el filtro montado debajo de la tapa y limpielo como sea necesario.

- Enlace la manguera montada encima del tanque.

- Llene el tanque con 5 a 10 galones de agua. Entonces encienda el motor. Nunca corra el motor a su velocidad maxima. Ajuste la valvula reguladora para que el motor corra siempre entre ½ y ¾ de velocidad.

- Hay una palanca que se engancha y desengancha con la bomba. Hay tambien otra palanca que ajusta la presion de la bomba. Utilize la bomba y lentamente aumente la presion de la bomba.

Para aplicaciones de césped, la presion de la bomba debe ser entre 50 y 100 psi. Para aplicaciones de arbustos y árboles ornamentales, la presion de bomba debe estar entre 100 y 250 psi.

- Cuando el motor esta corriendo y la bomba esta enganchada, haga una inspeccion visual del tanque rociador entero. Primero mire en el exterior del tanque. Busque por cualquier liqueos de la manguera o bomba. Si hay algun liqueo, no utilize el rociador. El liqueo debe ser reparado antes de que el tanque rociador vuelva a ser usado.

- Cheque la pistola de mano que esta montada en el extremo de la manguera del rociador, cerciorese que opere y que no este liqueando o derramando alguna materia liquida. Despues que el exterior del tanque rociador ha sido inspeccionado, inspeccione dentro del tanque. Cuando mire dentro del tanque, cerciorese que la agitacion este trabajando.

- Todos los tanques rociadores tendran un (jet) o un legado de agitacion mecanica dentro del tanque. Este legado de agitacion mantiene la materia liquida mezclada todo el tiempo. Si la materia liquida no es mezclada, el quimico y el agua pueden separarse. Si el quimico y el agua se separan y son entonces aplicados al césped o arbustos, daño muy grave puede ocurrir. Cerciorese que el legado de agitacion este mezclando la materia liquida. Si el legado

511

de agitacion no esta mezclando, el liquido en el tanque, no utilize el tanque rociador hasta que sea reparado y trabaje apropiadamente.

- Después que el tanque rociador sea inspeccionado y preparado, usted estara listo para mezclar la materia y el agua. Siempre lea y comprenda la etiqueta del producto antes de mezclar.

Calibrando su Esparcidor

Como un profesional usted necesitara calibrar su tanque rociador. Al calibrar su tanque rociador, usted sabra cuanta materia liquida sera aplicada a cierta área. Calibre su esparcidor al comienzo de el año antes de que empieze a usar el tanque rociador en el sitio de trabajo y otra vez cada pocas veces mensualmente.

Siga los siguientes pasos para calibrar su tanque rociador.

- Cerciorese y marque un área en el césped que es 1,000 pies cuadrados. El área necesitara ser 20 pies de ancho y 50 pies de largo (20 x 50 pies= 1,000 pies cuadrados).
- Llene el tanque rociador con exactamente 20 galones de agua.
- Enganche la pistola de mano al rociador de la manguera. La pistola de mano del rociador debe ser la que utilizara en una base diaria.

Si usted cambia la pistola de mano al rociador o la boquilla (nozzle) la calibracion cambiara. Usted debe re-calibrar el rociador si usted le cambia la pistola de mano/boquilla nozzle .

- Encienda el motor y ajuste la valvula del motor a una velocidad que usted usara en una base diaria. Esta velocidad de motor debe estar entre ½ y ¾ de velocidad. Haga una marca en la valvula o motor para que usted pueda fijar la misma velocidad de la valvula siempre que utilize el tanque rociador. O, si usted deja la valvula fija en la velocidad correcta y solo utiliza el switch de encender/apagar y el chute (choke) cuando enciende o apaga el motor.

- Después que la velocidad del motor ha sido fija correctamente, enganche la bomba. Luego ajuste la bomba a la presion que usted estara utilizando en una base diaria. Para aplicaciones de césped entre 50 y 100 psi. Usted necesitara utilizar la misma presion de bomba en una base diaria o la calibracion cambiara.

- Traiga la manguera al área de 1,000 pies cuadrados que usted marco. Entonces aplica el agua al área de césped de la **misma manera** que usted aplicaria una aplicación. Trate de caminar a una velocidad estandar. Aplique el agua hasta que haya hecho un buen contacto con el césped. Cubra el área entera de 1,000 pies cuadrados.

- Después que el área ha sido tratada, apague el motor y la bomba. Entonces determine cuanta agua queda en el tanque. si hay 17 galones aun en el tanque y usted empezo con 20 galones, usted utilizo 3 galones de agua. Ahora usted sabe que usted estara aplicando aproximadamente 3 galones de materia liquida por cada 1,000 pies cuadrados.

- Repita el proceso entero que acabamos de discutir y usted debe terminar con aproximadamente el mismo nùmero (3 galones por 1,000 pies cuadrados).

Este nùmero cambiara si la velocidad del motor es cambiada, si la presion de la bomba es cambiada, si la pistola de mano/boquilla es cambiada o si el aplicador cambia la veliocidad de caminar.

Como un aplicador profesional, debe mantener la misma velocidad del motor, presion de bomba y las tecnicas de aplicación en cada trabajo. Al ser consistente, cada aplicación debe ser aplicada correctamente y evitara daños y resultados pobres.

Equipo de Seguridad

Cuando opere un tanque rociador, debe siempre llevar puestos los pantalones largos, botas de hule, camisa de mangas largas, guantes de caucho resistentes a quimicos y lentes de seguridad. Usted debe llevar tambien puesto un respirador. Lea la etiqueta del producto para saber si un respirador es recomendado.

Hay dos tipos de respiradores que puede usar. El primer tipo es una mascara de hule con dos cartuchos de filtros. Cuando usted respira el aire fluye por medio de los cartuchos del filtro. Hay una valvula en la parte de caucho de la mascara donde usted exhala. Cerciorese que los cartuchos estan marcados para pesticidas y remplazelos como es recomendado por el manufacturador. Utilizando el respirador de caucho con el cartucho correcto es la manera disponible mas segura de protegerse a uste mismo de respirar rocio quimico.

El segundo tipo de mascara es la mascarilla de papel. Una mascarilla de papel es mas facil de llevar puesta, pero no le dara tanta proteccion. **Cerciorese** que la mascara este etiquetada para uso con rocio de pesticidas.

Mezclando

después que haya inspeccionado su tanque rociador, puede mezclar la materia liquida. Lea la etiqueta del producto para determinar cuanta materia debe ser mezclada con cuanta agua. Cerciorese que la tasa de mezclar este 100% correcta. Despues que usted sabe la tasa de mezclar, escribalo en su libreta, entonces le sera facil de localizar en el futuro. Materias diferentes vendran en formas diferentes. La materia viene en liquido, granulado, o polvo.

(Mezclando) Materia Liquida

- Empieze a llenar el tanque con agua.
- Pongase su ropas y equipo de seguridad. Siempre lleve puestos los lentes y el respirador cuando mezcla.
- Cuidadosamente ponga la cantidad correcta de materia liquida dentro de la taza de medida.

Usted debe tener una taza separada para (weed killer) matar hierba y una taza separada para insecticidas y el control de enfermedad. Etiquete cada taza medidora antes de usarlas.

- No debe haber gente o distracciones alrededor cuando usted este mezclando. Concentrece en lo que esta haciendo y no haga un error.

- Cuidadosamente traiga la taza al tanque y vaciela dentro del tanque. Rinsee la taza con agua que fluye dentro del tanque. Rinsee la taza varias veces.

- Guarde la materia liquida y la tasa medidora.

- Encienda el motor y bomba para que la mezcla del tanque empieze a ser agitada. Entonces continue llenando el tanque hasta que el agua alcanze la cantidad correta de galones necesarios.

- Remueva la manguera, enrosque la tapa y apague la bomba y el motor.

(Mezclando) Materia Granulado o Polvo

Un granulado o polvo es una materia seca que es mezclada con agua. Usted necesitara seguir las siguientes instrucciones de mezclar. Sin embargo, habra un paso adicional. Antes de vaciar la materia dentro del tanque, debe ser **pre-mezclada**. La materia granulada y polvo no se mezclan facilmente con el agua en su tanque. Si la materia no se mezcla correctamente, resultados pobres o daños graves pueden ocurrir. Al pre-mezclar la materia, sera mas facil de mezclar con el agua en su tanque. Para pre-mezclar la materia use un balde de 5-galones y llenelo ½ con agua. Entonces cuidadosamente ponga la materia medida dentro del balde. Mezcle la materia seca con el agua. Para mezclar la materia y agua, use un palo pequeño. La mejor manera de mezclar es de usar un (power drill and a paint mixing attachment). Esto rápidamente, facilmente mezclara la materia seca con el agua.

Después que la materia es mezclada, cuidadosamente vaciela dentro del tanque y siga las instrucciones que acabamos de discutir.

Conduciendo con un Tanque Lleno

Cuando llegue al sitio de trabajo, su tanque rociador debe ser inspeccionado y preparado como acabamos de discutir.

Para hacer una aplicacion con un tanque rociador, usted debe apropiadamente ser entrenado y debe ser licensiado como aplicador u operador de césped.

Siga estos pasos cuando haga una aplicación con su tanque rociador.

- Inspeccione visualmente el área que usted tratara. Si usted esta rociando cerca de una casa o edificio, cerciorese que todas las ventanas esten cerradas.
- Ponga una bandera de notificacion en el suelo en la entrada de la propiedad. Verifique las regulaciones del estado para asegurarse que instale las banderas de notificacion correctamente.

Dependiendo de las regulaciones de su estado, usted debe dejar saber al dueño de la propiedad que usted va hacer una aplicación en su propiedad. Esto puede ser hecho por medio de una carta unos pocos dias antes que usted llegue al sitio de trabajo. Usted puede tambien notificarle a la gente cuando llegue al sitio de trabajo, antes de rociar. En algunos estados, los vecinos de la propiedad que usted tratara tendran que ser notificados. Cerciorese que este advertido de todas las reglas de notificacion y que las siga apropiadamente.

- Después que el área ha sido inspeccionada visualmente y las notificaciones apropiadas han sido dadas, usted debe ponerse su equipo de seguridad.
- Encienda y fije el motor y bomba.
- Verifique su tanque para ver cuantos galones hay en el tanque.
- Hale la manguera del rociador lo mas lejos del área de la propiedad. Cuando hale la manguera, jamas la hale por la pistola del rociador. **Solamente la agarre/sostiene y hale la mangura.**
- Visualise y verifique el área que usted va a tratar. Planee usar el mejor modelo de rociar.
- Para las áreas de césped, usted debe caminar de atrás hacia delante de la misma manera que usted camina con el esparcidor. Aguante una pistola en una mano y sostenga la manguera en la otra mano. Recuerde de jamas halar la manguera por la pistola. Cuando este caminando a traves del área del césped, usted debe ser capaz de tratar un area de 6 pies de ancho. Al extender su brazo y la pistola de su lado derecho a su lado izquierdo. Usted debe tratar 3 pies en cada lado de usted por un total de 6 pies. Aguante la pistola a la altura de su cintura.

- La mayoria de materias requeriran que usted rocie el césped o hierbas hasta que las plantas esten completamente cubiertas. Tengo mucho cuidado para no tratar un area dos veces o si no usted causara daños al césped. Mantenga un modelo correcto de caminar y observe a lo que usted esta rociando para evitar este error.

- Cuando este (spot treating) tratando, ciertos lugares delcésped, utilize el mismo metodo de aplicación, excepto que busque por las hierbas en el césped y solamente las trata a ellas. Si hay demasiadas hierba pequeña en un área del césped, trate el área entera.

- Sea cuidadoso cuando rocia el mata hierba alrededor de las flores o plantas. Usted puede levemente bajar la altura de la pistola para que este cerca del suelo. Cuando baje la pistola cerca del suelo, sea cuidadoso para no apriclar demasiada materia a esta área.

- Si hay viento soplando, no trate las áreas de césped que estan cerca de las flores y plantas. En un dia ventoso, el rocio se puede desviar muy facilmente y causar daños graves con todo lo que haga contacto. En un dia ventoso, es mejor no rociar para nada.

- Después que haya terminado la aplicación de césped apaga la bomba y el motor. Rolee la manguera lo mas uniformemente posible. Remueva su equipo de seguridad y mire cuantos galones han quedado en el tanque. Entonces determine cuantos galones fueron utilizados en la propiedad y guarde esta informacion en su libreta de archivo de aplicaciones.

Verifique los requerimientos de su estado para archivar la información de aplicación.

Rociador de Muchila

Este tipo de rociador trabaja bien y es muy comunmente utilizados. El rociador de muchila generalmente aguanta tres galones de mezcla. Algo mas pequeño no es recomendado ya que usted tendra que detenerse a mezclar el quimico y agua muy a menudo. El rociador de muchila tiene dos cinturones y es llevado en sus hombros y espalda. Cuando abra y cierra la tapa, tenga cuidado de asegurarse que el caucho sello/gasket en la tapa este correctamente en su lugar. Apriete y asegure la tapa, pero no la sobre apriete o si no rompera el sello y la tapa liqueara. Cuando la tapa empieza a liquear, el quimico se llegara a sus ropas, cuello y espalda.

Puede haber un filtro debajo de la tapa para cachar alguna basura antes de que llegue al tanque. utilize este filtro y no lo remueva. El filtro a veces hace mas dificil de poner la tapa correctamente y por eso algunas personas lo remueven. **No remueva el filtro!** Usted solo causara mas problemas. En el fondo del tanque esta la bomba y un brazo de bomba para darle una presion de rocio correcto. Entonces hay una manguera que conecta la bomba a la pistola del rociador. Puede haber tambien otro filtro en la pistola o antes de la boquilla del rociador. Mientras utiliza este rociador, usted debe usar un brazo para controlar la bomba y darle la presion correcta de rocio y usted debe usar su otro brazo para sostener la pistola del rociador.

Antes de ir al sitio de trabajo, cerciorese que todos los filtros esten limpios. Tambien cerciorese que todas las conecciones de mangueras esten apretadas y aseguradas. Entonces chequee para cerciorarse que la punta del rocio este limpia y rocie correctamente. Los filtros estan en lugar para detener cualquier basua de atascarse en la punta del rociador. No hay nada peor que mezclar el quimico y llegar al sitio de trabajo y tener la punta atascasda cada pocos minutos. Siempre limpie y chequee el rociador antes de utilizarlo.

Rociador de Mano

El rociador de mano es basicamente lo mismo que el de muchila excepto que hay una bomba y asidero encima del rociador. Usted debe detenerse de trabajar y poner el rociador abajo en el suelo cada vez que lo bombea. Con el de muchila lo puede bombiar y rociar a la misma vez. El rociador de mano es mas compacto y tomara menos espacio en su camion o traila.

TIPOS DE APLICACIONES DE CUIDADO DEL CÉSPED
(CAPÍTULO 20)

Siempre lea y comprenda cada etiqueta del producto antes de hacer una aplicacion. Usted debe apropiadamente ser entrenado y licensiado antes de aplicar la mayoria de los productos listados en este capitulo. Comprenda todos los requerimientos del estado antes de hacer alguna aplicación. Siempre lleve puestos las ropas y equipos de seguridad correctas. Determine el total de los pies cuadrados de cada área de césped antes de que haga alguna aplicación. Mantenga notas y archivos de cada área de césped que usted mantiene. Para determinar el total de los pies cuadrados de una propiedad, mida la longuitud y anchura del frente, atrás y lados. Entonces separadamente calcule cada area y sume el total. Ver ejemplo:

Propiedad del Frente	**100 pies x 50 pies=**	**5000 pies cuadrados**
Propiedad de Atrás	**100 pies x 25 pies=**	**2500 pies cuadrados**
Lado Derecho	**55 pies x 25 pies=**	**1375 pies cuadrados**
Lado Izquierdo	**70 pies x 10 pies=**	**700 pies cuadrados**
Total:		**9575 pies cuadrados**

Abono (fertilizer)

El abono es el más usado comunmente en las aplicaciones de césped. El abono provee nutrientes al césped. Un césped no puede crecer saludablemente sin los nutrientes correctos. Hay tres nutrientes principales en todos los abonos; nitrogeno, fosforo (phosphorus), y postasio.

- Nitrogeno—El nitrogeno ayuda al césped a crecer y hace que el césped se vuelva de color verde. El nitrogeno promueve el crecimiento del césped pero no ayuda al sistema de raiz a crecer. Si usted aplica demasiado nitrogeno, el césped crecera muy rapido. Esto es insalubre para el césped. Tambien, si el nitrogeno es aplicado demasiado pesado, el área del césped puede dañarse o morir.

- Fósforo (Phosphorus)—El fósforo ayuda al crecimiento de un fuerte sistema de raiz del césped. Un fertilizador con mucho fósforo es aplicado cuando se esta sembrando o sodding ya que esto anima al crecimiento de la raiz. Fósforo tambien ayuda a reducir algunas enfermedades del césped.

- Potasio—El potasio es necesario para mantener el césped saludable. Sin la cantidad correcta de potasio, un césped llegara a ser insalubre y mas propenso a la enfermedad.

Un simbolo es utilizado para describir estos tres principales nutrientes. El nitrogeno es simplemente llamado (N), Phosphorus (P), y Potasio (K). Las plantas utilizan estos tres nutrientes en grandes cantidades. Muchos abonos tienen nutrientes aparte de NPK. Estos nutrientes secundarios son llamados micronutrientes. Los micronutrientes son tambien necesarios para mantener un césped saludable y fuerte pero no son usados tan a menudo como NPK.

Algunos micronutrientes comunmente usados son el hierro y el mangnesio.

El abono puede venir en una variedad de diferentes nutrientes. Los nutrientes estan listados en la etiqueta del producto, por ejemplo: 24-5-11. estos nùmeros indican la cantidad de (N) Nitrogeno, el segundo nùmero indica la cantidad de (P) Fósforo (Phosphorus) y el tercer nùmero indica la cantidad de (K) Potasio.

La etiqueta del producto tambien indica si hay algun micronutriente en el producto y si algun nutriente es liberado lentamente. Muchos productos de abono tienen algunos nutrientes que son de **liberacion lenta**. Esto significa que los nutrientes son gradualmente liberados en la tierra. Cuando los nutrientes NPK son liberados a la tierra todos juntos, hay oportunidad de dañar el césped si el abono es aplicado demasiado pesado. Un producto de liberacion lenta durara mas tiempo y no debe dañar el césped cuando es aplicado correctamente.

Hay dos tipos diferentes de abonos; sintetico y organico.

- El abono sintetico es mas comunmente utilizado. Un abono sintetico es hecho de quimico hecho por hombre. Un césped respondera rápidamente a este tipo de abono porque es un producto concentrado. Sin embargo, ningun error puede ser hecho cuando se aplica un abono sintetico o si no daños pueden ocurrirle al césped. Utilize un abono sintetico de liberacion lenta para mejores resultados.

- Los abonos organicos son todos naturales, son hechos de animales y plantas. Liberan los nutrientes a la tierra lentamente. Usted no observara una respuesta rápida del césped despues de aplicar un abono organico. Un abono organico gradualmente aumentara la salud del césped y de la tierra. El abono organico es mas seguro de aplicar pero es generalmente ma dificil de aplicar y mas costos que el abono sintetico.

El abono es aplicado en forma granulado o liquida. Los productos granulado secos generalmente vienen en bolsas y son aplicada con un esparcidor. Siempre lea la etiqueta para encontrar la tasa de recomendación para su aplicación. Entonces ajuste la configuracion de su esparcidor como sea necesario. Muchos productos de abonos granulados son de forma de liberacion lenta. La mayoria de césped requerira aproximadamente cuatro aplicaciones de abonos durante el año.

Cuando aplica una materia granulada con un esparcidor, debe llevar puesto botas, pantalones largos, camisa de mangas largas, guantes, lentes de seguridad. El abono no es un quimico peligroso por lo tanto un respirador no es necesario. Sin embargo, una marcara de polvo puede ser llevada puesta si es necesaria.

Los abonos de liquido generalmente vienen en una forma de polvo seco y debe ser mezclado con agua. Abono liquido no son generalmente de liberacion lenta tendran que ser aplicados mas a menudo que los productos granulados. El abono liquido necesita ser mezclado correctamente y aplicado con un tanque rociador.

Cuando aplica una materia granulada con un esparcidor, debe llevar puesto botas, pantalones largos, camisa de mangas largas, guantes, lentes de seguridad. Un respirador puede ser puesto para prevenir respirar el rocio del rociador.

Control Pre-inesperado de Garranchuelo
Pre-emergent Crabgrass Control

El control pre-inesperado de garranchuelo (pre-emergent crabgrass) previene que los garranchuelo (crabgrass) crezcan. Una vez que el garranchuelo (crabgrass) se establese, es dificil de matar. Por lo tanto es mas facil detener el crecimientos de las semillas de garranchuelo (crabgrass). Una aplicación de control pre-inesperado de garranchuelo creara una capa en la superficie de la tierra.

El área de césped debe ser limpiada antes de hacer una aplicación. El césped no debe ser molestado despues de la aplicación. El área puede ser cortado con un cortacésped, pero no debe ser rastrillado, limpiado, (de-thatched), o sembrado después de la aplicación. La semilla de césped no crecera en el césped que ha sido tratado con control pre-inesperado de garranchuelo (crabgrass) hasta que el quimico no este más en la tierra. Si la aplicación fue aplicada en la primavera, la siembra debe ser hecha en el otoño.

El control pre-inesperado de garranchuelo (pre-emergent crabgrass) debe ser aplicado en la primavera temprana. La aplicación debe durar

526

hasta el verano. Sin embargo, si el césped y la superficie de la tierra son molestados despues de la aplicación, resultados pobres ocurriran. Tambien, si hay bastante lluvia durante la primavera, el control de quimico no durara por mucho tiempo. Si el césped que esta tratando tiene problema de garranchuelos (crabgrass), dos aplicaciones pueden ser aplicadas. Verifique la etiqueta del producto para mas informacion en la tasa de aplicación y tratamientos.

La mayoria de garranchuelos pre-inesperado (pre-emergent crabgras) son granulados y son aplicadas con un esparcidor. Generalmente una combinacion de productos es utilizados tal como un abono con garranchuelos pre-inesperado (pre-emergent crabgrass). Cuando aplica una aplicación granulado, es muy importante hacer que las orillas del cesped recivan la cantidad correcta del producto. A los garranchuelos (crabgrass) les gusta crecer cerca de las orillas de un cesped y en áreas donde el cesped no es tan grueso.

El garranchuelo (Crabgrass) crecera mejor en una locacion soleada. El area de césped debe ser limpiada de cualquier basura antes de que haga una aplicación. Cuando haga una aplicación liquida, el césped debe ser preparada de la misma manera.

Los productos pre-emergent de garranchuelos (crabgrass) tienen un color amarillo. Este color tiñera la madera o superficies rocosas. Sople cualquier materia granulada cuando haya terminado con su aplicación. Las aplicaciones liquidas deben ser hechas cuidadosamente, no debe hacer contacto con ninguna madera o superficie rocosas.

Control de Hierba/Monte (Post-emergent)

Una aplicacion de control de hierba post-emergent matara cualquier hierba que este obviamente creciendo en un césped. Post-emergent significa que las hierbas han sido ya germinadas y crecidas. Este tipo de control de hierba no matara cualquier semilla de hierba. Una aplicación de control post-emergent liquida es la manera mas popular de matar la hierba en las areas de cesped. Generalmente las hierbas son tratadas en ciertos lugares seleccionados.

Una aplicación post-emergent es aplicada a las hojas de las hierbas existentes. El control de hierba debe hacer buen contacto con las hojas de la hierba. Sin embargo, no aplique demasiado materia o si no tambien matara al area de césped alrededor de la hirbas. Cuando la materia de control se aplica correctamente, la hierba empezara a absorver la materia por medio de las hojas. Entonces la materia fluira a traves de la hierba entera y morira. La hierba debe estar **activa y creciendo** si no absorbera la materia y no morira. Por eso, la mejor manera de aplicar es cuando las hierbas crecen rapidamente. A mediados de primavera es el mejor tiempo para hacer una aplicación del control de hierba. Y la segunda mejor vez es temprano en el otoño. **El control de hierba debe ser aplicada cuando la temperatura se hace calido (85 grados) o cuando la tierra esta muy seca.**

528

Cuando la temperatura esta muy calida, el control de hierba puede matar el area de césped alrededor de la hierba que esta tratando. El segundo problema es cuando se hace muy calido, la mayoria de las hierbas no creceran rápidamente. Si la hierbas no crecen rapidamente, la materia no sera absorbida por medio de las hierbas y no moriran. Las condiciones de tierra seca son otro problema. Si la tierra es muy seca, la mayoria de hierbas no creceran y los resultados de control de hierba seran pobres. Tambien el césped alrededor de las hierbas estara bajo condiciones de tencion si la tierra es seca. Por eso el césped puede morir muy facilmente si le aplica control de hierba al area. Para mejores resultados, el césped y hierbas deben ser permitido crecer antes de su aplicación. Evite hacer una aplicación cuando el césped acaba de ser cortado. Si las hierbas han sido cortadas de un cortaésped, habra menos superficie de hoja en la hierba. Cuando hay menos superficie de hoja en la hierba, la aplicación no trabajara bien.

Appliqué el control de hierba liquida hasta que la hierba entera ha sido cubierta, entonces dentengase inmediatamente. Si usted aplica demasiado liquido de control de hierba, puede dañar o matar el area de césped alrededor de la hierba. Sin embargo, si no aplica suficiente, la hierba no morira.

Permanezca lejos de las flores, plantas o raizes de las plantas. No aplique el liquido de control de hierbas en dias ventosos. Después de su aplicación, todas la gente y mascotas deben permanezer fuera del área. La mayoria de productos requerira que la aplicación sea secada y se quede en las hierbas por unas cuantas horas antes de que trabaje. Por eso, no aplique el control de hierbas si se espera lluvia. Siempre lea la etiqueta del producto para instrucciones, recomendaciones y precauciones de seguridad antes de utilizarlos.

Antes de hacer una aplicación, planee un modelo de caminar en el césped. Entonces sea muy cuidadoso y no tratar un área dos veces o daño grave puede ocurrir. En los dias calidos, las aceras y caminos de entrada se calentaran. Debe ser muy cuidadoso cuando trata hierbas alrededor de estas áreas ya que la tierra puede estar muy calida y seca. Si usted aplica control de hierba a las áreas que estan muy calidas y secas, el césped puede morir.

Los productos granulados son utilizados para matar hierbas. Sin embargo, son muy dificil de usar. Para que un producto granulado haga contacto con las hirbas, las hierbas deben ser mojadas. Si las hierbas no estan mojadas, el producto no se apegara con la hierba y resultados pobres ocurriran. El césped y hierbas no deben ser cortados antes de una aplicación y usted debe permanezer fuera de esa área por un periodo mas largo de tiempo. Evite hacer contacto con flores, plantas, o sistema de raices.

La mayoria de productos, liquida o granulado tomaran de 7 a 14 dias para matar completamente la hierba. Algunas hierbas dificiles de matar pueden necesitar una segunda aplicación para detener completamente el problema.

Control de Hierba/Monte pre-inesperado (pre-emergent)

Una aplicación de control de hierba pre-inesperado (pre-emergent) matara las semillas de hierbas antes de que puedan germinar y crecer. Este tipo de aplicación de control de hierba no es usado muy a menudo para controlar hierbas en un area de césped. La aplicación es muy cara y debe tratar el césped entero para que sea efectivo. Este tipo de aplicación es usado mas a menudo en las camas del paisaje.

El mejor tiempo para aplicar un control de hierba pre-inesperada (pre-emergent) es en la primavera temprana. La aplicación durara por unos cuantos meses y puede ser aplicada durante otras veces durante el año entero. El área de césped debe ser limpiada antes de que la materia sea aplicada y el césped no debe ser molestada despues del tratamiento.

La aplicación trabaja igual que un control pre-emergent de crabgrass excepto que la materia quimica controlara las hierbas en su lugar. Un producto granulado es utilizado mas a menudo, sin embargo un producto liquido esta tambien disponible.

Control de Insectos de Superficie

El control de insectos de superficie es utilizado para matar insectos que se alimentan de un césped. Cuando un insecto se alimenta de un césped, daños pueden ocurrir. Si el problema no se detiene rapidamente habra daños permanentes al césped. Los insectos de superficie son insectos que se alimentan de la parte de cima de una planta de césped, no se alimentan del sistema de raiz. Estos insectos pueden viajar de un césped a otro. Cuando encuentran un area de césped que les gusta, la haran su hogar. Entonces se alimentaran del césped y aumentaran los miembros de su familia.

Estos insectos generalmente empiezan a crear un daño al césped cuando la temperatura se pone calida en la primavera y en verano temprano. Cuando hay una o dos semana de termperaturas de mas de 75 grados, estos insectos llegaran a ser activos. Pueden hacer daños a traves de todo el año hasta que las temperaturas se queden bajo 75 grados.

La mayoria de los insectos de superficie prefieren un area de césped soleada. Los césped que tienen una capa gruesa de paja (thatch) obtendran mas insectos mas a menudo. La capa de paja (thatch) es la capa viejas decésped entre la cima del cesped y tierra. Los insetos les gusta hacer su casa en una capa gruesa de paja (thatch). Los insectos de superficie tambien prefieren un cesped que esta bien-abonado o sobre abonado. Sobre-abonando crea mucho nuevo suave de crecimiento, los insectos prefieren un cesped con muchos nuevo crecimiento tierno.

Los insectos de superficie discoloran las areas de césped cuando se estan alimentando. Despues de que el césped se discolara, se volvera marron y morira. Si usted ve algun area discolorada en el césped, inspeccionelo mas cerca para determinar si hay un problema de insectos.

Muchas veces, los insectos de superficie seran muy pequeños para que ojo humano los vean. Utilize una lupa, un libro de identificacion de insectos y piense acerca de las condiciones del lugar para determinar el problema. Si usted esta inseguro, tome un ejemplo del césped discolarado y traigalo al centro de jardin local o colegio. Cuando tome ejemplos, remueva parcialmente la area discolorada y no las areas del cesped que estan completamente marrones y muertas. Remueva la planta completa incluyendo las raices. Ponga el ejemplo en un contenedor o envuelvalo en un papel. Entonces chequeelo lo mas rapidamente posible.

Hay muchos tipos diferentes de productos para el control de insectos. Debe identificar el tipo de insecto antes de escoger un producto de control. Entonces lea la etiqueta del producto para cerciorarse que matara los insectos que causan el problema. Los dos productos granulado y liquido trabajan bien. Cuando aplique una materia liquida, matara los insectos inmediatamente. Cuando aplica una materia granulada, la aplicación no trabajara hasta que sea regado con agua correctamente.

Una vez que la materia es liberada al césped, matara cualquier insectos en la área. Entonces permanecera efectiva y protejera el césped por un periodo de tiempo. Los diferentes productos seran efectivos por diferentes periodos de tiempo. Algunos productos duran solo unos pocos dias mientras que otros se quedaran efectivos por semanas.

Control de Insectos de Tierra

Los insectos de tierra viven en la tierra y se alimentan del sistema de raiz de un césped. El insecto de tierra mas comun se llama gusano (grub). El gusano (grubs) se alimentan del sistema de raices del césped, y si son dejados sin tratar, pueden causar daños graves. La mayoria de daños es hecha en el verano tarde y en principio del otoño. Sin embargo, si hay una populacion grande de gusanos (grubs) en la tierra, daños pueden ser hechos en la primavera.

Los gusanos (grubs) prefieren las áreas de césped soleadas. Sin embargo, los gusanos viviran en cualquier césped. Usted puede obtener un problema de gusano (grub) si el césped esta altamente mantenido o no esta mantenido para nada. Para localisar un problema de gusano, busque por las áreas discoloradas de césped durante el **verano tarde y el otoño temprano**. Si hay muchos pajaros escarvando en el césped, es muy probable que haya un problema de gusano. Los pajaros les gusta comer gusanos (grubs). Agarre un área de césped discolorada y si el césped se levanta facilmente, usted tiene gusano. El gusano se comen todas las raices, entonces la cima del césped se levantara del suelo muy facilmente. Si usted levanta el césped y mira a la tierra, usted puede ser capaz de encontrar gusanos. Busque por gusanos pequeños blancos que son de una pulgada de largo. Estan usualmente en la tierra.

Hay dos tipos diferentes de control de gusanos y de otros insectos de tierra, pre-emergent o pos-emergent.

534

Control de Gusano (Grub Pre-emergent)

El control pre-inesperado (pre-emergent) es generalmente aplicado cuando usted sabe que hubo un problema de gusano durante el año previo o un area de césped altamente mantenida. Esta aplicación es hecha en la primavera o en el verano temprano. La materia sera liberada dentro la tierra y matara Los qusanos antes que puedan causar daños al césped. Esta aplicación es generalmente un tratamiento granulado. Al aplicar el control pre-inesperado (pre-emergent), usted sabe que el área de césped esta segura y ningun daño le ocurrira.

Control de Gusano (Grub Post-emergent)

El cotrol (post-emergent) es aplicado directamente al problema activo. Algunos daños de césped son generalmente hechos antes de hacer una aplicación. La mayoria de productos seran solamente efectivos por unos dias, por eso, la aplicación no debe ser aplicada hasta que usted visualize el problema.

Hay unos productos liquidos y granulados disponibles, sin embargo, los productos granulados son más comunmente utilizados. Cualquier materia granulado debe ser regado con agua inmediatamente despues de la aplicación o si no sera efectiva. Si hay un problema de gusano grande o si hay una capa de paja (thatch) pesada, una segunda aplicación puede ser necesaria.

Control de Garranchuelos (Crabgrass Post-emergent)

El control de garranchuelos (Crabgrass post-emergent) es utilizado para matar cualquier garranchuelo (crabgrass) que ha empezado a establecerse en un área de césped. Esta aplicación sera un tratamiento de ciertos lugares áreas selectas. La aplicación debe ser aplicada cuando el garranchuelo (crabgrass) esta aun tierno. Una vez que el garranchuelo (crabgrass) esta maduro, sera casi imposible de matar y la aplicación no se debe hacer.

Una aplicacion de garranchuelo pre-inesperado (crabgrass pre-emergent) es facil de aplicar y controlara el garranchuelo (crabgrass) mejor que la aplicacion post-emergent. Para controlar un problema de garranchuelo (crabgrass), siempre aplique una aplicación de pre-inesperado (pre-emergent) en la primavera temprana.

Si el césped tiene daños graves de garranchuelos (crabgrass) o si la aplicación pre-inesperada (pre-emergent) fue aplicada incorrectamente, algunos garranchuelos (crabgrass) pueden empezar a crecer durante el verano temprano. También, si hay mucha lluvia durante la primavera, la aplicación pre-inesperada (pre-emergent) puede que se lave de la tierra muy temprano, entonces el garranchuelo (crabgrass) puede ser capaz de crecer.si usted ve algunos garranchuelos (crabgrass) emperzando a crecer en un césped en el verano temprano, una aplicación de post-emergent debe ser aplicada inmediatamente. Si el garranchuelo (crabgrass) fue encontrado en el

536

verano cuando estaba ya maduro, sera mejor esperar hasta el proximo año para controlar el problema.

Cuando el garranchuelo (crabgrass) esta tierno y creciendo activamente, aplica un rocio de post-emergent. El control de garranchuelo (crabgrass) post-emergent es una aplicación liquida. Es generalmente mezclada en una pequeña cantidad y rociada de un rociador de muchila. El garranchuelo (crabgrass) que usted esta rociando debe estar **creciendo activamente** y la planta de garranchuelo (crabgrass) no debe ser cortada antes de su aplicación. El garranchuelo (crabgrass) debe ser dejado lo más largo posible para que el rocio pueda hacer un buen contacto con ello.

La mayoria de los productos necesitaran permanecer en el garranchuelo (crabgrass) por lo menos 24 horas para ser efectivos. Una segunda aplicación es generalmente necesitada para completamente matar el garranchuelo (crabgrass). Regrese en 7 a 14 dias para hacer una segunda aplicación. Siempre lea las instrucciones de la etiqueta del producto antes de hacer alguna aplicación.

Cuando hace una aplicación, usted rociara en partes cada planta de garranchuelo (crabgrass). Aplica el rocio hasta que el garranchuelo (crabgrass) este completamente cubierto, entonces detengase inmediatamente. El control de garranchuelo (crabgrass) matara el área de césped si es aplicado demasiado pesado. Evite rociar si la tierra esta muy seca y si el césped alrededor del garranchuelo (crabgrasss) esta bajo tension. El césped debe estar saludable y creciendo activamente o la aplicación no debe ser hecha. Rociar a un área de césped bajo tension matará el césped.

El control post-emergent no trabajara o causara mas daños que bien si no es aplicado correctamente. Si las condiciones no estan buenas, no haga la aplicación. Este producto es también muy caro, por eso, si tiene un área grande infectada con garranchuelo (crabgrass), sera mejor esperar hasta la proxima primavera cuando puede aplicar una aplicación pre-inesperaeda (pre-emergent).

Si todas las condiciones estan bien y si la aplicación es hecha correctamente, el garranchuelo (crabgrass) puede ser detenido con un rocio de post-emergent antes de que cresca a una hierba grande y fea. Si no puede hacer la aplicación, mantenga el césped cortado lo más alto posible. Esto hara más dificil para que el garranchuelo (crabgrass) pueda crecer. El garranchuelo (crabgrass) se volvera de color marron y morira en el invierno frio (frost). Entonces cerciorese de hacer una aplicación pre-inesperarda (pre-emergent) la proxima primavera.

Control de Hierbas Silvestre (Wild Grass Control)

La hierba silvestre son tipos de hierba no deseadas que infectan y se esparce por todo el área de césped. Las hierbas silvestre son agresivas y se esparcen rapidamente por medio del área de césped si son dejadas sin tratar. El control de garranchuelo (crabgrass) pre-inesperado (pre-emergent) o control de hierba no matara la mayoria de los tipos de hierba silvestre.

Un producto especial puede ser usado para tratar la mayoria de hierbas silvestre. El producto de control de hierbas silvestres es un rocio post-emergent. Es muy similar al control de garranchuelo (crabgrass) post-emergent. Las condiciones deben ser las correctas y el producto debe ser aplicado correctamente o no trabajará. El control de hierba silvestre es aplicado de un rociador de muchila.

Siga estas instrucciones cuando hace una aplicación para el control de hierba silvestres.

- Trate por partes la hierba silvestre antes de esparcirla a las áreas grandes. Tratar de controlar áreas grandes de hierbas silvestre en un césped sera muy caro y dificil.

- Lea la etiqueta del producto para encontrar instrucciones generales y si el producto mataria la hierba silvestre que rociara. Identifique las hierbas silvestre que usted esta tratando de matar y asegurese que esta usando el producto correcto.

- Trate las hierbas silvestre cuando estan tierna y creciendo activamente. Si las hierbas silvestre estan maduras, dos tratamientos puede ser necesarios. No haga una aplicación durante el tiempo que este caliente o seco.

- No corte las hierbas silvestre con un cortacésped. La hierba silvestre debe ser lo mas grande posible para que el rocio haga un buen contacto con ello. Cuando el rocio hace buen contacto con la hierba silvestre, sera más efectivo. Si la hierba silvestre ha sido cortada con un cortacésped, la aplicación no trabajara.

- Haga una aplicación con un rociador de espalda o un rociador de mano. La mayoria de los productos necesitan ser mezclados antes de cada trabajo y la mezcla debe ser terminada durante el dia.

- Aplique el rocio hasta que la hierba silvestre este completamente cubierta, entonces detengase inmediatamente. Si usted sobre aplica, el producto matara el césped alrededor de la hierba silvestre.

- Despues que la aplicación ha sido hecha, no corte o riegue con agua las hierbas silvestre que han sido tratadas por lo menos 24 horas.

Algunas hierbas silvestres no pueden ser matadas con los productos de control de hierba silvestre. Si usted identifica hierba silvestre y si no hay un producto de control de hierbas silvestre disponible, usted debe usar un producto de control no-seleccionado.

No-seleccionado significa que matara todo incluyendo el césped. Un no-seleccionado es mucho menos caro que el control de hierbas silvestres. Cuando use un producto de control no-seleccionado, usted tendra que re-sembrar las areas que ha tratado. Por eso, es mejor hacer una aplicación en el verano tarde y regresar en el otoño temprano para re-sembrar las áreas que usted trato.

Cuando rocia las hierbas silvestres en el área de césped con un producto no-seleccionado, debe ser muy cuidadoso. Aguante la punta del rociador cerca del suelo, utilize la presion de la bomba, y jamas haga una aplicación durante un tiempo ventoso.

Algunas veces removiendo las hierbas silvestres manualmente trabaja mejor. Si las hierbas silvestres no tienen un sistema de raiz profundo, remuevalas con un pico. Entones puede re-sembrar el mismo dia. Al remover manualmente las hierbas silvestres, no habra ninguna parte fea de color marron en el césped de un rocio quimico.

Control de Enfermedad

Hay muchos tipos diferentes de enfermedad. La enfermedad puede ocurrir y causar daños al área de césped durante cualquier tiempo del año. Sin embargo, la mayoria de enfermedades de césped se activan durante la primavera y el verano. Las condiciones del tiempo son muy lluviosas y mojadas, o cuando esta humedo, la enfermedad aumentara. También si un sistema de regadera esta regando con agua el césped muy a menudo o a la hora equivocada del dia, una enfermedad de césped se puede volver peor. Si el área de césped es saludable, puede soportar la enfermedad. Un césped saludable puede tambien repararse el mismo despues que la enfermedad ha sido detenida. Un césped insalubre obtendra enfermedad más facilmente, y no podra repararse el mismo despues que la enfermedad se detenga.

Las aplicaciones de control de enfermedad son muy caras y deben ser aplicadas muchas veces para prevenir o detener una enfermedad de césped. Es mejor siempre tratar de prevenir una enfermedad de césped antes de que suceda. Tal como un profesional del cuidado del césped, usted debe saber como ayudar a reducir y prevenir enfermedades antes de que sucedan. Entonces si una enfermedad de césped siempre ocurre, requerira una aplicación con menos control quimico.

Para ayudar a prevenir problemas de enfermedades de césped, siga estas instrucciones.
Mantenga el césped saludable al abonarlo en una base regular durante el año.

- Provea al césped un examen de tierra para determinar si hay deficiencias en la tierra. Entonces corrije cualquier deficiencia de tierra como sea necesario.
- Verifique el nivel de tierra pH y entoces hace una aplicación de césped para correjir y mantener el nivel de tierra pH.
- Remueva cualquier paja pesada del césped. La enfermedad vive en la capa de paja y se hara dificil de controlar a menos que la capa de paja pesada sea removida.
- Corte el césped en una base regular. Mantenga el césped cortado alto; no lo corte muy bajo. Cuando el césped es cortado muy bajo, obtendra mas facilmente enfermedades.
- Cerciorese que las cuchillas de cortar esten limpias y siempre afiladas. Las hojas sin filo romperan el césped en lugar de cortarlo. Cuando el césped ha sido cortado con una cuchilla sin filo, la enfermedad puede infectar el césped facilmente.
- Si el césped tiene alguna enfermedad, coleccione los recortes de hierba cuando corte el césped.

- Cuando haya terminado de cortar un césped con enfermedad, limpie debajo de la plataforma del cortacésped antes de que lo utilize para cortar otra vez, limpie debajo de la plataforma del cortacésped, luego rocielo con una mezcla 50/50 de clorox y agua.

- Si el césped tiene un sistema de regaedera, cerciorese que sea usado correctamente. Rieguelo con agua por la mañana solamente; entre 4:00 a.m. y 9:00 a.m. Nunca riegue con agua por la noche. Si el césped es mojado en la noche, un problema de enfermedad puede ocurrir muy facilmente que cuando esta seco.

- Provea al césped con una riegue de agua pesado unas cuantas veces a la semana. Esto le ayudara al césped a desarrollar un sistema de raiz profundo y le permitira al césped secarse entre los riegues de agua.

- No riegue con agua el césped levemente en una base diaria. Cuando le da al césped muchos riegues de agua leves, el césped estara constantemente seco. El sistema de raiz no tomara el agua y se hara insalubre. En lugar de crecer profundo en la tierra, las raices creceran cerca de la superficie. Con un sistema de raiz de poca profundidad el césped vendra a ser insalubre y obtendra enfermedades a menudo y facilmente.

- Mejore las condiciones de drenaje si el césped es constantemente mojado. La ventilacion puede ayudar a mejorar el drenaje. Esto tambien ayudara a reducir la paja y promover un sistema de raiz profundo.

Si hay una enfermedad activa en el césped y esta causando daño, debe aplicar un control quimico para detener el problema. Es mejor controlar cualquier enfermedad tan pronto empieza. Entonces puede controlar la enfermedad antes de que se esparce y las áreas puede ser solamente ser tratadas en ciertas áreas por pedazos.

Antes de tratar cualquier enfermedad de césped, debe identificar el tipo de enfermedad. Tal como un profesional del cuidado del césped debe llegar a familiarizarse con las enfermedades mas comunes en su area. Tome una clase en su colegio local y obtenga un buen libro de identificacion de las enfermedades del césped. Entonces mantenga el libro en su camion para que le ayude a indentificar una enfermedad que usted encuentre. Si no puede identificar correctamente la enfermedad, tome un ejemplo y traigalo a uno de los colegios agriculturales estatales.

Nunca haga una aplicación de control de enfermedad al césped si la enfermedad no fue identificada. Hay muchos tipos diferentes de enfermedad y productos de control quimicos. Siempre lea la etiqueta del producto para cerciorarse que detendra la enfermedad que usted identifico. Los productos de control de enfermedad son muy caros y no trabajarn si no son escogidos y aplicados correctamente.

Los productos de control de enfermedades seran liquidos o granulados. Algunos productos granulados deben ser aplicados cuando el césped esta mojado para que el producto se pegue al césped. Entonces el césped debe permanecer seco y ser dejado sin molestar; evite usar este tipo de producto. El segundo tipo de producto granulado es usado más frecuentemente. Es aplicado al césped cuando esta seco. Entonces el producto debe ser regado con agua. Los productos liquidos trabajarán mejor. Los pruductos liquidos pueden ser mezclados en un rociador de muchila o un rociador de tanque. los productos liquidos empezaran a trabajar tan pronto hagan contacto con el césped y no tienen que ser regados con agua.

Si la enfermedad es mala, una segunda o tercera aplicación puede ser requerida. Siempre lea la etiqueta del producto para instrucciones y recomendaciones del producto. Siempre lleve puesta las ropas y equipo de seguridad correcto cuando hace una aplicación.

Piedra Caleza (Limestone)

La piedra caleza es usada para ajustar o mantener el nivel de tierra pH. Al tener el nivel correcto de tierra pH, el césped sera ayudado en las siguientes maneras.

- El césped sera capaz de absorber todos los nutrientes de la tierra. Con un nivel **incorrecto** de pH, el césped **no sera capaz** de absorber los nutrientes que estan disponibles en la tierra.
- Mejores resultados de una aplicación de abono.
- Aumentara el color verde de el césped.
- Con un nivel correcto de pH, el césped no se enfermara tan facilmente.
- Los problemas de paja tomara mas tiempo para desarrollarse.

- El nivel correcto de pH le dara al césped una salud mejor. Un césped saludable sera más resistente a la enfermedad, insectos, hierbas y tension de un tiempo malo.

Para saber cuanta piedra caleza un césped necesita, el área debe ser medida para determinar el total de los pies cuadrados. Entonces una prueba de tierra pH debe tomarse. Al saber el total de pies cuadrados del área de césped y los resultados de tierra pH, usted sera capaz de determinar cuanta piedra caleza es necesitada para el área de césped. La taza de aplicación y instrucciones seran encontrados en la etiqueta del producto.

No aplique la piedra caleza si no sabe el nivel de tierra pH. Algunos céspedes no pueden necesitar ninguna piedra de caleza. Al aplicar la cantidad incorrecta de piedra de caleza al área del césped puede causar resultados pobres o aun añadir tension al césped. Siempre tome una prueba de tierra pH antes de hacer cualquier aplicación.

La piedra caleza es un producto granulado que generalmente viene en bolsas de 50 libras. Viene en (polvo o bolitas) (pulverized o pelletized). La bolita (pelletized) es mejor porque no se soplara cuando sea utilizado en condiciones ventosas. Evite que las piedras caleza entren a las camas del paisaje. el producto es muy seguro; sin embargo, el polvo puede irritar su nariz. Lleve puesta una mascarilla cuando aplica la piedra caleza. La piedra caleza tomara unos cuantos meses para que se mezcle con la tierra. Usted no obtendra rapidos, resultados visibles de la piedra caleza. La piedra caleza puede ser aplicada en cualquier tiempo del año; sin embargo, es generalmente aplicada durante el otoño o en el temprano invierno. Entonces la aplicación sera efectiva para la siguiente estacion.

AHOYAR Y SEPARACION DE PAJA
(CAPÍTULO 21)
CORE-AERATION AND DE-THATCHING

Para mantener un césped saludable, usted tendra que hacer más que aplicaciones de cuidado del césped basicas. Sobre los años, un césped puede declinar por una tierra compacta o por un aumento excesivo de paja. Ahoyar o separacion de paja puede ser necesario para detener estos problemas y mantener un césped saludable. Los dos servicios deben ser hechos tarde en el verano a la estacion de otoño. Durante la primavera, hay muchas hierbas activas. Cuando un césped es ahoyado o sacado paja, la tierra sera expuesta. Entonces la hierbas pueden crecer en las áreas de tierra expuesta antes que el césped. La siembra en ciertos lugares o la siembra en exceso (spot seeding, over-seeding) son generalmente hecha cuando se ahoya o se saca paja. En lo ultimo del verano o en el otoño son los mejores tiempos para sembrar.

Ahoyar (Core-aetation)
Los Beneficios de Ahoyar
Un césped jamas crecera saludable y fuerte con una tierra compacta. El agua y nutrientes no pueden penetrar a la superficie de una tierra compacta. La tierra necesita aire, si la tierra es compacta con poco o ningun aire, el césped crecera pobremente. Si este problema no es correjido, el césped no solamente no sera capaz de desarrollar un sistema de raiz profunda, en su lugar el césped desarrollara un sistema

de raiz poco profundo. Un césped con un sistema de raiz poco profundo no puede soportar condiciones de tension y morira muy facilmente o puede morir solo.

El césped gradualmente se compacta simplemente caminando sobre el. Cuando los cortacéspedes pesados son utilizados o si el césped es utilzado para deportes o fiestas, la tierra puede llegar a compactarse en uno o dos años.

Para mantener un césped saludable y evitar la tierra compacta, se debe ahoyar cada dos años. Después que el césped y la tierra son ahoyados, el césped entonces se beneficiara en muchas maneras.

- Las aplicaciones de césped son más efectivas ya que pueden alcanzar el área de raiz. El césped absorbe las aplicaciones de abono. Si la aplicación no puede alcanzar la zona de raiz resultados pobres ocurriran.

- El agua es también más efectiva ya que podra alcanzar la zona de raiz más facilmente. Esto permitira que el césped desarroye un sistema de raiz profundo. Con un sistema de raiz profundo, el césped podra ser capaz de soportar condiciones de tension. Cuando la tierra esta dura y compacta, mucho agua correra sobre el césped y no penetrara la tierra.

- Si un sistema de regadera es utilizado, usted sera capaz de reducir la cantidad de agua que esta poniendo al césped ya que cada riegue de agua sera más efectivo.

Nota: cuando riegue con agua cada seccion del césped, usted necesitara de 30 a 45 minutos de agua. Un riegue de agua pesada animara a un sistema de raiz profundo y un césped saludable. Si usted reduce el riegue de agua, es mejor eliminarlo un dia en lugar de reducir el tiempo.

- El aire sera capaz de penetrar la tierra. Como discutimos antes, el aire es necesario en la tierra para crecer un césped saludable.

- Ahoyar ayudara a mejorar el drenaje. Si el agua cae en la superficie del césped, la ventilacion ayudara a penetrar la tierra y mantener el área seca.

- El ahoyar estimula nuevo crecimiento. Un césped insalubre tendra todos los beneficios como acabamos de discutir; por eso, sera capaz de crecer más fuerte y saludable después de ahoyar.

Ahoyar (Core-aeration) (Procedimientos de Trabajo)

La mayor ahoyación es hecha con una máquina de poder de ahoyar. Una maquina de poder tiene muchos tubos metales huecos (**tines** es un elemento de metal que resiste el mojo) que lentamente da vueltas alrededor cuando la máquina se mueve. Los tines presionan dentro del suelo y hala los terrones de césped y tierra. Entonces los (terrones) se caen dentro el césped. Los (terrones) no deben ser rastrillados, se secaran y se desaceran en pocas semanas. Una herramienta manual de ahoyar debe ser utilizada para unos pedazos pequeños de césped o en áreas que son dificil de alcanzar con una máquina grande de poder.

Ahoyar debe ser hecho después que el césped ha sido cortado. Antes de ahoyar cualquier área de césped, usted **debe** inspeccionar el área entera de césped. Usando unas banderas de 12 pulgadas, marca cualquier cosa en el césped que necesite ser evitado. Tal como: sistemas de regadera o tubos expuestos, cualquier drenaje expuesto, cortadora, gas, o tubos de agua, cualquier alambres electricos que no estan enterrados correctamente, la cerca electrica invisible del perro; piedras grandes o objetos que pueden ser dañados con la máquina de ahoyar.

Siempre hable con el dueño de la propiedad antes de ahoyar para determinar que necesita ser marcado. Después que todo sea marcado claramente, usted sera capaz de empezar a trabajar.

Opere la maquina a tráves del césped de la misma manera que usted opera un cortacésped. Primero vaya alrededor porla orilla. Entonces hace un pase hacia atrás y hacia delante a tráves del césped. La mayoria de maquinas tienen una barra que baja o aumenta las puntas. Tienen que ser levantados del suelo cada vez que haga una vuelta peligrosa. Entonces lo baja hacia abajo para el proxima paso. Cuando hace una vuelta gradual, usted debe ser capaz de dejar las puntas abajo y manualmente dar vuelta a la máquina cuando se esta moviendo.

Una palanca de control se engancha o desengancha las puntas. No enganche las puntas hasta que hayan sido bajados al suelo. Desenganche las puntas antes de subirlos. Cuando las puntas estan dando vuelta en el suelo, la máquina se movera hacia delante. Cuando usa la máquina recta, superficie plana, usted puede correr la máquina a la velocidad completa. Cuando trabaja en una cuesta, colina, sea muy cuidadoso. Trabaje a tráves de la colina, no de arriba hacia abajo ya que la máquina no tiene frenos. También, corra la máquina a una velocidad lenta. Mantenga las puntas lejos de piedras, aceras, o caminos de entrada o daños puede ocurrir conlas puntas y la acera o caminos de entrada.

Cuando termine con el césped completo, remueve todas las banderas de marcar y ha terminado. Después que el trabajo este hecho, riegue con agua y abono el área de césped. Siembre en ciertas áreas o siembra en exceso puede ser también hecha después de la ventilacion. Discutiremos la siembra en lugares y la siembre en exceso en el proximo capítulo.

Removiendo Paja
De-thatching
La paja se desarrolla del exceso de partes viejas de césped. Asi como la hierba crece, causa estas partes muertas. Estas partes muertas del cesped se descompone muy lentamente y se desarrolla en una capa esponjosa dentre la hierba y el sistema de raiz. La paja sedsarraya naturalmente y no es causada por los recortes dejados en el césped. Los recortes de hierba se deterioran rápidamente y hacen más bien que daño al césped.

Si un césped es abonado incorrectamente, al usar constantemente un abono de alto nitrogeno un exceso de paja ocurrira más rápidamente que lo normal. La tierra compacta y el uso constante de pesticidas ayudara a un exceso de paja más rapido que lo normal. Cortar demasiado hierba en un corte, o cortar infrecuentemente también aumentara la capa de paja. Algunos tipos de grama tal como (Blue grass, Bermuda grass y Zoysia grass) producen paja rápidamente más que otros tipos de grama.

Para determinar si un césped tiene un problema de paja, use una pala plana (una herramienta usada para cavar, tiene una hoja de hierro que presiona dentro del suelo con el pie) para remover una seccion pequeña de césped. La capa entre el sistema de raiz y hojas de hierbas es la capa de paja. Mire a su pedazo ejemplar. Si la capa de paja es ½ pulgada de grueso, el césped tiene un problema de paja. También, cuando camina en un césped con un problema de paja, se sentira muy esponjoso.

Una capa de paja delgada es normal y necesaria. La capa de paja delgada proteje la planta, pero una capa de ½ pulgada o más prevendra las aplicaciones de césped, agua y el aire de penetrar dentro la tierra y el sistema de raiz del césped. Un sistema de raiz poco profundo se desarrollara ya que todo el agua es atrapada en la capa de paja; un cèsped con una raiz poca profunda es insalubre. La capa de paja humeda vendra a ser el hogar de insectos y enfermedades. Los problemas aumentaran y la belleza del césped disminuira. La capa gruesa de paja debe ser reducida para resolver todos estos problemas.

Removiendo paja (Procedimientos de Trabajo)

La separacion de paja es hecha con una máquina de separacion de paja o un rastrillo de poder. La máquina de separacion de paja rápidamente reducira la capa gruesa de paja. Puede ser ajustada alto o bajo, para cortar la paja al nivel que usted quiere.

La separacion de paja debe ser hecha después que el césped ha sido cortado. Inspeccione y marque cualquier objeto de dañar en el césped. Tal como las cabezas de regaderas, tubos o piedras. Operar la máquina de sacar paja de la misma manera que usted corta un césped. Primero va alrededor del césped, entonces hace pasos de atrás hacia delante a tráves del césped. La mayoria de máquinas de separacion de paja tienen dos palancas; una para enganchar el rastrillo de poder y otro para levantar o bajarlo al suelo. Encienda la máquina en la configuracion más alta, enganche el rastrillo de poder y empuje la máquina a tráves de una seccion pequeña del césped. Baje la configuracion hasta que la máquina remueva casi toda la capa de paja. No vaya tan profundo o si no puede dañar el césped. Si usted ve mucha tierra, usted esta illendo muy profundo. Después que encuentre la configuración correcta, empuje la máquina a tráves del césped entero. Cuando el rastrillo de poder es enganchado y bajado al suelo, la máquina sera más facil de empujar. Evite golpear cualquier acera, caminos de entrada o piedras. Las áreas pequeñas de césped puede ser separadas la paja manualmente con un rastrillo de separar paja.

Cuando termine de usar la máquina, usted necesitara rastrillar y desacerse de toda la paja que fue removida del césped. Esto debe ser hecho con un rastrillo de hoja. Al usar un rastrillo de hoja juntamente con un soplador de tierra obtendra el trabajo más rápidamente. Traiga unas carretillas para poner dentro los montones de paja, entonces se desace de la paja.

Después que el trabajo es hecho, riegue con agua y abone el área de césped. Siembre ciertas áreas o siembra en exceso puede ser hecha después de separar la paja. Nosotros discutiremos la siembra en lugares y la siembra en exceso en el proximo capítulo.

SIEMBRA EN LUGARES, SIEMBRA EN EXCESO,
(CAPÍTULO 22)
SIEMBRA EN PEDAZOS (SPOT SEEDING)
(OVER-SEEDING) (SLICE-SEEDING)

La siembra en un área de césped existente es hecha por varias diferentes razones. La siembra en ciertos lugares es hecha para reparar las áreas pobres de un césped existente. Cuando se hace la siembre en lugares, es muy importante usar el mismo tipo de semillas de césped como el césped existente. Si usted usa un tipo diferente de semilla, las áreas de siembra se pueden ver diferente del resto del césped.

Siembra en exceso es hecha para mezclar una nueva, mejor calidad de semilla con un césped viejo. La siembra en exceso ayudara a convertir un delgado, césped debil a un césped grueso y saludable. Muchos de los tipos de semillas nuevos son más resistentes a los insectos y enfermedades. También son más resistentes a la sequia, tienen una mejor apariencia y son más verdes en el color. La siembra en exceso es hecha cuando las condiciones de la propiedad han cambiado. Sobre los años, los árboles crecen más grandes y crean más sombra. Si el césped consiste de una semilla de césped que requiere el sol, comenzara a declinar cuando la sombra aumente. Para tener un césped grueso, saludable, una semilla de sombra necesitara ser sembrada en exceso dentro del césped.

La siembra en pedazos es utilizada en el proceso de la renovacion del césped o para incorporar una semilla nueva en una vieja, césped de pobre calidad. La máquina de siembra en pedazos cortara por medio de la capa de paja dentro de la superficie de tierra. Entonces la semilla de césped caera dentro de estos pedazos y hara contacto con la tierra. El contacto de la semilla y tierra es necesario para que la semilla germine. Un césped que ha sido sembrado en pedazos se establecera más rápidamente y más grueso que uno que ha sido con metodo de siembra en exceso.

La semilla de césped viene en una variedad de diferentes mezclas tal como: (Full Sun, Sun, Sun & Shade, Shade and Dense Shade). Cerciorese que usted escoja la mezcla de semillas correctas para cumplir con las condiciones especificas de cada trabajo. Siempre escoja una mezcla de semilla de alta calidad.

Antes que compre la semilla de césped, lea la etiqueta de la semilla y busque por lo siguiente:

- Condiciones donde la semilla crecerá.
- Nombres y porcentajes de los tipos de césped.
- El porcentaje de germinacion de por lo menos 85%.
- Contenido de semilla de hierba de no más de 0.5%.
- (Inert Matter) no más del 1%.
- Tipos de semillas no deseados más del 1%.
- Una fecha reciente que es menos de un año de viejo.

En la mayoria de las regiones del pais, el mejor tiempo para crecer la semilla de césped es en el otoño temprano. En el otoño, el suelo esta aun calido lo cual ayuda a agilizar el proceso de germinacion. El aire es fresco durante la noche. El aire fresco ayuda a la tierra a permancer humeda por un tiempo más largo de tiempo. La semilla debe permanezer humeda o no germinara, cuando la semilla de césped se establece en el otoño, tiene más tiempo para desarrollar un sistema de raiz fuerte antes que las condiciones de tension del verano lleguen. En la primavera es el segundo tiempo mejor para crecer la semilla de césped. Nunca trate de establecer semilla de césped durante el verano.

Las Herramientas y Equipo

Usted necesitara las siguientes herramientas y equipo para sembrar en lugares, sembrar en exceso y sembrar en pedazos. Una máquina sembrar en pedazos, una máquina de separar paja, un esparcidor rotorio, un esparcidor de gota, un esparcidor de mano, un balde limpio de cinco galones para semilla, un rolo de césped, un cuchillo de utilidad, carretillas, un rastrillo plástico de hoja, un rastrillo de metal, un rastrillo de grado, un rastrillo de separar paja, palas, y un soplador de muchila.

Usted debe llevar puesto los guantes y considerar llevar puesta una mascarilla de polvo.

Siembra en Lugares (Procedimientos de Trabajo)
(Spot Seeding)

* Inspeccione el sitio de trabajo y determine el tipo correcto de semilla que sera usado. Si el tipo de semilla de césped incorrecto es usado, las áreas de semillas se veran diferente al resto del césped. Determine cuanta semilla sera necesaria.

* Determine si algun tipo de tierra vegetal (topsoil) sera necesaria en las áreas que seran sembradas en ciertos lugares. Si las condiciones de tierra son pobres o desgastadas, tierra vegetal adicional puede ser usada.

* Antes de comenzar a trabajar, el césped debe ser cortado. Corte el césped levemente más bajo que lo normal.

* Prepare las áreas para la siembra de semillas de césped. Si las áreas que seran sembradas son de más tierra, use un rastrillo de arco de metal para aflojar la superficie de la tierra. Si hay paja en las áreas de césped que seran sembradas, remueva la paja con un rastrillo de separar paja. Si las condiciones de la tierra son pobres o desgatadas, esparce una capa de tierra vegetal sobre las áreas.

Nota: todas las áreas que seran sembradas deben ser preparadas correctamente o si no la semilla no crecerá.

* La semilla puede ser esparcida sobre las areas a mano o usando un esparcidor. Si usted esta esparciendo la semilla a mano, ponga la semilla dentro de un balde de cinco-galones. Entonces tira la

semilla sobre cada área. **Cerciorese que la semilla se esparce uniformemente.** No deje caer ninguna semilla dentro de las camas de paisaje o en áreas no deseadas. Si usted esta usando un esparcidor, fije el esparcidor en la configuracion correcta. Entonces cuidadosamente esparce la semilla sobre cada área. Sea cuidadoso cuando usa un esparcidor rotorio. El esparcidor rotorio esparcira semilla de seis a ocho pies de ancho. Un esparcidor de gota solamente esparcira semilla de 3 a 4 pies de ancho; por eso trabaja mejor cuando siembra cerca de las camas de paisaje o de aceras. Cuando siembra en lugares, siempre es mejor aplicar una cantidad generosa de semilla para mejores resultados.

- Aplica el abono a la taza correcta sobre cada área con un esparcidor rotorio o de gota o por mano. No aplique abono (starter fertilizer) muy pesado que la taza recomendada o puede dañar la semilla.

- Aplica paja sobre cada área. Esparce la paja lo más uniformemente posible. Aplica más a las áreas inclinadas o las áreas de tierra vegetal abiertas. El pajote (starter mulch) es un nuevo producto que protejera la semilla de césped y trabajara mejor que la paja. Este producto viene en bolsas y puede ser esparcidor a mano o de un esparcidor de gota. El producto viene en pequeñas bolas (pellets). Estos bolas (pellets) se disuelven después de un riegue de agua pesado y forman una capa protectiva sobre la semilla de césped. El producto permanece en el suelo y no se soplara como la paja hace. El pajote (starter mulch) trabaja muy bien con la siembra de ciertos lugares pero es muy caro para cubrir áreas muy grandes.

- Después que las áreas han sido sembradas y cubiertas con pajote (starter mulch) o paja, usted debe rolear cada área. Al rolear usted presionara las semillas dentro de la tierra. Las semillas **deben** hacer buen contacto con la tierra o si no ho creceran. Llene el rolo de césped con agua y rolee todas las áreas que usted sembro.

- Cerciorese que el dueño de la propiedad riegue con agua cada área en una base diaria hasta quela semilla este a unas pulgadas de alto. Entonces continue regando con agua cada pocos dias por ocho semanas. Los resultados pobres ocurriran si el riegue de agua no es hecho apropiadamente. Las instrucciones detalladas de regar seran explicadas en un capítulo mas adelante.

Siembra en Exceso (Procedimientos de Trabajo)
(Over Seeding)

- Inspeccione y mida el área de césped para determinar el tipo correcto de semilla y la cantidad de semilla necesaria.

- Solamente use semilla de alta calidad.

- Lea la etiqueta de semilla y encuentre la cantidad de semilla recomendada y requerida para su trabajo. Usted necesitara medir el área para determinar los pies cuadrados. Entonces usted sera capaz de comprar la cantidad correcta de semilla para su trabajo.

- Para determinar los pies cuadrados de una propiedad, mida la longuitud y anchura del frente, parte de atrás, y de los lados de la propiedad. Entonces separadamente calcula cada área.

Por ejemplo:

Propiedad del frente:	100 pies x 50 pies=	5000 pies cuadrados
Propiedad de atrás:	100 pies x 25 pies=	2500 pies cuadrados
Lado derecho:	55 pies x 25 pies=	1375 pies cuadrados
Lado izquierdo:	*70 pies x 10 pies=*	*700 pies cuadrados*
Total de la propiedad		9575 pies cuadrados

Redondee el nùmero 9,575 pies cuadrados seria redondeado a los 10,000 pies cuadrados. Ahora usted puede comprar suficiente semilla para sembrar-en exceso un césped que es 10,000 pies cuadrados en tamaño. Siempre compre un poco extra de semilla. Usted necesitara semilla extra para que pueda aplicar generosamente y para esparcir semilla extra en cualquier área que no crecio ninguna semilla.

- Separe la paja del área entera del césped (como discutimos en el capítulo anterior).

Nota: la siembra en exceso no trabajará bien a menos que la capa de paja sea removida y la semilla de césped pueda hacer contacto con la tierra.

- Corte el área de césped levemente más bajo que lo normal. Después que el césped ha sido sembrado en exceso, usted necesita permanecer fuera del área por el tiempo más largo posible. Al cortar el césped bajo, usted sera capaz de permanecer fuera del césped por dos semanas.
- Añade tierra vegetal a cualquier área pobre del césped.

- Para mejores resultados, una prueba de tierra debe ser tomada unas cuantas semanas antes de empezar el trabajo (como discutimos en el capítulo 5 de este libro). Aplique el tipo correcto de aplicación como es recomendado por la prueba de tierra. **Si el abono es necesario para correjir alguna deficiencia de tierra, los nutrientes pueden estar disponibles en el abono de empezar (starter fertilizer) que sera aplicado. Tenga cuidado de no aplicar demasiado abono o la semilla se puede dañar y no puede crecer.**

- Aplica una aplicación de abono de empezar (starter fertilizer). El abono de empezar es utilizado para ayudar a establecer el sistema de raiz de semilla y sardo (sod) de césped. Siempre chequee la recomendación en la bolsa del abono de empezar. Jamas aplique mas de lo recomendado. Si usted aplica mas de lo recomendado, puede quemar la nueva semilla porque la aplicación de abono es muy fuerte.

- Aplica semilla a todas las orillas de la nueva área de césped. Use un esparcidor de mano o ponga semilla dentro de un balde limpio y la esparce a mano. Tenga cuidado de ninguna semilla caiga dentro de las camas del paisaje o de otras áreas donde la hierba no es querida. La semilla se debe aplicar uniformemente a la taza correcta. **Evite aplicar la semilla demasiado pesado o leve. Evite los montones o semillas en el suelo.** Aplica la semilla por lo menos dos pies de ancho de todas las orillas. Las orillas pueden ser tambien sembradas usando un esparcidor de gota. Un esparcidor de gota esparcira las semillas cerca de las orillas sin dejar ninguna semilla caer dentro de las camas del paisaje.

- Despues que las orillas han sido completadas, usa un esparcidor rotorio para esparcir semilla en un área grande de la propiedad. Un esparcidor rotorio esparcira semilla aproximadamente de seis a ocho pies de ancho en una pasada. Un esparcidor de gota esparcira semilla aproximadamente tres pies de ancho en una pasada. Ajuste el esparcidor a la taza correcta. Cuando aplica semilla, camina a la misma velocidad a traves de toda el área entera. Al caminar a una constante velocidad, la semilla sera aplicada uniformemente. Levemente traslape la semilla cuando haga cada pasada con el esparcidor.

- Cubra el área entera con paja. Entonces la paja ayudara a mantener la humedad alrededor de la semilla y ayudara a prevenir daños a la nueva semilla de una lluvia pesada. Tambien ayudara desanimar los pajaros de comer las nuevas semillas. Ponga los manojos depaja en las carretillas para moverlas alrededor de la propiedad. **Esparce la paja a mano lo mas uniformemente posible.** Si en el área hay una cuesta que se lavara de una lluvia, aplica mas paja para proteger el área.

- Entonces, usted necesitara rolear el área entera. Al rolear el área, usted empujara las semillas dentro de la tierra. La semilla debe hacer buen contacto con la tierra o no va a crecer. Llene el rolo de césped con agua y rolee el área entera.

Siembra en pedazos (Procedimientos de Trabajo)
(Slice Seeding)

Nota: si el césped tiene una capa gruesa de paja, la separacion de paja debe ser hecho primero.

- Inspeccione y mida el área de césped para determinar el tipo correcto de semilla de usar y la cantidad de semilla necesitada.
- El césped debe ser cortado levemente mas bajo que lo normal.
- Marque cualquier sistema de regadera, tubos, etc. en el área de césped.
- Llene la máquina de sembrar en pedazos con semilla y ajustela a la taza correcta. La mayoria de las máquinas tienen una cartelera de tazas que le diran la configuracion correcta para cada tipo de semilla. Hay una palanca de control que es usada para apagar o encender la semilla.
- Una palanca es usada para guiar la máquina hacia delante o en reversa. La máquina tambien puede ser levantada o bajada similarmente a la máquina de separacion de paja. Siempre encienda la máquina a la configuracion alta.
- Debajo de la máquina estan las cuchillas que dan vuelta y cortan dentro del suelo. Una palanca encendera y apagara las cuchillas.
- Ponga la máquina en el césped. Con la máquina en la configuracion alta, enganche las cuchillas y la maneja hacia delante unos pocos pies. Inspeccione el césped, las cuchillas deben cortar por medio del césped y paja y aruñar la superficie de tierra. **Las cuchillas deben aruñar la superficie de la tierra**

pero no cortar muy profundo dentro de la tierra. Cuando la altura correcta es fijada, usted debe empezar a sembrar. Abra la palanca de control de semilla.

- Opere el sembrado en pedazos alrededor del perimetro del área del césped primero. Entonces haga pasadas de atrás hacia delante a traves del césped similar a la manera que el césped es cortado.

- Apaga la semilla cuando de vuelta a una maquina. Permanezca lejos de algun area que ha sido advertida con banderas. Rellene la máquina con semilla como sea necesario.

- Despues que el césped ha sido sembrado en pedazos, aplica el abono de empezar y cualquier apliciones necesarias para correjir las deficiencias de la tierra (por el examen/prueba de tierra).

Las instrucciones correctas deben ser seguidas despues que la semilla ha sido instalada o resultador pobres pueden ocurrir. Lea la siguiente informacion, entonces cerciorese que el cliente este informado de estas instrucciones y de lo que necesita para que la semilla se establesca.

- El riegue con agua del àrea entera debe ser hecho como es necesario para mantener la semilla, césped, y tierra humeda todo el tiempo.

- Las áreas de césped deben permancer humedad de 4 a 8 semanas para asegurar la germinacion correcta y el desarrollo de raiz. La semilla germina en diferente periodos de tiempo; continue regando hasta 8 semanas para mejores resultados. Despues de un periodo de 8 semanas, riegue generosamente por lo menos dos veces por semanas a traves del resto del año.

- No discontinue regando cuando algo verde sea notado.
- Cerciorese de permitir que el césped y el suelo se sequen completamente antes de ser cortados. Para lograr esto debe no debe regar el dia antes de cortar. Las primeras 4 a 8 cortes deben ser hechos muy cuidadosamente ya que el césped no ha madurado, y el sistema de raiz no esta desarrollado completamente. Mantenga la altura de corte a la configuracion mas alta posible.
- Trate y mantenga la gente y mascotas fuera del nueva area de césped por 4 a 8 semanas, o daños o resultados pobres ocurriran.
- Las aplicaciones de abono de empezar deben ser aplicadas aproximadamente 30 dias despues de sembrar.
- No aplique pesticidas a su nuevo área de césped hasta las proximas 12 semanas despues de la germinacion., cuidadosamente lea la etiqueta en los productos de césped que usted aplica.
- Siembra en ciertos lugares adicional de un nuevo areas de césped puede ser necesitada para asegurar un césped grueso hermoso. Haga la siembra en lugares lo mas pronto posible despues que la primer siembra esta al 75% establecida; esto ayudara a evitar un problema de hierba.

RENOVANDO, PRUEBA DE TIERRA Y MANTENIENDO UN CESPED EXISTENTE (CAPÍTULO 23)

En este capítulo, explicaremos como cambiar (renovar) un césped de pobre calidad insalubre a un césped hermoso y saludable.

También discutiremos como mantener profesionalmente un césped existente. Antes de comenzar a mantener un césped, debe hacer una inspeccion del área. Algunos césped tienen diferentes problemas. Las aplicaciones solas no pueden mejorar el césped. Usted debe considerar renovar cuando.

- El césped existente no esta grueso, verde y saludable. Ha sido deteriodado a traves de los años.

- El césped existente no se mejora mucho de las aplicaciones de césped.

- El césped existente tiene problemas de enfermedad constante de insectos.

- El césped existente es hecho de una baja-calidad mezcla de semilla y hierba.

- El césped existente necesita ser mejorado al mezclar una semilla de césped de alta calidad con el césped.

- Un césped existente ha sido cambiado de un área soleada a un área de sombra porque los árboles han crecido mas grandes. El césped necesita ser mejorado al mezclar semilla de (sombra) con el césped.

- Si usted esta tratando de reducir el uso de pesticidas, mejore un césped al mezclar un (endofyte) con la semilla de césped dentro del césped. (Endofyte) es resistente a algunos insectos y enfermedades.

Despues que haya determinado que un césped necesita la renovacion, debe planear el trabajo. Si hay hierbas y otros problemas en el césped, el proceso de renovacion puede llevarse un año para completar. Planee remover cualquier hierbas, insectos, hierba silvestre, etc. en la primavera y al principio del verano. Entonces el área de césped estara listo para el verano tarde/temprano del otoño. Todas las renovaciones deben ser levemente diferentes. Algunas tomaran un año para completar mientras que otras pueden ser hechas en una visita.

Ahora discutiremos los pasos necesarios para completar la renovacion de césped. El césped que discutimos esta en muy malas condiciones y la renovacion se llevara un año para completar.

Renovacion de Césped (Procedimientos de Trabajo)

- Mida el área de césped para determinar el total de los pies cuadrados (como es explicado en el ultimo capítulo).
- Tome una prueba de tierra. Al tomar esta prueba de tierra, encontrara si hay deficiencia de tierra. Entonces puede correjir la deficiencia antes de sembrar en el césped. Un césped jamas

crecera saludable y fuerte si hay deficiencias de tierra. Debe tomar una prueba de tierra.

Prueba de Tierra

Para tomar una prueba de tierra, necesitara una pala pequeña o una herramienta especial que es usada para remover ejemplos de tierra. Trate de remover una pedazo de tierra de aproximadamente seis pulgadas de profundo y uno o dos pulgadas de ancho. Remueva un pedazo pequeño de tierra de este ejemplo y pongalo en una bolsa. Repita este proceso por lo menos seis veces y tome ejemplos de diferentes áreas de césped. Entonces mezcle los pedazos de tierra juntos en la bolsa y traigalo al laboratorio de prueba de tierra.

Una prueba de tierra puede ser hecha por su Servicio Local (Local cooperative Extension Service) usualmente es parte de un colegio agricultural o por un laboratorio privado de pruebas-de tierra. Los resultados incluyen: Nitrogeno, Phosphorus, Potasio, Tierra pH, contenido Organico, y Micronutrientes.

Nitrogeno, Fosforo (Phosphorus) y Potasio son los tres nutrientes mayores que todas las plantas necesitan. Si uno de estos elementos esta bajo habra un problema.

Tierra pH. Aun si todos los otros nutrientes estan disponibles en la tierra, no pueden ser capaz de ser absorbidos por la planta si la tierra pH esta incorrecta. El nivel de tierra pH es de 1 a 14 y un nivel entre 6.0 y 7.5 trabaja mejor. El nivel entre 6.0 y 7.5 es llamado Neutral.

Cualquier que este bajo 6.0 es llamado Tierra Acidica; cualquier mas o menos 7.5 es llamado Alkaline. Al tener el nivel correcto de pH, el césped sera capaz de absorber todos los nutrientes en la tierra y llegara a ser mas saludable y fuerte.

Para ajustar el nivel de tierra pH a neutral:

- Cuando la tierra es Acidica, aplica piedra de caleza (limestone) para **levantar** el pH.

- Cuando la tierra es Alkalina, aplica (sulfur) para **bajar** el pH.

Contenido Organico—la prueba de tierra deberia dejar tambien saber cuanto materia organica hay en la tierra. La materia organica es necesaria para que un césped cresca saludable.

Micro Nutrientes—los micronutrientes son nutrientes secundarios que la planta necesita. Incluyen Calcio, Magnesio, Hierro y otros nutrientes. Los micronutrientes son muy importantes y debe ser añadidos a la tierra si es necesario.

Una buena prueba de tierra le puede ayudar a ajustar el nivel pH, organicos o micronutrientes de la tierra. Despues que el césped ha sido medido y la prueba de tierra ha sido tomada, continue con los procesos de trabajo de renovacion del césped.

- Haga cualquier aplicación necesitada para corregir la deficiencia de tierra y aplica una aplicación de abono balanceada.

- Aplica una aplicación de control pre-inesperado de garranchuelo (crabgrass control application) (temprano del verano).

- Haga una aplicación de control de hierba (primavera).

- Si hay alguna posibilidad de que el césped tenga problemas de gusano (grub), haga una aplicación de control de gusano (tarde primavera/temprano verano).

- Trate cualquier superficie de insectos si un problema surge (tarde primavera/temprano verano).

- Trate cualquier hierba silvestre o garranchuelo si surge durante el verano. Necesitara usar un control post-emergent (verano).

- Aplica una aplicación de abono balanceado (verano).

- Fije una fecha para sembrar. El mejor tiempo sera durante tarde del verano o temprano del otoño. Tambien escoja una mezcla de semilla que trabajara mejor en el sitio de trabajo. Tal como (Sunny, Sun and Shade, o Dense Shade). Al usar el total de la medida de los pies cuadrados usted sera capaz de determinar cuanta semilla debe comprar. Recuerde siempre es mejor comprar un poco extra.

- Dependiendo en las condiciones existentes del césped, debe hacer uno o mas de los siguientes procedimientos antes de sembrar.

Removiendo la paja— Si hay una capa gruesa de paja, debe ser removida antes de sembrar. Separe la paja en todo el césped que tiene capa gruesa de paja. (separacion de paja fue discutida en detalle temprano en esta guia de instrucción).

Ahoyar—Si en la tierra existente es muy dura y compacta, debe ser ahoyada. La semilla no sera capaz de establecer un sitema de raiz fuerte si el suelo es duro y compacto. El ahoyar creara un buen ambiente para la semilla para que se establesca. (El ahoyar fue discutido en detalle temprano en esta guia de instrucción).

Reparaciones—Llene y repare cualquier hoyos o areas malas en el césped. Llene las areas, y entonces compacta la tierra con un rolo de césped. Despues que la tierra fue compactada levemente, regradue el area con un rastrillo de metal de grado. Cuando siembre aplica extra semilla y paja a estas áreas. Entonces cuidadosamente empuje el rolo de césped sobre estas áreas para ayudar a presionar la semilla dentro de la tierra.

Siembra en Pedazos o Siembra en Exceso—Siembra en pedazo es la mejor manera para qaue la semilla dentre en el césped existente. Si usted esta sembrando en exceso, separe la paja del césped primero y entonces aplica la semilla. Use un rolo de césped y rolea el área despues de sembrar en exceso. (Siembra en pedazo y Siembra en exceso fue discutido en detalle temprano en esta guia de instrucción).

- Despues que el césped ha sido sembrado, aplica semilla adicional a ciertas areas selectas como sea necesario. Cualquier áreas que son toda tierra con poco o ningun cesped existente necesitaran semilla adicional. Tambien aplica paja y rolea el área.
- Aplica una aplicación de abono. *Nota*: no sobre aplique abono o si no sera muy fuerte para la semilla.

Las instrucciones correctas deben ser seguidas despues que la semilla o sardo (sod) de césped han sido instaladas o si no resultados pobres ocurriran. Lea la siguiente informacion, entonces cerciorese que el cliente entienda completamente estas instrucciones y de lo que necesita para que la semilla se establesca.

- El riegue con agua del àrea entera debe ser hecho como es necesario para mantener la semilla, césped, y tierra humeda todo el tiempo.

- Las áreas de césped deben permancer humedad de 4 a 8 semanas para asegurar la germinacion correcta y el desarrollo de raiz. La semilla germina en diferente periodos de tiempo; continue regando hasta 8 semanas para mejores resultados. Despues de un periodo de 8 semanas, riegue generosamente por lo menos dos veces por semanas a traves del resto del año.

- No discontinue regando cuando algo verde sea notado.

- Cerciorese de permitir que el césped y el suelo se sequen completamente antes de ser cortados. Para lograr esto no debe regar el dia antes de cortar. Las primeras 4 a 8 cortes deben ser hechos muy cuidadosamente ya que el césped no ha madurado, y el sistema de raiz no esta desarrollado completamente. Mantenga la altura de corte a la configuracion mas alta posible.

- Trate y mantenga la gente y mascotas fuera del nueva area de césped por 4 a 8 semanas, o daños o resultados pobres ocurriran.

- Las aplicaciones de abono de empezar deben ser aplicadas aproximadamente 30 dias despues de sembrar.

- No aplique pesticidas a su nuevo área de césped hasta las
  proximas 12 semanas despues de la germinación., cuidadosamente
  lea la etiqueta en los productos de césped que usted aplica.
- Siembra en ciertos lugares adicional de un nuevo areas de césped
  puede ser necesitada para asegurar un césped grueso hermoso.
  Haga la siembra en lugares lo mas pronto posible despues que la
  primer siembra esta al 75% establecida.

Usted vera un mejoramiento continuo en el césped de cuatro a cinco
meses despues de la renovacion. Para mantener un césped saludable y
prevenir problemas que ocurran, debe seguir un regular, programa
continuo del cuidado del césped.

**Manteniendo un Césped (Programa Anual de Cuidado del
Césped)**

Temprano en la Primavera

- Haga una prueba de tierra si es su primer año manteniendo el
  césped, tome una prueba de tierra para determinar la condicion de
  la tierra. Entonces aplica aplicaciones necesarias para correjir
  cualquier deficiencia de tierra.
- Pre-inesperado control de garranchuelo balanceado, aplicación de
  abono de liberacion lenta.

Primavera

- Aplicación de control de Hierba.
- Control de insectos de superfice (lo necesario).

Tarde en la Primavera

- Balanceado, un abono con micronutrientes de liberacion lenta.
- Control de insectos de superficie y control de hierba (lo necesario).
- Control de enfermedad (lo necesario).

Temprano del Verano

- Control de insectos de superficie y control de hierba (lo necesario).
- Post-emergent control de garranchuelo (lo necesario).
- Control de Enfermedad (lo necesario).
- (Opcional) Pre-emergent aplicación de control de gusano (grub).

Verano

- Balanceado, abono de liberacion lenta
- Control de insectos de superficie (lo necesario).
- Post-emergent control de hierba silvestre (lo necesario).
- Control de Enfermedad (lo necesario).

Tarde del Verano/Temprano del Otoño

- Siembra en Lugares, renovaciones, reparaciones (lo necesario).
- Post-emergent control de desmaleza y control de insectos de superficie (lo necesrio).
- Control de Enfermedad (lo necesario).

Otoño

- Balanceado, abono de liberacion lenta.
- Control de hierba (lo necesario).

Tarde del Otoño/Temprano del Invierno

- Piedra de caleza (dependiendo en el área del pais que vive).
- Aplicaciones de abono para el invierno.

Nota: Las aplicaciones de arriba son para un Programa Anual del Césped **Completo**. Un Programa Basico de Césped es el mas usado. Un Programa Basico de Césped solamente debe incluir abono, control de aplicaciones de insectos y hierba. Cualquier otra cosa necesaria sera un cargo adicional. Un Programa de Presupuesto (budget) de Césped incluiria solamente abono y aplicaciones de control de hierba. Un Programa de Pesticidad Reducido solamente aplica pesticidas necesarios cuando un problema activo es encontrado en el césped. Un Programa Organico usa abonos organicos solamente y no pesticidas. Cada cliente sera diferente al tener un Completo, Basico, Presupuesto (budget), Pesticida Reducido y Programa Organico de Césped. Usted tendra un buen programa para todos.

PREPARANDO EL TERRENO PARA UN CÉSPED NUEVO
(CAPÍTULO 24)

Antes de establecer un área nueva de césped, el terreno se debe preparar correctamente. Las piedras y los escombros de basura necesitarán ser rastrillados y quitados del terreno. El terreno debe tener el nivel correcto para que el agua fluya lejos de la casa o edificio y no contra ella y para mantener la propiedad entera lo más seca posible. Cúalquier hoyo o áreas desigual necesitarán ser llenadas. Las enmiendas o cambios de tierra se deben agregar para mejorar la tierra. (Mesclador) de lo tierra sería también muy útil. Sin embargo, una mescla se hace raramente porque requiere también mucho trabajo y tiempo. Por lo tanto nosotros no discutiremos (roto-tilling).

Las Herramientas y Equipo

Usted necesitará las siguientes herramientas y equipo para preparar el terreno para un césped nuevo. Un tractor pequeño con un rastrillo del paisaje, carretillas, palas, piochas, rastrillos pequeños (del arco de metal), y rastrillos de metal grande (que gradúan).

Procedimientos del Trabajo

- *Sí hay alguna hierba no deseada o césped silvestre que crecen en el área, ellos deben ser quitados. Sí usted corta sòlo el pedacito de la cima de la hierba, usted no matará el sistema de raíz y la hierba crecerá de regreso. Rociar las hierbas con una sustancia química trabajará mejor. Utilize un producto tal como (Round-up Pro). (Round-up Pro) matará la hierba entera y usted podrá sembrar dos semanas después de que usted ha rociado. Rocíe las hierbas y césped silvestre 14 días antes de usted empieze a preparar el terreno. Entonces después que el terreno se ha preparado, usted puede instalar la semilla inmediatamente. Tome una prueba de tierra (como se discutio en el Capítulo 5 de este libro). Tomando una prueba de tierra, usted sabrá cuáles alimentos nutritivos la tierra carece. Entonces usted puede aplicar el tipo correcto de aplicación para que la tierra tenga todos los alimentos nutritivos necesarios para establecer un césped. Una prueba de tierra se debe hacer unas pocas semanas antes de preparar el terreno.*

- Rastrille cúalquier escombros de basura grande. Utilize un tractor con un rastrillo del paisaje o rastrille los escombros de basura en montones a mano. recoja los montones de escombros y los quita. Sólo rastrille y quita los escombros grandes, no quite los pedazos más pequeños de escombros.

- El terreno debe tener el nivel correcto para que el agua corra lejos de la casa y de la propiedad. Usando el cubo de un tractor, trate de quitar algunos de los lugares altos en el terreno. Entonces use esa tierra para ajustar el nivel o llenar cúalquier hoyo o lugares bajos. La tierra adicional se puede necesitar para levantar cúalquier áreas bajas o para nivelar adecuadamente. Esparza la tierra con el cubo del tractor y anivele con el rastrillo de paisaje. Para terminar de nivelar utilize un rastrillo grande de metal.

- Después que el nivel correcto se establece, usted debe llenar primero el área entera con una capa superficial del tierra de alta calidad o de materia orgánica. Muchos paisajistas no cubren primero el terreno. Los resultados serán un césped pobre de calidad que puede tener problemas progresivos. Para un trabajo profesional, cubra la cima del área entera antes de instalar el césped.

- Cuándo cubra la cima del área, usted estará esparciendo una capa delgada de tierra de alta calidad sobre el terreno. Una capa de aproximadamente 1 o 2 pulgadas de tierra serán benéficiosos y económicos. Sí el terreno existente es extremadamente pobre, una capa más grueso de tierra se debe instalar. (topdressing) al cubrir se debe usar también para suavisar cúalquier imperfección en el terreno. Use un cubo de tractor y rastrillo de paisaje para esparcir la tierra. Entonces termine de nivelar el área a mano.

Opcional: remover (Roto-tilling) y emparejar (grading) son la mejor manera de preparar el terreno para un césped nuevo. Pero este procedimiento no se hace a menudo a causa de la cantidad grande de tiempo y trabajocomplicados. El hoyar (Core-aeration) es una opción buena porque quitará tapones de tierra del suelo existente. Cubra (top dress) después que usted (Core aerate) a hechouna hoyacion, entonces la capa superficial de tierra podrá incorporarse con el terreno existente. Entonces el terreno será más adecuado para el desarrollo de la raíz.

Nota: Para mejores resultados, sólo cubra primero cuándo las condiciones del tiempo han sido secas. Cubrir el patio con tierra mojada en el terreno mojado es casi imposible.

- En breve después que el terreno se ha preparado, la semilla o el sardo (sod) necesitarán ser aplicado.

- Applicaciones tal como el abono y caliza se aplicarán cuándo instalemos la semilla o sardo (sod).

INSTALANDO SEMILLA Y SARDO (SOD)
(CAPÍTULO 25)

Instalando un Césped con Semilla

Establecer un césped de semilla es la manera más económica de crear un césped nuevo. Sembrar céspedes crecidos requerirán más tiempo y esfuerzo para llegar a establecerse. Pero una vez que esten establecidos, son a menudo más fuerte que los céspedes hechos de sardo (sod). Las semillas vienen en una variedad de mezclas diferentes tal como: (Full Sun) Sol Lleno, (Sun and Shade) Sol y Sombra, (Dense Shade) o Sombra Densa. Usted puede instalar una mezcla que reunirá las condiciones específicas de cada trabajo.

En la mayoría de las regiones del país, el mejor tiempo de comenzar un césped de semilla es en el comienzo del otoño. En el otoño, el suelo está aún tibio lo cuál ayuda a acelerar el proceso de la germinación. El aire es fresco durante la noche. El aire fresco ayuda a la tierra a permanecer húmeda por un período más largo de tiempo. La semilla debe permanecer húmeda o no germinará. Cuándo un césped se establece en el otoño, tiene más tiempo para desarrollar un sistema fuerte de raíz antes que las condiciones de tensiòn del verano lleguen. La primavera es la proxima oportunidad mejor para comenzar un césped de semilla. Nunca intente establecer un césped durante el verano.

Las Herramientas y Equipo

Después que el suelo se ha preparado, usted necesitará las siguientes herramientas y equipo para instalar un césped con semilla. Carretillas, rastrillos de hoja de plástico, (rotary spreader) espacidor rotatorio, un esparcidor de gota (drop spreader), un esparcidor manual (hand spreader), un cubo limpio de cinco galónes para la semilla, un rolo de césped, y un cuchillo.

Usted debe llevar puestos los guantes y una máscara de polvo y considerar llevar las rodilleras y un soporte de espalda.

Prepare el terreno como nosotros discutimos en el capítulo previo. Después que el terreno se ha preparado, siga los procedimientos de abajo para obtener los mejores resultados.

- Aplique la semilla o el sardo (sod) inmediatamente después de cubrir con tierra el área. Después de cubrir, la tierra estará floja y las raíces podrán establecerse fácilmente. Sí el área no se cubre con tierra, usted tendrá que aflojar la superficie de tierra. Nunca siembre semilla o sardo (sod) en tierra compacta.
- Escoja el tipo correcto de semilla para las condiciones en cada trabajo específico.
- Sólo use semilla de alta calidad.
- Lea la etiqueta en la semilla y averigua la cantidad recomenda de semilla requirida para su trabajo. Usted necesitará medir el área

para determinar los pies cuadrados. Entonces usted podrá comprar la cantidad correcta de semilla para su trabajo.

- Para determinar los pies cuadrados de una propiedad, mide la longitud y la anchura del frente, atrás y los lados de la propiedad. Calcule separadamente cada área.

Por ejemplo:

Propiedad anterior (frente): 100 pies × 50 pies =   **5000 pies cuadrados**

Propiedad posterior (atrás): 100 pies × 25 pies =   **2500 pies cuadrados**

Lado derecho: 55 los pies × 25 pies = 1375 pies cuadrados

Lado izquierdo: 70 los pies × 10 pies =   700 pies cuadrados

El total de la propiedad: **9575 pies cuadrados**

Redondee el número 9,575 pies cuadrados serían redondear a 10,000 pies cuadrados. Ahora usted puede comprar suficiente semilla para establecer un césped nuevo que es de 10,000 pies cuadrados en tamaño.

Siempre compre un poco más de semilla. Usted necesitará semilla extra para que usted la pueda aplicar generosamente y por si usted tiene algún lugar extra para sembrar semilla en algún área que no nacio.

- Aplique una aplicación de abono de principio (starter fertilizer). El abono de principio (starter fertilizer) se usa para ayudar a establecer el sistema de raíz de la semilla y el sardo (sod). Siempre verifique la recomendación en la bolsa del abono de principio (starter fertilizer). **Nunca aplique más de lo que es recomendado.** Sí usted aplica más de lo que es recomendado, usted puede quemar la semilla o el sardo (sod) nuevo porque la aplicación de abono son demasiado fuertes para las raíces tiernas.

- Una prueba de tierra debe haber sido hecha unas pocas semanas antes de comenzar el trabajo (como fue discutido en el Capítulo 5 de este libro). Aplique el tipo correcto de aplicación como es recomendado por la prueba de tierra. Sí el abono se necesita para corregir una deficiencia de tierra, los alimentos nutritivos pueden estar disponible en el abono del principio (starter fertilizer). Tenga cuidado para no aplicar también mucho abono si no la semilla el sardo (sod) pueden ser dañados y no crecerán.

- Aplique semilla a todas las orillas del área nueva de césped. Use un esparcidor manual (hand spreader) o ponga la semilla en un cubo limpio y lo esparce a mano. **Tenga cuidado** para evitar tirar cúalquier semilla de césped en las camas del paisaje o en otras áreas donde el césped no se necesita. La semilla se debe aplicar uniformemente y en la cantidad correcta. Evite aplicar la semilla en demasia o muy leve. Evite los grupos de semillas en el suelo. Aplique la semilla por lo menos dos pies de ancho de todas las orillas. Las orillas pueden ser sembradas también usando un esparcidor de gota (drop spreador). Un esparcidor de gota (drop spreador) esparcirá las semillas cerca de las orillas sin que tirar las semillas en las camas del paisaje. Ajuste el esparcidor a la cantidad correcta y usted podrá esparcir la semilla alrededor de las orillas rápidamente y fácilmente.

- Después que las orillas se han completado, use un esparcidor rotatorio (rotatory spreador) para esparcir la semilla en las áreas más grande de la propiedad. Una esparcidor rotatorio (rotatory spreader) esparcirá la semilla aproximadamente de 6 a 8 pies de ancho en una pasada. Un esparcidor de gota (drop spreader) esparcirá la semilla aproximadamente de tres pies de ancho en una pasada. Ajuste el esparcidor a la cantidad correcta. Cuándo aplica la semilla, camine a la misma velocidad a través del área entera. Caminando a la misma velocidad, la semilla se aplicará uniformemente. Traslape levemente la semilla cuándo hace cada paso con el esparcidor.

- Después que la semilla se ha esparcido, usted necesitará rolear el área entera. Roleando el área, usted empujará las semillas dentro de la tierra. Las semillas deben hacer un buen contacto con la tierra o no crecerán. Llene el rodillo con agua y rolee el área entera.

- Cubra el área entera con paja. La paja ayudará a mantener la humedad alrededor de la semilla y ayudará a prevenir el daño a la semilla nueva de una lluvia fuerte. Ayudará también a desalentar a los pájaros de comer las semillas nuevas. Ponga los manojos de paja en las carretillas para moverlos alrededor de la propiedad. Esparza la paja a mano lo más **uniformemente** posible. Sí hay una cuesta o un área en el cuál corre mucha agua de una lluvia, aplicar más paja para proteger el área. Las instrucciones correctas se deben seguir después que la semilla se ha instalado o resultados pobres ocurrirán. Lea la información siguiente, entonces cerciórese que el cliente está completamente enterado de estas instrucciones y de lo que ellos deben hacer para que la semilla se establesca.

9. Regar el área entera se debe hacer como sea necesario para mantener la semilla, el sardo (sod), y la tierra húmeda todo el tiempo.

10. Las áreas del césped deben permanecer húmedas por 4 a 8 semanas para asegurar el desarrollo apropiado de la germinación y el desarrollo de la raíz. Las semillas germinan en diferentes períodos de tiempo; continúe regando con agua hasta 8 semanas para obtener mejores resultados. Después de un período de 8 semanas, riegue con agua generosamente por lo menos dos veces por semana a través del resto del año.

11. **No** discontinúe regando con agua cuándo algo verde sea notorio.

12. Cerciórese de permitir que el césped y el suelo se seca completamente antes de cortar. Para llevar a cabo esto usted no debe regar con agua el día antes de cortar. Los primeros de 4 a 8 cortes se deben hacer muy cuidado samente ya que el césped no ha crecido, y el sistema de raíz no se ha desarrollado completamente. Mantenga la altura del cortacéspedes en la configuración más alto posible.

13. Trate y mantenga a la gente y mascotas lejos del área nueva de césped de 4 a 8 semanas, o resultara en daño y resultados pobres ocurrirán.

14. Las aplicaciones regulares del abono se deben programar para ser aplicadas comenzando aproximadamente 30 días después de sembrar.

15. No aplique pesticidas a su área nueva de césped hasta aproximadamente 12 semanas después de la germinación, lea cuidadosamente la etiqueta en cúalquier productos de césped que usted puede aplicar.

16. Siembra adicional de áreas nuevas de césped se puede necesitar para asegurar un césped grueso hermoso. Siembre la semilla lo más pronto posible después que la primer siembra esté aproximadamente 75% establecido; esto ayudará también a evitar un problema de hierba.

Instalando un Césped Con Sardo (Sod)

Al instalar sardo (sod) provee al cliente con un césped instantáneo. El césped se mirará grueso y saludable inmediatamente, y después de unas pocas semanas, profundizara las raíces en la tierra existente. La mayoría del sardo (sod) se establecen de (Kentucky Bluegrass). (Bluegrass) crecerá bien en una ubicación soleada y crecerá pobre en condiciones sombreadas. El sardo (sod) está generalmente sólo disponible en el tipo de (Bluegrass) de césped. Sí las condiciones del sitio del trabajo no son soleadas, puede ser mejor sembrar el área.

El sardo (sod) viene en tiras de aproximadamente de ocho pies largos por dos pies de ancho. El sardo (sod) es vendido por el pie cuadrado. Mida los pies cuadrados de su trabajo para determinar cuánto sardo (sod) usted necesitará. Compre del 5 al 10% más para tener para los cortes y los pedazos malgastados. Prepare el terreno como nosotros discutimos en el capítulo previo. Después que el terreno se ha preparado, instale el césped en la manera siguiente.

- Usted puede ordenar el sardo (sod) de su centro local del jardín o usted puede comprar el sardo (sod) directamente de una granja de sardo (sod) sí hay uno en su área. Los pedazos de sardo (sod) serán enrollados y se ponen en paleta. Una vez que usted obtiene paletas de sardo (sod), el sardo (sod) se debe quitar de la paleta y ser instalado. Sí el sardo (sod) se deja en la paleta por un período largo de tiempo, se dañaráo o morirá.

- Aplique el abono y los alimentos nutritivos como nosotros discutimos en la página previa.

- Remueva los rollos de sardo (sod) de la (paleta). Colóquelos en una carretilla y los coloca cerca del área donde usted empezará a trabajar. Mantenga el sardo (sod) enrolladó hasta que usted esté listo para instalarlo.

- Como siempre, organiza el trabajo. Una persona debe estar quitando el sardo (sod) de la paleta mientras la segunda persona coloca el sardo (sod). Recuerde de organizar cada trabajo antes que usted comienze y otra vez durante el trabajo si es necesitadó. Como un profesional del paisaje, usted siempre debe pensar en las maneras más fácil, más rápido y más seguro de hacer el trabajo.

- Coloque la primera fila de sardo (sod) de extremo a extremo a lo largo de la orilla de una caminata recta, aceras, camino de entrada, calle o cama de paisaje. Sí no hay orilla recta de donde trabajar, establesca una cuerda en medio de dos estacas. Comience la primera fila de sardo (sod) usando la cuerda como una guía.

- Cerciórese que cada pedazo de sardo (sod) esté convenientemente apretado uno contra el otro y que esté instalado recto. Los pedazos de sardo (sod) no deben tener ninguna partes altas. El pedazo entero de sardo (sod) debe hacer contacto con el terreno.

Ponga cada fila de sardo (sod) para que el centro del pedazo de sardo (sod) traslape uno encima del otro.

- Tenga cuidado cuándo trabaja encima del sardo (sod) que usted acaba de instalar. Algunos profesionales de paisaje utilizan pedazos de madera para trabajar. Entonces así ellos no dañan el sardo (sod) que acaba de ser instalado. Mueva la madera hacia adelante como usted trabaja.
- Utilice un cuchillo agudo para cortar cúalquiera curva o pedazos pequeños. Trate de mantener cada pedazo de sardo (sod) lo más grande posible. Los pedazos pequeños se moverán muy fácilmente.
- Después que el sardo (sod) se ha instalado, usa el rolo de césped para rolear el área entera. Rolea el área en dos direcciones diferentes. Rolear el sardo (sod) asegurará un buen contacto entre las raíces del sardo (sod) y la tierra existente.
- Después que el sardo (sod) se ha instalado, regar el área entera. Entonces siga las recomendaciones de regar dadas anterior en este capítulo.

ABOUT THE AUTHOR

Bryan Monty is a horticulturist, a successful lawn and landscape business owner and has been actively involved in the industry for over 20 years. During this time, he has trained and managed hundreds of different employees, English and Hispanic. He has developed, tested and perfected the Training Guide with other industry professionals to help bring new recruits and experienced employees up to a professional level.

Printed in the United States
24262LVS00002B/245